TO BUILD, TO PLANT

INTERNATIONAL THEOLOGICAL COMMENTARY

Fredrick Carlson Holmgren and George A. F. Knight
General Editors

Volumes now available

Genesis 1–11: From Eden to Babel
by Donald E. Gowan

Joshua: Inheriting the Land
by E. John Hamlin

Judges: At Risk in the Promised Land
by E. John Hamlin

1 Kings: Nations under God
by Gene Rice

Ezra and Nehemiah: Israel Alive Again
by Fredrick Carlson Holmgren

Proverbs and Ecclesiastes: Who Knows What Is Good?
by Kathleen A. Farmer

Song of Songs and Jonah: Revelation of God
by George A. F. Knight
and Friedemann W. Golka

Isaiah 1–39: The Lord Is Savior: Faith in National Crisis
by S. H. Widyapranawa

Isaiah 40–55: Servant Theology
by George A. F. Knight

Isaiah 56–66: The New Israel
by George A. F. Knight

Jeremiah 1–25: To Pluck Up, To Tear Down
by Walter Brueggemann

Jeremiah 26–52: To Build, To Plant
by Walter Brueggemann

Ezekiel: A New Heart
by Bruce Vawter and Leslie J. Hoppe

Daniel: Signs and Wonders
by Robert A. Anderson

Hosea: Grace Abounding
by H. D. Beeby

Joel and Malachi: A Promise of Hope, A Call to Obedience
by Graham S. Ogden
and Richard R. Deutsch

Amos and Lamentations: God's People in Crisis
by Robert Martin-Achard
and S. Paul Re'emi

Micah: Justice and Loyalty
by Juan I. Alfaro

Nahum, Obadiah, and Esther: Israel among the Nations
by Richard J. Coggins
and S. Paul Re'emi

Habakkuk and Zephaniah: Wrath and Mercy
by Mária Eszenyei Széles

Haggai and Zechariah: Rebuilding with Hope
by Carroll Stuhlmueller, C.P.

Forthcoming in 1991

Deuteronomy: Word and Presence
by Ian Cairns

TO BUILD,
TO PLANT

A Commentary on

Jeremiah 26–52

WALTER BRUEGGEMANN

WM. B. EERDMANS PUBLISHING CO., GRAND RAPIDS

THE HANDSEL PRESS LTD, EDINBURGH

First published 1991 by William B. Eerdmans Publishing Company,
255 Jefferson Ave. S.E., Grand Rapids, Michigan 49503
and
The Handsel Press Limited
139 Leith Walk, Edinburgh EH6 8NS

Printed in the United States of America

Eerdmans ISBN 0-8028-0600-7

CONTENTS

ABBREVIATIONS

LXX   Septuagint
NRSV   New Revised Standard Version
RSV   Revised Standard Version
SBL   Society of Biblical Literature

EDITORS' PREFACE

The Old Testament alive in the Church: this is the goal of the *International Theological Commentary*. Arising out of changing, unsettled times, this Scripture speaks with an authentic voice to our own troubled world. It witnesses to God's ongoing purpose and to his caring presence in the universe without ignoring those experiences of life that cause one to question his existence and love. This commentary series is written by front-rank scholars who treasure the life of faith.

Addressed to ministers and Christian educators, the *International Theological Commentary* moves beyond the usual critical-historical approach to the Bible and offers a *theological* interpretation of the Hebrew text. Thus, engaging larger textual units of the biblical writings, the authors of these volumes assist the reader in the appreciation of the theology underlying the text as well as its place in the thought of the Hebrew Scriptures. But more, since the Bible is the book of the believing community, its text has acquired ever more meaning through an ongoing interpretation. This growth of interpretation may be found both within the Bible itself and in the continuing scholarship of the Church.

Contributors to the *International Theological Commentary* are Christians—persons who affirm the witness of the New Testament concerning Jesus Christ. For Christians, the Bible is *one* scripture containing the Old and New Testaments. For this reason, a commentary on the Old Testament may not ignore the second part of the canon, namely, the New Testament.

Since its beginning, the Church has recognized a special relationship between the two Testaments. But the precise character of this bond has been difficult to define. Thousands of books and articles have discussed the issue. The diversity of views represented in these publications makes us aware that the Church is not of one mind in expressing the "how" of this relationship. The authors of this commentary share a developing consensus that any serious explanation of the Old Testament's relationship to the New will uphold the integrity of the Old Testament. Even though Christianity is rooted in the soil of the Hebrew Scriptures, the biblical interpreter must take care lest he or she "christianize" these Scriptures.

Authors writing in this commentary will, no doubt, hold varied views concerning *how* the Old Testament relates to the New. No attempt has been made to dictate one viewpoint in this matter. With the whole Church, we are convinced that the relationship between the two Testaments is real and substantial. But we recognize also the diversity of opinions among Christian scholars when they attempt to articulate fully the nature of this relationship.

In addition to the Christian Church, there exists another people for whom the Old Testament is important, namely, the Jewish community. Both Jews and Christians claim the Hebrew Bible as Scripture. Jews believe that the basic teachings of this Scripture point toward, and are developed by, the Talmud, which assumed its present form about 500 C.E. On the other hand, Christians hold that the Old Testament finds its fulfillment in the New Testament. The Hebrew Bible, therefore, belongs to both the Church and the Synagogue.

Recent studies have demonstrated how profoundly early Christianity reflects a Jewish character. This fact is not surprising because the Christian movement arose out of the context of first-century Judaism. Further, Jesus himself was Jewish, as were the first Christians. It is to be expected, therefore, that Jewish and Christian interpretations of the Hebrew Bible will reveal similarities *and* disparities. Such is the case. The authors of the *International Theological Commentary* will refer to the various Jewish traditions that they consider important for an appreciation of the Old Testament text. Such references will enrich our understanding of certain biblical passages and, as an extra gift, offer us insight into the relationship of Judaism to early Christianity.

An important second aspect of the present series is its *inter-*

national character. In the past, Western church leaders were considered to be *the* leaders of the Church—at least by those living in the West! The theology and biblical exegesis done by these scholars dominated the thinking of the Church. Most commentaries were produced in the Western world and reflected the lifestyle, needs, and thoughts of its civilization. But the Christian Church is a worldwide community. People who belong to this universal Church reflect differing thoughts, needs, and lifestyles.

Today the fastest-growing churches in the world are to be found, not in the West, but in Africa, Indonesia, South America, Korea, Taiwan, and elsewhere. By the end of this century, Christians in these areas will outnumber those who live in the West. In our age, especially, a commentary on the Bible must transcend the parochialism of Western civilization and be sensitive to issues that are the special problems of persons who live outside of the "Christian" West, issues such as race relations, personal survival and fulfillment, liberation, revolution, famine, tyranny, disease, war, the poor, religion and state. Inspired of God, the authors of the Old Testament knew what life is like on the edge of existence. They addressed themselves to everyday people who often faced more than everyday problems. Refusing to limit God to the "spiritual," they portrayed God as one who heard and knew the cries of people in pain (see Exod. 3:7-8). The contributors to the *International Theological Commentary* are persons who prize the writings of these biblical authors as a word of life to our world today. They read the Hebrew Scriptures in the twin contexts of ancient Israel and our modern day.

The scholars selected as contributors underscore the international aspect of the series. Representing very different geographical, ideological, and ecclesiastical backgrounds, they come from over seventeen countries. Besides scholars from such traditional countries as England, Scotland, France, Italy, Switzerland, Canada, New Zealand, Australia, South Africa, and the United States, contributors from the following places are included: Israel, Indonesia, India, Thailand, Singapore, Taiwan, and countries of Eastern Europe. Such diversity makes for richness of thought. Christian scholars living in Buddhist, Muslim, or Socialist lands may be able to offer the World Church insights into the biblical message—insights to which the scholarship of the West could be blind.

The proclamation of the biblical message is the focal concern of the *International Theological Commentary*. Generally speaking, the authors of these commentaries value the historical-critical studies of past scholars, but they are convinced that these studies by themselves are not enough. The Bible is more than an object of critical study; it is the revelation of God. In the written Word, God has disclosed himself and his will to humankind. Our authors see themselves as servants of the Word which, when rightly received, brings *shalom* to both the individual and the community.

—George A. F. Knight
—Fredrick Carlson Holmgren

AUTHOR'S PREFACE

I am glad to express my thanks to Fredrick Holmgren and to Allen Myers for their patient editorial work, and to Gayle Medlin who assisted in the typing of this manuscript. I am grateful to Tim Beal and Tod Linafelt for a final checking of the manuscript. Most of all, I am grateful to Tempie Alexander who, without protest or visible exasperation, oversaw every phase of the life of the manuscript, with endless drafts and retypings. Without her steadfastness, there would have been no manuscript.

Walter Brueggemann
Columbia Theological Seminary
Epiphany Day, 1991

TRUTH SPEAKS TO POWER
Jeremiah 26:1–29:32

These four chapters can be grouped together, both for reasons of convenience and because of a common theme. The grouping is in part a matter of convenience, for it is clear that the four chapters do not form an obvious and natural literary corpus. They do, nonetheless, form an in-between group of chapters. On the one hand, ch. 30 begins a quite new grouping with its accent on promise and hope, and its poetic casting. On the other hand, ch. 25 stands by itself, so that most scholars understand it to be a climactic statement at the end of the first half of the book of Jeremiah. In any case, it is not likely that ch. 26 has any integral connection to ch. 25. Between chs. 25 and 30, then, are chs. 26–29, which may be grouped together by default.

More than that, however, can be said about this grouping. The four chapters do seem to make a sustained statement concerning a single theme. The text, completely expressed in prose, features a deep, partisan, ideological dispute concerning Judah's true situation vis-à-vis Yahweh, and therefore vis-à-vis Babylon. The "official view," voiced by the Jerusalem establishment and especially on the lips of Hananiah, is that (a) Jerusalem is safe and guaranteed by the promises of God, and (b) the Babylonian intrusion into Judean life is short term, after which there will be a prompt return to "normalcy." This official view, which counts heavily on establishment ideology, does not receive much direct expression in the text, but is the assumed and implied dominant view with which the prophet must struggle.

Against that self-serving view, Jeremiah (and the tradition of Jeremiah) voice a counterview of reality which functions to un-

1

dermine and subvert the settled ideology of Jerusalem.[1] In this counterview, (a) Jerusalem is not guaranteed at all, but its existence and well-being are intensely conditioned by a resolve to keep torah, and (b) the Babylonian threat is a theological judgment on Jerusalem which is both long term and severe, and therefore not to be taken lightly. This counterview is variously articulated, but is rooted in the conditionality of torah, on which see 26:4-6.

In these chapters there is joined a crucial public issue concerning the political-theological assessment of Judah's actual place in the world. The person of Jeremiah is at the center of the dispute. The dispute does not, however, turn on his personal role, but on the theological-political realities of the situation.[2] There is, in ancient Judah, no unambiguous way to adjudicate this substantive dispute, no court of appeals which will give an objective verdict. The text as it stands is a testimony to Jeremiah's claim, and ultimately is his vindication. That is, in the end the text shows that Jeremiah is right in his assessment of the situation of Judah.

This unit begins in ch. 26 with the polemical proclamation of the prophet, a reiteration of ch. 7. This proclamation predictably evokes the hostility and resistance of the establishment, and Jeremiah is put on trial for his life (26:7-16). The intervention of powerful elders (vv. 17-19), among them Ahikam (v. 24), rescues Jeremiah. The following episode concerning the prophet Uriah indicates that, while Jeremiah may be personally rescued, the issue is not settled in his favor (vv. 20-23). That concluding episode in the chapter indicates that the dominant ideology has both the will and the capacity to silence a counterview and to crush its speakers.

As happens so often in Jeremiah, after the episode of ch. 26 set in the time of Jehoiakim (26:1), we are moved abruptly to another time, that of Zedekiah in chs. 27–28. Clearly the tradition is not put

---

1. On the ideological dispute, see Henri Mottu, "Jeremiah vs. Hananiah: Ideology and Truth in Old Testament Prophecy," *The Bible and Liberation,* ed. by Norman K. Gottwald (Maryknoll, N.Y.: Orbis, 1983), 235-251.

2. For that reason, there is a problem with excessive stress on the historical person of the prophet. Larger policy issues are the main agenda of the text. The problem facing the Jerusalem establishment is not the critical voice of Jeremiah, but the conditional character of Jerusalem's well-being.

together to make a chronological case.[3] Chapter 27 features a series of prophetic speeches in which the prophet asserts the reality of threat, and assaults the "good news" prophets who engage in massive denial. The same dispute which is generalized in ch. 27 is made direct, dramatic, and personal in the conflict with Hananiah in ch. 28. Finally, Jeremiah urges his contemporaries to prepare for the long haul of displacement (29:1-9) and again rejects false and easy assurances (29:15-32). The issue is clearly a major policy question in which this prophetic tradition asserts what the established ideology does not want voiced. The purpose of the book of Jeremiah is to present a counterview of reality, to say that which is most unwelcome to the ruling view of policy.

Only in 29:10-14 do we see a break in this theme of dispute, warning, and judgment. Here we can see the book of Jeremiah engaged once again in its two-stage notion of Yahweh's intention. After exile, there will be a homecoming. After "plucking up and tearing down," there will be "planting and building." But it will come only after.

Two matters surface in these chapters that relate to the larger themes of the book. First, the issue of true prophecy and false prophecy (ideology) is a recurring theme.[4] While the matter of what is true and what is false cannot be finally or objectively resolved, the book of Jeremiah as an enduring piece of literature clearly wants to insist on the truth of Jeremiah and his trajectory of interpretation.

Second, the unwelcome truth of Jeremiah concerns the reality of Babylon, a geopolitical reality taken as Yahweh's work in the world. Consistently in chs. 27–29 (with an initial warning in ch. 26), these chapters pivot on the Babylonian threat and the need

---

3. The same abrupt juxtaposition is evident in chs. 34–35. The former is in the days of Zedekiah and the latter in the time of Jehoiachim.

4. On the recent discussion of this dispute, see Thomas W. Overholt, *The Threat of Falsehood*. Studies in Biblical Theology, 2nd series 16 (London: SCM and Naperville: Allenson, 1970); James L. Crenshaw, *Prophetic Conflict*. Beihefte zur Zeitschrift für die alttestamentliche Wissenschaft 124 (Berlin: de Gruyter, 1971); and James A. Sanders, "Hermeneutics in True and False Prophecy," in *Canon and Authority*, ed. George W. Coats and Burke O. Long (Philadelphia: Fortress, 1977), 21-41 and the references to Quell and Buber.

to face it, a theme quite congruent with the Baruch narrative of chs. 36–45. The single exception to that emphasis in these four chapters is 29:10-14, in which the oracle envisions post-Babylonian reality (not unlike chs. 50–51). Thus, as in both the "Baruch narrative" and the "Oracles against the Nations," Jeremiah's theological argument in these chapters is saturated with Babylonian reality. The theme of Babylon is enmeshed in an argument about truth and falseness, so that the argument of the Jeremiah tradition is that the truth of Yahweh enunciated by the prophet concerns the cruciality of Babylon in any assessment of Judah's place in the world.

Thus the book of Jeremiah, exemplified in these four chapters, stays very close to political reality and urges Jerusalem to face that reality which it is prone to deny. That political reference is brought into close contact with Yahwism, so that Near Eastern geopolitics is understood theologically. According to this argument, Judah must at the same time reckon with the reality of Babylon, but also with Yahweh, who stands behind and sponsors Babylon and who then rejects Babylon for the sake of newness.

Thus the issue of truth and falsehood in theological discernment is not, in the book of Jeremiah, simply a matter of having right information or right discernment. It is, rather, an interpretive issue of recognizing that the transcendent will of Yahweh is completely coherent with socioeconomic, political processes.[5] It is in, with, and under Babylon that God is at work. The falseness of Jeremiah's opponents is not that they did not believe in and trust Yahweh, but that they tried to keep Yahweh apart from the world processes of their time. If trust of Yahweh is linked to geopolitics, as this tradition insists, then Jerusalem and Judah are much more at risk than the dominant ideology is wont to imagine. In the face of such a high risk, Judah is urged to face reality and to face "the truth" which comes packaged as torah repentance. This tradition will entertain no other sense of security, certainly no notion that Judah can count on unconditional promises from Yahweh. Judah

---

5. On the linkage of Yahweh and socioeconomic political processes, see especially Norman K. Gottwald, *The Tribes of Yahweh* (Maryknoll, N.Y.: Orbis, 1979), 608-621.

is summoned by the prophet to live in a dangerous place, with no excessive assurances, but with only a summons to see in its immediate context the dangerous and decisive role of Yahweh. Interpretation of this tradition requires the continued adjudication of theological truth and falseness, an issue which brings theological claims very close indeed to socioeconomic realities. Without this latter reference, any attempt at theological truth will turn out to be false.

RESPONSE TO THE TEMPLE SERMON (26:1-24)

This narrative account of Jeremiah's public endangerment is presented as a comment upon his pivotal "temple sermon" in ch. 7. In the sermon of ch. 7, we were given no report on the response of his hearers. This text, conversely, treats the prophetic word itself only briefly (26:1-6) and deals at length with the response of the community. Thus chs. 7 and 26 relate as *proclamation* and *response*. The response puts the prophet in profound conflict with his community and its leaders and with its preferred theological conviction. This theme of conflict will be explored in greater detail in chs. 27–29. The conflict that arises from the dangerous decree of God places the messenger in jeopardy, because his construal of the city is a most unwelcome one. The conflict which dominates the text, however, is not a personal one. The overriding issue, and the overriding interest of the narrative, is not the person of Jeremiah. It is rather the sovereign purpose of Yahweh which will not be overcome, and cannot be silenced or dismissed.

26:1-6 These verses summarize the public proclamation of the prophet given in more detail in ch. 7. The words occur "in the beginning of the reign of Jehoiakim" (26:1). This king is the model of disobedience in the tradition of Jeremiah. From the outset of this reign, the word of Yahweh is an unwelcome word, systematically rejected and resisted by the government. We have no direct report of the prophet's actual speech. We have only notice of what Jeremiah is authorized by God to say. We assume he spoke exactly as he was instructed by God. The prophet is

5

God's "device" or strategy for intruding into Judah's public process.

The decree of God places the future of the city precisely in the hands of those who are addressed. That is, the city is not fated by the will of God. The future all depends on what the people do. What they do will in turn determine what God does. The substance of the proclamation entrusted to Jeremiah is a sharp either/or. Either Jerusalem will turn and avoid God's evil, or it will not turn and receive God's evil. While policy questions may seem complicated, when construed by the prophet they are simple and abrupt. As in 18:7-8, the choice of obedience places in human hands the destiny of Jerusalem to be received from God. Judah has a chance (26:3). If, however, the chance is rejected, then Jerusalem stands under severe notice (vv. 4-6).

The "if-then" formula of vv. 4-6 places Jerusalem in a situation like that of the ancient shrine of Shiloh (cf. 7:12-15; Ps. 78:59-66). The choice is clear and exceedingly demanding. Judah must choose God's torah or be destroyed like Shiloh. The city must recenter its life around the purpose and will of Yahweh or cease to exist. The proclamation on the lips of the prophet asserts that the moral, covenantal factor is the key reality in the public process of Judah's life. In making this statement, the prophet contradicts the royal-temple ideology which imagined that the requirements of torah and the threats of the old covenant tradition were no longer operative for Judah. The prophet does not announce something new; rather, he announces something very old which had long since been dismissed as obsolete to the royal establishment. Insistence upon torah obedience relativizes the claims of authority held by human leadership. All present certitudes are thereby destabilized.

The response to his speech is quick and aggressive (Jer. 26:7-19). The prophet is brought to trial for his life. His threat to the city is judged by the religious leadership (priests and prophets) to be treasonable and worthy of death (vv. 7-9). His words are not for a moment considered by his hearers as a serious word from God, but only as an alternative political opinion which is immediately found unacceptable. The religious leadership has broad public support for finding him promptly guilty. The verdict, "You shall die," is a pre-trial opinion, perhaps a product of crowd psychology (cf. Matt. 27:22-23), or perhaps the filing of a formal charge. These accusers have already reached their verdict. It is the analogy to Shiloh that unnerves the religious leadership. The devotees of the city had imagined that Jerusalem had a privileged place with God and so was immune from the fate of Shiloh.

We are made privy to a courtroom scene in which the royal officers convene court "in the gate" (Jer. 26:10). The charges are lodged: he "prophesied against this city" (v. 11; cf. Amos 7:12-13).[6] This city is supposed to be immune to such criticism. Clearly the legitimacy of the city required keeping such a harsh critique unspoken.

In response, Jeremiah testifies in his own defense (Jer. 26:12-15). He concedes that the charge is correct. He does not argue the point. His self-defense is twofold. First, the assault on the city which he has spoken is not his speech, but the word of God (v. 12). Second, this unwelcome word which is heard as threat is in fact an offer of rescue (v. 13). It proposes a way out of impending death, for it is not yet too late. It is indeed later in the reckoning of God than the leadership thinks. It is indeed very late, but not too late.

Jeremiah makes an important distinction between the words he must speak from God (vv. 12-13) and his own personal destiny (v. 14). The prophet speaks no word on his own behalf and is completely submissive to the authorities before whom he stands. His submissive gesture, however, is only a brief digression from his real issue, namely, the truth of Yahweh which he fears. In v. 15 the prophet returns to the main issue, the summons to torah as the only chance for life in Jerusalem. His opponents want to dispose of his message by a political-judicial maneuver. Such an urgent, ominous word, however, cannot be eliminated by disposing of the messenger. The message itself will have to be engaged, because it is from God.

---

6. It is worth noting that the charge made against Jeremiah distorts his actual words, much as the testimony of Amaziah distorted the words of Amos in Amos 7:10-17. Jeremiah did not simply prophesy against the city, but gave an invitation to repent. This invitation from the prophet has dropped out in the charge against him. His enemies mispresent him.

The ultimate claim the prophet makes for his words is that God has spoken to him "in truth" *(emet)* (v. 15). Even his opponents do not claim that his word is false, only that it is prohibited. Thus the issue of genuine authority haunts the entire life and tradition of Jeremiah; the issue cannot be clearly disposed of, either by the tradition itself or by the opponents of the tradition. For that reason, the claim of the prophet is always fragile and sure to be challenged wherever it touches established ideology. In this chapter the opponents of the demanding word of God do not dispute the claim of authority. They do not seem to care if it is a word from God, for the defense of their way of life overrides any such theological question. They perceive, rightly, that the word of the prophet constitutes a significant threat to their ideological claims and therefore to their political power. Even if Jeremiah is authorized by God, his word is unwelcome. Thus the tradition poses a dramatic confrontation between the word of God and the false ideology by which the city lives. The opponents of the word imagine that if the word can be silenced, it will be nullified.

As long as the dispute is between Jeremiah and the religious leaders (priests and prophets), there can be no serious adjudication, because rival claims to authority end in a stalemate. Perhaps it is the religious leadership, the ones accustomed to giving legitimacy to societal claims, that have the greatest stake in the status quo. Alongside Jeremiah and his religious opponents, however, the narrative introduces a third voice, one that surprises us (vv. 16-19). It is the civic leadership, the princes, along with "all the people." Their intervention and verdict affirm the right of the prophet to speak. The princes do not assert that Jeremiah's word is true. They allow only that he has a right to speak and to be heard, because he speaks a word other than his own. Thus the princes resolve the dispute about authority by recognizing that a voice of prophecy must be taken with seriousness in the community.

The argument then takes an unexpected and decisive turn. In this controversy, certain "elders of the land," that is, those not a part of the urban establishment, cite a precedent in the tradition. The precedent that is cited is from Mic. 3:12, a prophet from a Judean village who a century earlier had spoken a harsh threat against the Jerusalem establishment. Moreover, it is asserted, King

Hezekiah honored the prophetic word of Micah and did not execute the prophet as a traitor. On the basis of that remembered event, Jeremiah is acquitted. That is, a prophetic word spoken against the status quo of Jerusalem is not cause for execution of the speaker, but cause for repentance and a change in public policy.

Several things are of importance in this testimony. First, this is an example of "intertextuality," of the Bible itself quoting earlier texts from the Bible.[7] This prophetic tradition does not stand in a vacuum but relies on precedents. Second, the text quoted is from the prophet Micah, that is, a villager who looks askance at the claim of the urban center. Third, the ones who remember and testify are "elders." Hans Walter Wolff has suggested that it is the elders as village leaders who are rooted in old covenantal traditions and who maintain a vision of social reality and a historical perspective that was not preempted by royal definitions of reality.[8] Fourth, the Jeremiah tradition is shaped to assert that the city of Jerusalem must, because of its very character, host prophetic voices which are critical of its own practice. It belongs to this community to receive prophetic voices, even when those voices are sharply critical of present social reality.

In one important regard, the offer of Jeremiah in this text is more generous than the text quoted from Micah. Micah offered no way out, but only announced a judgment. As this text casts the message of Jeremiah, there is an appeal for repentance, suggesting that it is not yet too late.

The tradition of Jeremiah has built this court trial into a focal drama. Through this confrontation, we are able to see that two perceptions of social reality are in deep and earnest conflict with

---

7. Michael Fishbane has made the most helpful and extended exploration of the practice of intertextuality. On this text, see his *Biblical Interpretation in Ancient Israel* (Oxford: Oxford University Press, 1985), 245-47, 458-460.

8. Hans Walter Wolff, "Micah the Moreshite — The Prophet and His Background," in *Israelite Wisdom*, ed. John G. Gammie (Missoula: Scholars Press, 1978), 77-84. On the social conflict of village and larger concentrations of power, see the broader argument by George E. Mendenhall, "The Palestinian Grass-roots Origins of New Testament Christology," in *Jesus in History and Myth*, ed. R. Joseph Hoffman and Gerald A. Larue (Buffalo, N.Y.: Prometheus, 1986), 79-86.

each other. In short form, this is the old conflict between royal ambition and the memory of torah piety. The text suggests that Jeremiah is not an isolated figure, but he stands in a long tradition of covenantal memory and is the speaker for what must have been a live and insistent political opinion in Israel.[9] This tradition, voiced by the prophet and sanctioned by the elders, resisted the self-indulgent, cynical policies and practices of royal Jerusalem. They did not think that such easy "peace and prosperity" was a way to well-being, because the guarantees and requirements of the torah were being mocked and dismissed. Furthermore, where such requirements are mocked and dismissed, profound trouble is sure to come. Thus the theological verdict of the prophet and the socioeconomic, political interests of the village mentality converge against royal ideology. This exchange, then, is not only high prophetic drama, but can be understood in terms of sociological realism. A poet from the village of Moresheth in Gath (Micah) and a prophet from the village of Anathoth (Jeremiah) may share a critique of the capital establishment.

The implication of the precedent from Micah is that in the present, the power structure of Jerusalem should act as did Hezekiah a century earlier. Not only is Jeremiah acquitted, but the present king, presumably Jehoiakim, should replicate the "good king" Hezekiah. The latter is presented as a king who was not hopelessly enmeshed in Jerusalem ideology and who could respond to the claims and demands of the old tradition (cf. 2 Chr. 29–31). That is, the charge brought against Hezekiah and subsequently against Jehoiakim (cf. Jer. 22:18-19) is that Jerusalem's policy is unjust, and that injustice is an affront to the God of the Exodus. In terms of economic policy, that governmental perspective is a threat to the lesser landowners. The elders are asking the king to take those alternative traditions seriously, and not to be so singularly committed to the narrow economic interests of the Jerusalem operators.[10] The socioeconomic issues are not unlike

---

9. On the social location of the prophet amid the social forces of his day, see Robert R. Wilson, *Prophecy and Society in Ancient Israel* (Philadelphia: Fortress, 1980), 245-49.

10. On Micah's concern for land policies and his critique of royal usur-

those posed for Rehoboam (1 Kgs. 12:1-15), who like Jehoiakim was so committed to self-serving royal ideology that he would not heed the voice of the tradition. Such cynical obtuseness in each case can only jeopardize the throne and its security.[11]

Because the material concerning Jeremiah's dispute is then taken up in the later tradition of Jeremiah and reused in the exilic community, this dramatic exchange permits one other reading. Addressed to exiles, the text suggests that it is disregard of the torah tradition that has brought such trouble to the community. Therefore, in the Exile the reappropriation of the torah tradition is the only door of hope. Thus the prophetic voice seconded by the elders continues to insist, in each successive generation, that there is no alternative for this people except the embrace of torah, which entails systemic repentance.

The unrelated episode of Jer. 26:20-23 is an unexpected intrusion in the narrative. It concerns an otherwise unknown prophet, Uriah, who also reflects village life (Kiriath-jearim).[12] The case of Uriah is cited to make a contrast with Jeremiah in order to demonstrate the characteristically brutal policy of the crown, and to show that the danger to Jeremiah was real and serious. On this second occasion, the same king, Jehoiakim, was not deterred by the elders from his wrath against a prophet. Uriah had spoken words not unlike those of Jeremiah (v. 20). In this case, the prophet was extradited from Egypt and executed as an enemy of the state (v. 23). It is remarkable that the king was not content to have this unbearable voice of the

pation of land, see Albrecht Alt, "Micha 2,1-5 ΓΗΣ ΑΝΑΔΑΣΜΩΣ in Juda," *Kleine Schriften zur Geschichte des Volkes Israel* 3 (Munich: C. H. Beck, 1959): 373-381.

11. It is instructive that Barbara W. Tuchman, *The March of Folly: From Troy to Vietnam* (New York: Knopf, 1984), 8-11, cites King Rehoboam as a primary case of "the march of folly." The kings at the end of the dynasty in the time of Jeremiah only finish the destructive folly begun with Rehoboam. Tuchman concludes her comment, "The alternative course that Rehoboam might have taken, advised by the elders and so lightly rejected, exacted a long revenge that has left its mark for 2800 years" (11). Jeremiah is an interpreter of that "long revenge."

12. William L. Holladay, *Jeremiah 2*. Hermeneia (Minneapolis: Fortress, 1989), 109, suggests that both Micah and Uriah come from villages in the Shephelah, a linkage intended in the tradition.

torah simply leave the country in flight (as was the priest Amaziah in Amos 7:10-17, and as are many authoritarian governments in our own day). Rather, the king would settle for nothing short of Uriah's elimination. Thus the contrast is made deep and massive between the old critical covenantal tradition and the royal apparatus which unwittingly prepared for its own death by its crass and greedy policies. Judah is now so distorted in its perception of reality that the very voices of the covenant tradition which might save (i.e., the prophets) are regarded as a threat that must be silenced. The only voice which holds a promise of life is perceived as an unacceptable threat. The very torah which is the foundation for life in Judah is now intolerable.

We misunderstand if we imagine that the prophet is a lone religious authority standing against his community. Rather, he stands in the center of a deep public debate and dispute. Not only Jeremiah, but many elders could see plainly that the leadership of Jerusalem has abandoned the true identity of the community. Indeed, it is argued by the elders that such a prophetic voice which stands against current policy is constitutive for Judah. The prophet is as much an indispensable ingredient in the public life of Judah as are king and temple (cf. Deut. 18:9-22). When that voice of prophecy is silenced and that role nullified, Judah abandons its reason for being and its source of life.

The final verse of our text (Jer. 26:24), after the digression of vv. 20-23, concludes the narrative by reporting the outcome of the encounter. Unlike Uriah, Jeremiah is not executed. The source of rescue, however, was not the intervention or protection of Yahweh.[13] The narrative is much more realistic. It is not reported that the royal court was persuaded by the precedent of Micah. Rather, the rescue is reported in terms of political realism. Jeremiah had a powerful advocate in the family of Shaphan, no doubt representative of the influential families who were increasingly alarmed at the growth of royal power. Thus the prophetic word has

---

13. In Jer. 36 the action of the princes in hiding Jeremiah and Baruch (v. 19) is said in v. 26 to be the action of Yahweh. Thus the human act and divine protection are equated. In our verse, no such linkage to God is suggested. The protection of Jeremiah here is human and political.

its destiny resolved not only because of religious reality, but in the day-to-day realities of political influence and exercise. The rescue of the prophet is a quite human event. The word of God lives and works amid real historical realities. There the messenger is variously jeopardized and protected. It is there that the claims of torah must be decided upon. There is a coherence between the word of the prophet and the social yearning of part of the community, the part which understands the destructiveness of royal policy. This prophetic tradition knows that the true interest of the community is not contained in the narrow, self-serving, self-indulgent interests of the royal leadership. It insists that the true interests of the community lie elsewhere, rooted in the old tradition of torah.

THE YOKE OF YAHWEH (27:1–28:17)

These two chapters belong together thematically, though they contain rather different materials. Chapter 27 is a fourfold decree from Yahweh that is formally all one speech. Chapter 28 is a narrative account of a face-to-face dispute evoked by the decree of ch. 27. The chapters have in common with ch. 26 the theme of the judgment of Jerusalem and the conflict between this torah-prophetic perception of Jerusalem and the dominant assumptions in the city. The substance of the judgment anticipated against the city, however, is quite different. In ch. 26 the judgment is the destruction of the city "like Shiloh" (v. 6); in chs. 27–28 the debate concerns not such final destruction, but how long the Exile will last. All of chs. 26–28 suggest an intense and ongoing debate about the future of the city and the nature and extent of its tribulation.[14]

Chapters 27–28 are removed chronologically from ch. 26.[15] They are set at the beginning of the reign of Zedekiah (27:1),

---

14. Christopher R. Seitz, *Theology in Conflict: Reactions to the Exile in the Book of Jeremiah*. Beihefte zur Zeitschrift für die alttestamentliche Wissenschaft 176 (Berlin: de Gruyter, 1989), has explored the ways in which the book of Jeremiah is an exemplar and evidence of the interpretive disputes present in the community.

15. While the Hebrew text reiterates "Jehoiakim" as in ch. 26, there is a scholarly consensus, following an alternative textual tradition, that the name of the king in 27:1 should be Zedekiah.

that is, just after the first incursion of Babylon into the city (598 B.C.E.). The first wave of Jewish exiles have been carried away (cf. 1:3; 52:28). By 598 it is established beyond dispute that the city of Jerusalem is not invincible. The deportation itself must have profoundly shattered the ideology within the city. Now the controversy concerns how long this displacement will last. The theological controversy concerns how long Yahweh will permit the Babylonian power to have its way against Jerusalem and its citizens. The question of *Realpolitik* concerns the durability and capacity of the empire. In the perceptual field of Jeremiah, the theological question of Yahweh's permission and the political question of imperial capacity and durability are the same question. Jeremiah insists that the *rule of Yahweh* and *Judah's response* to that rule are the only pertinent issues. That is, the prophet redefines the issue of politics. (It is of course true that his opponents also view international politics with reference to the character of Yahweh. Thus the difference is not in their political judgments, but in their discernments of God.)

27:1-22 This chapter begins with the dramatic action of Jeremiah in response to the command of Yahweh (27:2). Jeremiah publicly wears a yoke, which symbolizes Babylonian domination.[16] The yoke of Babylon is worn, however, not at the behest of Nebuchadnezzar, but at the command of Yahweh. It is Yahweh's yoke which Judah must now wear! The remainder of this chapter is a theological elucidation of that daring act.

27:3-7 This is a message ostensibly sent to the kings of the neighboring nations, all of whom were in the same subservient position to Babylon as was Judah. Perhaps the words suggest a conspiratorial meeting of subservient nations in Jerusalem to organize against Babylon, or perhaps the prophet simply appeals to the ambassadors regularly in residence in Jerusalem. Or perhaps the framing of the oracle to these nations is simply a device of

---

16. S. Dean McBride, Jr., "The Yoke of the Kingdom," *Interpretation* 27 (1973): 273-306, has shown how the metaphor of "yoke" serves for submission both to political power and to the command of Yahweh.

the staging of the proclamation.[17] Either way, the speech reflects
the global vision of prophetic faith. Moreover, it intentionally
controverts all the usual assumptions of such international di-
plomacy, for it asserts that the real issue is Yahweh's will and not
the apparent problem of Babylonian power. That is, in this oracle
Yahweh preempts any claim of the empire.

The oracle addressed to the nations (vv. 5-7) is a freighted
theological statement that has four elements:

(a) The foundational statement is in v. 5a: "It is I!" It is Yahweh
and none other who is the creator of all that is, the earth,
humankind, and the animals.[18] All are from Yahweh. All belong
to Yahweh. All are accountable to Yahweh. The language of "great
power" and "outstretched arm" is a reminder of Exodus language,
bespeaking Yahweh's sovereign, unquestioned, incomparable
power. The reminiscences of Exodus language are now in the
service of a creation claim, befitting address to the nations who
do not share Exodus faith but may acknowledge a creator God.

(b) From this large, uncompromising claim, it follows in v. 5b
that Yahweh may dispose of any part of creation in any way that
Yahweh chooses. Specifically Yahweh may assign power to anyone
Yahweh chooses (cf. 50:44). These two elements together in 27:5
constitute one of the most remarkable statements of Yahweh's free
sovereignty. Yahweh does not need to give explanation or justification, does not need to give account to the nations. The rhetorical
intent of the announcement is to take the mind of Judah
completely off Babylon. In such an assertion, the power and
significance of Babylon are completely nullified. This claim for
Yahweh assumes that in the beginning the nations were all par-

---

17. Predictably Holladay relates the framing to an actual event, whereas
Robert P. Carroll, *Jeremiah*. Old Testament Library (Philadelphia: Westminster
and London: SCM, 1986), believes the framing to be only a literary strategy.

18. In a study of the Plague Cycle in the book of Exodus, Terence E.
Fretheim, "The Plagues as Ecological Signs of Historical Disaster," *Journal
of Biblical Literature* (forthcoming), has observed that the conflict between
Pharaoh and Moses includes the devastation of the nonhuman world. In
parallel fashion, it is noteworthy that the Jeremiah tradition refers to "the
animals" when characterizing the way in which the creator God has turned
creation over to the power of Babylon.

celled out (cf. Deut. 32:8-9). They can, however, be redistributed at any time Yahweh wills, in any way. Yahweh does not need to respect old maps nor adhere to old power arrangements. The nations are put on notice about Yahweh's freedom.

(c) On the basis of the premise of Jer. 27:5, the specific decision of vv. 6-7a is one the nations will need to accept. "All these lands" (i.e., all the nations named in v. 3) are willed by Yahweh to be governed by Nebuchadnezzar and the empire of Babylon. The empire is not an accident. It is Yahweh's intent, and therefore should not be challenged or resisted by the nations.

This is one of the most astonishing claims of the book of Jeremiah, pointing to one of the most pervasive assumptions of the Jeremiah tradition. Nebuchadnezzar is "my servant." The book of Jeremiah has a pronounced "pro-Babylonian cast." That is, the book envisions and entertains the convergence of the *will of God* and the *rise of the empire*. Prophetic faith does not live in a religious vacuum, but must take sides on the public issues of the day. This equation of Yahweh and the rise of Nebuchadnezzar may be political prudence, especially if this text is a late exilic text. It manages to turn submission to real, unavoidable power into a theological virtue. Or perhaps the prophet is simply a sympathizer whose political inclinations are pro-Babylonian and anti-Egyptian. Both factors of prudence and sympathy may indeed be operative. The canonizing process, however, claims more than prudence or bias. It claims that this affirmation of Babylon in light of Yahweh's will is a theological datum. The God of the Bible effectively tilts the international process. The literature dares to discern God's solidarity with a major world power. Accordingly, Yahweh's support of Babylon is to last three generations, that is, a long time past the present rulers (v. 7).

(d) In v. 7b, the announcement of the prophet takes a surprising turn. It is introduced by "until" (Heb. *'ad*). The promise of vv. 5-7 is not permanent. It has a time limit. The phrasing which follows indicates a quite complete and intentional philosophy of history. The text is not simply propaganda for the empire, but is a struggle concerning the tricky relation between the reality of God and *Realpolitik*. The text knows that the Babylonian Empire, even willed by Yahweh, is not absolute or permanent. In the eyes of Yahweh, the empire has a statute of limitation beyond which it cannot endure. In time, Babylon will in turn become subservient to others. Thus the same God who authorizes the empire anticipates its destabilization (eventually enacted in chs. 50–51).

We may propose practical explanations for such an "until." The simplest explanation is to say that this is a late exilic text, composed by those able to discern the erosion of Babylonian power.[19] Or one may say that the Bible writers are shrewd enough to know that every empire eventually exhausts itself in carelessness or overextension and comes to an end.[20] Such practical considerations are in principle not excluded from our interpretation. The canonical process, however, asserts more and other than this. The fall of Babylon will occur because Yahweh wills its ending as Yahweh has willed its rise. The particularities of 27:6-7 are not simply political prudence and "realism," but are theological affirmations that Yahweh does indeed govern the nations, sometimes to their advantage and sometimes to their destruction. We should not dismiss by reductionism the daring or the intense theological, intellectual work in such a claim. The prophet insists that the nations live in a world of moral accountability. This theory of the rise and fall of Babylon as willed by Yahweh is given more precise characterization in Isa. 47. There the rise of Babylon is because

---

19. This is the propensity of Carroll's commentary. In such a view, however, texts can only follow perceived reality and never be original. Such a procedure domesticates texts and tames them to "reality." Such a view does not allow for the authority or courage of the critical vision of the text. *Mutatis mutandis,* one may observe that one did not need to watch for the demise of the Soviet Empire to anticipate that it would surely come to an end, for such power cannot endlessly subjugate the human spirit. In like manner, one need not wait until after the fact to assert that the U.S. "colossus of the North" sooner or later will pay for and relinquish its grip on the peoples of Latin America.

20. Reference should be made here to the careful study of Paul M. Kennedy, *The Rise and Fall of the Great Powers: Economic Change and Military Conflict from 1500 to 2000* (New York: Random House, 1987). Kennedy of course does not include a theological factor in his analysis. The way he marshals his argument, however, makes clear that the rise and fall of the nations is not unrelated to the powerful, unavoidable operation of a moral dimension to public reality. While his analysis is not explicitly parallel to the prophetic tradition of the OT, the two are not without points of contact.

of Yahweh's anger with Israel (Isa. 47:6a). Conversely, the fall of Babylon is because it was excessively ruthless, that is, it showed no mercy (Isa. 47:6b).[21]

The claims of these two verses require a conviction that the human, historical enterprise is not meaningless or autonomous, but reflects an abiding governance beyond the will of either Babylon or Jerusalem. This abiding governance includes a great, expectant "until," at which time Jerusalem will be liberated. Thus this turn in the rhetoric of the sentence converts what has been a harsh judgment on Jerusalem into an act of hope. The time of the turn is not specified, but the homecoming of Jews is as sure as the word itself. The very God who authorizes the deportation into exile is the very God who assures a return (cf. Isa. 54:7-8).[22]

27:8-11 These verses finally continue the decree to the nations from Jer. 27:3. While it is formally addressed to the nations, we may imagine that this is a rhetorical way of addressing Judah and more specifically King Zedekiah. In these verses, the pro-Babylonian claim of the prophet is made even more explicit. The unit consists of two unequal parts. In the first part, the listener is warned about what happens to nations who refuse the hegemony of Babylon which is willed by Yahweh (v. 8). Such nations are subject to the great plagues of sword, famine, and pestilence and will be destroyed.[23] These threats should not be understood "supernaturally." They are the predictable result of an occupying army. Thus the nation that does not submit to Babylon will be devastated by invasion and occupation. In the second part of this unit (v. 11), a nation that submits to Babylon will not be destroyed or exiled. That nation may be incorporated into the empire and its tax structure, but it will remain in its own place. It will not

---

21. See Walter Brueggemann, "At the Mercy of Babylon: A Subversive Rereading of the Empire," *Journal of Biblical Literature* 110 (1991):3-22.

22. See Walter Brueggemann, "A Shattered Transcendence? Exile and Restoration," in *Biblical Theology: Problems and Prospects,* ed. Steven Kraftchick et al. (forthcoming).

23. On such curses, see Delbert R. Hillers, *Treaty-Curses and the Old Testament Prophets.* Biblica et Orientalia 16 (Rome: Pontifical Biblical Institute, 1964).

have the fabric of its own life disrupted. Thus the choices are devastating — death or submission. There is no third alternative. Submission permits continued life in the land.

Between the warning of devastation (v. 8) and the alternative assurance (v. 11), the text warns against false prophets (vv. 9-10). The language of the warning recalls the catalogue of Deut. 18:9-13. The substance of the warning, however, is simply that the false prophets are not pro-Babylonian; they seduce Judah into imagining a third alternative, namely, resistance to the empire. That is, such voices engage in religious fantasy not related to the power realities. There is actually no third alternative, and resistance will lead to death. Such a third alternative of resistance and independence is a false reading of social reality, as it is a false discernment of the will of Yahweh. Not to submit is to be crushed.

One should not draw easy parallels, but the situation is not unlike the slogan "Better dead than Red" used so recently in the face of the perceived threat of the Soviet Union. "Dead" and "Red" were nicely said to be the options. The equivalent of "Red" is to be incorporated into the Babylonian Empire. The prophet urges "Red" rather than "dead." The prophet asserts that submission is now Judah's act of prudence, but it is also Judah's act of obedience to Yahweh. The alternative of resistance is a sure way to be "dead." The prophet makes a strong theological claim, but it is a theological claim that has important historical, political extrapolations. It is impossible, in the tradition of Jeremiah, to sort out what is political realism and what is theological discernment. The tradition refuses to have them separated. The convergence of the two constituted a devastating critique of the royal ideology of Jerusalem which imagined that the will of Yahweh was predictably on the side of Jerusalem safety. Such an ideology could hardly imagine that Yahweh's resolve could be aligned against Judah and not in its favor.

27:12-15   Here the same general message is asserted yet again, this time addressed specifically to King Zedekiah. It is likely that the announcement in Jer. 27:1-11, ostensibly addressed to the nations, is in fact addressed to the Jerusalem community in the years of Zedekiah. Now that address is made explicit. Once more the prophet voices a pro-Babylonian stance. We cannot here (as

19

anywhere else in the tradition) determine to what extent this urging is prudence, bias, or an act of discerning faith. Perhaps it is all three, for discerning faith is not required to be imprudent or neutral. What resounds in these texts is the sure conviction that Yahweh governs the nations, both the great empire and the chosen community. No assertion of ideology, arms, or strategy can prevail against the will of Yahweh which is now being enacted. That irresistible will, as Jeremiah discerns it, is to submit to the yoke of Babylon, to yield to imperial policy. The specific command of v. 12 alludes back to the statement of v. 2, though the wording is somewhat different. The "yoke" of the empire is in this instant understood as the yoke of Yahweh. Subservience to Nebuchadnezzar is obedience to Yahweh. This inscrutable claim is not defended in the text, but it suggests a realism about faith. Submissiveness to political power may be (but is not always) an act of fidelity to the God who orders the affairs of the nations.

The alternative to submissiveness in this case is death, again by the great triad of covenant curses (v. 13). The lean political alternatives of vv. 12-13, either submission or death, are correlated to the religious question of true and false prophecy. More than anyone else in the OT, Jeremiah troubles over rival readings of historical realities, each of which claims to be faithful to Yahweh. The prophet clearly had powerful and articulate competitors and adversaries who urged either that Egypt was a better alternative than Babylon or that resistance was more faithful to Yahweh than was submissiveness.

Recommendation of resistance, claims this tradition, constitutes a "lie" *(sh-q-r)* (v. 14). Such a recommendation is an invitation to fantasy. Judah cannot resist Babylon, because God does not will such resistance. Such a fantasy will lead inevitably to disaster. Of course such a reading of reality cannot be made with objective certitude. Faithful discernment of God in the public process must always be done "in the middle of things," before the data are all in. That is what makes prophetic discernment so problematic and so urgent. Such a prophetic judgment requires the courage to declare without certitude. It is a religious judgment rendered with enormous political risk. But it is the only kind of religious judgment worth bothering with. The alternative is to remain silent and have faith dictated by events. Jeremiah dismisses a more "trusting" option not only as foolish, but as disobedient.

27:16-22   In this fourth section of the decree, the prophet addresses yet another constituency, the priests and the people. (We have already seen in ch. 26 that the priests are his primary adversary.) While the people are named here as an addressee, this word seems peculiarly addressed to the priests, for it concerns temple equipment. The substance of the first part of this section is by now familiar to us (27:16-17). Again the listener is warned against false prophets who were saying that the deportation of 598 would not last long. Only now it is not exiled people who would be returned, but it is the "temple vessels," all the gold and silver accoutrements which signify and enhance the worship of Yahweh.[24] Those temple vessels have now been profaned, mocked, and scandalized by removal, treated as so much indifferent hardware. The loss of such objects is passionately felt because it violates the highest symbolic, sacramental sensitivity of the adherents of the temple system. Again the conclusion is drawn: live by submission! Whoever says otherwise is engaged in a fantasy. Verses 16-17 simply reiterate the preceding announcement made to the nations (vv. 3-11) and to Zedekiah (vv. 12-15).

In v. 18, however, the argument advances in a new direction. Jeremiah throws down the gauntlet to the other prophets. If they want to speak about something important, if they want to make a difference, they should not fantasize about what is lost. They should rather devote their effort (through intercessory prayer) to making sure that Babylon does not come again to take what remained after 598. If they are able by their intercession to stop the empire from further usurpation, that will be an act of genuine authority, and all will know that these prophets are genuine. If Babylon is only the passing threat they imagine, they should be

---

24. Peter R. Ackroyd, "The Temple Vessels: A Continuity Theme," *Supplements to Vetus Testamentum* 23 (1972): 166-181 (repr. in *Studies in the Religious Tradition of the Old Testament* [London: SCM, 1987], 46-60), has demonstrated how the "temple vessels" function in the exilic literature as a sign and gesture of continuity in the disruption of exile. See his comments on our passage, *Studies in the Religious Tradition*, 54-56.

able to stop the flow of goods from the temple to the empire. That is, Jeremiah calls their bluff and requires that their easy word of assurance be put to hard test.

Immediately in vv. 19-22 the prophet refutes his own playful invitation to the adversaries. Even if the other prophets would accept the difficult task Jeremiah has given them, that task is futile. Thus by implication Jeremiah invites his false adversaries to a task they cannot possibly achieve, an impossible mission. From the perspective of Jeremiah and his tradition, not only will the first installment of temple equipment taken in 598 not be returned soon; but the remainder of temple vessels not taken at that time will be taken subsequently. There will not be a quick return (as the other prophets anticipate), but more harsh, intense treatment by the empire. Thus his opponents are doubly wrong.

In our handling of this text, it does not greatly matter if it is in fact dated after 587 when a second usurpation was enacted in Jerusalem. As it stands, the rhetoric of Jeremiah is anticipatory, asserting that God's sovereign will of "empire versus Jerusalem" will be brought to full, harsh fruition. Such a devastating eventuality is certain, even though many thought, hoped, and believed otherwise. The complete raiding of Jerusalem by the empire is as sure as God's rule is sure. Thus the prophet establishes dramatic and unbearable distance and tension between *the rule of God* and the *well-being of Jerusalem*. His opponents imagined that the rule of God and the well-being of Jerusalem were intimately allied. Events of the time supported the harder judgment of Jeremiah. Jerusalem has no "safe conduct" from its God.

Jeremiah's conviction about a second Babylonian seizure in Jerusalem is documented in the historical summary of 52:17-23. Indeed, that chapter is likely added to the literature from 2 Kgs. 25:8-20 as a vindication of Jeremiah's daring assertion in Jer. 27:16-22. Chapter 52 is a detailed summary of the Babylonian operation which includes the items mentioned in 27:19. Everything precious from the temple is placed under imperial control, thus scandalizing the faithful and placing in further jeopardy the ideology of Yahweh's commitment to Jerusalem.

This sequence of pro-Babylonian (i.e., pro-Yahwistic) announcments ends on a decisive and surprising note (vv. 22b).

It is introduced by the word "until" *('ad),* echoing v. 7. This "until" asserts the prophetic expectation that Babylonian power is not absolute but provisional. The exile to Babylon is not for perpetuity, even though it is for a long time. The vessels of the temple will not forever be absent from Jerusalem, even though they will be absent for a long time.

This powerful "until" ultimately breaks the connection between *the destiny of Babylon* and *the will of Yahweh* which the prophet has so determinedly established. In the end, empire and Yahweh are not coterminous. As in v. 7, this "until" announces that the Babylonian Empire is an episode in God's history of sovereignty — an important episode, but only an episode, not to be taken with ultimate seriousness. What is ultimately serious is God's final resolve to restore Judah to its land. The restoration, however, does not negate the exile. This final note is not a capitulation to the voices of false hope earlier combatted by the prophet. This ultimate hope, judged by the canon to be genuine, is not a hope based on the collapse of the empire, but a hope rooted in God's positive and faithful regard for Judah, a regard which will outlast the Babylonian moment of domination. The long-term survival of the empire and its ultimate termination, in the reckoning of this tradition, both attest to the rule of Yahweh. The prophet is willing to discern the will of Yahweh in the midst of the empire, but not so that the two are equated. Jeremiah ends in agreement with his critics: there will be restoration. But it will not be soon or easy. In the end, Jeremiah's argument is of a quite different kind. He does the difficult work of affirming hope, but without grounding it in the ideology of the city.

28:1-17 This chapter includes a concrete and dramatic confrontation reflecting a continuing dispute about the programmatic decree announced in ch. 27. This narrative account is intentionally linked to the preceding chapter (28:1), but is made much more specific. The new voice in the dispute is Hananiah, a prophet who uses the same messenger formula as does Jeremiah to authenticate his speech: "Thus says the LORD" (v. 2). Like Jeremiah, he claims to be sent and authorized by Yahweh (cf. 23:21-22). His name is perhaps telling, for Hananiah means "Yahweh is gracious." His message is precisely that Yahweh is more immediately and powerfully gracious than Jeremiah can allow. Thus the dispute about the future of Jerusalem in the end is a dispute about the character and intention of God, for the life of Jerusalem flows from the life of God.

The first speech of Hananiah (28:2-4) directly challenges the preceding assertion of Jeremiah in 27:16-22. The Babylonian yoke of 27:12 is quickly a broken yoke at the hand of Hananiah (28:2). Babylonian domination will end, and with it, Judah's exile. The disaster of 598 will be undone, and of course, there is no prospect in the horizon of Hananiah for a later, second invasion and exile. Israel's life in all its parts will be resumed. Temple vessels will be restored (v. 3). The exiled king will be restored to power (v. 4). The positive and faithful inclination of Yahweh will result in full restoration and return to normalcy in Jerusalem.

Thus the issue is joined sharply and decisively. In a political dimension, there is a sharp disagreement about the future of the empire and how lasting Babylonian domination will be. Such political judgments, however, are rooted in competing convictions concerning the character of Yahweh and Yahweh's commitment to the Jerusalem establishment. It is not clear why Hananiah speaks this message and makes this judgment. The text does not probe his motivation or rootage at all. Perhaps he is a sheer opportunist who tells the king what the king most wants to hear. That possibility is a standard stereotype among us of a "false prophet." Likely matters are too serious and stakes are too high for such a surface assessment. Likely Hananiah had better and more serious reasons for his statement.

Two other explanations seem more cogent and more serious. On the one hand, Hananiah may be rooted in the royal theology of Israel, trusting in God's commitment to the temple and to the dynasty.[25] Thus the central issue is whether God would honor those long-standing commitments and much-celebrated promises to Zion. Hananiah's position then is not opportunistic, but is a reiteration of

---

25. Carroll, 537, concludes: "So the prophets of v. 16 were right after all but were wrong about the timing!" The difference about the timing, however, is decisive. The other prophets want to collapse the two events of exile and return. The distance between the two, upon which this text insists, makes two experiences qualitatively and decisively different.

God's trustworthiness rooted in the normative theological tradition of Jerusalem. On the other hand and more specifically, Hananiah's message is congruent with the words of Isaiah a century earlier.[26] We know that Isaiah's words were vindicated in the astonishing deliverance of the city from the Assyrian threat in 701. There is no doubt that that miraculous rescue generated in Jerusalem supreme confidence that God is and would be the patron and guarantor of the holy city. Hananiah thus may be a disciple of the tradition of Isaiah and simply anticipates that God would again perform such an act of deliverance. Working from historical parallelism, the crisis of 598 did not seem so very different from the events of 701.

Whether Hananiah appeals primarily to the David-Zion traditions or to the memory of Isaiah, we may imagine that he spoke in good faith and believed he was articulating a serious form of bold and responsible faith. He is likely not a charlatan or a huckster. He is, nonetheless, judged by the canonical tradition to have been false in his faith. That falseness may be a judgment rooted in historical outcomes, for his anticipation was not in fact what happened. That is, the exile in Babylon was not short term, and the restoration was not quick, as he anticipated. Alternatively, Hananiah's falseness may be a theological judgment, for his word did not reckon with the stern, conditional quality of Yahweh's promise so championed by the tradition of Jeremiah. Either way, his hope rooted in an old, treasured memory, in this context, is an ideological distortion; it does not reflect what God is doing here and now. If the present-tense reality of God cannot be discerned, then any prophetic discernment is likely ideology. Thus yesterday's certitude has become today's distorting ideology.[27]

Jeremiah responds to the challenge of Hananiah (vv. 5-9). His response is in a quite public forum, for we are witnessing a crucial debate about policy (v. 5). The response of Jeremiah consists of three

---

26. On the ideology of the temple and its delicate relation to the claims of the dynasty, see Ben C. Ollenburger, *Zion, the City of the Great King.* Journal for the Study of the Old Testament Supplement 41 (Sheffield: JSOT Press, 1987), 59-66 and *passim.*

27. On the ideological dimension of Hananiah in this narrative, see Mottu, "Jeremiah vs. Hananiah," 235-251.

parts. First, he responds to Hananiah with the wish (perhaps ironic or even sarcastic) that Hananiah may be correct, that deliverance will be soon, and that exile will not be protracted (v. 6). The first word of the response is "Amen." If the word is sarcastic, it might be rendered, "Right!", dripping with mocking and disbelief. That hope for the quick rescue promised by Hananiah (perhaps voiced in disbelief) is quickly countered in vv. 7-8 with an adversative introduced by "yet" *(ak)*. The tradition of Jeremiah is eager to place Jeremiah in a succession of prophets, so that he is not an isolated case. In this second part, the prophet appeals to "former prophets." The argument is that "real prophets" speak mainly of the covenant, of its requirements, and of its ominous sanctions for disobedience — war, famine, and pestilence. This argument does not in and of itself negate Hananiah, but it puts us on notice that Hananiah is against the mainstream of prophetic announcement. Thus the argument is that Hananiah is suspect because he does not say what prophets characteristically say. He is soft on the dangers of covenant disobedience.

In the third element of Jeremiah's response, Hananiah's word of "well-being" *(shalom)* can be tested (cf. 6:14; 8:11). It is not likely that Hananiah is correct, but the test is whether his word comes to fruition. Thus Jeremiah appeals to the test of prophets proposed in Deut. 18:22. For Jeremiah and the tradition of Jeremiah, a tradition so committed to and self-conscious of its memory, the burden of proof is on Hananiah, because he has taken a stand against the main strand of prophetic speech.

Hananiah's word can only be tested through the passage of time. It is as though Jeremiah anticipates Gamaliel, who counselled: "If this plan or this undertaking is of men, it will fail; but if it is of God, you will not be able to overthrow them. You might even be found opposing God!" (Acts 5:38-39). That, however, does not help much in the present, for decisions must be made and policies must be enacted. This criterion for assessing Hananiah seems almost for the sake of the canon. When the book of Jeremiah was ultimately framed, presumably in exile, enough time had passed to judge Hananiah and vindicate Jeremiah. "Peace" had not come as Hananiah had promised. God does not so promptly override God's own moral judgments. Whoever imagines that God will, is in fact false. Thus the text, even though set in a critical moment, has the long-term effect of establishing the authenticity of Jeremiah as the one who rightly discerned God's way with Judah. The "true prophet" must take into account the reality of God's free rule and the fact that even the well-being of Israel depends upon fidelity. There are no "quick fixes" for a people which distorts Yahweh's will. No ideology of continuity can deliver a quick rescue in the face of such fundamental distortion. While the dispute was urgent in the moment of Zedekiah, it is as though the canonical text is building a record of vindication for Jeremiah. The later community can remember and attest that there was in those difficult days one voice who spoke the truth. That one voice emerges canonically as an enduring witness and a recurring reminder.

Hananiah, however, is convinced, intransigent, and imaginative (Jer. 28:10-11). He is cast in the role of the antagonist necessary to the drama, but sure to be defeated. Jeremiah had worn yoke-bars as a sign of exile (27:2). Now the narrative returns to that initial notice. Hananiah dramatically breaks the symbolic yoke, thus articulating God's liberating action (28:10). Hananiah comments on his action by reiterating his judgment that in two years the Exile will end (cf. v. 3). His act is offered as a gesture of good news. The narrative leaves Hananiah's gesture unanswered and unrefuted. It is left lingering in the narrative, unresolved (v. 11).

Unfortunately, it is far easier to break a symbolic yoke than it is to override Yahweh's tough verdict or to break the reality of Babylonian power. Hananiah's symbolic act of breaking is a symbol without corresponding reality. Jeremiah, "after the breaking," makes one more response to Hananiah (vv. 12-16). The real yoke of exile is like iron, not like wood. It is unbreakable. It is unbreakable, not because it is hard metal, but because Yahweh's sovereign decree is for Babylonian domination. Jeremiah is unshakable in this discernment of reality. The God of this text is not an inevitable patron of state religion, but has enough distance and freedom from the royal apparatus to be for or against God's own people (cf. 23:23).

Jeremiah's response to the "breaking" is in two parts. First, he reasserts God's intention for public reality (28:14). God gives the world over to Nebuchadnezzar. Moreover, this authorized hegemony includes not only the human, political enterprise, but even the "beasts of the field." Thus Nebuchadnezzar has become God's "new adam" who will have his way in the world. The verdict could not be more sweeping. Second, after the assertion about public policy, Jeremiah addresses the person of Hananiah, the office of the prophet, and the matter of truth (vv. 15-16).

These verses constitute a lawsuit form aimed at Hananiah. The indictment is in v. 15. Hananiah has not been dispatched by Yahweh but is making up the good news on his own. The outcome is a "lie" *(sh-q-r)*.[28] Both the prophet and his word are a lie. In v. 6, Jeremiah had uttered the word "true" *(amen),* perhaps in mocking or perhaps in hope. Now, however, that hope is dismissed. The verdict is "false" *(sh-q-r),* not true *(amen).* The sentence of the lawsuit is in v. 16: "Therefore, behold . . ." The sentence corresponds to the offense.[29] The offense was, "I did not send." The sentence is "I will send you." The RSV translation does not reflect the rhetorical correspondence. It renders, "I will remove," but the wording is, "I will send you now, for I did not send you to prophesy." That is, I will send you away from the earth, that is, to death. Hananiah had announced life for Judah, but his own destiny is certain death. Hananiah is a rebel against God and so must be dismissed. Jeremiah is impatient and heavy-handed with those who distort, mislead, soothe, and falsely reassure in Jerusalem.

The narrator adds tersely, "He died in the same year" (v. 17). Death was announced as a verdict in v. 16. In the same year the word comes to fulfillment. The report serves several purposes. It discredits Hananiah. It attests to the legitimacy of Jeremiah and his vocation. Moreover, it removes the hope of an immediate deliverance. As the messenger is eliminated, so the false message evaporates. It is worth noting that the terse conclusion makes no theological claim. It does not say that Yahweh destroyed Hananiah. Rather, it is a lean factual account. But of course, in this freighted, self-conscious narrative,

---

28. On the role of the term *sh-q-r* in the tradition of Jeremiah and especially in chs. 27–28, see Overholt, *The Threat of Falsehood.*

29. On the characteristic correspondence of sin and judgment, see Patrick D. Miller, Jr., *Sin and Judgment in the Prophets.* SBL Monograph 27 (Chico: Scholars Press, 1982). So far as I can determine, Miller does not cite this particular case.

such a factual report points beyond itself to the great theological issue of truth and falsehood. The issue of truth and falsehood is, however, not a theoretical issue. It concerns the will of Yahweh, the power of Babylon, and the future of Jerusalem.

The career of Hananiah in ch. 28 is only an episode which exercises no lasting impact upon the tradition of Israel. The distorting force of Hananiah passes quickly from the scene and the toughness of Jeremiah endures. By 28:17 we are made freshly aware that the prophetic announcement of ch. 27 is in effect. Yahweh is a hard sovereign. Jerusalem is under stern judgment. Jeremiah, the messenger of a hard sovereign, bears the message of stern judgment. No ideology or wishful religion can deny the intention of Yahweh in history as Jeremiah has voiced it. All the world can see is Babylonian imperialism. The community of this text, however, knows more. It knows that the real agent is not Nebuchadnezzar, visible as he is, but the God who "plucks up and tears down."

And we, long after Hananiah is gone, are left with this relentless text. We are left to ponder that, in a world of raw imperial power and in a world of well-wishing religious passion, there is this other claim made upon Jerusalem and every holy operation, upon Babylon and every concentration of world power. One cannot generalize from this specific case about power politics. The canonical shape of the story, however, keeps Jeremiah lingering as a witness into the very long future.

CORRESPONDENCE WITH THE EXILES (29:1-32)

This chapter has important connections to chs. 27–28. Those chapters asserted that the exile in Babylon after 598 would be extended over a long time. This chapter gives attention to those in exile since 598 who must find ways to live faithfully and hopefully in the midst of exile. In giving counsel to the exiles, this chapter implies a confirmation of Jeremiah's proclamation in chs. 27–28. The chapter has closest affinities with ch. 24, where the same exiles are addressed as the carriers of God's future.[30] On critical grounds,

---

30. See Walter Brueggemann, "A Second Reading of Jeremiah after the Dismantling," *Ex Auditu* 1 (1985): 156-168.

it is likely that the materials in chs. 24 and 29 reflect a later traditioning process in a subsequent generation of exiles. As the texts are now presented, both chs. 24 and 29 characterize Jeremiah as practicing pastoral care among the exiles. That pastoral care is expressed around two convictions: (a) there must be a realistic and intentional *embrace of the Exile* as a place where Jews must now be and where God has summoned them to obedience (29:5-7), and (b) there is *a long-term hope for return and restoration* that can be affirmed and accepted (vv. 10-14).

Both affirmations are important for the exiles and for the shape of the Jeremiah tradition. The first, which enacts "tearing down and plucking up," offers an alternative against romantic escapism and abdication. The second, which enacts "building and planting," speaks against ultimate despair. The two themes together correspond to the governing verbs of 1:10 and reflect the basic structure of the completed message of the Jeremiah tradition. While Jeremiah's word is characteristically one of judgment, it is striking that this voice of judgment brings with it a powerful voice of hope. The suffering of exile is for the OT the matrix in which the hope of God is most powerfully and characteristically at work.[31] The Exile is the place where God's faithful promises work a profound newness. Nowhere is this more passionately voiced than in the tradition of Jeremiah. Thus the completed tradition anticipates Paul: ". . . suffering produces endurance, and endurance produces character, and character produces hope, and hope does not disappoint us . . ." (Rom. 5:3-5).

29:1-3   These verses provide a frame for the pastoral letter of Jer. 29:4ff.[32] The letter is addressed to all those who were removed to

---

31. See Walter Brueggemann, *Hopeful Imagination: Prophetic Voices in Exile* (Philadelphia: Fortress, 1986).

32. The form of the letter is perhaps to be taken seriously. It is not implausible that such a written communication could have been sent from Jerusalem to the exiles in Babylon. Cf. William L. Holladay, "God Writes a Rude Letter (Jeremiah 29:1-23)," *Biblical Archaeologist* 46 (1983): 145-46. Nonetheless, it is difficult to determine where the letter ends in this chapter. Perhaps it ends in v. 23, suggesting that the letter is a witness against the false teaching. In form, however, the letter is transmuted into a prophetic oracle. Except for the framing in vv. 1-3 (and the mention of other letters in vv. 25,

Babylon in 598. There was important tension after 598 (and before 587) between those who had been deported and those who remained in the city of Jerusalem (cf. ch. 24). In his pro-Babylonian posture, Jeremiah concludes that the ones exiled are the bearers of Judah's hope for the future and the special object of God's attentive love and concern. This judgment about the exiles is congruent with the larger tendency of the Jeremiah tradition. It is to the latter that the letter is addressed, the ones who count for the future.

The letter is carried by royal messengers.[33] It is not known whether they are dispatched for the purpose of carrying this letter or whether it is incidentally taken along with other business. Because the letter is such a public matter, and because Jeremiah had intense interactions with King Zedekiah, carrying such letters may have been routine business for any diplomatic courier. The verse following the substance of the letter was a quite public matter (29:29).

The letter purports to extend from v. 4 to v. 28. It is framed by the reiteration in v. 28 of the main admonition of v. 5; the accent is on the imperative verbs, "build, live, plant, and eat." This is the key pastoral advice of the message. Between these two framing verses (vv. 5, 28) is a series of prophetic oracles. The first is cast as a letter, but the later ones make little claim to the form of a letter and are simply oracles. The burden of the whole is that exile will be long and unavoidable, but not to perpetuity. Judah must accept exile as its proper place, and there must live its life and practice its faith.

29:5-7   Here is the most poignant statement of the long unit. In a series of imperatives, vv. 5-6 urge the development of sustained communal life in exile. Judah is to build and plant (cf. 1:10), to marry and to have their children marry. That is, Judah is to prepare for a long haul, because exile will extend beyond the present generation. Even in exile, Judah is to multiply just as the

---

29-30), the chapter becomes a series of oracles which continue the debate and conflict of chs. 27–28.

33. It is important that one of the messengers is a son of Shaphan, suggesting a convergence of the fortunes of Jeremiah, the interests of the king, and the engagement of a powerful family that was pro-Babylonian in its politics (cf. 26:24, where another son of Shaphan protected Jeremiah).

old enslaved community of Exod. 1 multiplied. Even in displacement, Judah continues to be the people over which God's promise
for the future presides with power.

Then comes a stunning and remarkable turn in the letter (Jer.
29:7). This additional imperative reflects the Babylonian propensity of the Jeremiah tradition. It also reflects political realism,
urging the exiles to accommodate their imperial overlord. "The
city where I have sent you" is Babylon. Jews in exile are to work
for the well-being *(shalom)* of the empire and its capital city. The
well-being *(shalom)* of Judah is dependent upon and derivative
from that of Babylon. This positive attention toward Babylon is
very different from the deep resentment toward the imperial
masters generally and Babylon particularly as expressed elsewhere
(in the Jeremiah tradition, see chs. 50–51, and also Isa. 13-14,
47). Prophetic faith is powerfully realistic about the political situation of the Jews in exile. The Jews have no option to Babylon,
which is God's chosen habitat for the exiles.

There is, however, more than realism in this assertion. The
imperative bestows upon this vulnerable, small community a large
missional responsibility. In this way, the community is invited into
the larger public process of the empire. Such a horizon prevents
the exilic community from withdrawing into its own safe, sectarian
existence, and gives it work to do and responsibility for the larger
community.

29:8-9   The text now returns to the recurring problem of false
prophets, as already seen in chs. 23, 27–28. This particular warning
reflects the concern of Deut. 13:1-5, which may identify the editorial hand at work in the completed text. The concern of the text
is not a theoretical one about the nature of prophecy. The concern
is a quite practical one, concerning the seduction of religious fantasy.
The threat to the Jews is that they will be talked out of the reality of
exile, invited to deny the real place where they must live their faith.
Thus Jer. 29:5-7 affirms the real place of exile; the warning of vv.
8-9 is against an emotional, imaginative departure from that place,
that is, engagement in an illusion. Prophetic faith is hard-nosed
realism that is resistant to romantic, ideological escapism. No
pretense based in religious fantasy can extricate God's people from

their actual place in history. Those who permit religion to abrogate historical-political reality speak a lie.

29:10-14   While vv. 5-9 assert the reality of exile and the responsibility of being fully engaged with it, vv. 10-14 move the horizon of Judah beyond exile to assert the hope of return from exile. This is one of the most powerful, intense, and freighted announcements of return in all of Scripture. It is a rich inventory of Israel's primary formulas for hope of return. The reference to "seventy years" (25:11) is apparently a convention, perhaps not to be taken literally.

Moving beyond the actual circumstance of 29:5-9, the text makes a claim that is profoundly theological: Yahweh will keep the promise of homecoming (v. 10). That promise is rooted in God's long-term resolve for Judah. It had seemed through much of the Jeremiah tradition that God intended only evil for God's people. In the face of the *evil* of exile, however, the text asserts Yahweh's more fundamental interest in doing *good* for this people. This assertion does not nullify the long Jeremianic tradition of judgment. Rather, it moves through, past, and beyond judgment to assert Yahweh's final resolve. God has a long-term "plan" for Judah that is not defeated by particular historical circumstance. (On the "plan of Yahweh" for Judah, see Gen. 50:20; Deut. 4:29-31; Isa. 55:6-9.) Yahweh exercises sovereignty even beyond the reality of Babylon. There is a future willed by God that refutes any despair which Judah has experienced. The juxtaposition of Jer. 29:5-9 and 10-14 explicates the deep judgment and the powerful purpose of Yahweh which are held together in tension, both in the heart of God and in the destiny of Israel.

Yahweh had seemed to the exiles to be hidden, absent, unavailable, and ineffective. In vv. 12-14a, however, God is now available (cf. Isa. 54:7-8). It is only required that Israel must "come, seek, and pray." That is, the exiles must engage in serious acts of piety and penance. More than that, Judah must reorient its life in exile. When Judah repents, Judah will find Yahweh to be faithful, available, ready and able to save. Precisely in a situation of hopelessness, Yahweh is announced to be the one who will overcome hopelessness and open a new possibility to Judah. Judah must only decide to seek its future exclusively from Yahweh. The exclusiveness is asserted in the characteristic language of Deuteronomy, "all your

heart" (cf. Deut. 6:5; 13:3). Yahweh wills a people utterly devoted.
And when there is such an utterly devoted people, life is made
newly possible. This is an assertion of the gospel: God is available
in the midst of despair and will override both the despair and the
circumstances which generate it.

In the juxtaposition of Jer. 29:5-9 and vv. 10-14, we may observe
a play on the word *shalom*. On the one hand, there is a contrast
between the *shalom* which is a *task* for the exiles (v. 7) and a *gift* from
God to the exiles (v. 11). On the other hand, the *shalom* of v. 7 is
the welfare of the empire, whereas in v. 11 it is *shalom* for the
community of exiles. Thus the two units together provide a subtle
reflection on the subject of *shalom*, a subject which the exiles have
on their mind even in their chaotic situation of displacement.[34] In
the midst of the Exile, there is energy to meditate on and anticipate
the possibility of *shalom* for Israel and for the world.

The God newly available in exile will act for the exiles (v. 14b).
The conclusion of this oracle is dominated by first person verbs
in the mouth of Yahweh: "I will restore, I will gather, I will bring
you back." It is not denied that Yahweh has caused the Exile: "I
have driven you; I sent you into exile." Yahweh is not, however,
fated to any decree of the past, nor is Judah in exile fated by
Yahweh's old decree. God can do a new thing. This is a moment
of a new decree from Yahweh which opens a new future from
God for Judah. As *exile* is Israel's most devastating judgment, so
homecoming and restoration to the land are Israel's deepest yearning
and God's best gift. The God who has displaced Judah will now
restore Judah. This is, in God's heart and in Judah's faith, a
moment for radical newness, rooted only in God's good resolve.

The two units of vv. 5-9 and 10-14 express the core convictions
of the Jeremiah tradition. They are hard-won affirmations. The
counsel to settle in exile (vv. 5-9) is against the popular notion that
the Exile is short and temporary. The counsel to look beyond exile

---

34. In the exilic proclamation of 2 Isaiah, the subject of *shalom* is again
articulated (cf. Isa. 52:7). Moreover, if *shalom* is the opposite of chaos (cf.
Isa. 45:18-19), then *shalom* is understood as the opposite of exile. The promise
of *shalom* and the task of *shalom* in our passage then are alternatives to the
present disordered experience of exile.

(vv. 10-14) is against the temptation to despair. Both affirmations from the prophet are in fact counter to prevailing opinion. The capacity to entertain both of these affirmations is more than pragmatism, opportunism, and self-interest. Rather, it witnesses a robust dynamic in the textual tradition. It asserts that God has more than one thing to do with Judah, and Judah has more than one moment in its destiny. "True prophecy" is the capacity to say the right thing at the right time, a capacity not exercised by the prophets of optimism nor by the voices of despair. The canonical process is a conviction that Jeremiah rightly sounded both notes of faith at the right moment.

The remainder of this chapter shows the Jeremiah tradition in combat with alternative opinions. These verses reflect the deep tension in the Jewish community between 598 and 587, and no doubt in the same communities later on. Those who remained in Jerusalem after the deportation of 598 continued to believe they were favored by God and regarded themselves as the blessed carriers of Judaism. This was a natural, commonsense assessment. The tradition of Jeremiah, however, a tradition that voices a scandalous alternative, asserted that the ones in exile are favored by God and the ones in Jerusalem are to come under harsh judgment. Moreover, there were those among the Babylonian exiles who articulated the "Jerusalem line," to the chagrin and despair of the deported. In these verses Jeremiah counters that conventional Jerusalem view with his more difficult reading of historical reality. The claim of this tradition is that the ones apparently defeated through deportation are the community from which future Jerusalem will emerge.[35]

29:15-19   The dispute over the truth of faith is treated in three distinct units. The first unit is framed in vv. 15-19 by two indictments (vv. 15, 19). Both indictments are critiques of the prophets who disagree with Jeremiah and who are regarded by the Jeremiah tradition as unprincipled ideologues and propagandists. The main indictment is that they did not "listen," for if they had heeded, they

---

35. A Christian appropriation of this affirmation is evident in the christological claim that it is the rejected, scandalized One who is crucified, who is God's way to new life. See, e.g., 1 Cor. 1:18-25; Phil. 2:5-11.

would not have disagreed with Jeremiah's proclamation. Between these two indictments is the sentence against the king (Zedekiah) and the community remaining in the city (vv. 16-18). The actual curse is conventional language in two formulas. First, the prophet names the three massive curses of sword, famine, and pestilence, which all arise with an occupying army (v. 17). Thus, in effect, the curse anticipates the second invasion of the imperial army. Second, in v. 18 that triad is repeated, but then the heavier threat is that the city will be "a curse, a terror, a hissing, and a reproach" (cf. Deut. 28:37). Using traditional language, the text anticipates the time when the city will be utterly destroyed and an embarrassment among the nations. The two formulas together in Jer. 29:17-18 anticipate (a) another occupation (sword, famine, pestilence) and (b) an ultimate devastation (curse, terror, hissing, reproach). These troubles will come because there has not been obedient torah-listening. Those clinging to the old uncritical hopes of the Jerusalem establishment, to the disregard of the torah, receive the heaviest indictment from the prophet.

29:20-23   In the second of these conflict narratives, the same charges as in vv. 8-9, 15, 19 are voiced, only this time with particular reference to two prophets. Presumably Ahab and Zedekiah were two prophetic adversaries, but we know nothing about them. Again the judgment is the same. They will be submitted to violent death at the hands of the Babylonians, because they pronounced a lie. That is, they did not comprehend and articulate who Yahweh really is and what Yahweh is doing. Their unreality about the historical prospects of Judah is rooted in their unreality about the demands of Yahweh. Their historical judgment is skewed because they did not treat torah religion seriously. They could not believe that God's demands are so serious that disregard would lead to trouble with the public process of history.

After the initial indictment and threat (v. 20), the text then reflects on how these two prophets will become a byword among the exiles (vv. 21-23). They will be a point of ridicule, but also a source of warning to others. The warning among the exiles is "Don't be like Ahab and Zedekiah." Since we know nothing about them, we cannot assess the charges made, except to note that the anticipated mocking of them departs considerably from the standard formulations we have had thus far concerning falseness. Thus the threat is worse than a conventional one. They are "roasted" by the king of Babylon (v. 22). Moreover, their affront is of a different kind: "They have committed folly in Israel [and] they have committed adultery with their neighbors' wives" (v. 23). It is difficult to know how to relate this quite personal charge to the more standard phrasing about false prophets. It may be that the true prophets had the wrong ideology but then attracted this more specific moral indictment. Or perhaps they were troublemakers in the community that had attached to them the more generalizing indictment about falsehood. Perhaps the charge of "adultery" is to be taken metaphorically in relation to falsehood. In any case, these prophets are treated as models of disobedience, used to warn against both moral corruption and theological distortion. The outcome of the oracle is to underscore the rule of Yahweh who will not be deterred from power, either by the empire or by distorting Jewish faith. Yahweh's governance is not altered or diminished by religious posturing or by political wishing. Those who resist the rule of Yahweh, both in its judgment and in its hope, will come to a sorry end.

29:24-32   Finally, one more opponent of Jeremiah is named. Presumably this adversary, Shemaiah, is also in Babylon. The letters he sends (vv. 25, 29) are intended in the present form of the text as a contrast and foil to the earlier letter of Jeremiah. The prophet among the exiles (Shemaiah) urges the priest in Jerusalem (Zephaniah) to exercise his priestly office by suppressing the prophets who are mad, that is, who contradict established opinion (v. 26; cf. Hos. 9:7). Specifically, Shemaiah urges Zephaniah to restrain Jeremiah, who has been speaking subversively. It is the same old issue one more time. The charge made against Jeremiah in Jer. 29:28 is a quote from the letter of vv. 4-5. Jeremiah, in his realism about the Exile, is ideologically unacceptable to this prophet. Thus the letter from Shemaiah is not only a counter to the letter of Jeremiah, but is in fact evoked by it and intends to refute it. The intent of Shemaiah is that the Jews should receive "better news," which means to deny their true situation in exile.

    Zephaniah, the priest who is the target of Shemaiah's letter, shares the letter with Jeremiah but does not act on it (v. 29). Apparently he is allied with Jeremiah, or at least sympathetic to him. Predictably the consultation of v. 29 leads to yet another oracle from Jeremiah (vv. 30-32). This oracle deals only with Shemaiah, who is condemned as a liar (v. 31). He and his family are excluded from any future in Judah, because his teaching is an act of "rebellion" against God and God's intent for Judah. At the end of v. 32 this heavy oracle against a particular opponent takes a final positive turn. God will do *good* for God's people (v. 32). Thus we have a contrast between *good for Judah* and *evil for the deceiving prophet*. The *good* here echoes the *shalom* of vv. 11-14, which is homecoming. There will be a homecoming! It will, however, be in Yahweh's own time. It will not be soon or easy, but it is sure.

This is an exceedingly complex chapter, reflecting a deep divide and conflict in the Jewish community. It continues the dispute of chs. 27–28. Indeed, the issue with Ahab, Zedekiah, and Shemaiah is reminiscent of the issue with Hananiah. The canonical Jeremiah tradition accepted as *true* the pro-Babylonian stance of Jeremiah! On the one hand, this view resists the easy assurance that generates *false hope,* as in the case of Hananiah. This is the central issue in the conflict against Ahab, Zedekiah, and Shemaiah, who echo Hananiah. Against their optimism, Jeremiah urges realism. The hard claim of biblical faith characteristically resists easy, romantic renderings. On the other hand, as a subordinate counterpoint, Jeremiah affirms that there will be a homecoming in God's good time. This affirmation is against *weary resignation* which ends in despair, as though exile is a permanent fate.

Against both illusionary expectation and despairing resignation, Jeremiah speaks of God's powerful governance which both settles into exile and ends exile. Jeremiah seeks to extricate Yahweh's sovereign rule from every political compromise and qualification. It may, of course, be argued that Jeremiah's pro-Babylonian posture is itself a pragmatic compromise. Inside the claim of the text itself, however, this posture is affirmed as theologically correct, as congruent with God's own purpose. The purposes of God cannot be trimmed and fitted to any political resolution, either falsely assuring or misleadingly negating. God has God's own way, which is with utter freedom and, in the end, caring fidelity.

"THE BOOK OF COMFORT"
Jeremiah 30:1–33:26

The primary work of the book of Jeremiah is to speak Israel into exile. While Jeremiah is given a twofold task in 1:10, "to pluck up and to tear down, to build and to plant," the negative theme is much more decisive for and prevalent in the book of Jeremiah. Indeed, the book of Jeremiah is framed in 1:1-3 and 52:12-30 to situate the literature toward and in exile. The primary burden of the literature is that Israel, Judah, and Jerusalem will be dismantled according to the intention of Yahweh.

The countertheme of "plant and build," however, is indeed present in the literature. It is that theme which governs chs. 30–33. The editorial process of the book of Jeremiah has grouped together in these chapters the primary materials voicing God's intention of newness and, derivatively, Israel's restoration after exile.[1]

We may identify three dimensions of the promissory materials which concern us. First, there are important historical considerations. In fact, the Exile was not the end of the Jewish community or of Jewishness. On the one hand, Jerusalem was not "emptied" by the Babylonians, but many Jews continued in the city. On the other hand, the Jewish community in Babylon developed an intentional and intense self-consciousness as a faithful community in exile. This community understood and presented itself as a community in waiting, and preempted for itself the claim to be the "real Israel" which would shape post-587 B.C.E.

---

1. On the critical problems related to the promises in Jeremiah, see Siegfried Herrmann, *Die prophetischen Heilserwartungen im Alten Testament*. Beiträge zur Wissenschaft vom Alten und Neuen Testament 85 (Stuttgart: Kohlhammer, 1965), 159-241.

Judaism.[2] Thus historical reality required that an honest portrayal of Israel with God should be amazed by and grateful for the survival and continuation of Jewishness. It turned out that "plucking up and tearing down" was not the last moment in Judaism. Something had to be said about that resilient historical reality.

Second, there is no doubt that the promissory passages function in a pastoral way to voice comfort, consolation, assurance, and hope for the exiles. It was not unreasonable that after 587 Jews in exile and in Jerusalem should have the sense that God had abandoned God's people, or at least was absent. The promissory oracles are in part evoked by such a sense of abandonment, intending to counter such a mood. In a very practical way, the promises serve to give Jews courage and energy to keep on keeping on.

Third, however, the historical and pastoral dimensions of these promises do not touch the reality of the Jeremiah text. Indeed, if there were no real substance to the promises of God, then they simply misread in terms of the historical facts, and they mislead in terms of pastoral crisis. In the end, the ground of hope and promise in Israel and in these texts is theological, that is, it is concerned with and for the character of God.[3] Historical criticism,

---

2. The assertiveness and claim to preeminence of the Babylonian community of exiles is evidenced in the narrative reports of Ezra and Nehemiah as the initiators of what came to be Judaism. It is certain that this community in Babylon played a decisive role both in preserving the normative text for Judaism and in shaping the normative canon. While its claim to preeminence may be overstated, it is clear that the claim is rooted in actual reality.

3. A great deal of literature exists on the identity of the God of Israel as a God who makes and keeps promises. The primary and most influential in this regard is Albrecht Alt, "The God of the Fathers," *Essays on Old Testament History and Religion* (Garden City: Doubleday, 1969), 1-100. See also Gerhard von Rad, *Old Testament Theology* 1 (New York: Harper & Row and Edinburgh: Oliver & Boyd, 1962), 165-174; *Old Testament Theology* 2 (New York: Harper & Row and Edinburgh: Oliver & Boyd, 1965), 263-277; Claus Westermann, *The Promises to the Fathers* (Philadelphia: Fortress, 1980); and Walther Zimmerli, *Man and His Hope in the Old Testament.* Studies in Biblical Theology, 2nd series 20 (London: SCM and Naperville: Allenson, 1971). Note in the work of Zimmerli the important reference to Ernst Bloch. This strand of OT study was taken up in systematic theology in the decisive work of Jürgen

in my judgment, has worked too hard at relating such promises to specific historical situations, seeking to explain the text in terms of context.[4] This sort of correlation tends to diminish the bold theological claim that the ground for assurance is not found in needy circumstance but in the character and resolve of God and in nothing other and in nothing less.

In the book of Jeremiah, the mandate "to build and to plant," that is, to restore, revive, and rehabilitate God's people and God's city, is presented as a resolve of God's own heart (cf. 29:11). The God of Israel (and of the book of Jeremiah) is in fact a self-starter whose speech grows out of a passion for a new beginning and whose speech guarantees newness, for what God says, God will do. The theological ground for the promissory claim depends on two factors. First, *God is faithful* to God's people and to God's promise (cf. 31:28). God does not quit or abandon or disregard. In these texts, particularly in 30:12-17 and 30:20, God's fidelity emerges with fresh power out of God's hurt and yearning for this people. Second, *God is powerful* and able, in spite of Israelite recalcitrance and in spite of imperial resistance, to work a newness in the real world of public power. *The faithfulness and the power of Yahweh* assure that in the depth of Israel's exile God will work a homecoming, in the face of Israel's death God will work new life. That is the substance and burden of these chapters.

In making such a theological affirmation that brusquely overrides historical circumstance, we are not yet at the wonder of these promissory texts. The wonder of these texts is that the resolve of God rooted in God's faithful and powerful character comes to

---

Moltmann, *Theology of Hope* (New York: Harper & Row, 1967). The promissory element in Jeremiah is to be understood in the context of the more general promissory dimension of Israel's faith.

4. Brevard S. Childs, *Introduction to the Old Testament as Scripture* (Philadelphia: Fortress and London: SCM, 1979), has paid primary attention to the canonical shape of the text. For Childs this means that the context of any passage of Scripture is not some historical situation, but the place where it is situated in the larger, completed text. Thus the promises of Jeremiah are to be understood, not in a sixth-century historical context, but as they are situated in chs. 30–33, between the disputes of chs. 26–29, and the Baruch document which follows in chs. 36–45.

expression in human speech, in poem and oracle and narrative. Thus God's resolve is voiced speech. It is the voiced speech heard in Israel that forms the text of chs. 30–33. This voiced speech is not to be understood as human description and observation of events as they unfold, as though the prophet is a historical commentator or chronicler. Nor is the voiced speech of promise simply human hope or wishful thinking, the anticipation that somehow "things will get better." Rather, this speech on the lips of the prophet is God's self-announcement, God's self-resolve to which God's own self is committed in the face of resistant circumstance. That is, God has pledged to work a newness precisely where there is no evidence of such newness on the horizon.

As the promissory text embodies God's self-commitment, so the promissory text lingers in the exilic and postexilic community as an anchor for faith and hope in a context of fickleness and despair. That is, the text is not a prediction, but it is a promise to which Israel clings because of Israel's confidence in the promise-maker. The promissory text is not "used up" or exhausted in any fulfillment or partial fulfillment, but continues to stand, in situation after situation, in generation after generation, as a witness and testimony to what God intends that has not yet come to fruition.

The parlance of promise poses an intense theological problem for us in our interpretive modernity. Enlightenment epistemology is committed to a kind of technological positivism which believes that what is possible is contained in what is humanly available. Enlightenment epistemology programmatically excludes promise as a viable intellectual category, because promise rests upon and refers to power and resolve beyond human control. As a result, promises in the text have either been subjected to historical criticism to explain them (away) or have been generalized as to become innocuous or domesticated through trivialization. The outcome of all these strategies of criticism, generalization, and trivialization is that promise disappears as a category for faith in the midst of history.

An affirmation of promise as a mode for life and faith, however, persists in the text. It refuses to be banished from our horizon of reading and hearing. Moreover, it is striking and odd that while the notion of promise is enormously inconvenient in the midst of modernity, those who are marginalized by modernity — the poor, the oppressed, and the disadvantaged — find Israel's promissory speech to be credible speech. Those who find it unconvincing or inadequate to view the world through human control, or to see the world as finally meaningless, often do not find it irrational to trust another governance that enacts newness. It is the enactment of newness that is the subject of these chapters. To these chapters concerning promise (and others like them), the community of faith returns again and again, in a refusal to believe that present circumstance is the last word on human destiny. Newness is not only possible, but is promised. In the end, "building and planting" requires a wholly different perception of historical reality, a perception that regularly subverts and destabilizes all present-tense reality, for the sake of what God yet intends.

On the basis of 30:2, these chapters are referred to by scholars as "The Book of Comfort," presumably a collection or a scroll of promises through which God will work a new community and a new Jerusalem out of exile. This term for the collection applies most directly, according to common critical judgment, to chs. 30–31, and derivatively to ch. 33. Chapter 32 is of a different genre, a narrative rather than an oracle. Even in the narrative, however, the oracle of God in 32:15 (cf. also vv. 25, 37-41, 43-44) becomes the driving force of the narrative. The account of land purchase in ch. 32 keeps Jewish hope linked to the concreteness of historical reality. The newness this God will work out beyond the failure of Jerusalem and the domination of Babylon is never otherworldly or private, but always public, social, political, and economic. The form and substance of promissory oracles hold together the powerful resolve of Yahweh and the concrete possibilities of Jewishness revitalized. Others in addition to Jews (such as Christians) may use these texts, but in doing so, their future is always mediated to them through the peculiar discourse of Jewish promise.[5]

---

5. On the development, nuance, and history of promissory speech in the OT, see Claus Westermann, "The Way of the Promise through the Old Testament," in *The Old Testament and Christian Faith*, ed. Bernhard W. Anderson (New York: Harper & Row, 1963), 200-224.

It is the power of this promissory tradition that is distinctive for Jewishness, and that authorizes and permits the strange, remarkable survival and witness of Jews. In his novel *The Thanatos Syndrome*, Walker Percy has a maladjusted priest conclude:

> The Jews as a word sign cannot be assimilated under a class, category, or theory. No subsuming Jews! Not even by the Romans. . . . This offends people, even the most talented people, people of the loftiest sentiments, the highest scientific achievements, and the purest humanitarian ideals.[6]

These chapters of promise voice, in the sixth century and beyond, the relentlessness of Yahweh in the history of the Jews, relentlessness for newness which the world can neither evoke nor preclude. The promises require us to redefine the categories through which we sort out what is possible and what is not possible. In the end, nothing is impossible for this God (cf. 32:17, 27).[7] This God can indeed plant what has been plucked up and build what has been pulled down. The people who stay close to these promises are very odd people, who will never be "subsumed" either under the false promises of empires or under the large despairs of a failed city. After the failed city and the false promises of the empire, there persist these promises, the God who makes them, and the people to whom they are made. The promises, the God, and the people constitute an always new possibility in history, a possibility undaunted by the summarizing, subsuming categories of the empire. These chapters bear witness to that which the empire dismisses as impossible. The community of this text is insistently urged not to trust in what the world calls possible, for that way leads to despair, conformity, anxiety, and finally death. This community trusts instead in the impossibilities which exist first on God's lips.

---

6. Walker Percy, *The Thanatos Syndrome* (New York: Farrar, Straus & Giroux, 1987), 126. The same priest declares, "Since the Jews were the original chosen people of God, a tribe of people who are still here, they are a sign of God's presence which cannot be evacuated" (123).

7. Cf. Walter Brueggemann, "'Impossibility' and Epistemology in the Faith Tradition of Abraham and Sarah (Gen 18$_{1-15}$)," *Zeitschrift für die alttestamentliche Wissenschaft* 94 (1982): 615-634.

COMFORT FOR ISRAEL AND JUDAH (30:1–31:40)

The introduction to these two chapters is an instruction from God to Jeremiah: "Write in a book all the words that I have spoken to you. For behold, days are coming, says the LORD, when I will restore the fortunes of my people, Israel and Judah . . ." (30:2-3). These verses of instruction and authorization provide the clue to prevailing critical judgments about the chapters. These two chapters are called by scholars, "The Book of Comfort."[8] The phrase suggests two things. First, it is a book, a writing. Many scholars believe that these two chapters may have first existed as an independent literary unit. In any case, there was some kind of editing process which has brought together in one place most of the promissory material of the book of Jeremiah. Second, the purpose of the book is to announce that "I will restore the fortunes of my people." That is, the subject of these chapters is God's good resolve for the future, which is homecoming for the exiles. Thus the chapters are a powerful statement of hope made to the exiles, announcing that the Exile will come to an end because God intends to bring the community back to its own land. We have seen that while 29:5-7 anticipates a long exile, 29:10-14 anticipates an end to exile and a homecoming.[9] Chapters 30–31 exposit in lyrical ways the foundational promises of 29:10-14. That is, God is still powerfully at work on behalf of Israel. The God who willed exile now wills homecoming. The God who plucks up and tears down is the very God who will now plant and build (cf. 1:10; 31:28). Exile is not a defeat or failure for God, but the arena out of which God works a glorious newness for God's beloved people and for God's treasured city.

---

8. William L. Holladay, *Jeremiah 2*, 148, provides a basic bibliography on these chapters. For a helpful summary statement in English, see Theodore M. Ludwig, "The Shape of Hope: Jeremiah's Book of Consolation," *Concordia Theological Monthly* 39 (1968): 526-541.

9. The completed tradition of Jeremiah makes in turn two quite different theological emphases which are impossible to coalesce. On the one hand, the tradition of judgment works against complacency; on the other, the tradition of promise intends to counter despair.

These chapters enunciate a hope rooted in God's own resolve and fidelity, a hope addressed toward a people at the brink of despair, a hope issued in the face of and against the reality of the imperial prowess in Babylon and the utter failure of Judah. The text insists that the resolve of God is strong and active enough to create new possibility in the world, a possibility not generated by the Jerusalem establishment nor permitted by the Babylonian regime. The prospect of homecoming is the evangelical assertion that exile is not the last fate of God's people or of God's world: God's resolve overrides the deathly circumstance of the world, and authorizes and permits new life which did not seem possible in the season of displacement. The hope of this cluster of texts is rooted in nothing but God's intention, uttered against the recalcitrant circumstances of lived experience. The rhetoric of this little collection is complex, and the critical questions have yielded no consensus.[10]

The main claim of the text is, however, not difficult or obscure. It is a stunning theological insistence that the historical process is subject to the powerful resolve of God to work a newness, to intrude into old power arrangements and firmly established patterns of reality, to rearrange, reshape, and make new. According to this assertion, any attempt to understand or assess or participate in the historical process without reckoning with this powerful resolve of God is sure to misconstrue and distort. The mode of the argument is mostly lyrical poetry. That lyrical poetry, however, should not be underestimated. It is the chosen mode of the tradition to voice what the closed discourse of power politics refuses and seeks to silence.[11] The oddness of this lyrical discourse in the ancient as in the contemporary world is that it moves in and through and beyond the very power arrangements which seek to silence it. And wherever it moves, it transforms and rehabili-

---

10. On the critical questions, see the careful review by John Martin Bracke, "The Coherence and Theology of Jeremiah 30–31" (diss., Union Theological Seminary, Richmond, 1983); and *"šûb šĕbût:* A Reappraisal," *Zeitschrift für die alttestamentliche Wissenschaft* 97 (1985): 233-244.

11. On the power of such discourse to reopen the silence closed by censoring power, see Walter Brueggemann, *Finally Comes the Poet: Daring Speech for Proclamation* (Minneapolis: Fortress, 1989).

tates. This poetry is a means whereby the God of the Jeremiah tradition does indeed "plant and build" out of the very ruins of betrayed covenant.

30:1-3 These verses are a preamble to "the Book of Comfort." The prophet is authorized by Yahweh, the same Yahweh who destroyed Jerusalem, to record a new collection of words of Yahweh. In these verses there is joined together a statement about the mechanics of the origin of the literature and a high theological promise. The editors of the book of Jeremiah have a self-conscious interest in how *God's intention* becomes a *sacred scroll* (cf. 1:1-3; ch. 36).[12] This part of the text is established as the direct disclosure of God's new resolve.

The substance of the resolve concerns a new future for Israel and for Judah, certain but without a specified time: "Days are coming," the days when Yahweh's resolve will come to fruition. The new resolve of Yahweh is expressed in two notions, both introduced by first person verbs: "I will restore" *(shub)*, "I will bring back" *(shub)*. The first phrase is thematic for hope in Jeremiah.[13] "Restore fortunes" means to give back to the covenant people the life, destiny, and well-being that belong to its identity as Yahweh's people. The phrase bespeaks rehabilitation of every aspect of life.

That phrase, however, lacks specificity. It is the second powerful phrase that makes concrete the programmatic theme of reversal. The second phrase concerns the end of exile and restoration to the land. Indeed, restoration to land is the central, quintessential hope of the Jeremiah tradition, and of much of the Bible. The land promise gives materiality to biblical faith; it concerns real life in this world. This tradition of hope knows that in the real world, no people or community will have dignity,

---

12. On redactional activity and the canonizing process, see Gene M. Tucker, "Prophetic Superscriptions and the Growth of a Canon," in *Canon and Authority,* ed. Coats and Long, 56-70; and the older discussion of Eduard Nielsen, *Oral Tradition: A Modern Problem in Old Testament Introduction.* Studies in Biblical Theology 11 (London: SCM and Chicago: Allenson, 1954).

13. On the formula, see Bracke, "Coherence and Theology," 148-155.

security, respect, or well-being unless it has guaranteed land.[14] This is a conviction well understood by the contemporary state of Israel and by the Palestinians as well, by peasants in Latin America, and by Blacks in South Africa. The promise of God is to give that without which human life is endlessly precarious. The promise of Yahweh intends to overrule present land distributions, even those arrangements seemingly guaranteed by imperial decree. Indeed, the claim of the Jeremiah tradition (echoed by recent events in Eastern Europe) is that even imperial guarantees cannot resist the drive for secure land which is a dynamic of history over which Yahweh presides. God's envisioned future for this people concerns land redistribution on behalf of those who cannot secure land for themselves.

30:4-11 These verses include three distinct rhetorical units, which are grouped together in terms of their shared theme of God's rescue in the face of great odds. The poetic unit of 30:4-7 invites the listener into a situation of fear and unrest. The power of terror and dread is vivid perhaps as in the face of an invading army (cf., e.g., 4:13-22). Jeremiah 30:5a describes the external situation in general, and v. 6 portrays a response of enormous fear to the situation. The rhetorical strategy of v. 6 is to state a premise as a question: men do not experience the labor of childbirth? And yet "brave men" (*geber*) act like they are in labor. They hold their stomachs as in the enormous pain of childbirth. Of course their pain is not related to childbirth. It is rather the pain of panic before the great day of turmoil caused by the power of God at work against God's people.

The ludicrous image of v. 6 may be turned in two directions. First, the metaphor of labor pains suggests the futility of this reaction to the danger. There are labor pains but no labor, birth pangs but no birth. Second, the military elite is mocked in what is a sexist image, soldiers acting like women in distress and fear

---

14. Concerning the significance of land as the substance of God's promise, see W. D. Davies, *The Gospel and the Land* (Berkeley: University of California Press, 1974); and *The Territorial Dimension of Judaism* (Berkeley: University of California Press, 1982).

(cf. 50:43; 51:30). The graphic portrayal of 30:5-7a leads us to be surprised by the dramatic conclusion of v. 7b: "Yet!" . . . Nevertheless . . . The powerful adversative preposition shows that the fidelity of God overrides the terror and panic. "He [presumably Judah, the frightened strong man] shall be rescued [presumably by Yahweh]" (NRSV). There is nothing in the scene of terror and panic which leads us to expect this reassuring conclusion. The outcome arises outside the scene of panic, wrought by the fidelity of Yahweh. With this abrupt preposition, a situation of grief and pain is turned to a situation of assurance. Thus the rhetoric itself voices the "turn" promised in v. 3. The terrified one is reassured.

Then follows a prose comment with a very different kind of affirmation (vv. 8-9). These verses give substance to the verb "rescued" *(y-sh-ʻ)* from v. 7. In that coming time, assured by God's fidelity, oppression will be overcome. Whereas vv. 5-7 stayed with the image of the frightened soldier acting like a pitiful woman, these verses step outside the image to the world of imperial oppression. Imperial oppression will be overcome (v. 8), and Israel will again have its own free government (v. 9). Yahweh is the subject of two strong, liberating verbs: "I will break, I will burst." Yahweh will overcome the subjugation caused by the Babylonian hegemony. The power of God is mobilized with reference to an actual concrete political reality, namely, the imperial "yoke."

Verse 9 reflects the conviction of some in exilic Judah that the Davidic dynasty will be reestablished. While this is not a primary expectation of the Jeremiah tradition, it is a live hope in the world of exilic Jeremiah (see 23:5-6; 33:14-16, 17, 22, 26; cf. Ezek. 34:23-24). These verses serve to introduce political specificity into Israel's hope, a political realism kept alive in the Christian tradition by seeing in the person of Jesus the power of God's promise to liberate from oppression (cf. Luke 4:18-19). The juxtaposition of Jer. 30:5-7 and vv. 8-9 is likely not happenstance. More likely, the daring poetry of vv. 5-7, which lacks political concreteness, generated and permitted the more realistic expectation of the prose verses. Thus if Yahweh is indeed to "rescue" these frightened strong men (vv. 6-7), there must be identifiable ways for such rescue.

These verses suggest that the instrument of such rescue is the restored monarchy.

The quick rhetorical move from poetic imagery (vv. 5-7) to concrete political expectation (vv. 8-9) culminates in the poetic promise of vv. 10-11. These verses, centering in the magisterial "fear not," are an exile-ending announcement which has close affinities to the material of 2 Isaiah.[15] In this speech form, Yahweh asserts not only solidarity with Israel but a readiness to act on behalf of Israel in ways that will drastically transform Israel's exilic situation. In this form of speech, we are at the center of the notion that God's word of promise and presence does indeed impinge upon the historical process to save. The yoke of oppression is broken (v. 8), because Yahweh has announced an intention to intervene (vv. 10-11). The substance of the promise is that exiled Israel will come home and dwell in safety, the recipient of Yahweh's most powerful blessing (v. 10). The rhetoric marking the new life of the community is governed by Yahweh's strong verbs: "I will save" (*y-sh-ʿ*), "I am with you to save" (*y-sh-ʿ*). The double use of the verb *y-sh-ʿ* echoes the promise of v. 7.

The remaining lines of v. 11 engage in two rhetorical moves which are interesting, but somewhat anticlimactic. First (v. 11b), there is a contrast between Israel and "the nations." The nations who oppress will be terminated,[16] whereas Judah will not be terminated. Thus the assurance of Yahweh goes against common-sense assessments of international politics in the sixth century. On the face of it, Babylon seemed guaranteed to perpetuity, and Judah seemed precarious. Seen in light of Yahweh's faithfulness, however, the situation of the powerful and the vulnerable is exactly inverted. The destinies of the oppressed and the oppressor are reversed.

Second, the last lines of v. 11 are an acknowledgement of reality

---

15. On the text, see Edgar W. Conrad, *Fear Not Warrior: A Study of 'al tîrā' Pericopes in the Hebrew Scriptures.* Brown Judaic Studies 75 (Chico: Scholars Press, 1985), 108-115. On this formulation in a context of exile, see Walter Brueggemann, "Genesis 50,15-21: A Theological Exploration," *Supplements to Vetus Testamentum* 36 (1985): 46-53.

16. While "nations" is plural, in the context of the book of Jeremiah the reference is mostly likely to Babylon (cf. chs. 50–51).

which cannot be ignored, even in this lyrical promise. There really is exile. God really does punish God's own people. God does indeed take covenantal disobedience seriously. Judah will be (and is) firmly punished. The conviction that the guilty must be punished is very old and central in the Mosaic memory that feeds the tradition of Jeremiah (cf. Exod. 34:7; Num. 14:18). Moreover, even the Davidic promise which gives large guarantees does not expect a future which is without moral payouts (cf. 2 Sam. 7:14).

Thus Jer. 30:11 contains several theological convictions which stand in some tension with each other. No doubt the ideas in tension — that Judah will not be ended, that Judah will be punished — reflect the ongoing conversation and dispute in exilic Judah about God's intended future for the community. There is punishment, but it is not ultimate. There is rescue, but it is not cheap. God is sovereign and will not be mocked; God is caring and not to be doubted. The ideas are not mutually exclusive, but they are not easily harmonized; it matters enormously in these several theological tensions where the accent is placed. The text leaves the matter of accent open, so that we are left to read and interpret with some freedom.

These three distinct units taken together — vv. 5-7, 8-9, 10-11 — articulate powerful faith, vivid rhetoric, and historical realism. In the end, it is asserted that God's sovereign purpose reshapes and reorders both Israel's despairing present and Israel's doubted but yearned-for future. In the process of adjudicating Israel's future, "the nations" are brought under the same sovereignty as that on which Judah must stake its life.

30:12-17   The theme of exile and return is here considered afresh through a different metaphor, that of sickness and healing. The most interesting fact about this poem is that it is bounded by two statements that blatantly contradict each other. The beginning point is a ruthless, candid diagnosis of diseased Israel (v. 12). God's people is terminally ill, beyond healing, sure to die. The end of the poem is a promise that God will indeed heal and restore (v. 17). Taken together, vv. 12 and 17 affirm that the one who is utterly beyond healing will be healed. The work of the poem (and our interpretation) is to trace the way in which Israel's faith and

51

imagination move from the hopeless candor of v. 12 to the astonishing assurance of v. 17.[17]

Verses 12-15 revolve around the twin themes of guilt and illness. The sickness of Israel is beyond help. Israel, in its disease, is utterly abandoned, disregarded by former allies ("lovers"). The figure suggests abandonment by fair-weather friends who will not stand by a loser, and who leave off friendship when sickness strikes. This people, in its theological pathology, stands alone in the international scene, helpless before the imperial threat that is authorized by Yahweh. There is for Israel no point in complaining about its deep jeopardy, for healing is not possible (v. 15). Moreover, the cause of the illness is no mystery. Sickness unto death is the outcome of sin, disobedience, and flagrant disregard of God. The diagnosis is unambiguous. Israel's desperate situation has a theological cause which produces a sociopolitical outcome. The nullification of Israel is willed by Yahweh. Clearly there can be no rescue from a sickness willed by Yahweh and warranted by disobedience. The poet daringly uses a medical metaphor to make a staggering affirmation about Judah. The politics of the Near East is read theologically! Judah is caught in a deep pathology of its own making, the pathology of infidelity and self-sufficiency.

The poem takes an abrupt turn in v. 16. We are not prepared for the "therefore" of that verse. In the prophets the term "therefore" characteristically introduces more judgment. More judgment, however, is not required or perhaps even possible after the pathos, harshness, and indignation of v. 15. What else could be said? We discover, however, that the "therefore" of v. 16 is a verbal trick. The term prepares us for one more message of judgment, but in fact the following lines offer exactly the opposite message — a word of God's powerful, healing intervention. The four word pairs of "devour-devour," "foe-captivity," "despoil-spoil," and "prey-prey" indicate a total, symmetrical inversion wrought by God's faithful power, an inversion whereby vulnerable, exposed Judah is protected, and all its powerful

17. See Walter Brueggemann, "The 'Uncared for' Now Cared for (Jer 30:12-17): A Methodological Consideration," *Journal of Biblical Literature* 104 (1985): 419-428.

attackers are done in by the will of Yahweh.[18] Thus the poem witnesses to the inversion we have already seen in vv. 8-9, 11, whereby the strong are crushed and the weak one is guarded and guaranteed. This inversion again gives flesh to the promise of v. 3 concerning the restoration of Israel's fortunes. The one who has been a threat to Israel is now under severe threat from Yahweh. Yahweh is now actively at work on behalf of Israel's healing, and so deals decisively with the proximate curse of illness. It is odd that in vv. 12-15 it is Yahweh who causes Israel's terrible problem, but in v. 16 the nations are held accountable for the jeopardy of Judah. Yahweh was the enemy in vv. 12-15, but has become Israel's friend and advocate in vv. 16-17. Yahweh has decisively changed roles, which in turn decisively changes Israel's prospects for the future. Thus in vv. 16-17 the poem changes tone and direction, reflective of the change in Yahweh's disposition and the consequent change in Israel's fortune.

Nothing has changed about the propensity of Israel. Israel is still guilty, still sick, still under threat. Everything, however, has changed about God. Between v. 15 and v. 16 there is a radical alteration in God's attitude, perspective, and inclination. The indignant One has become the compassionate One.[19] God who would abandon Judah is now prepared to intervene to save Judah. The poem traces in dramatic fashion, albeit with elliptical articulation, the transformation of God from enemy to advocate. Indeed, the changed fortune of Judah (v. 3) depends upon the changed disposition of Yahweh. It is the changed disposition of Yahweh which moves Israel's lot from exile to homecoming. The life of Israel depends in both aspects (exile and homecoming) upon the inclination of Yahweh.

The crucial and most interesting point in the poem is the reason

---

18. On the close correlation of sin and punishment, see Patrick D. Miller, Jr., *Sin and Judgment in the Prophets*. What is interesting here is that this prophetic mode of argument is now turned against the enemy of Judah.

19. The same transformation of God is disclosed in Deut. 4. In Deut. 4:24 Yahweh is a jealous God but in v. 31 Yahweh has become a merciful God. In the Flood narrative of Gen. 6–9, the same transformation of God occurs. See Walter Brueggemann, *Genesis*. Interpretation (Atlanta: John Knox, 1982), 75-87.

given for God's decisive transformation. The final line of v. 17 seems to give the reason for that change. In v. 14 God has asserted about the nations that "they care nothing for you." God observes that the nations have become indifferent. In v. 17, however, it is now the nations who mock Israel in the same words, who say, "Zion, for whom no one cares." It is powerful irony that God's own verdict in v. 14 is now on the lips of the nations in v. 17. When that same verdict is sounded by the nations, however, it evokes in Yahweh a response of caring solidarity. Yahweh had been free to critique and condemn this people. However, when the nations do the same as Yahweh had done, Yahweh is made freshly aware of deep concern for Israel. In the mocking voiced by the nations, Yahweh is driven to fresh saving action, becoming newly cognizant of a deep solidarity that Judah's guilt and Yahweh's indignation have not mitigated. It is as though in the depth of exile, in the bottom of Israel's terrible humiliation before the nations, Yahweh found depths of love for Israel about which Yahweh did not heretofore know. It is the situation of Israel's hurt which evokes in Yahweh fresh measures of love and resolve. Yahweh's transformed attitude and inclination dominate the poem and are good news for the exiles. There will be healing, because the diagnostician of vv. 12-15 has become the powerful healer in vv. 16-17. That healing wrought by a change in God bespeaks homecoming, restoration, and rehabilitation for this terminally ill people!

30:18-22   Given God's new resolve to heal Judah (vv. 16-17), the poetry now articulates a wondrous, sweeping scenario of the new historical possibility of restored Jerusalem. The poetry massively overrides any present inadequacy in the city, and focuses our attention on the newness decreed in an anticipatory vision. The poem begins with the "formula of rehabilitation" (cf. v. 3) which envisions an end of exile, an end that is rooted in Yahweh's "mother-love" ("compassion," *rhm*) directed toward the city which God loves (v. 18). There follows a picture of restored Jerusalem. The rebuilding, which is assured as God's own work and not a task urged on Judah, will mean the resumption of joyous liturgy, the glad sounds of birth and weddings (cf. 33:10-11), the return of ordered, prosperous life — all the antithesis of the shabby, poverty-ridden days just past. God will be at work to assure prosperity, prestige, dignity, and well-being (30:19). The promise is that "the good old days" (i.e., "as of old") can be experienced again.

Any who intrude or disrupt or "oppress" (presumably the nations) will have to deal with Yahweh, who is guarantor and protector of the revived city (v. 20b). Yahweh has changed roles; the destroyer has become the guarantor, and when Yahweh makes healing, restorative gestures toward the city, Israel's life is utterly transformed. Verse 21 suggests the reestablishment of the rule of law, though specifics are lacking.

In contrast to the present disorder, there will be an honorable leader with political authority, but also with liturgic legitimacy, for the term "draw near" implies access to cultic functions.[20] Perhaps this is an anticipation of the theocracy to come, when the leadership will be priestly (cf. 33:18, 21-22). Such specifics, however, are not at issue here. What is important is the restoration of legitimated order which will permit the community to function. These verses provide an impressionistic inventory of all that is required and promised for the resumption of a full communal life. The promise is capped in 30:22 with the formula of covenantal fidelity which redefines both parties.[21] Thus the tradition flings in the face of exilic disorder and despair the eloquence of God's new possibility. The poem intends to evoke and nurture a dangerous hope that becomes increasingly restless and ill at ease with the distortions, deprivations, and humiliations that presently go with occupation, defeat, and displacement. The poem summons and authorizes a community which believes promises and trusts the promise-maker to move beyond the present into a better world. Life begins again. That new beginning consists in real life in public categories, life guaranteed by the passion, care, and fidelity of Yahweh.

---

20. The term rendered "prince" in the RSV (*dr*) may refer to any formidable leader. It does not necessarily or intentionally suggest a monarch, as the RSV rendering might imply.

21. On the formula, see Rudolf Smend, *Die Bundesformel*. Theologische Studien 68 (Zurich: EVS, 1963).

30:23-24 The preceding poetic units have voiced Yahweh's positive action toward Jerusalem. These two verses pause in the midst of that wondrous promise to articulate the dark, ominous side of Yahweh's saving action. Political reality dictates that Jerusalem cannot be restored until the occupying armies of Babylon are removed. Life cannot be normal again in Jerusalem until the imperial cause of the disruption is overcome. These verses are an assault on and warning against "the wicked" (plural). The language lacks specificity and might be variously assigned.[22]

In this context, however, the "wicked" must refer to the imperial power which oppresses (vv. 8, 11, 16, 20), and which precludes and prohibits restoration. The language must perforce be impressionistic, because the poet has no concrete strategy against Babylonian power. In its extremity, Israel does not engage in political analysis, but in sweeping, daring theological rhetoric. The real issue is not specific imperial policy, so the text urges, but imperial disobedience against Yahweh and imperial disorder against the people of Yahweh. The turn in power which will permit Judah to resume life is voiced in ominous, ill-defined threats of "wrath" and "tempest" which are vehicles for the anger which Yahweh has toward the wicked who violate God's people. In the end, there is a moral reckoning and even Babylon must answer to it. God is about to unleash a whirlwind of destruction against the oppressor, for the sake of beloved Jerusalem.[23]

---

22. The same lines occur in 23:19-20. In that text the critique concerns the false prophets in Jerusalem. Here the lines appear to be aimed against "the nations." The reuse of the same lines suggests the supple way in which the tradition is open to varied use through fresh interpretation. On the general problem of "the wicked" as the enemy, see Steven J. L. Croft, *The Identity of the Individual in the Psalms*. Journal for the Study of the Old Testament Supplement 44 (Sheffield: JSOT Press, 1987), 15-48. It is clear that the terms have no stable referent, but are open to varied uses.

23. The unleashing of storm and whirling tempest is not to be understood as "supernaturalism." Rather, the terms bespeak a political revolution, the unleashing of a political, military assault which Babylon cannot withstand. This hint of threat becomes explicit in chs. 50–51, wherein it is Persian power which will be unleashed by God. The unleashing of such power against an established, seemingly impenetrable power is evident in recent time in the dismantling of the power of the Soviet Union.

This daring articulation of God's wrath which operates world-wide, however, is not capricious passion. The wrath is an action in the service of God's intention.[24] The vocabulary of judgment is escalated: "storm, wrath, whirling tempest, anger." The entire sequence drives toward the "until" *('ad)* in v. 24. It is the same "until" we have seen in 27:7, 22. The hard, demanding, uncompromising wrath of Yahweh is serious, but it is not ultimate. It has a purpose beyond itself. There is a turn in the rhetoric which marks a turn in God's disposition. The "until" opens vistas for Israel beyond the present situation. The wrath serves God's purpose, a purpose which exists in God's heart beyond the wrath. Thus the wrath against the marked oppressor is instrumental to God's larger intention (30:24a). The destruction that can topple even a great empire is identified by the poet as a strategy of God. The political process of intentionalism is understood in the enormous categories.

The poem ends with the enigmatic assertion of v. 24b: "In the latter days you will understand."[25] "The latter days" are whenever God's intention is implemented. Then God's largest intention will be clear, and this people which has understood so little will see and know. In the meantime, between now and "the latter days," the outcome of the historical process is hidden in God's heart, and Israel can only trust. The future is securely hidden in God's heart. Israel must walk by faith where it may not yet see. Israel may trust in the meantime that there is more in God's heart than wrath. This enigmatic conclusion asserts that the historical process,

---

24. On God's anger as an ordered act of sovereign policy, see George E. Mendenhall, *The Tenth Generation* (Baltimore: John Hopkins University Press, 1973), 69-104. In a little noticed article, G. Ernest Wright, "The Nations in Hebrew Prophecy," *Encounter* 26 (1965): 225-237, speaks of God's maintenance of God's "imperium." The same theme is voiced by Wright, *The Old Testament and Theology* (New York: Harper & Row, 1969), 121-150; and Patrick D. Miller, Jr., "The Sovereignty of God," in *The Hermeneutical Quest.* Festschrift James Luther Mays, ed. Donald G. Miller (Allison Park, Pa.: Pickwick, 1986), 129-144.

25. Cf. Jer. 31:26; Deut. 29:29. In key places the text acknowledges that there is something hidden about the very matters it seeks to disclose. That hiddenness recognizes not only that the future is not obvious, but that God's intention for the future lies well beyond human discernment.

which on the face is destructive and chaotic, in fact is meaningful and structured in ways that only God can discern. The seeming chaos is a mode of God's majestic rule.

Chapter 30 is a statement of enormous complexity, utilizing a rich variety of literary forms. It moves in and out of the themes of God's anguish and fidelity, Israel's prospect for the future, God's resolve to save, God's readiness to rescue, and Israel's joy in the rebuilding. All of these themes serve the conviction that the future, characterized by Yahweh's covenantal fidelity, is firmly under the rule of God. On the one hand, Israel must not deny its bleak present. On the other hand, however, it must not take the present with ultimate seriousness. God's sure governance of the future stands as a powerful, palpable alternative to present despair. Even in this season of wrath, other days are coming, days of God's well-being and restoration. The poet provides a rich set of images as a bulwark against present-tense resignation. God's sovereignty precludes a deathly fate for Israel. Israel holds to powerful promises in order not to succumb to present despair.

31:1   This verse is a prose introduction for the nine promises that have been collected here. On the one hand, the assertion made by God is almost banal in its flatness. The covenant formula sounds so hackneyed. On the other hand, the statement can be understood as the most foundational promise God can make to exiles. It is the same covenant formula much used by Jeremiah and Ezekiel.[26] Most recurrent in exile when Israel felt abandoned, the formula intends to counter that sense of abandonment: "I shall be your God and you shall be my people." In exile, it is asserted that God will be present to and intervene for Israel precisely in its failure and humiliation. The process of God's loyalty is the process of tribes ("families," *mishpahot*) becoming one "people" *('am);* thus the work of God is to gather and unify separated and scattered small social units of Israelites to form them into one viable community.[27] God in exile pledges to "form Israel"

---

26. Smend, 5-6, lists the several uses, especially as they pertain to the Exile.

27. Norman K. Gottwald, *The Tribes of Yahweh,* 237-340, has provided

once again (cf. Exod. 19:6; 1 Pet. 2:9-10). Thus God will now do in exile what God did at the outset in Egypt, when God formed a new people out of disparate and hopeless social units.[28]

31:2-6 This promissory oracle affirms God's fidelity to Israel and, as a result, Israel's resumed life which is marked by joy and abundance. God is utterly faithful to Israel (Jer. 31:2-3). These two verses contain two of the most fundamental statements of God's fidelity to Israel: (1) "The people . . . found grace in the wilderness." This statement makes an allusion back to the wilderness sojourn in the ancient days of Moses, when God surprisingly gave sustenance in the wilderness (cf. Exod. 16:12;[29] Jer. 2:2). At the same time, however, "wilderness" is a reference to contemporary exile, so that the assertion not only remembers surprising graciousness in the past, but is a statement concerning God's powerful, gracious presence in Israel's contemporary circumstance of displacement. This is an example of how an old memory illuminates and redefines Israel's present circumstance. The formula asserts that the present reality of exile is not godless and not graceless.

(2) "I have loved you with an everlasting love." God asserts an abiding fidelity to Israel. This statement is in considerable tension with much of the Jeremiah tradition, which suggests that God has terminated a relation with Israel. The tension cannot be resolved, because both statements of abandonment and fidelity are made, and both inclinations are present to Yahweh. This

---

the most programmatic statement concerning the sociopolitical process of tribes becoming a unified people.

28. On the process of the formation of a new people, see the suggestive statement by Norman K. Gottwald, "Religious Conversion and the Societal Origins of Ancient Israel," in *Perspectives on the Hebrew Bible*. Festschrift Walter J. Harrelson, ed. James L. Crenshaw (Macon: Mercer University Press, 1988), 49-65. While Gottwald comments on the early period of Israel and not the exilic period, I cite the discussion because Gottwald shrewdly shows the interface between sociopolitical and theological aspects of conversion.

29. It is not unimportant that this narrative affirmation is lodged in the Priestly tradition, i.e., in an exilic text that shares the context and concerns of the "Book of Consolation."

positive statement is characteristically made *after* the crisis of abandonment. Thus it is regularly in retrospect that such assurances of God's grace and presence are given, so that the statement does not in fact cancel or deny the recent, distressful past. Rather, the statement of grace and presence provides a basis on which to move beyond that terrible moment of distress into a new future, buoyed by God's reliable love. This statement does not abrogate older statements of discontinuity, but it now overrides them for the future.[30] Therefore God's freshly offered love (*'hb*) issues in faithfulness (*hsd*) which gives impetus for the rehabilitation of Israel. Clearly the prophet is not a systematic theologian, but a poet who lives very close to the hurts and hopes of God's own heart. It is God's heart made visible here which gives Israel a new chance in the future.[31]

Israel will have all aspects of its life restored and revitalized (31:4-6). This poetic unit is dominated by the threefold "again" (*'od*) which acknowledges that there has indeed been a decisive break in well-being. But that break will now be overcome. Thus "again" there will be building and restoration (v. 4a), as anticipated in the programmatic statement of 1:10. There will "again" be merriment, dance, celebration, and rejoicing, after all the party noise has ceased (31:4-6; cf. 7:34; 16:9; 25:10; 33:11). There will "again" be plenty and the earth will produce in abundance (31:5). "Plant," in the third element, is used as a term to balance "build" in the first element. The two terms together bespeak restoration of urban life and of agriculture, that is, all aspects of the community.

The restoration culminates in an invitation of pilgrimage to Zion (v. 6). That means the temple will be rebuilt and restored; to it will come worshippers from the north (Ephraim) in a reunited Israel. The love (*'hb*) and faithfulness (*hsd*) of God (v. 3) issue in the revitalization of every aspect of Israel's daily and public life. The poem effectively holds together theological, socioeconomic, and political dimensions of communal life; everything begins anew.

---

30. See Walter Brueggemann, "A Shattered Transcendence?"

31. See Walter Brueggemann, "A Shape for Old Testament Theology, II: Embrace of Pain," *Catholic Biblical Quarterly* 47 (1985): 395-415.

31:7-14 This promissory oracle in God's mouth asserts with exuberance the well-being, joy, and abundance that God will give to the restored, returned community. The oracle addresses the community itself (vv. 7-9) and the watching nations (vv. 10-12), followed by a summary statement of newness (vv. 13-14). The poem is a collage of Israel's best stock phrases for newness from God.

The community is summoned, invited, and urged to engage in praise (v. 7). Five imperatives are employed: "sing aloud, raise shouts, proclaim, give praise, say!" The substance of the proposed speech of Israel is either an imperative seeking God's rescue, or it is a declaration, celebrating it. Perhaps the verb intends to point in both directions, as imperative and as celebrative declaration. Either reading is powered by the decisive verb, *y-sh-ʿ*. God announces what is to happen, introduced by "Behold, I" (v. 8). God is bringing and God is gathering. The term "gather" *(q-b-ts)* (vv. 8, 10) is a key word for the restoration of the exiles. Because of the destruction of Jerusalem, Jews have become fugitives, refugees, and displaced persons all over the known world. In these images God will bring them from all parts of the world, including the north (i.e., Babylon). Among those gathered will be the weak and the vulnerable, the blind, lame, and pregnant. They will be given power and legitimacy, which they themselves do not possess. The faithfulness of God makes possible a great homecoming procession of those valued by God whom the nations have devalued (cf. Isa. 35:3-6; 43:5-7). The homecoming throng will be deeply moved, overwhelmed with both memory and hope (Jer. 31:9a).

The language necessary to this overwhelming picture requires two metaphors. On the one hand, language of "lead," "brooks of water," and "straight path" evokes the picture of the good shepherd who seeks out the lost and brings them home (v. 9; cf. Isa. 40:11). On the other hand, the reference to the "first-born" suggests an Exodus motif (cf. Exod. 4:22), concerning the one especially valued and beloved, who receives God's special protection, care, and gifts. The shepherd who protects is the father who values. The metaphors are particularly telling because the community of the firstborn is constituted by the disabled. The two metaphors together bespeak a situation in which the last ones become the

61

first ones; that is, the disabled ones become the firstborn. The "father" of the "first-born" takes those "orphaned" by the process of exile and makes them a home (cf. Hos. 14:3b).

The nations are addressed by God's firm resolve for homecoming for God's people (Jer. 31:10-12). The one who "scattered" now speaks (v. 10). It was none other than this God who caused exile; now the "scatterer" has moved to a new inclination and a new kind of activity. The One who scattered (i.e., caused exile) is the One who will now gather (i.e., bring home from exile). Again the shepherd image is invoked for the One who seeks and saves the lost ones. No single Jewish exile is lost from the wonder of a safe homecoming. The homecoming requires Israel's richest, most passionate vocabulary, to say fully what must be said about rescue. In v. 7 we have already had the verb "save" (*y-sh-ʿ*), and now in v. 11 we have "ransom" (*pdh*) and "redeem" (*gʾl*). The latter phrase in v. 11 suggests that the hands of the oppressor were too strong for Israel to resist. The strong hand of Yahweh, however, is stronger than "hands too strong for him." The strong hand of Yahweh will prevail, and so Israel will be safe.[32]

Though the address to the nations continues in v. 12, that particular address seems almost forgotten. The poet simply describes the scene of the joyous return in power. Though many Jews in fact never left the homeland, and though Jews may have trickled back over a longer time, this is not the scene we are offered. The text of course is not descriptive reportage. This is rather a lyrical scenario, constructed for the most dramatic effect possible, in terms of the governing metaphor of exile and return. Israel's poetic tradition in exile imagines all the exiles coming home together in one great event, in a procession led by Yahweh.[33] In this verse the dominant image is of a well-watered

---

32. Two clusters of uses evidence that "Yahweh's hand" concerns rescuing power. On the one hand, the notion occurs in the classic credo of Deut. 26:8 and similar uses. On the other hand, the motif is central to the "Ark narrative" of 1 Sam. 4–6, as Patrick D. Miller, Jr., and J. J. M. Roberts have shown in *The Hand of the Lord* (Baltimore: Johns Hopkins University Press, 1977).

33. Isaiah 40:10-11 offers one standard image of Yahweh at the head of

land, which is a "good" from God, who knows where the good streams are. In that well-watered land (like a luxuriant garden), the best crops (grain, wine, oil) and the best animals (flocks and herds) will flourish, and there will be no more drought (languishing). Well-watered, productive land is one of Israel's ways of speaking about God's rich blessing that makes abundant life possible (cf. Ezek. 34:25-31). Note well, the rhetoric moves beyond salvific language to creation, for the scope of the newness is utterly comprehensive. The poet strains to find language to match the envisioned newness.

The conclusion to this celebrative poem characterizes the new gifts of God given to the rescued (Jer. 31:13-14). This conclusion is introduced by "then" *(az)*. The "then" that is promised is sharply contrasted with the "now" which is still deathly and exilic. The key verb is "turn" *(hpk):* "I will turn" (v. 13), that is, God will invert and transform the total situation of Israel. The language here is closely related to and perhaps echoes the more intimate speech of Ps. 30:11:

> You have turned *(hpk)* my mourning into dancing;
> you have taken off my sackcloth
> and clothed me with joy. (NRSV)

This God has power to move against mourning and sorrow, the mood dictated by exile (cf. John 16:20). In their place God authorizes dancing, merriment, joy, comfort, and gladness. It will be "like priest, like people" (Jer. 31:14; cf. Hos. 4:9). The priests who receive a share of sacrifices will have more than enough; the people will be satiated with God's goodness ("bounty," *tob*). The structure of this section is a contrast of then and now; the poem celebrates both the coming "then" and the one who gives it. God has power to transform, and has promised to do so.

---

a great, triumphant, celebrative procession coming home to Jerusalem. On the antecedents to this imagery for exiles, see Thomas W. Mann, *Divine Presence and Guidance in Israelite Traditions* (Baltimore: Johns Hopkins University Press, 1977).

31:15-22   This poem reflects the tradition of Jeremiah at its most daring in the use of poetic metaphor, imagery, and strategy.[34] It begins by a careful listening at the very edge of Israel's horizon (Jer. 31:15). Jerusalem has listened too long to its own immediate crisis. Now it is invited in the poem to listen to a much older, much more pathos-filled voice. The sound comes out of the ancient past; Mother Rachel grieves over the generations, for all the lost children who are so vulnerable and so brutalized.[35] Mother Rachel is disconsolate for all the lost children of Israel, including the current generation of exiles. The weeping of the uncomforted mother easily traverses the generations, for all the lost ones are the same to this mother, regardless of their generation.[36]

God answers the disconsolate mother (vv. 16-17). The structure of vv. 15-17 is one of lament and response. The response in Israel is characteristically a response of presence, concern, intervention, and rescue. And so it is here. God's word to Mother Rachel is an invitation to wipe away the tears, to end the weeping (cf. Isa. 25:8; Rev. 7:17; 21:4). The children who "are not" will again "be," for they will come home. Thus the construct of lament-response is taken up to assert the resolution of homecoming for the grief of exile. The gift of hope overrides the despair of the lamenter.

After the mother grieves and God answers, the lost child speaks (Jer. 31:18-19). It is a speech of sorrow, regret, and repentance.

---

34. On this difficult unit, see Bernhard W. Anderson, "'The Lord Has Created Something New': A Stylistic Study of Jer 31:15-22," *Catholic Biblical Quarterly* 40 (1978): 463-478 (repr. in *A Prophet to the Nations,* ed. Leo G. Perdue and Brian W. Kovacs [Winona Lake: Eisenbrauns, 1984], 367-380); and Phyllis Trible, *God and the Rhetoric of Sexuality.* Overtures to Biblical Theology (Philadelphia: Fortress, 1978), 40-50.

35. On the reach of Rachel's grief across the generations, see Matt. 2:18. On that same voice in more contemporary accents, see Emil L. Fackenheim, "New Hearts and the Old Covenant: On Some Possibilities of a Fraternal Jewish-Christian Reading of the Jewish Bible Today," in *The Divine Helmsman.* Festschrift Lou H. Silberman, ed. James L. Crenshaw and Samuel Sandmel (New York: KTAV, 1980), 191-205; and Jonathan Kozol, *Rachel and Her Children: Homeless Families in America* (New York: Crown, 1988).

36. It is for that reason that Fackenheim and Kozol can claim that Rachel weeps even for twentieth-century children. All are equally treasured by this mother, who refuses to be comforted.

It is an admission of resistance to the discipline of God. The speaker admits turning away, but now is ashamed at his own actions. God's response to the repentance of vv. 18-19 is one of pathos, comfort, and assurance (v. 20). As Mother Rachel has had unrequited pathos, so the God of Israel is moved by deep pathos. Indeed, God's response is not unlike that of Mother Rachel. There is, on God's part, an inclination to reject wayward Israel, and to be done with such painful, exhausting recalcitrance.

That inclination, however, is countered in the very heart of God. God's heart is profoundly torn. On the one hand, the cessation of speech which tries to blot out the painful name and deep memory of Israel will not ever finish with the son.[37] On the other hand, God's own memory of Israel is as compelling and powerful and palpable as the memory Rachel has of her children. God is reduced to trembling yearning, and finally finds that mercy wins over rejection.[38] The two infinitive absolutes of "remember" and "have mercy" indicate the power of God's positive resolve. The God who *utterly remembers* is the God who *utterly has mercy*. Thus v. 20 is a response to vv. 18-19, just as vv. 16-17 answer v. 15. In both vv. 16-17 and v. 20, God's response finally authorizes an utterly new beginning, putting behind (but not denying) all the grief of Rachel and all the waywardness of Israel.

God counsels a return along well-marked paths (the torah) (v. 21). The return is geographical (end of exile) and theological (end of resistance).[39] Astonishingly, Israel is addressed both as "virgin" (v. 21) and as "backsliding [RSV 'faithless'] daughter" (v. 22). Finally, the poem ends in an utter newness (v. 22). The virgin Israel (not the abandoned widow; cf. Isa. 54:4-8) is welcomed home. She is purged of her foolishness, is resolved to faithfulness, and is brought back to the land. The grieving Rachel

---

37. The verb for "remember," *zkr,* is expressed in the infinitive absolute, voicing the great force of the act of memory.

38. Again, the verb "have mercy" *(rhm)* is in the infinitive absolute.

39. On repentance and return as a primary theological motif in the Exile, see Hans Walter Wolff, "The Kerygma of the Deuteronomic Historical Work," in Walter Brueggemann and Wolff, *The Vitality of Old Testament Traditions* (Atlanta: John Knox Press, 1975), 83-100.

is consoled; the wayward woman becomes the faithful woman now established in the land, prepared to have heirs and so to guarantee security. This rich and expensive range of metaphors (admittedly sexist in its manipulation of female roles) is used to render the awesome gift of homecoming, a new beginning both theological and geographical.[40] The use of these images suggests that the poet wants to voice not just a changed venue for Israel (homeland rather than exile), but also a genuine transformation that alters the very character of Israel and the modes of relationships in the community. Thus it is both a changed venue and a genuine transformation that matter for the ending of Israel's exile.[41]

31:23-26 This promissory oracle again anticipates resumed, renewed life in the land. This brief unit utilizes a number of interesting rhetorical maneuvers. It reuses the thematic statement, "I will restore their destinies [RSV 'fortunes']." It promises that a celebrative song of Zion will again be sung in the land (Jer. 31:23). The "again" (RSV "once more") implies that there was a time when the song was not sung, that is, when the temple was discredited, God was absent, and the singing stopped. Now Israel will resume the old liturgical refrain which acknowledges that Zion is the place where God and God's people can meet. All around the temple and the city, life will resume in harmony and free from conflict (v. 24). This will include the towns and their inhabitants. It will equally include farmers and their flocks. Thus all aspects of the economy are named and included. They will all stand under the promise of God. God will minister to the weary and the faint, and will make them strong and vibrant. Again, the poem asserts God's resolve to invert completely every aspect of Judah's life.

Verse 26 is a most peculiar verse. Its rhetoric is apocalyptic,

---

40. On the newness, see Anderson, "'The Lord has Created Something New,'" 477-78.

41. The second dimension of a genuine and profound transformation is expressed variously as "a new heart" (cf. Ezek. 11:19; 18:31; 36:26), "new covenant" (Jer. 31:31), and "new name" (Isa. 62:2).

and it seems to allude to something like resurrection, with language of being asleep and being awakened. It is exceedingly difficult to know what is being talked about. Perhaps the verse suggests that this promise is a dream or a vision. Perhaps we should regard the scenario of vv. 23-25 as an act of imagination in which the speaker can envision reality beyond the present. We are told nothing about the present and its possibilities, but only about the future which is so unlike the present. This entire collection of promises, and indeed the hope of Israel in every exile, depends upon the capacity to imagine reality beyond present circumstances. Moreover, that act of imagination is not simply inventive fantasy,[42] but it is linked to the power and freedom of God as known in Israel's memory. Thus v. 26 indicates that this author fully understands what he is doing. He is voicing a dreamlike scenario of healing reality, not yet in hand, but already assured by the power of God. Hope is clearly understood as a dreamlike alternative imagination which accepts God's intent as more powerful than the present, seemingly intransigent circumstance.

31:27-30   This promissory oracle anticipates a new beginning for Israel and Judah, a new beginning after the old communities have been put to death. God asserts a powerful resolve to begin again, afresh, after a complete failure. Verse 28 appeals to the six verbs which set the theme of the Jeremiah tradition in 1:10. The four negative verbs are intensified by the addition of a fifth one, "to bring evil." The most important matter in this verse is that the five negative verbs have all been fully enacted. There is no more threat in them. God has monitored ("watched," *sh-q-d*) the fulfillment of all the negatives and has kept track ("watched") until the promise of destruction has been fully actualized.

That review of the negatives, however, is only backdrop for the oracle. What counts now for the poem are the two positive verbs, "to plant and to build." The terms bespeak a full resumption of all of life. God is watching over these two verbs to bring them to

---

42. On the crucial distinction between imagination and escapist fantasy, see the discerning statement of J. R. R. Tolkien, "Tree and Leaf," *The Tolkien Reader* (New York: Ballantine, 1966), 29-99.

fruition and to fulfillment. Thus the text uses all six verbs from 1:10. They are used here, however, in two distinct stages, so that the positive verbs come in sequence after the negatives. The poet proposes a two-stage philosophy of history which is crucial for the full acknowledgment of exile and the full practice of hope in the face of exile.[43] The negative has happened; the positive is only promised. The poem places us between the destruction already accomplished in 587 B.C.E. and the homecoming only promised but keenly anticipated. The oracle places us between a death already wrought and a resurrection only anticipated.[44] The text places the listener "in between" and promises that, in that in-between place, God is watching with powerful, intentional concern.

This assertion of God's watching echoes 1:10 (cf. *sh-q-d* in 1:11-12) and contrasts with 44:27 wherein God's watching is negative. It is easy in exile to conclude either that God is hostile to Israel or that events are completely out of control. This insistent text, however, refuses both the conclusion of God's hostility and the conclusion that matters are out of control. What is in fact happening, so the text asserts, is happening under the watchful superintending eye of God, who will not quit until all is accomplished. The God who watches over recalcitrant Jews in Egypt for evil (so 44:27) is the God who intends only good for the community that adheres to Jeremiah (so 24:6).

It is exceedingly difficult in our intellectual situation to believe in a larger purposefulness to public events, beyond our intention and discernment. That assertion of a larger purposefulness, however, is indispensable to fend off resignation and despair in situations of exile. God does indeed intend good (cf. 29:11).

That, however, leaves the question, is such goodness from God possible in a situation so burdened by the consequences of plucking

---

43. Childs, 345-354 and esp. 346, has shown how the literary history of the book of Jeremiah serves a two-stage theological statement.

44. Jacob Neusner, *Understanding Seeking Faith: Essays on the Case of Judaism*, vol. 1: *Debates on Methods, Reports of Results*. Brown Judaic Studies 116 (Atlanta: Scholars Press, 1986), 145, has shown how the language of death and resurrection pertains to the Jewish experience of exile and restoration. Indeed, the dominant Jewish paradigm Neusner presents operates in those categories.

up and tearing down? Will not the consequences be visited upon the children and the children's children (cf. Exod. 34:7)? In response to that question which must have been much alive among exiles, Jer. 31:29-30 is added to the promise of vv. 27-28. The two positive verbs, "plant and build," anticipate a newness from God. The proverb repeated in v. 29 apparently was popularly held and affirmed: children into the next generation are fated to the consequences of the deeds of their parents. In the context of exile, this proverb asserts that the generation of the Exile is fated to the consequences of choices made in Jerusalem prior to 587. The conclusion is that newness is impossible in the face of such a sure, heavy fate; the parents have already chosen the fate of the children and the children's children.

The text, however, finally refuses the proverb and declares it to be null and void. Each one (i.e., each new generation) can act out its own destiny and choose its own future with God. The refutation of the proverb, and therefore the dismissal of conventional wisdom, asserts that newness is possible for the generation of the Exile. God can indeed "plant and build" for and with and in that generation. Paul Joyce has shown that this statement is not an eruption of "individualism" in the community, as much interpretation has heretofore accepted, but simply is an assertion of newness possible for the new generation of exiles.[45] The newness to exiles made possible by the nullification of the proverb prepares the way for the promise of the next literary unit.

31:31-34 This oracle of promise is the best known and most relied upon of all of Jeremiah's promises. It has frequently been preempted by Christians in a supersessionist fashion, as though Jews belong to the old covenant now nullified and Christians are the sole heirs of the new covenant. Such a distorted reading of the text has been abetted by the rendering of old and new "covenant" as old and new *"testamentum,"* which was taken too easily and uncritically as the two "testaments" of Christian scrip-

---

45. Paul Joyce, *Divine Initiative and Human Response in Ezekiel.* Journal for the Study of the Old Testament Supplement 51 (Sheffield: JSOT Press, 1988), 35-60.

ture. Thus the "new covenant" (i.e., new relation of God with God's people) became one of "two testaments," with the "New Testament" (and its community) being the "real" one.[46] Such a preemptive reading ignores the text itself. Moreover, such a rendering of the future could hardly be expected or cogent in the midst of these several promissory oracles which anticipate the reconstitution of the Israelite community.[47] Such a supersessionist reading in fact asserts the rejection rather than the reconstitution of Israel, a point not on the horizon of these oracles.[48]

It is clear, against such a Christian misreading, that the contrast of "old and new" concerns the Israelite community of covenant in both its parts. The "old" covenant belongs to that Israelite community which through its sustained disobedience forfeited covenant with God, even as it lost the city of Jerusalem. The "new" covenant now wrought by God also concerns the Israelite community. This is the community formed anew by God among exiles who are now transformed into a community of glad obedience. Thus we are right to posit a deep discontinuity between old and new, but that deep discontinuity is not between Jews and Christians, but between recalcitrant Jews prior to 587 and transformed Jews after 587 who embrace the covenant newly offered by God.[49]

This promise concerns a new covenant, a new relation, offered

---

46. See the discussion of Paul M. Van Buren, *A Christian Theology of the People Israel,* Part 2: *A Theology of the Jewish-Christian Reality* (San Francisco: Harper & Row, 1983), 28 and *passim.*

47. Van Buren, 255, comments on the text: "What was it that was to be new about it? Surely not a change of partners!"

48. This is a somewhat different reading from that of Van Buren. Van Buren suggests (155) not only that it is the same covenant, but that there is no room for discontinuity. I believe this view fails to appreciate the radicalness of the text, a radicalness that does not depend on Christian supersessionism.

49. Kornelis H. Miskotte, *When the Gods are Silent* (New York: Harper & Row, 1967), 409-415, offers a most helpful theological comment on the text. He observes: "The new covenant is new in that it finally becomes in simple truth a covenant. . . . So dreadful is the estrangement, so irreparable is the apostasy! Creating, establishing, disposing, God will have to call into being what is self-evident, so that Israel will finally be Israel in its own place, in time" (413).

and given and established by God. It is given by God without
reason or explanation, out of God's own resolve for the relation.[50]
The second party who receives the new relation with God is the
community of Israel and Judah (31:31). The contrast between
old and new covenant is in its mode of reception. The old covenant
from Sinai was resisted until it was broken and abrogated. The
new covenant will not be resisted, because the torah — the same
commandments as at Sinai — will be written on their hearts. That
is, the commandments will not be an external rule which invites
hostility, but now will be an embraced, internal identity-giving
mark, so that obeying will be as normal and as readily accepted
as breathing and eating. Israel will practice obedience because it
belongs to Israel's character to live in this way. All inclination to
resist, refuse, or disobey will have evaporated, because the members of the new community of covenant are transformed people
who have rightly inclined hearts. There will be easy and ready
community between God and reconstituted Israel.

From that basis, we are offered four derivative points about
the coming covenant, all of which witness to the new communion
wrought by God's powerful resolve:

(1) There will be genuine solidarity, expressed in the covenant
formulary (v. 33).

(2) There will be full "knowledge of Yahweh." This theme is
an important one for Hosea and for Jeremiah after him. On the
one hand, as Hans Walter Wolff has urged, "knowledge of Yahweh"
denotes a cognitive capacity to recite the saving tradition (2:6-8).[51]
That is, such knowledge consists in knowing the identity-giving
story. On the other hand, it is probable that "knowledge of
Yahweh" means affirmation of Yahweh as sovereign LORD with
readiness to obey the commands for justice that are the will of
Yahweh. Thus when Jer. 22:15-17 speaks of "knowing Yahweh,"

---

50. See Hans Walter Wolff, *Confrontations with Prophets* (Philadelphia:
Fortress, 1983), 49-62.

51. See Miskotte, 412 and esp. n. 3, with references to Wolff and Zimmerli.
See Herbert B. Huffmon, "The Treaty Background of Hebrew *Yāda'*," *Bulletin
of the American Schools of Oriental Research* 181 (1966): 31-37; and Huffmon and
Simon B. Parker, "A Further Note on the Treaty Background of Hebrew *Yāda'*,"
Bulletin of the American Schools of Oriental Research 184 (1966): 36-38.

it suggests obedience to God's commands for justice. It is not necessary (or even possible) to choose between these two meanings. Either or both are possible for the newly constituted community of covenant. Thus community both embraces a concrete memory and acknowledges a present loyalty.

(3) There will be common, shared access to this knowledge which evidences fundamental egalitarianism in the community. On the crucial matter of connection to God, the least and the greatest stand on equal footing. No one has superior, elitist access, and no one lacks what is required. All share fully in the new relation. All know the story, all accept the sovereignty, and all embrace the commands.

(4) The concluding statement may be the most crucial. The phrase is introduced by *ki,* as though this line states the basis for all the foregoing. All the newness is possible *because* Yahweh has forgiven. Indeed, beginning again in and after exile depends upon Yahweh's willingness to break out of a system of rewards and punishments, for the affront of Israel and Judah could never be satisfied by punishment.[52] God has broken the vicious cycle of sin and punishment; it is this broken cycle that permits Israel to begin again at a different place with new possibility. This is an uncommon statement, utterly Jewish, utterly grace-filled; upon it hangs the whole of reconstituted Judaism out of exile. Jewish faith is deeply rooted in forgiveness.[53]

In this, of all Jeremiah texts, we must reflect on the Christian appropriation of the promise. The use of this text in Heb. 8:8-13;

---

52. The exhaustion of punishment and the intrusion of forgiveness is expressed in other language in Isa. 40:2. Miskotte comments: "And so it is that knowledge grows out of forgiveness. And forgiveness remains the incredible miracle that wipes out time, establishes time, and illuminates time" (414).

53. On the originary power of forgiveness, see Hannah Arendt, *The Human Condition* (Chicago: University of Chicago Press, 1958), 236-243. Arendt (239, n. 76) comments concerning Jesus: "It is his insistence on the 'power to forgive,' even more than his performance of miracles, that shocks the people, so that 'they that sat at meat with him began to say within themselves, Who is this that forgives sins also?' (Luke 7:49)." On the quite practical, public outcome of forgiveness, see Carter Heyward et al., *Revolutionary Forgiveness: Feminist Reflections on Nicaragua* (Maryknoll, N.Y.: Orbis, 1987).

9:15-22; and 10:16-17 provides a basis for a Christian preemption of the promise. This preemption, however, misreads and misinterprets the text. Thus we arrive at a profound tension between the OT text and the NT quotation, a tension reflective of a long history of Jewish-Christian competitive acrimony. The matter is not easily adjudicated, because the supersessionist case is given scriptural warrant in the book of Hebrews. My own inclination is to say that in our time and place the reading of Hebrews is a distorted reading, and we are back to the recognition of the Jewishness of the new covenant. At best, we may say that Christians come derivatively and belatedly to share the promised newness. This is not to deny Christian participation in the newness, but Christian participation is utterly grounded in Jewish categories and claims, and can have participation on no other terms. Moreover, this Jewish mediation of newness is left open as an act of profound grace to all who come under these commandments and allegiance to this God. It is of course possible to read this in terms of Jewish triumphalism, but such is not the intent of the text. Indeed, the text invites Jews (and belatedly Christians and others) to stand in grateful awe before the miracle of forgiveness, to receive it, and to take from it a new, regenerated life. Thus the promise occasions no arrogance or pride, but only genuine gratitude. The offer of newness is not narrowly construed, but it has at its core the commandments which God has given first of all to the Jews.[54]

31:35-37 Whereas Jer. 31:31-34 places its accent on discontinuity between old and new, the capacity of God to terminate and begin again, these two brief oracles place accent on continuity, on God's abiding and constant fidelity through historical disruptions. Whereas vv. 31-34 focus on Israel's recent experience of

---

54. The claim of the priority of Jews in the covenant is variously nuanced in the works I have cited by Van Buren, Miskotte, and Wolff. All of these scholars are agreed against any form of supersessionism. On the more general problem of supersessionism, see the discussion in *Hebrew Bible or Old Testament?* ed. Roger Brooks and John H. Collins (Notre Dame: University of Notre Dame Press, 1990), with special attention to the paper by Rolf Rendtorff.

loss and displacement, these two brief oracles completely disregard historical specificity and focus on the abiding structures of creation.[55] The stress on continuity and creation embodies the largest and most comprehensive ground for God's fidelity to Israel imaginable;[56] they do, however, cut against the grain of most of the Jeremiah tradition, for that tradition inclines to discontinuity rather than to continuity, to historical specificity rather than to creation. Thus in these two oracles, we are at the edge of the imaginative world of the Jeremiah tradition, in which the text strains to voice the most unshakable assurance it can muster. In both oracles, God's love for Israel is as sure and durable and credible as God's governance of the world itself.

The first oracle (vv. 35-36) consists in a doxology (v. 35) and an "if-then" statement of assurance (v. 36). The doxology seeks to establish the awesome power of the Speaker of the oracle, to indicate that this Speaker does indeed have the capacity to do what is promised. The doxology is governed by two participles, describing actions which God characteristically and continually does. First, "God gives": God gives the sun, the moon, and the stars their place and their ordering (cf. Ps. 136:7-9). Second, "God stirs up": God rules the sea and causes it to roar. Whereas the reference to sun, moon, and stars bespeaks order, the reference to

---

55. The tension between 31:31-34 and 35-37 is reflective of the two strands of Israelite faith as articulated by Claus Westermann, "Creation and History in the Old Testament," in *The Gospel and Human Destiny,* ed. Vilmos Vajta (Minneapolis: Augsburg, 1971), 11-38; (with Friedemann W. Golka), *What Does the Old Testament Say About God?* (Atlanta: John Knox, 1979); and *Elements of Old Testament Theology* (Atlanta: John Knox, 1978), as respectively a theology of "deliverance" and a theology of "blessing." The latter does not appear extensively in the tradition of Jeremiah. When we learn to look for that theology of blessing, however, we may find more of it than our conventional categories have permitted us to see.

56. James L. Crenshaw, "Introduction: The Shift from Theodicy to Anthropodicy"; and "The Problem of Theodicy in Sirach: On Human Bondage," in *Theodicy in the Old Testament,* ed. Crenshaw. Issues in Religion and Theology 4 (Philadelphia: Fortress and London: SPCK, 1983), 1-16, 119-140, has urged that when the historical categories of rescue became inadequate, Israel was driven to creation as a way of affirming sense in its experience. Such a development may suggest why 31:35-37 is included in the tradition of Jeremiah.

the sea suggests disorder and surging chaos (cf. Jer. 5:22). God governs both order and chaos. Then, as in the doxologies of Amos, the story line of the doxology abruptly breaks off in awed exclamation.[57] Yahweh is Yahweh of the troops![58] Yahweh's awesome name matches and conveys Yahweh's awesome power to dispatch the creatures of heaven and earth.

With such a doxological prefix, we are now prepared to take seriously the "if-then" formulation of 31:36. The "if" concerns the "fixed order" of sun, moon, and stars, the order just asserted in the doxology of v. 35. The point of the protasis is that this cosmic arrangement is utterly reliable. Thus the "if" is not a statement of conditionality (as it might appear to be), but in fact is a confident negation. It intends to assert that "never" will this fixed order cease. The cessation of sun, moon, and stars which God has authored is unthinkable and unimaginable. The "then" clause concerns Israel's status as the object of Yahweh's special love. The implied "never" of the protasis carries over into the apodosis: "never" will Israel cease.

This twofold implied "never" may be taken as an ontological assertion, thus giving Israel status not unlike sun and moon and stars as a fixture of creation. More likely this statement does not claim so much, but is a pastoral affirmation. Some must have taken the catastrophe of 587 as a sign of Israel's rejection by Yahweh (cf. 33:24).[59] Such a reading, this oracle asserts, is a terrible misreading, for even 587 cannot terminate the relation to which Yahweh is committed. This bold assertion, which is a very different assurance from that of 31:31-34, anticipates Rom. 8:38-39. Nothing, not even 587, can separate Israel from God's relentless love.

---

57. Concerning the doxologies of Amos, see James L. Crenshaw, *Hymnic Affirmation of Divine Justice*. SBL Dissertation 24 (Missoula: Scholars Press, 1975); and Werner Berg, *Die sogennannten Hymnenfragmente im Amosbuch*. Europäische Hochschulschriften 23/35 (Frankfurt: Lang, 1974).

58. When the "hosts" are understood as stars, then the accent on creation and the sovereign rule of God are more closely connected.

59. See the troubled, lingering, unanswered question of Lam. 5:20-22 and the liturgical verdict concerning the question in Isa. 49:14. The texts suggest that Israel's sense of abandonment was a powerful theological problem.

The second oracle is structured according to the same "if-then" pattern and makes the same affirmation (Jer. 31:37). Again, the "if-then" construct is not a statement of conditionality, but a twofold statement of "never." The heavens and the earth are never to be measured or explored;[60] Israel will never be rejected. The final line of the oracle is not indifferent to Israel's serious misdeeds, ". . . all that they have done." All that they have done is bad indeed, enough to evoke hostility and rejection; all of that evil, however, cannot undo God's powerful choosing. The connection between God and Israel cannot be abrogated from Israel's side; what God chooses, Israel cannot reject.[61] Israel is impotent to terminate the relation. Only Yahweh has made the relation, only Yahweh can nullify the relation, and Yahweh will not.

Two misreadings of this text are possible. On the one hand, it would be a mistake to consider this text as claiming ontological significance for the covenant structure, as if Israel is fixed in the cosmos like heaven and earth. The text does not claim this. On the other hand, in our modernity, it is not useful to consider that now the heavens can be measured and earth can be explored, thereby nullifying the promise made from an ancient view of the world. We must take the assertion on its own terms in its own context, as a pastoral, evangelical assertion of God's fidelity toward and solidarity with Israel, in and through the Exile. Israel's well-being rests with God's inclination; and God's inclination, as the sun, moon, stars, heavens, and earth attest, is relentlessly steadfast.[62] The episode of 587, harsh as it is, does not finally detract from the overriding reality of God's watchful, persistent fidelity.

---

60. See the lyrical, doxological conclusions of Job 28, and the discussion of Gerhard von Rad, *Wisdom in Israel* (Nashville: Abingdon and London: SCM, 1972), 145-49.

61. This affirmation clearly runs counter to the statement of v. 32, that Israel "broke" *(prr)* the covenant. The two affirmations are there in the text, back-to-back. Israel struggled with both statements. The interpreter is not free to opt for either one to the neglect of the other. The two affirmations provide the arena for Israel's ongoing theological work.

62. On the attestation of sun, moon, and stars in praise, see Terence E. Fretheim, "Creation's Praise of God in the Psalms," *Ex Auditu* 3 (1987): 16-30. See also von Rad, *Wisdom in Israel,* 144-176.

31:38-40   This final promissory oracle in the chapter provides a surprising and remarkable climax to the series of promises in these two chapters. We have seen that 31:31-34 and 35-37 make very different points of emphasis, the former concerning discontinuity and historical specificity, and the latter concerning continuity and creation. Both of those promissory passages, however, are preoccupied with the relation between Yahweh and Israel. That is, the subject is intensely theological. This final promise (vv. 38-40) demonstrates the way in which Israel's faith in general, and the Jeremiah tradition in particular, are concerned with day-to-day concrete reality. This final promise does not attend to a more general God-Israel relation, but to the specific economic-political reconstruction of the city of Jerusalem. The oracle is filled with quite concrete geographical references to the city. The actual reference points are not known to us, but they are written or spoken by someone who is clearly familiar with the city. While it is most congenial to situate this oracle in the time of Nehemiah and that rebuilding of the city,[63] we must not disregard the enduring promissory character of the oracle. Thus the oracle is not simply reflective of a single rebuilding effort, but looms as a pervasive and enduring promise that marks the life and destiny of the city of Jerusalem in every time and circumstance. This oracle assures that Jerusalem in every time is a city under the powerful promise of God for rebuilding and for well-being.

The city of Jerusalem has indeed become a place of profanation (cf. 3:2; Ezek. 8–11). Now it is promised that this profaned city will be a place "sacred [RSV 'holy'] to Yahweh." The city which had become repellent to Yahweh, where Yahweh would no longer abide, now becomes an acceptable habitat where God will again dwell.[64] Thus the quite concrete geographical references are turned toward theological significance. The reconstituted city becomes

---

63. See Holladay, *Jeremiah 2*, 199-200.

64. The notion of the profane city being made holy to the LORD is parallel to the dramatic presentation of Ezek. 9–10, 43–44, in which the glory of God departs and returns to the city. See Ralph W. Klein, *Ezekiel: The Prophet and His Message* (Columbia: University of South Carolina Press, 1988), 172-79.

once again the place where God will be present with healing, protective power.[65]

The acceptability of Jerusalem as a place of God's residence means that the whole bleak history of destructiveness (which has preoccupied the tradition of Jeremiah) will end. Thus in Jer. 31:40 it is asserted that the two negative verbs "uprooted" and "overthrown," which have been a leitmotif for Jeremiah since 1:10, are now eliminated from the vocabulary of Yahweh and from the life of Jerusalem. The long history of destructiveness evoked by Israel's disobedience has ended (cf. 31:27-28); now the counter-verbs from 1:10, "plant and build," can have full sway. It takes no great imagination, given the power of "plant and build" to overpower "uproot and overthrow," to see a new future for Israel, as stunning and profound as the ways in which resurrection nullifies and overrides crucifixion. Moreover, the final word about the silencing and annulment of these negative terms in the life of Jerusalem is "forever" *(l'olam)*, which the RSV renders "never again." That is, there will be no "plucking up" or "overthrowing" ever again. One can see in the oracle an inchoate Zionism that will loom large in emerging Judaism. The city of Jerusalem now becomes the visible sign and evidence that God has turned the destiny of Israel decisively in a new direction of well-being. Where there has been uprooting and overthrowing, there will be building and rebuilding . . . forever!

JEREMIAH PURCHASES LAND (32:1-44)

This long prose passage seeks to find in God's resolve a way into the future for Israel, which has been seriously dislodged in the present. The chapter has its center in a quite specific, public, concrete, economic act (32:6-15). That specific act, which becomes the taproot of reflection in this chapter, generates an expansive and sweeping claim for the future (cf. esp. vv. 42-44).

---

65. The lyrical anticipation of a "new Jerusalem" in Isa. 65:17-25; Rev. 21:2-4 thus is connected to a quite concrete passion for reconstruction of the ruins of Jerusalem. The metaphor must not be permitted to float off away from historical concreteness.

32:1-5 The chapter begins in an odd way. The tradition of Jeremiah several times reiterates an encounter between the prophet and King Zedekiah (21:1-7; 37:3-7, 17-21; 38:14-28). This is yet one more report of such an encounter. The beginning point of the report is the delivery of another prophetic word (32:1). Two circumstances pertain: the city is under siege, and the prophet is under arrest (vv. 2-3a). The only speech in this unit is not "the word of the LORD," but the questioning speech of the king (vv. 3b-5). Thus v. 1 introduces a "word from the LORD," but what follows is a word from the king.

The king asks a question, but the substance of the question is a quote from the prophet, that is, a word uttered previously by the prophet. Thus "the prophetic word" is placed in the mouth of the king, who ostensibly had heard the message so often that he knew it by heart. The recurring message of the prophet that the king quotes is that the city will be taken and the king will be deported. While elsewhere the death of the king is anticipated, here what is promised is only an unequal, ominous meeting with the king of Babylon. The quote in the mouth of the king adds an ominous conclusion: "You shall not succeed" (v. 5). The staging of the entire speech of the king is "Why? *(maddua',* v. 3b). Why does Jeremiah say this? Why does the prophet threaten the king? Why are the king and the city under assault?

Two observations are evoked by the question of the king. First, if the king had listened closely enough to quote the prophet as he does, the king might have listened closely enough to know the answer to his question. Second, though the king asks "why," this narrative in fact offers no answer. Thus vv. 1-5 present only a general background for the narrative to follow; the query of the king does not in fact relate in any specific way to what follows. All we know (yet again) is an inordinate threat to crown and to city. The king does not really ask for information, but makes a plea for rescue.

32:6-15 The core element in this chapter is the specific episode of land purchase here narrated. The word of Yahweh announced in v. 1 is now voiced in v. 6. The specific impetus for this public act is given in vv. 6-8. On the one hand, Jeremiah is forewarned (by the LORD) about his cousin's request (v. 7). On the other hand, the cousin makes the direct request as anticipated (v. 8). The convergence of Yahweh's forewarning and Hanamel's request authenticates that this act is indeed wrought by God. The actual imperative in v. 8 implicates Jeremiah in a land transaction at the moment when the land and its worth are jeopardized by a military occupation (vv. 1-5). Thus the "right of redemption" is an act to keep a family inheritance of land intact, just when circumstances made such an investment seemingly foolish. The family obligation (sanctioned by God) is taken seriously against all negative indicators from the sorry context. The obligation is to preserve and maintain the family inheritance of land.

Jeremiah acts to fulfill his cousin's imperative that is authorized by God (vv. 9-13). The narrative reports in a detailed way a carefully proper transaction in which appropriate public procedure is meticulously followed. There is a transfer of cash, the signing of titles and deeds, the verification of witnesses, and the public filing of copies of the transaction. Verse 12 suggests that there are ample witnesses, so that that can be no later question concerning the property or completeness and legality of the transaction. In this episode, we also have the first mention of Baruch, who is given a special position as the one who retains the deed of purchase (v. 12).

We may wonder why this episode receives such careful attention. Apparently the episode provides, in narrative form, clear title that this community facing deportation has an inalienable piece of land. That is, while the act contains one plot of land for one family, in the narrative presentation, that piece of land is paradigmatic of all the land which Israel held and now loses. Moreover, the public act (and its narrated report) put Jeremiah on public record as claiming that there is indeed "life after Babylon."[66] The prophet has put his money where his mouth is.

The narrative makes clear that while this is a carefully performed economic, legal act, it is not simply an economic or legal transaction. It is a land deal freighted with enormous theological

---

66. See Peter Diepold, *Israels Land.* Beiträge zur Wissenschaft vom Alten und Neuen Testament 95 (Stuttgart: Kohlhammer, 1972): 129-131.

significance. Baruch is commanded to deposit the deed where it is safe and where it will be an enduring witness into the long-term future. The act closely parallels and anticipates that of Seraiah the brother of Baruch in 51:59-64. Both acts that the brothers record and for which they make enduring deposits affirm the same reality of life after Babylon.[67] In terms of our reading the text, we may conclude that the safe place in which Baruch deposited the evidence, even after the "earthenware vessel" (32:14), is the biblical text itself. That is the only place in which the evidence of the land deal has remained. That evidence, however, is sufficient for Israel's long-term hope.

The entire transaction concerning the land comes into theological focus in v. 15. Now, in the mouth of God, we are given to discern the meaning of the economic, legal act. The triad of "houses, fields, vineyards" bespeaks the most common and characteristic elements of economic life. These items will "again be bought." The term "again" suggests a disruption and a cessation.[68] The invasion by the Babylonians will indeed cause the economy to come to a halt. A time will come when there will be no market for fields, houses, or vineyards, because people lack money or nerve. The invasion causes the economy to come to a standstill. But the land will be "born again." "Bought again" means that the economy will resume and regain its health. The community will begin to function again, and when the economy resumes Jeremiah will have staked out a crucial point of access for himself.[69] The entire process of vv. 6-15 holds together the theological reality of God's promise and the restoration of an economic infrastructure.

---

67. The references to Baruch (32:12; 36:4ff.) and his brother Seraiah (51:59-64) suggest that the family of Neriah (1) was skilled as a family of scribes and (2) belonged to the pro-Babylonian party in Jerusalem. On both counts, they were important to the developing tradition of Jeremiah.

68. The recurrence of the adverb "again" (*'od*) in exilic texts acknowledges both an honest recognition of discontinuity, and a deep conviction about rehabilitation after the discontinuity (cf., e.g., Isa. 54:9).

69. The act is at the same time a way of securing family property and of vindicating the faith voiced in the tradition of Jeremiah. That the land can later be reclaimed serves to announce that Jeremiah was right in his reading of history.

81

This is a characteristic way in which the Bible holds together faith claims and the realities of public life. Unless both factors are present, the significance of this episode collapses. In the exercise of family economic responsibility, the prophet enacts the long-term fidelity of God as well. Jeremiah invests in God's promised future exactly when that future seems completely closed off.

32:16-25   The prayer of the prophet which follows the purchase of the land may have been placed here through an editorial process. It is, however, not inappropriate in its present place, for the conclusion to the prayer in v. 25 alludes directly to the climactic statement of v. 15.

After the transitional comment of v. 16, the prayer begins with a doxology (v. 17). God is named and then is identified as creator of all that is; the wonder of creation is sighted as evidence of God's power and freedom to do whatever God chooses. The way of creation is "by great power and by outstretched arm." This same sort of phrasing is more familiar to us in an Exodus recital, yet another area of God's power and freedom (cf. v. 21). Finally in the doxology, the prayer asserts that nothing is "impossible" for God. This extreme statement seems to allude back to Gen. 18, wherein what is not "impossible" for God is the birth of a child to an old, barren couple.[70] In the context of this chapter concerning exile, the doxology — which appeals to creation by implication to the Exodus, and to a birth to the barren — asserts that even the circumstance of exile cannot curb or limit or defeat God's great and powerful resolve, any more than chaos, bondage, or barrenness could thwart God's powerful intention.

After this thematic assertion, Jer. 32:18-23a provides a catalogue of the "impossibilities" God has wrought. The supporting evidence for praise to God is a highly stylized recital of Israel's canonical statement of God's gracious miracles. Yahweh is characterized by *hesed*, "steadfast love," which God has persistently "showed" to Israel. That statement of God's goodness, however, is balanced or even countered by the adversative statement that God repays *(sh-l-m)* guilt (v. 18). The two parts of v. 18 thus

---

70. Walter Brueggemann, " 'Impossibility' and Epistemology," 615-634.

voice the fundamental tension in the character of Israel's God, a tension early articulated to Moses (Exod. 34:6-7), a tension evidenced in the wilderness tradition, especially Num. 14.[71] God is utterly faithful and exactingly severe.

Israel seems untroubled in its presentation of this tension in God, and is not obligated to find a way to resolve the tension. The doxological formulation of Jer. 32:18b-19a perhaps revels in the tension, and takes the very tension of God's faithfulness and judgment as the inescapable working of Yahweh's greatness and might. On the one hand, it is the God of such greatness and might who endlessly assesses the world, and who "rewards" all according to their just desserts. Thus the verbs "repay" *(sh-l-m,* v. 18; RSV "requite") and "reward" *(ntn,* v. 19) suggest a God of responsible retribution. On the other hand, v. 20 begins a recital of God's *hesed,* which is not at all guided by merit but by mercy.

The core memory of Israel completely disregards a retributive moral scheme and rejoices exuberantly in good gifts given by God which have not been warranted. This inventory of good gifts includes the signs and wonders of the Exodus and the gift of the land. These miracles, like the miracle of creation (v. 17), are accomplished by a strong and outstretched arm. The upshot of such generosity from God is a land of milk and honey. Thus in the recital, the prayer keeps the tension in God's inclination wondrously balanced, open, and unresolved.

After the recital of God's wonders, vv. 23b-24 speak out of a very different frame of reference, again returning to retributive sanctions. These verses are a programmatic lawsuit statement, offering a rationale for the Exile. The indictment of the lawsuit is that Israel did "not listen," did not "walk in the torah," did not "do." The sentence of the lawsuit, introduced by "therefore," refers to all these "evils" ("disasters"), specifically siege and its derivative visitations of sword, famine, and pestilence. These verses, like the

---

71. On this text and its bipolar theological function, see Katherine D. Sakenfeld, "The Problem of Divine Forgiveness in Numbers 14," *Catholic Biblical Quarterly* 37 (1975): 317-330; and Dennis T. Olson, *The Death of the Old and the Birth of the New.* Brown Judaic Studies 71 (Chico: Scholars Press, 1985), 129-152.

events of 587 B.C.E., indicate that Yahweh in "repaying the guilty"
has the last word. It is judgment against torah-breakers that finally
prevails. This is indeed a primary claim of the book of Jeremiah,
sustained by Israel's experience (587).

Except for v. 25! Indeed, the entire prayer beginning in v. 17
moves toward v. 25, surprising as it is after the reasoning of vv.
23b-24. For the most part, this prayer is focused on retribution.
Except for the initial statement of "nothing is impossible" (v. 17)
and the initial reference to "steadfast love" (*hesed*, v. 18), we expect
nothing more beyond retribution. The move beyond a system of
judgment begins with "Yet thou" *(we-attah)* (v. 25). Of course,
finally Israel must reckon not with a system of sanctions but with
the "Thou" who created the world, birthed the heir to the barren,
and freed the slaves to become Israel.[72] This "Thou" is characteristically willing and able to move beyond prearranged payoffs
and consequences to utterly new, inexplicable possibilities. This
moment in exilic theology is such a moment when God moves
beyond strategies and constraints of retribution. The land is in-
vaded and occupied and has become worthless. The "Thou" of
Yahweh, however, counters that outcome of worthlessness with a
resolve and a promise: "Invest!" *(qnh)*. The promissory imperatives continue: Buy land and get witnesses, secure titles. Thus the
verse names the matters Jeremiah performed in vv. 6-15. Do all
these in faith, against the present data. The data is all Babylonian.
God, however, speaks beyond Babylon to anticipate the liberation
and revaluing of the land when it has been regarded as worthless.

This prayer is often dismissed as late, tendentious rhetoric. Such
a verdict, however, misses the delicate, torturous, vibrant struggle
of the text to find hope in exile. The voice of the text is honest
and does not wish to evade or deny the awesome threat against
Jerusalem which is the result of "not listening" (v. 23b) and which

---

72. See the convergence of these several themes in Rom. 4:17. Hans
Heinrich Schmid, "Rechtfertigung als Schopfungsgeschehen," in *Rechtfer-*
tigung. Festschrift Ernst Kasemann, ed. Johannes Friedrich, Wolfgang Pöhl-
mann, and Peter Stuhlmacher (Göttingen: Vandenhoeck & Ruprecht, 1976),
402-414, has suggested that *creatio ex nihilo*, resurrection from the dead, and
justification by grace are in fact parallel and synonymous claims. The same
kind of identity of themes is present in this verse.

issues in terrible curses (v. 24). That moral severity is rooted in very old character traits of Yahweh (cf. v. 18; Exod. 34:7). That harsh element of Yahweh is readily acknowledged; it is not denied that Judah warrants every harsh action from Yahweh that it receives.

The prayer is not, however, a scolding. It is an act of amazement. It is mindful that Yahweh is not controlled or finally victimized by the reality of disobedience and evil. This same God is marked by and free for *hesed*. The *hesed* seen in creation and Exodus now comes powerfully into play among the exiles. God intends a good life for this people after exile. Such a post-exilic destiny for Israel might seem to the exiles and to us utterly impossible. The possibility here announced is not first of all economic or political. It is rooted only in God's passionate freedom which issues in concrete newness. The world does not culminate on Babylonian terms, because God has post-Babylonian intentions for Judah.[73] Because of this "Thou," history for Judah and Jerusalem is open to outrageous newness wrought through the courage of the faithful. The act of faith commanded concerning the land is concrete and specific. It is because so much of faith rides on this act that the extreme care of Jer. 32:6-15 is taken. The move beyond exile to life in the land is the cause for doxology. Indeed, such a restoration of the land is a miracle on a par with creation. Life begins again, out of chaos!

32:26-41   The "prayer" of Jeremiah (vv. 16-25) evokes a response from Yahweh in the form of an oracle. Thus these two long prose sections are formally related as prayer (vv. 16-25) and as answer (vv. 26-41). In substance, however, they are two long theological reflections on the twin themes of judgment and hope, placed respectively in the mouth of the prophet and in the responding mouth of God.

Verse 27 is precisely symmetrical to v. 17 in all four of its parts:

---

73. In the end, chs. 50–51 are canonically decisive. Most of the book of Jeremiah concerns the judgment of God wrought through Babylon. The defeat of Babylon in those concluding chapters creates space for the newness God will enact on behalf of this people.

	v. 17	v. 27
Initial ejaculation:	"Ah" *('hh)*	"Behold" *(hnh)*
Naming of God:	Lord Yahweh	Yahweh
Reference to creation as scope		
of sovereignty:	doxology	"all flesh"
Statement on impossibility:	conclusion	rhetorical question.

Thus v. 27 seems to echo and answer all the elements of v. 17 and prepare for the assertions that follow (vv. 28-41), even as v. 17 opens the way for the prayer of vv. 17-25. Verse 27 has Yahweh announce self as the cosmic sovereign. The question, "Is anything too hard for me?" echoes Gen. 18:14; it is a rhetorical question with an implied answer of "no." Thus the question corresponds to the assertion of Jer. 32:17. The oracle like the prayer concerns the God who acts beyond what Israel (or the world) thinks is possible.

The impossibility which God will work, according to both prayer and oracle, is twofold. First, God will work a massive judgment which is here expressed in a lawsuit form (vv. 18-36). It is not "impossible" for God to terminate Jerusalem. The more extended part of this divine asseveration is an indictment, detailing the wrongs of Judah (vv. 30-31a, 32-35). The affronts committed by "this city" against Yahweh are a quite generalized "evil" (vv. 30, 32); more specifically, the people of Israel and Judah "did not listen, they refused discipline" (v. 33, author's translation). That is, they regarded themselves as autonomous, outside the claims of the torah and beyond the obligations of covenant. Thus autonomy was the worship of other gods, which in fact are only projections of self-interest.

The sure outcome of such a rejection of Yahweh is that Yahweh will dispatch Babylon to destroy (vv. 28-29), so that the offending city is removed from Yahweh's field of vision (v. 31). The argument is a straightforward articulation of disobedience (vv. 30-31a, 32-35) and punishment (vv. 28-29, 31b). The disobedience is of the grossest kind, and therefore the punishment is most severe. If any in Jerusalem still believed the ideology that Jerusalem is inviolate, this oracle rejects such a view in the most unambiguous terms.[74]

---

74. For a positive presentation of the theological claims of the Zion establishment, see Ben C. Ollenburger, *Zion, The City of the Great King.*

In light of such an insistent statement, we are scarcely prepared for the second aspect of God's "impossibility" (vv. 36-41). The rhetoric marks a drastic turn in the oracle with "and now therefore" (v. 36). The "and now" *(we'attah)* characteristically marks a drastic break with a discussion of what is past, and makes an intense focus on the present which may stand in sharp tension with the past. The "therefore" is odd,[75] for it suggests that the facts of vv. 28-35 are the cause of v. 36. Nothing, of course, could be further from the intended shape of the argument. Verse 36 does not follow in any way from the argument of vv. 28-35. Indeed, in v. 36 the text makes an enormous leap away from vv. 28-35 to God's second impossibility. Now the news is good. It has not been impossible to destroy the city. It also is not an impossibility, we are now told, that God will revive this city which is in ruins.

Verse 36 functions to tie the two impossibilities together, for v. 36 reiterates the judgment sounded against the city in vv. 28-29. Indeed, it is as though the text wants to establish continuity, so that we understand that the city now to be revived is in fact the city that has been destroyed. For the theological point being made, it is crucial that it is the same city. The issue of continuity in a crisis of deep discontinuity is not unlike the issue of the continuity of the crucified Jesus and the risen LORD, attested by Thomas's probing touch (John 20:24-28). As the resurrection of Jesus is the resurrection of the Crucified One, so the gathered city is the gathering of the city destroyed. That city is in the throes of heavy curses (Jer. 32:36). Those curses are, however, disrupted by the intrusive speech of God: "Behold!" (v. 37). The term matches the term in v. 27, thus creating a parallel in rhetoric as the two impossible acts of God are contrasted. This is followed by three powerful verbs through which Yahweh enacts a fresh and inexplicable intention: I will gather, I will return, I will settle. The verbs directly counter the negative "I drove them" (v. 37), so that the reverse of verbs serves God's intent to reverse exile. The rejected city is the place of God's great, impossible gathering.

These programmatic assertions are then followed by a series of theological statements reflective of Israel's best exilic faith, state-

---

75. Some versions of the text do not include the word.

ments which find important parallels in exilic Isaiah and in Ezekiel (vv. 38-41). These statements include the following:

(1) The covenantal formula, "They shall be my people, and I will be their God" (v. 38).[76] This statement asserts utter solidarity between God and Israel, a solidarity sharply disrupted by the Exile, but now fully restored.

(2) A gift of a new heart, a new disposition toward Yahweh which permits full trust in God, which makes trustful obedience joyous (v. 39; cf. Ezek. 11:19-20; 36:26-27).[77]

(3) An assertion of an "everlasting covenant," one not to be disrupted or violated as exile disrupted and violated the old covenant.[78] Thus it is precisely the exilic situation of radical discontinuity that evokes and permits such a full statement of confidence and of continuity.

(4) The promise that God will act in complete fidelity *(emet)* to do good and to plant Israel in the land which had seemed forfeited (Jer. 32:41; cf. 1:10).

These four phrasings, characteristic of Israel in exile, give substance and depth and form to the large promise that God will "gather." This is what "gathering" means. Yahweh is resolved that Israel will now be fully blessed as God's people, so that none of the hurts or scars of the events around 587 and the Exile should remain. The word "faithfulness" *(emet)* suggests that Israel is now to benefit from God's powerful capacity to keep covenant.[79]

This double statement of prophetic prayer (vv. 17-25) and divine oracle (vv. 26-41) demonstrates how the tradition of

---

76. See Smend.

77. On the "new heart," see Donald E. Gowan, *Eschatology in the Old Testament* (Philadelphia: Fortress, 1986), 69-83; and Joyce, 107-124.

78. The *berit 'olam* emerges as especially important in the Exile when the covenant of Moses seemed to have been abrogated. See Delbert R. Hillers, *Covenant: The History of a Biblical Idea* (Baltimore: John Hopkins University Press, 1969), 98-119.

79. On the delicate interplay of continuity and discontinuity in the covenant, see David Noel Freedman, "Divine Commitment and Human Obligation: The Covenant Theme," *Interpretation* 18 (1964): 419-431; and the fresh and vigorous argument of Jon D. Levenson, *Sinai and Zion: An Entry into the Jewish Bible* (Minneapolis: Winston, 1985), esp. 187-217.

Jeremiah understands and voices the problem of exile in relation to the fidelity of God.[80] The circumstance of Israel's experience in the time of the formation of this tradition required a two-stage statement of God's resolve. It would not do, on the one hand, only to state the destructive "impossibility," both because it was not by itself true and because it is not theologically adequate for the way of God's governance. On the other hand, it would not do to speak only of God's second possibility of restoration, for that would deny too much of the painful discontinuity and would in fact be a mode of "cheap grace." Both "impossibilities" are present in this oracular response of God. Both are essential, in sequence, to Israel's life with God. This twofold structure of "impossibilities" is faithful both to Israel's experience and to the programmatic statement of 1:10. We may see in the two-stage presentation an anticipation of the Christian shaping of life in terms of death and resurrection.[81] While the casting of this twofold matter is of course in terms that are particularly Jewish (and only derivatively Christian), the twofold drama of grief and hope is in fact intrinsic to human experience, for those who have eyes to see. The commonality of this drama is well said by George Steiner.

> There is one particular day in Western history about which neither historical record nor myth nor Scripture make report. It is a Saturday. And it has become the longest of days. We know of that Good Friday which Christianity holds to have been that of the Cross. But the non-Christian, the atheist, knows of it as well. This is to say that he knows of the injustice, of the interminable suffering, of the waste, of the brute enigma of ending, which so largely make up not only the historical dimension of the human condition, but the everyday fabric of our personal lives. We know, ineluctably, of the pain, of the failure of love, of the solitude which are our history and private fate. We know also about Sunday. To the Christian, that day signifies an intimation, both assured and precarious, both evident and beyond comprehension, of resurrection, of a justice

---

80. Though the term is not often used for this text, the text in fact articulates a powerful proposal for a theodicy, holding together God's power and fidelity, and the experience of suffering in Judah.

81. See Neusner, 145 and *passim*, for those two stages in the decisive paradigm of Judaism.

and a love that have conquered death. If we are non-Christians or non-believers, we know of that Sunday in precisely analogous terms. We conceive of it as the day of liberation from inhumanity and servitude. We look to resolutions, be they therapeutic or political, be they social or messianic. The lineaments of that Sunday carry the name of hope (there is no word less deconstructible).

But ours is the long day's journey of the Saturday. Between suffering, aloneness, unutterable waste on the one hand and the dream of liberation, of rebirth on the other. In the face of the torture of a child, of the death of love which is Friday, even the greatest art and poetry are almost helpless. In the Utopia of the Sunday, the aesthetic will, presumably, no longer have logic or necessity. The apprehensions and figurations in the play of metaphysical imagining, in the poem and the music, which tell of pain and of hope, of the flesh which is said to taste of ash and of the spirit which is said to have the savour of fire, are always Sabbatarian. They have risen out of an immensity of waiting which is that of man. Without them, how could we be patient?[82]

32:42-44 An additional oracle reiterates the same twofold drama of Israel's life with God. The rhetoric of 32:42 indicates the twofold character by "just as" _(ka-asherr)_ and "so" _(ken)_. The one follows the other and is linked to it. In this brief oracle the destructive judgment of God is only alluded to in order to make the contrast between God's past deed of destruction and God's new action of restoration. The accent, however, falls completely on God's second act, that of restoration. The "good" (fortune) _(tob)_ promised (cf. _tob_ in vv. 40, 41) is restored, safe life in the land.[83] The substance of "good" is "fields shall be bought" (vv. 43, 44). That is, the promises of God are not theoretical or spiritual, but concern real life in a reordered, political-economic situation. Moreover, the revival of a full economy and an adequate property system touches all geographic regions of Judah's terri-

---

82. George Steiner, _Real Presences: Is There Anything in What We Say?_ (Chicago: University of Chicago Press and London: Faber & Faber, 1989), 231-32.

83. On the use of "good" _(tob)_ in exilic theology, see Walter Brueggemann, "The Kerygma of the Deuteronomistic Historian: Gospel for Exiles," _Interpretation_ 22 (1968): 387-402.

tory.[84] The whole land which is diminished shall now be utterly enhanced. The oracle anticipates a complete reversal of Israel's life into well-being.

The prayer (vv. 17-25) and the long oracle (vv. 27-41) with the double reference to "impossibility" shape the double thema of this entire chapter. On the one hand, the phrase "too hard" looks back to an anticipation of the destruction of the city and of the king (vv. 3-4) which is reiterated in vv. 23-24, 28-29. The loss of Jerusalem is indeed a major fact in Israel's faith and in Israel's experience. The city long regarded itself as privileged and guaranteed by God, but now has been devastated by God. The experience is visible and incontrovertible.

On the other hand, however, the prayer and oracle both dare to look ahead in hope to God's second resolve of restoration. This resolve is voiced in v. 15 and is reiterated in vv. 25, 37-41, 42-44. The text dodges or denies nothing of Judah's trouble. It insists, however, that the trouble is not the end of the tale. Thus in every element of this long reflective statement, beginning at v. 6, the crucial issue is that God has promised and will enact complete restoration. That promise is rooted in God's own resolve and in nothing less. The action of the prophet in vv. 6-15 vouches for God's promise in the most concrete way possible. The text is a massive reflection which moves Israel into the displacement, and out of it, both by the resolve of God for whom nothing is too hard. Israel's destiny is to lose what it treasures, and then to have it handed back by God in mercy, massively broken and then powerfully blessed.

RESTORATION FOR JUDAH AND JERUSALEM (33:1-26)

This chapter consists in seven promissory oracles, each of which announces God's resolve to invert the fortunes of Judah and to create a new season of well-being for Jerusalem. While these several oracles differ in detail, two factors are constant. First, the voiced resolve of the text is indeed God's very own resolve, rooted

---

84. The regions named are the same as those named in 33:13.

in God's long-term intention and uttered in God's own speech. Second, that resolve of God concerns precisely the public, historical, sociopolitical future of the community. Thus these promissory statements join together the resolve of heaven and the future of the earth.

33:1-10   The word comes "a second time" while the prophet is still under arrest. The "first time" is reported in 32:2. The formula joins together (through editorial activity) the narrative, prayer, and oracle of ch. 32 and the present chapter. These promissory passages, according to the introduction, are situated in a hostile confinement. A poet held as a political prisoner writes poems of hope, resolutely contradicting not only the present condition of his people, but resolutely overriding his own personal circumstance.[85] Such a rhetorical act stridently asserts the freedom and effectiveness of God's intent, against all apparent limitations imposed by "realism." These promises have little patience with or respect for conventional "realism."

The oracle begins by God's self-assertion and self-identity (33:2). The speaker of promise is not just any God, but the God who had the power to make the earth, to form the earth, to found the earth. This is a God who has moved decisively against chaos (cf. 5:22). The name of this God is Yahweh, a name associated in doxologies with the power to bring order out of chaos and life out of death. This large claim for Yahweh's identity is reminiscent of 32:17, 27.

This powerful God in whose will the world lives, now promises to be available precisely to the exiles who thought they were God-abandoned.[86] The creator of heaven and earth is the God

---

85. The utterance of promises rooted in faith from prison is not unlike some of the epistles of Paul in the NT. Moreover, in our own time some of the most important and dangerous poetry has come from those imprisoned and politically at risk. See Nicanor Parra, *Emergency Poems* (New York: New Directions, 1972).

86. Thus the Exile is an experience of Jerusalem's God-forsakenness in response to Jerusalem's having abandoned God. This dialectic perhaps provides a model for an interpretation of the cross in the NT. Jürgen Moltmann, *The Crucified God* (New York: Harper & Row, 1974), 243, concludes: "The

who assured attentiveness to and care for the exiles. The God of all power is the God who attends to the powerless. The God who seemed to be absent is present, findable, and approachable. (See the exilic theme in Deut. 4:29-31; Jer. 29:12-14; Isa. 55:6-9; and subsequently Isa. 65:24.) The "call" that is invited and authorized is Israel's call of need, petition, and distress.[87] God will answer such a call; when God answers, it will not be an innocuous assurance, but it will be a disclosure of what is not yet known in Israel, that is, a disclosure of the future which is certain in God's resolve, even if not yet visible in Israel. If exilic Israel acts in faith, God will make available God's intent for the future.

Then follows the very disclosure that has been promised. Jeremiah 33:4-5 provides the context for talk about the future by a brief review of the recent past. The recent past is filled with houses torn down to provide emergency military equipment and supplies, with defense maneuvers, with invading Babylonians, and with an abundance of corpses, military casualties.[88] That utter disorder has occurred because of God's hidden "face." That is, God has withdrawn from the city the sustaining power of God's promise, making the city available for and vulnerable to massive destruction. The city without God's face, that is, without God's own self, is left to the outworking of its own wickedness. And that wickedness, without the protective hedge of God, has inundated Israel. If vv. 4-5 can be related to the rhetoric about creation in v. 2, then we have a picture of the creator God who has

---

Fatherlessness of the Son is matched by the Sonlessness of the Father. . . ." *Mutatis mutandis,* such a formulation is not unlike the situation of God and Jerusalem in the Exile.

87. Karl Barth, *Church Dogmatics,* III/3 (Edinburgh: Clark, 1960), 262-288, has most powerfully urged that petition is the center of biblical prayer. Petition which God will hear is the proper mode of speech in exile. Barth asserts, "Prayer, or praying, is simply asking" (268). See Perry LeFevre, *Understandings of Prayer* (Philadelphia: Westminster, 1981), 28-45, for a discussion of Barth on prayer.

88. In this usage, "house" bespeaks influence, affluence, power, and stability. Such houses are sure to be the target of an invading army; they are also the target of prophetic criticism, because they embody social inequality, indifference, and exploitation. Cf. Jer. 22:13-17; Amos. 3:15; and the counterreality of the Rechabites in Jer. 35:7-9.

withdrawn ordering governance and abandons life to the surging power of chaos which takes the form of Babylonian invasion. Babylon is simply the power of chaos which Yahweh has finally unleashed against God's own people. Israel's enacted evil has caused God to relinquish this beloved city to the surging power of cosmic evil.

All of this analysis and threat in vv. 4-5, however, is background and context for the oracle. The chaos of evil has indeed worked its will. The "great and hidden things" of v. 3 are only now approached in v. 6. The interlude of vv. 4-5 tells of things not hidden (which everyone can see), and of things not great. The "great and hidden things" concern God's unexpected but sure resolve to quench the evil and to move against and beyond the destruction.

The "great and hidden things" now disclosed concern God's resolve to act with powerful, beneficent verbs (vv. 6-9). God now resolves to bring healing in the face of the destructive powers which have wrought chaos, and to give to the city utter well-being, a well-being *(sh-l-m)* marked by God's own fidelity *(emet;* RSV "security"). The language of the promise envisions a complete inversion of the destruction of the recent past. Thus the promise uses the programmatic formula, "I will restore the fortunes," that is, renew the good conditions of old (v. 7). The formula is given more concrete substance by three verbs: "I will build [rebuild], I will cleanse, I will forgive" (vv. 7b-8). The first verb refers to the physical reconstruction and rehabilitation of the city; the other two refer to making the city religiously, ritually acceptable to God, so that God can again be available and present in the city. God will do for Israel and Judah what they cannot do for themselves: make them qualified for God's good gifts and God's powerful presence. Verse 8 is saturated with the language of guilt and sin, using all three standard words for sin: "sin" *(ht')*, "guilt" *('on)*, and "rebellion" *(p-sh-')*.[89] These words, however, are overpowered by the strong verbs which

---

89. See the same three terms in Exod. 34:7, in one of Israel's primary articulations of the seriousness with which God takes Israel's infidelity. In the old confession, such sin is punished; here it is forgiven. Thus this text plays against the old warning.

permit God's newness. The outcome of God's resolve and God's action is the rehabilitation of Jerusalem. The city had become a place of grief and wretchedness, and now comes joy! It had become a place of shame and humiliation, and now comes glory and splendor! The action of God makes an utterly new Jerusalem. The new city is a gift of life to its inhabitants.

The city is at the same time a powerful and unambiguous witness to the nations. The other nations are always watching Jerusalem, and God knows they are watching. They have watched while God abandoned the city, and they have no doubt drawn ignominious conclusions about Yahweh.[90] Now, however, the nations will notice the newness. They will see the "good" *(tob)* and the "prosperity" *(shalom)*, and they will be required to draw new conclusions about God and about Israel. Through the rescue of Jerusalem, all the nations will see and know that there is a God in Israel (cf. 1 Sam. 17:46). The greatest attestation to be made concerning the rule of Yahweh comes whenever God's power for life vetoes the grip of death.[91] That veto is about to be enacted by Yahweh in Jerusalem and the nations cannot fail to notice. They will be unable to avoid the conclusion that the God of Jerusalem must be reckoned with. Thus healed Jerusalem becomes a theological datum which requires the nations to reposition themselves vis-à-vis Yahweh. (This argument in the end leads to the oracles of chs. 46–51, which assert that Yahweh is the key factor in the life of the nations.)

33:10-11 This second promissory oracle states a massive inversion in Jerusalem toward well-being, wrought by God. The promise culminates in the use of the programmatic formula, "restore the fortunes." Leading to that concluding verdict is a concrete example of the inversion wrought by God. The Hebrew text

---

90. The drawing of such conclusions is the basis of the petition of Moses in Num. 14:13-19 and of God's fresh resolve in Ezek. 36:22-32. On the latter, see Brueggemann, *Hopeful Imagination,* 69-87.

91. This is the same claim made in the Christian affirmation of the resurrection of Jesus which breaks the power of death; cf. Acts 2:24; 1 Cor. 15:54-57.

begins with the promise, "There will again be heard," and then
the entire negative phrase which constitutes the bulk of 33:10 in
English is a dependent clause only identifying the place. The
negativity only characterizes the place where the happy affirmation
of v. 11 will be heard. The negative designation of v. 10 is stated
in a parallelism concerning the cities of Judah marked as a "waste"
and the streets of Jerusalem marked as a "desolation." The first
of these, the cities of Judah, are characterized by a double *en*
(without): without humankind and without animals. The second
set concerning the streets of Jerusalem has a threefold use of *en*
("without"): without humankind, without inhabitants, without
beasts. The cities and the streets together are five times "without"
(en), suggesting that they have been forcibly emptied of all viable
life, human and nonhuman. It is in this empty, abandoned, bereft,
hopeless place, a place reduced to mute despair, that sounds will
again be heard. The good news of the sounds cannot be fully
appreciated unless the contrasting situation of mute despair is fully
mapped out.

Three times Jeremiah has characterized the destruction of
Jerusalem and Judah by anticipating the elimination of the sounds
of a wedding (7:34; 16:9; 25:10). The cessation of wedding joy
signifies a crushing judgment in which conventional social relations are impossible and the entire infrastructure of the community
has failed. The community will cease to practice the most elemental
acts necessary for its maintenance through time. In this massive
assertion of judgment, there is no will for celebration, not enough
security or trust or buoyancy or confidence to undertake a wedding
which always constitutes some investment in the future. This
particular silence, the absence of celebrative social noise, is as acute
as "without, without, without, without, without."

It is in this place of desolate silence that a new sound will be
heard. What has not been heard will again be heard, as God's
good resolve for viable human community overrides the empty
silence. Israel will resume the social practice of mirth, enacting a
broad commitment into the future.[92] The desolateness will be

---

92. The recent social transformation in Eastern Europe offers important
parallels to the anticipations of these promises. After the "opening" of the

overcome enough to foster a season of mirth and celebration, as the reconstituted community overrides the pall of exile.

The voices that sing of weddings also sing a more theological song, for the resumption of social life is intimately linked to the resumption of life with God (33:11b). Thus the voices that sing wedding songs also sing a song of thanks to God. This thanksgiving song entails a concrete gesture of gratitude, an offering which bespeaks a blessing received. The song of thanks, accompanied by offerings as a gesture of gratitude, sings of the character of Yahweh. Thanks is given because Yahweh is good (does good), because Yahweh's loyal love is endlessly abiding.

Two claims operate in this doxology. First, it is voiced in the Exile, just when Yahweh seemed neither good nor faithful. What Israel believes about God is here not derived from circumstance, but is sung against circumstance. Second, the juxtaposition of wedding song and doxology evidences how Israel's faith is enmeshed in the fabric of life. The two songs are different but they are not unrelated. The joy of futuring human relations derives from and is authorized by the large intention of God about the future. It is God's sure fidelity that permits the practice of human fidelity in a context of abundant fickleness. Both songs together show Israel moving past emptied cities and emptied streets. The outbreak of blessing, joy, and gratitude overrides the silence of desolation.

33:12-13   This third promissory oracle brings together two themes recently voiced in the tradition of Jeremiah and organizes them in relation to a fresh metaphor. On the one hand, the negative characterization of the city and towns echoes that of v. 10. This is the same empty place, void of life. On the other hand, the map of restoration reiterates the same six geographical reference points of 32:44: Benjamin, Jerusalem, Judah, hill country, Shephelah, and the Negeb. These six elements, in the horizon of Judah, mean "everywhere." All the land will be restored and healed.

Soviet Union, a cabaret was opened after fifty years. A commentator observed that it had been "fifty years of mirthlessness in Moscow." In like manner, Jerusalem has long had "mirthlessness."

The fresh metaphor which reshapes the material is that of flock, shepherd, and pasture land. The tranquil pastoral scene of grazing with adequate food, water, and protection will again be established. To be counted by the shepherd means that the shepherd knows the name of each sheep, counts them, and pays attention to any missing one.[93] After a season of chaos, such an image bespeaks a settled, well-ordered, caring, and attentive community with healing governance. While the image of peasant tranquility may be an economic-domestic statement, there is no doubt that the image refers to reordered political life in which there is adequate governance to protect against both rapaciousness and anarchy (cf. 23:1-4; Ezek. 34:1-24). The metaphor serves yet again to witness to the radical, healing transformation intended by God.

33:14-15   This fourth promissory oracle looks back to Jer. 23:5-6. Indeed, this oracle is a simple repetition of that statement (on which see vol. 1, *To Pluck Up, To Tear Down,* 199-200), except for the phrase, "I will fulfill the promise I made to the house of Israel and the house of Judah." This oracle thus refers back to a previous oracle. The reference may be back to the taproot oracle in 2 Sam. 7:8, or it may be an editorial acknowledgement that the promise already appears in 23:5-6 and is seconded here.

In either case, the promise to the Davidic house is peculiar and unexpected in the tradition of Jeremiah, for the larger casting of the Jeremiah tradition regards the dynasty as a main problem for Israel (cf. 22:13-18, 24-30), and does not characteristically envision a David-shaped future. Nonetheless, God's good inclination toward the dynasty and family of David belongs to Israel's central stock of promises. It is therefore included here among the many ways in which Israel voices its hope. Indeed, this chapter seems to want to collect all Israel's possible ways of speaking of God's good future. It is promised that one will arise in that dynasty who will do what kings are supposed to do, namely, practice justice and righteousness (Ps. 72:1-4; cf. Jer. 22:15-17). Thus the Jeremiah tradition draws even the dynasty into its passion for the

---

93. It is this metaphor with reference to the ingathering of exiles that lies behind the parable of Luke 15:3-7 and the declaration of John 10:1-18.

primary torah guarantees of Israel. Indeed, "justice and righteousness" have belonged to the central mandate of Davidic kings from the outset (cf. Isa. 9:7; 1 Kgs. 10:9). Jeremiah makes that general Davidic promise serve his own passionate sense of covenantal requirements for any viable future with Yahweh.

When the king practices justice and righteousness, the city and the land will be healed and saved. Thus the royal intention of Jerusalem is reshaped for the large covenantal design of the Jeremiah tradition which connects covenantal obedience and covenantal blessing. The prophetic construct of "justice → well-being" is not new. What is new is the assurance that royal Israel will act in ways that make new life possible. The outcome is that this sordid, disappointing city of indifference and exploitation receives a means whereby a new social reality is authorized.[94]

33:17-18   This fifth promissory oracle makes only a single statement about a well-ordered future upon which God is resolved. The oracle is of interest to us for two reasons. First, the dynastic future of David and of the priestly order are intimately linked together and both are guaranteed. This intense connection may reflect the way in which priests are functionaries of the kings. More likely it reflects the exilic and postexilic situation of Judah in which civil and priestly authority worked closely together.[95] In that linkage, it is noticeable that whereas the assumed king is given no task to perform, the task assigned to the guaranteed priest is quite explicit and extensive. The function of the priest would seem to be the more important factor in the shaping of the future. This suggests that in the horizon of this oracle, the "state" is on the way to becoming a "church."

Second, the guarantee that "David" "shall never lack a man" is strikingly peculiar in the tradition of Jeremiah. The statement seems to guarantee the dynasty into the future. On the one hand, Jeremiah had explicitly voiced the termination of the monarchy

---

94. See Ezek. 48:35, where the city is renamed and thereby recharacterized. See Klein, 187-89.

95. See Roland de Vaux, *Ancient Israel, Its Life and Institutions* (New York: McGraw-Hill, 1961), 376-79; and Holladay, *Jeremiah 2,* 229-230.

when there would be none to occupy the throne (Jer. 22:30). On the other hand, the general thema of Jeremiah refuses to regard the monarch either as guaranteed or as important. The monarchy is completely dependent on and subordinated to the torah. Thus on both concrete textual and programmatic grounds, this royal promise surprises us in this context. One can only conclude that the crisis of discontinuity in Judah is past and behind Judah. Without denying Judah's great discontinuity worked in 587, the monarchy continued to impact the imagination of Israel. When Israel imagined the future, it could not finally imagine a future without both guaranteed king and guaranteed priest. The promised king is a human agent who is designated to do the human task which will reshape a human future. In contrast to 33:14-15, the king here is not required to do anything. The assurance for the future is simply a gift from God. Clearly the tradition has moved a long distance from the strictures of 22:13-18, 24-30.

33:19-22   This sixth promissory oracle seeks to assure continuity in the community by two large appeals. The assurance of continuity concerns the covenant made with the Davidic house and the covenant with the Levites. The two, king and Levite, are here grouped together as in 33:17-18. That linkage likely reflects the realities of power and leadership at the time when the text voices its claim, presumably in or after the Exile. The covenant with David (cf. 2 Sam. 7:11-16; Ps. 89:24-37; Isa. 55:3) has seemed in the Exile to be in jeopardy. Indeed, Jeremiah had placed the Davidic claim in jeopardy by his subversive voicing of reality.

This text, concerned with fidelity and continuity, against much of the Jeremiah tradition, asserts the abiding certitude of these two covenants which legitimate leadership and therefore certify the structure of the community. It is as though a voice of wonderment and disbelief asked, "How sure are these covenants?" — which of course is an inquiry about the reliability of God's promise.

The answer to that question of reliability is twofold. First, the covenants with king and priest are as sure as the covenants of night and day, that is, ultimately reliable. In other words, the rhythms of night and day are not "natural" phenomena, but happen in regular ways because God has promised that each of them will have an assured and regular time of presence. This rhetoric regards the reliability and predictability of night and day to be the most extreme statement possible concerning God's faithful, powerful capacity to do what God promises. God will keep God's word, not only for night and day, but for king and priest about which God has also made promises. Historical structures rooted in God's promises are as sure as cosmic sequences authored by God who creates and presides. God's love to Israel is as sure as God's ordering of creation.

The second guarantee is an appeal to the Abraham-Sarah promise about fertility and productivity into the future (Jer. 33:22). This family is assured of multiplicity as the stars of the heavens (Gen. 15:5) or as the sand of the seashore (Gen. 22:17; 32:12). The text only alludes to the ancestral tradition and explicitly moves directly from "stars/sand" to the royal, priestly families. The threat for all dynasties, royal and priestly, is to be without heirs. Because these dynasties are assured countless heirs, their futures are utterly, utterly secure. These massive and grand assurances of continuity are in amazing and profound tension with the main claims of the Jeremiah tradition and with the threat of the exilic experience. These promises do not resist or deny the reality of discontinuity, but are voices of hope after the breaking point, and therefore speak against the painful judgments of the historical process. The promises of Yahweh are not always and everywhere the appropriate thing to say; they function, however, in particular times and places, times of death and places of despair. The promises rooted in reliable cosmic realities seek to override the despair. Israel's way into the future rests only upon God's good word which abides in the face of disruptive circumstance.

33:23-26　　This final promissory oracle in the sequence of this chapter again appeals to the ordering covenant with creation as a criterion for God's fidelity to Israel, as in Jer. 33:20-22 and 31:35-37. This assurance in this text, however, is framed very differently from the earlier statements. The oracle of 33:25-26 is a response to the problem expressed in v. 24. This oracle, unlike the others in the series of this chapter, responds to a specific and stated issue. The problem is that "these people" treat Yahweh's covenant people with contempt. We do not know the identity of "these people." They may be any of the surrounding nations who have observed the recent history of this community, or they may be more specifically the Babylonians who had dismantled the Judean community. The speaker is not interested in identifying the practitioners of contempt. The Israelites have a long history, either of paying attention to what the nation thinks or of alleging what the nations think as a ploy to evoke a response from God (cf. Num. 14:13-16; Jer. 30:17; Ezek. 36:22). The "two families" refers to the north and south of divided Israel, so that the Israelites are being judged as failures in exile (cf. Ezek. 37:15-23).

The important point is not what the nations think (for perhaps they thought very little at all about Israel), but what Israel thinks of itself and what it thinks the nations think of it. That is, the contempt allegedly held by the nations is in fact intrinsic in exile, which is a context evoking Israel's shame, humiliation, and self-despising (cf., e.g., Isa. 54:4). It is the reality of exile that leads to the judgment that God's chosen has become God's rejected (Jer. 33:24). In sum, the Exile evokes the conclusion that Israel's special status as God's beloved has been forfeited. It matters not at all if that conclusion is drawn by the nations or drawn by Israel and projected upon the nations.

It is in response to that theological crisis evoked by the Exile, a crisis concerning Israel's theological identity as Yahweh's people, that the oracle of vv. 25-26 is given.[96] The oracle consists of a protasis ("if") in v. 25 and an apodosis ("then," *gam*) in v. 26. If the ordering of creation (day and night, heavens and earth) was not established, then Yahweh would reject Israel. The oracle appeals back to the negative term "reject" in v. 24. The unstated countertheme is that, since God's ordering of creation manifestly persists, the operative word for Israel persists as "chosen" and not

---

96. Thus in a laconic way, these verses are in fact a response to the question of theodicy, making an affirmation not unlike that of Ps. 73. On the issues of theodicy in Ps. 73, see Ronald J. Williams, "Theodicy in the Ancient Near East," in Crenshaw, *Theodicy in the Old Testament,* 50-51; and Martin Buber, "The Heart Determines: Psalm 73," in Crenshaw, *Theodicy in the Old Testament,* 109-118.

"rejected." Thus creation is offered as argument and analogue for the status of Israel with Yahweh. This argument and analogue decisively reject the verdict of v. 24. Thus the verdict of v. 24 is wrong, whether drawn by the nations or by Israel and projected upon the nations. Exile does not entail rejection. Exile is not the end of Israel's chosen status. Israel's chosenness persists in and through exile!

The specifics of the enduring chosenness in the Exile, on the one hand, appeals to the primal promises to the ancestors in Genesis and, on the other hand, to the Davidic dynasty (v. 26). Thus the promises to David are not rooted in memories and commitments which are undermined in the Exile. The promises and old commitments of God are in force and are powerfully operative in and through the difficult present. Thus the oracle appeals to memory and tradition in order to assert a theological reality that overrides present historical circumstance. The theological reality is that the promise endures. The political fact derived from that promise is the legitimacy of the Davidic enterprise, a legitimacy not undermined by the loss of the throne. Thus the oracle asserts a theological claim that relativizes the present historical moment of negative experience.

That verdict which finally refutes the misreading of v. 24 is reinforced by the concluding formula of v. 26. Not only is the phrase "restore their fortunes" used one more time, but it is reinforced by the final phrase, "I will have mercy upon them." It is precisely in exile, when all seems lost, that mercy comes to the fore as God's primal way with Israel.[97] God's resilient mercy makes the seeming discontinuity of exile less than decisive. The oracle reads reality against observable circumstance.

These seven oracles together comprise for exilic Israel a remarkable affirmation: God's commitment to Israel in the present and God's resolve for Israel's good future are fully asserted and reaffirmed. The editorial process of the book of Jeremiah has gathered together into a powerful collection oracles of God's relentless fidelity as a conclusion to the "Book of Comfort." Those oracles sustained and sustain Israel even in its times of abandonment.

---

97. See Brueggemann, "At the Mercy of Babylon."

A CASE STUDY IN FIDELITY

Jeremiah 34:1–35:19

This narrative begins with an address to King Zedekiah (34:1-7), offers two narratives concerning the community — one negative (34:8-22) and one positive (35:1-11) — and two conclusions from the contrasting "case studies" (35:12-19).

34:1-7 These verses deliver yet again a harsh announcement against the city and the king in the face of the threat of Babylon, a threat which the prophet characteristically takes as a threat from Yahweh. The passage has parallels in 21:1-7; 37:3-10; and 38:14-28, where the same points are articulated. In each of these, Zedekiah receives or acknowledges a hard word from the prophet.

This passage is framed by statements about command (34:1-2a) and obedience (vv. 6-7). In the command, the word of the prophet is in a context of massive Babylonian pressure. Note the repeated use of the word "all" (v. 1). The word given to the prophet is congruent with the awareness that *all* the armies and *all* the peoples are against *all* the cities. In vv. 6-7 we are told that Jeremiah spoke as God had commanded him. Again in the conclusion of the section, we are reminded of the context of great military threat. The use of the word "all" — "all these words" (v. 6), "all the cities" (v. 7) — suggests an interface between a context of ominous danger and a message of severe threat. The known world of Jerusalem is under assault both by word and by the imperial army.

The message from God given through the prophet forms the center of the passage (vv. 2b-5). It is this message that is commanded (vv. 1-2a) and performed (vv. 6-7). The message itself is divided into two parts. First, there is a straightforward announcement of judgment and doom (vv. 2b-3). The judgment includes the city of Jerusalem (which will be destroyed) and the king (who will be apprehended by Babylon). There is no escape from Babylon. The judgment against the king, however, is less severe than is promised on the same king elsewhere. It is elsewhere anticipated that the king will suffer a cruel death (21:6-7). Here it is anticipated only that Zedekiah must give answer before the king of Babylon. Perhaps the cruel death made explicit elsewhere is only implied here in the king's appearance at the imperial court. In any case, the judgment is ambiguous, but for that, no less ominous.

Second, however, a different announcement is made which offers a different future for the king (34:4-5). Here it is announced that the king will die a peaceful death, will be honored in death, and appropriately buried and grieved by his kingdom. (On the humiliation of being ungrieved, see the contrast in 22:18-19.)

Scholars have been quick to notice that the verdict on King Zedekiah in 34:4-5 is very different from that pronounced in v. 3. Characteristically, there are two ways to handle the contradiction. On the one hand, the term "in peace" *(b-sh-l-m)* is emended to read "in Jerusalem" *(b-y-r-sh-l-m)*. Such an emendation does not fully overcome the contradiction, for in v. 3 he is to be taken to Babylon and is not to die in Jerusalem. The proposed emendation does, however, eliminate the key word that suggests a tranquil death.

More plausibly, in my judgment, scholars read the statement in vv. 4-5 by assuming a protasis-apodosis construction and implying an "if-then" argument:

[if] you hear the word of the LORD . . .
[then] you shall die in peace.

This construal of the message is congruent with Jeremiah's argument elsewhere concerning obedience and blessing. Moreover, such a reading permits vv. 4-5 to make sense even after the assertion of vv. 2b-3. That is, vv. 2b-3 give the expected sentence, but vv. 4-5 add a proviso for an alternative outcome to altered behavior. The alternative of hearing the word, however, in fact means submitting to Babylon, the urging made all along by the prophet. If the reading of "if-then" be accepted, then vv. 2b-3 assert disaster if there is resistance to Babylon, and painful living until death if there is not submission to the empire. Such an interpretation fits well with what is said elsewhere in the tradition, and provides a clear choice to the king that is both theologically consistent and politically credible. Clearly the cruel fate suffered by Zedekiah suggests, according to the tradition of Jeremiah, that Zedekiah did not listen (39:5-7; 52:11). The king found it impossible to accept the only choice of life offered by the prophet, the choice of submission to the empire.

34:8-22   The narrative tradition now presents a remarkable "case study" in fidelity and infidelity. The whole of 34:8–35:19 may be placed here by an editorial process in order to provide ground for and support the harsh judgment of 34:1-7. The case study consists of two parts, an example of infidelity (34:8-22) and a "control group" as an example of fidelity (35:1-11). The first example comes from the days of Zedekiah (34:8), and the second from the time of Jehoiakim (35:1). Because the two narratives are removed from each other chronologically, it is clear that the narrative is not making a historical-sequential statement, but intends a much more programmatic and didactic statement. The whole can be understood as a proclamation about the nature of fidelity, the cost of fidelity, and the price of infidelity.

The first element in this negative case of infidelity is a narrative summary which sets the context for the subsequent prophetic word (vv. 8-11). Verse 8 begins as though it is a "word of the LORD." In fact, however, that word is not given until v. 12.[1] Before the word announced in v. 8 is given in v. 12, we are offered a narrative report on the social crisis which evoked the prophetic word (vv. 8b-11). King Zedekiah made a covenant to release slaves. We do not know of this act from any other report.[2] The

---

1. The deferral of the word from the LORD as a narrative strategy in 34:8 until v. 12 is paralleled in ch. 32, in which the word announced in v. 1 is withheld until v. 6.

2. The closest parallel to this account is the action of Nehemiah in Neh. 5:1-13. These two narratives suggest that the provision for a year of release was at least in the purview of Israel's practice.

action of the king is based in the old torah commandment that debt slaves can only be held in bondage for six years, and then must be released with their debt cancelled (cf. Deut. 15:1-11; Exod. 21:1-6).[3] Note well that the legal provision and this action by the king relate to "Hebrew slaves" — "Judeans." That is, this narrative concerns fellow Jews who are in hock because they are poor and cannot pay their debts to other members of the Jewish community.

In a remarkable, humane provision, the torah of Moses limited the ways in which the community could exploit such poor persons. And now Zedekiah enacts the provision of liberation and debt cancellation. We do not know what prompted the action of the king, but it is in any case an economically disruptive act, for it simply writes off unpaid debts around which the economy is organized. It is usual to think this was a frantic gesture (foxhole religion), to show in an emergency good faith toward the torah commandments. It is thinkable that in this episode Zedekiah is as responsive as was his father Josiah to the demands of torah (Jer. 22:15-16; cf. 2 Kgs. 22:11). The narrator does not linger over this act of Zedekiah, but takes it only as a premise for what follows.

Zedekiah's political constituency obeyed his covenant and did indeed liberate their debt slaves and cancel their debts (Jer. 34:10). The verse twice uses the term *shemaʿ*; they heard and heeded (RSV "obeyed") and acted differently, at some obvious risk to their economy. (Notice that the protasis of v. 4 concerning Zedekiah depends on "hearing.")

The entire episode concerning the release, however, issues in a surprising reversal of intent and practice (v. 11): "But afterward!" The economic leadership reneged and reinforced slavery, thus violating the torah, nullifying the covenant, and reducing social relations between the haves and have-nots in the community to sheer economic power. Unbridled wealth and greed prevailed over neighbor solidarity. As the covenant is rejected, instead of covenant

---

3. On the text of Deut. 15:1-11 and its significance for Israel's faith, see Jeffries Mock Hamilton, "Social Justice and Deuteronomy: The Case of Deuteronomy 15" (diss., Princeton Theological Seminary).

blessings, Judah receives one more unwelcome oracle from the prophet.

We are not told why the people of Jerusalem reneged, any more than we are told why the king originally took such a positive initiative. If the intent of the king was initially pragmatic (i.e., the action was only to avert judgment), then it may follow that the reneging on the torah initiative was equally pragmatic. Perhaps the leadership in Jerusalem learned only late how costly the action of slave liberation and debt cancellation was. Either they thought the crisis had past, or they decided that the cancellation of debts was irrelevant to the Babylonian crisis, or they acted for their own vested interest because the cost of debt cancellation was simply too high. The narrative does not tell us anything about motivations, but only reports the actions taken and their outcomes. It is as though two views of social relations are caught in a massive struggle. On the one hand, the act of covenanting is an acknowledgement that all persons are members of the community and each must care for all. On the other hand, commodity interest prevails over covenant, and the strong work their will against the weak and at their expense.[4]

The poignancy of the crisis is reflected first of all in the strong and definitional contrast between two modes of social relations, oriented respectively toward covenant and toward commodity. The phenomenon of debt slavery raises the overarching question of social power: are there limits to the ways of the strong against the weak? Are there zones of human solidarity which override and curb raw economic power? The torah of Moses compelled Zedekiah and his cohorts into modes of covenantal thought for just an instant. Their commitment to sheer economic power,

---

4. By a rejection of covenantal relations, the poor were reduced to a commodity. This act of reneging provides an opportunity to reflect on the ways in which denial of covenant produces commoditization. Karl Marx has provided the decisive analysis of commodity, on which see David McLellan, *The Thought of Karl Marx: An Introduction* (London: Macmillan, 1971, and New York: Harper & Row, 1972), 105-121. See also Franz J. Hinkellammert, *The Ideological Weapons of Death: A Theological Critique of Capitalism* (Maryknoll, N.Y.: Orbis, 1986); and Gregory Baum, *Theology and Society* (New York: Paulist, 1988), 51.

however, caused them to yield "afterwards" to the rule of wealth at the expense of community. This strong contrast is made even more poignant by the abrupt and inexplicable reversal of policy and practice, which only sharpens the complete disregard for torah in the community. This is indeed a dramatic form of resistance in Jerusalem to the torah and to the responsible leadership of the king. This dramatic and inexplicable reversal evokes the harsh prophetic word signalled in v. 8.

34:12-22   The prophet now speaks "the word of the LORD" anticipated in v. 8. The initial formula in God's speech is "I [myself] made a covenant." This statement seems likely only an historical introduction. It is, however, precisely parallel to the statement of v. 8, "King Zedekiah made a covenant." Nothing is made of the parallelism. As a backdrop for what follows the parallel is nonetheless important, for it contrasts God's covenantal faithfulness, upon which God did not renege, with Zedekiah's covenant, upon which he did renege. Moreover, the covenants of Yahweh and of Zedekiah are parallel in that they both concern a "proclamation of liberty." In Yahweh's covenant, "proclaiming liberty" is a torah provision (cf. Deut. 15:1-11); in Zedekiah's covenant, "proclaiming liberty" is an implementation of that torah provision. Indeed, in Yahweh's covenant the torah provision is quoted exactly (Jer. 34:14). The parallelism is continued in the narrative comment. "Your ancestors did not listen," that is, they did not heed the covenant provision of cancelling debts on fellow covenant members (v. 14b). In parallel fashion, Zedekiah's contemporaries also did not listen and so refused the costly commandment.

This last point provides the opening for the prophetic word, which alludes back to vv. 9-11. The statements in vv. 15-16 are precisely parallel in construction, but to opposite effect. Verse 15 asserts, "You, you turned" *(tashubu)*. Israel turned back to torah obedience, obeyed the commandment of release, and solemnly swore to practice the commandment in the temple. That is, the economic act is undertaken as a major, self-conscious theological statement. But then that act is promptly countered in v. 16: "You turned" *(tashubu);* you turned away from torah obedience and from covenant fidelity. The oath sworn in "the house which is called by my name" (v. 15) is now profaning my name; that is, it mocks God and diminishes God's reputation by reenslaving fellow Jews who owe money. The interface between theological intent and economic act is intense and remarkable. The two cannot be separated. Reenslaving debt slaves diminishes God's reputation; that is, it profanes God's name.

The careful and complicated rhetoric of vv. 12-16 constitutes a prophetic indictment which asserts the guilt of Judah and Jerusalem. It makes use of five rhetorical devices: (1) the parallel of Yahweh who made a covenant and Zedekiah who made a covenant; (2) the contrast of Yahweh who kept covenant and Judah who violated covenant; (3) the double use of the word *tashubu*, for Judah turned twice in fickleness and inconsistency; (4) the double use of God's name, before whom an oath is taken and which is profaned in the reneging; and (5) the larger contrast between the historical review (vv. 8-11) and the prophetic comment (vv. 12-16). The result of the completed assertion of vv. 8-16 is to establish that Judah has reneged in its oath to Yahweh and in its obligation to fellow Jews. Nothing is stated about motivation. The act of reneging, committed for whatever reason, makes Judah into a disobedient people that does not heed torah and does not honor its own covenant commitments to its needy fellows.

There follows, as we expect, a massive "therefore" (v. 17) and a sweeping, harsh sentence (vv. 17-22). The indictment is restated in v. 17 as a way into the sentence. The first element in the sentence plays on the word "release" *(dror)* and matches the punishment to the crime.[5] "You did not release [your neighbors from their debts], so I will release — sword, pestilence, and famine!" What God releases is the unfettered devastation and unrestrained terror of covenant curses. The list is a classic, highly stylized recital, but it is also reflective of the forms of damage that come in the wake of an invading army.

---

5. On the symmetry of the affront and the punishment, see Patrick D. Miller, Jr., "Sin and Judgment in Jeremiah 34:17-19," *Journal of Biblical Literature* 103 (1984): 611-13.

The second element of the sentence plays on the word "cut." The word is used in vv. 8, 13 as the technical term for "made" a covenant. The verb perhaps refers to a ritual act of cutting an animal as part of an act of blood-solidarity (cf. Gen. 15:7-11). In Jer. 34:18 the prophetic speech seems to refer back to something like the primitive rite of Gen. 15, only now it is the people of Judah themselves who are cast as the ritual calf who is to be "cut," which of course means brutalized and killed.[6] The argument is not very clear, and the wording is elusive. It does seem clear, nevertheless, that in Jer. 34:19 all parts of the population, and especially its leaders and opinion-makers, are the cut animal in this covenant of death now being enacted by Yahweh. Verse 20 explicates the meaning of the foregoing: they will be handed over to enemies who will kill them, and their corpses will be left exposed in dishonor. Both plays on words, "release" and "cut," are simply rhetorical maneuvers to pronounce an awful judgment of death which matches the great affront committed against Yahweh. Clearly, the prophet makes a great deal of the refusal of Judah to release its poor from bondage. Indeed, Judah's whole future turns to curse because of this act which dishonors God and exploits neighbor.

The final judgment pronounced concerns the king who now will be handed over to Babylon (v. 21), and the city of Jerusalem, and the towns of Judah (v. 22). Babylon is described as being "withdrawn" (v. 21), but the LORD will "bring them back." This statement alludes to the previous invasion of 598, after which there was a respite for Jerusalem from Babylon. That respite, however, is now to end with a second decisive invasion in 587.

The main plot of this oracle is clear. We should not, however, miss the poignancy of the argument. The practice of torah and the implementation of the commandment of release would generate safety and well-being for the city. Reneging on the covenant and consequently practicing economic exploitation evoke the invasion of Babylon. This is no silly "supernaturalism," but reflects the prophetic conviction that internal disorder invites

---

6. I am following the usual rendering. On the textual difficulty in this verse, see Holladay, *Jeremiah 2*, 242-43.

external threat which implements God's sovereign rule. The first step toward death is internal economic disorder that pits the "haves" against the "have-nots." Such internal economic disorder reflects a fundamental recalcitrance in Judah. The reference to the Exodus (v. 13) is a reminder that God's initial act of rescue was a gesture of liberation in which the slaves of Egypt were rescued from their economic plight of helplessness. Israel is expected to continue to reenact that miracle of new economic beginnings in its own ordering of social life. When it fails to "hear" *(shema'),* when it no longer remembers its rootage or its historical destiny,[7] it becomes vulnerable to the exploitation of more powerful "haves."[8] A failure to order its economic life differently jeopardizes the city, the king, the villages, the temple, and finally the whole people.

35:1-11 The narrative now takes up a contrasting episode, which is located ten years earlier, in the time of Jehoiakim. It is as though the blatant disobedience of Zedekiah and his cohorts evokes in the memory of the narrator a much earlier prophetic act.

The prophet has a remarkable encounter with the Rechabites in the temple at the command of Yahweh (35:2-4). We are told nothing about the Rechabites or why they are summoned into the drama. Jeremiah is commanded to give them wine (v. 2), and he does so (v. 5). It is as though God has deliberately set up a test case for the Rechabites.

The center of the episode is the response of the Rechabites to the offer of wine (vv. 6-10). The Rechabites promptly recite the commands of their ancestor and founder. This response is like the recital of a catechism, or a brief series of commands:[9]

---

7. On the decisive power of rootage in memory, see Cynthia Ozick, "Metaphor and Memory," *Metaphor and Memory, Essays* (New York: Knopf, 1989), 265-283.

8. While Zedekiah and his cohorts may have been the influential "haves" in Jerusalem, their resources or staying power against Babylon are flimsy and fleeting. In the book of Jeremiah, it is Babylon who is the real "have," which makes all in Jerusalem vulnerable "have-nots."

9. Erhard Gerstenberger, *Wesen und Herkunft des "apodiktischen" Rechts.*

> You shall not drink wine,
> You shall not build a house,
> You shall not sow seed,
> You shall not plant or have a vineyard,
> You shall live in tents.

This pentalogue seems designed to warn against accommodation to the values of the dominant society. Thus the Rechabites are something of a "sect" whose identity entails resistance to the comfortable accommodations of settled, urban society.[10] The Rechabites may indeed be regarded as a religious curiosity. In this narrative, however, they constitute a sect that practices an "alternative life-style," which is regarded in a most positive light.

The narrative exhibits no particular interest in the actual practices of the Rechabite community and makes no particular judgment on those commands. That is, the narrative does not debate whether it is right or good to drink wine or live in houses.[11] What counts for our narrative is that the Rechabites live zealously under command (vv. 6-7); they are a community of intense obedience (v. 8):

> We have obeyed . . .
> [the charge] to drink no wine,
> not to build houses to dwell in.
> We have no vineyard or field or seed.

Thus the narrative first reports the commands of Jonadab (vv. 6-7) and then reiterates the commands in terms of their being obeyed (vv. 8-10). The climactic statement is "We have obeyed and done all that our ancestor Jonadab commanded us" (NRSV). Thus in vv. 8-10, the verb *shema'* is used twice. This is quintessentially a community of listeners!

Wissenschaftliche Monographien zum Alten und Neuen Testament 20 (Neukirchen-Vluyn: Neukirchener, 1965), 110-17 and *passim.*

10. This same theological tendency and strategy is voiced in the contemporary discussion by Stanley Hauerwas and William H. Willimon, *Resident Aliens: Life in the Christian Colony* (Nashville: Abingdon, 1989).

11. See my comments on 33:4 in which "houses" are taken as a symbol and metaphor for disobedient power. The policy of the Rechabites no doubt reflects the same critical attitude toward such social fixtures.

The comment in v. 11 seems extraneous both to the narrator and to the contrast made between ch. 34 and ch. 35. It appears to be a parenthetical comment about why this countercultural movement is in fact in the city of Jerusalem. The Rechabites are in Jerusalem for protection that only a walled city can provide. Clearly the narrator does not regard their presence in Jerusalem as a contradiction to the practices commanded concerning the avoidance of settled urban culture. If dwelling in Jerusalem were to violate the commands of Jonadab, then the whole contrasting case fails; that clearly is not intended by the narrator.

This summary statement about the Rechabites in terms of command and obedience establishes a contrast with Zedekiah, which is the didactic point of the larger narrative. On the one hand, the ancestors of Israel *did not listen* (34:14) and you *did not listen* (34:17). On the other hand, the Rechabites have *listened and heeded faithfully* (35:8, 10). It is the formal act of listening and not the substance of obedience that is accented in this contrast.[12]

35:12-19   The narrative has juxtaposed two episodes, one from the time of Zedekiah and one from the much earlier time of Jehoiakim. We are now prepared for the instructional conclusion that the narrator draws. This section is in fact a militant meditation on the meaning of listening, the requirements of listening, and the costs of not listening. Everything depends on listening.

The argument begins with a question that is part urging and part accusation (v. 13). Could you not "learn a lesson" (RSV "receive instruction")? The term "lesson" is "discipline" *(musar)*.[13] It is

---

12. The accent of the text falls upon the formal contrast of listening and not listening (RSV "obey"). It is, however, inevitable that the narrator would have also noticed the substantive difference. Not only did the Rechabites listen, but the commands to which they listened constitute a critique of settled culture, the kind of culture the prophet keeps under assault. Thus attention to form includes within it some attention to the substantive contrast between the Rechabites and the community around the king.

13. On the term, see Hans-Joachim Kraus, "Geschichte als Erziehung," in *Probleme biblischer Theologie.* Festschrift Gerhard von Rad, ed. Hans Walter Wolff (Munich: Kaiser, 1971), 267-274. Kraus concludes with a comment concerning "God as Educator," a theme not unlike the usage in this verse.

instruction that the older generation offers to the younger as part of inculcation and socialization into the norms of the community. Thus the question is asked with some impatience and indignation: Can you not accept nurture into the true identity of this community? The RSV makes the two phrases sound sequential and synonymous: receive instruction and listen to my words. The Hebrew, however, makes the second phrase derivative from the first, so that accepting discipline means to be prepared to *shemaʿ*. The community is urged to accept what it means to be Israel: to come under discipline means to learn to listen, to become persons and a community whose very life consists in hearing what God addresses. Thus the listening urged is not to a particular command, but it is a posture and habit and inclination of life that acknowledges that the source of life lies outside of self.[14] Thus the question means, "Could you not renounce your fraudulent autonomy?"

Putting that programmatic question (imperative and accusation), the narrator now exposits the significance of that urging. First the narrator cites once again the positive example of the Rechabites who listen (v. 14a). But then it is the negative case with Israel that receives more extended coverage (vv. 14b-15). This formulation concerning recalcitrant Israel contains a complete statement of a prophetic philosophy of history in three parts:[15]

(1) God spoke — but Israel did *not listen*.
(2) The prophets are a mitigating factor inviting repentance to avoid harsh judgment.
(3) Still, even in the face of the prophets, Israel did *not listen*.

Thus this speech is sandwiched with two uses of *shemaʿ*, before and after the prophets; the prophets change nothing and do not

---

14. See the contrast sharply voiced in Deut. 8:17.

15. Klaus Koch, *The Prophets*, vol. 2: *The Babylonian and Persian Periods* (Philadelphia: Fortress and London: SCM, 1984), 25-32 and *passim*, clearly articulates the shape of prophetic understandings of history. It is telling that Koch, *The Prophets*, vol. 1: *The Assyrian Period* (Philadelphia: Fortress and London: SCM, 1983), 1-6, understands the prophetic enterprise as "The Longing for a Moral World Order." The three points I have listed summarize the prophetic notion of a moral world order.

cause Israel to listen. In between the double use of the verb *(shema')* is a summary of prophetic speech as understood in the tradition of Jeremiah. The prophet summons Israel to repentance *(shub)*, especially to obey the First Commandment. That summons becomes an offer and a condition of staying in the land. The reference to the land alludes to the fact that this tradition has landlessness and land loss (exile) very much on its mind.[16]

In the three great prose chapters of 7, 26, and 36, the mode of prophetic speech here summarized is precisely enacted by Jeremiah, who invites Israel into land-keeping through life-preserving repentance:

> Amend your ways and your doings, and let me dwell with you in this place. (7:3 — author's translation; cf. vv. 5-7)

> It may be that they will listen, all of them, and will turn from their evil way, that I may change my mind about the disaster that I intend to bring on them because of their evil doings. (26:3 — author's translation; cf. vv. 4-6)

> It may be that when the house of Judah hears of all the disasters that I intend to do to them, all of them may turn from their evil ways, so that I may forgive their iniquity and their sin. (36:3— author's translation)[17]

The concluding part of this didactic section draws a twofold conclusion from the twofold story of *shema'* (35:17-19). The section is introduced with a "therefore," indicating consequences to be announced. On the one hand, Israel receives all the disasters *(ra'ah)* of the entire curse tradition, for not listening and for not answering (v. 17). On the other hand, the Rechabites receive the consequence of their listening, again with a "therefore" in v. 19: because they listen, they are guaranteed a continuing line of heirs

---

16. See Diepold, *Israels Land;* and Walter Brueggemann, "Israel's Sense of Place in Jeremiah," in *Rhetorical Criticism.* Festschrift James Muilenburg, ed. Jared J. Jackson and Martin Kessler. Pittsburgh Theological Monograph 1 (Pittsburgh: Pickwick, 1974), 149-165.

17. On the theology and provenance of the prose units in Jeremiah, see Ernest W. Nicholson, *Preaching to the Exiles: A Study of the Prose Tradition in the Book of Jeremiah* (Oxford: Blackwell, 1970).

and descendants for all foreseeable generations. The opposite consequences for the two parties are not quite symmetrical. If they were symmetrical, Israel would be denied land (as it is) and the Rechabites would be assigned land. The Rechabites, however, are not destined for land and do not want it, but want only a guaranteed, protected community. The formula of v. 19, "a man shall not be cut off," is not unlike the formula for the guarantees of the Davidic line and heir (Ps. 132:12; cf. Jer. 33:17). Thus the positive assurance to the Rechabites silently and completely suggests an end to the Davidic dynasty, which will indeed "lack a descendant" to stand before Yahweh.[18] Land loss and the end of the dynasty go together in the ominous consequence of not listening.

Thus the didactic conclusion to the narrative is organized in the following way:

> The general thesis as question (summons and accusation)
> (35:13)
>> Contrasting actions (vv. 14-15)
>>> Rechabites *listen* (v. 14a)
>>> Israel does *not listen* (vv. 14b-15)
>>> The contrast of *listening and not listening* (v. 16)
>> Contrasting consequences:
>>> "Therefore" land loss for Israel (v. 17)
>>> "Therefore" promised continuity for the
>>>> Rechabites (vv. 18-19)

Everything hinges on the ability and willingness to listen. On that basis, we are able to see how this twofold "case study" (34:8–35:19) relates to the oracle to Zedekiah (34:1-7). The whole problem of Zedekiah and his contemporaries is that they *failed to listen* (34:4) and so were captured and brutalized by Babylon. The general theological notion of listening thus is harnessed to a quite concrete policy issue and a very heavy social crisis.

---

18. This devastating announcement of the end of the dynasty reflects the primary tendency of the tradition of Jeremiah. That primary tendency, however, is powerfully countered in the oracles of 23:5-6; 33:14-16; cf. also 33:17-22.

Our interpretive inclination concerning this extended passage may be delineated in four dimensions:

(1) Israel is a creature of God's word voiced *in the torah*. The general theological foundation for Israel's existence in listening is at the center of the theology of Deuteronomy, which believes that Israel is addressed with everything needful for existence, security, and prosperity.[19] Israel is not a self-starter and can never exist autonomously. Its life is always derivative as a gift from God which requires responsive obedience. To listen is to resist autonomy.

(2) In the move from the torah to the prophets, or more specifically in the move from Deuteronomy to Jeremiah, the listening that is required is no longer to the word of the torah. It is *the word of God that has come to the prophet,* specifically the word given to Jeremiah. Thus the whole of *shemaʿ*-theology is mobilized to establish and enhance the speech of this known, named individual person. The transference of *shemaʿ*-theology from scroll to specific prophet is a major and daring shift in canonical theology, for it is now claimed and urged that the command of God is not an established scroll, but a fresh utterance issued concretely.[20]

(3) Insofar as *shemaʿ*-theology is in the mouth of Jeremiah and addressed to Zedekiah, its whole substance turns on one concrete affirmation: *submission to Babylon is Yahweh's will* for Jerusalem and is the only route to survival and well-being. Thus the grand "theology of hearing" in 34:8–35:19 boils down to the concrete-

---

19. The theology of listening is given its clearest rendering in the tradition of Deuteronomy. However, the final form of Jeremiah is deeply impinged upon by the theology of Deuteronomy (as Nicholson has shown) and reflects the same theological inclination.

20. John Barton, *Oracles of God: Perceptions of Ancient Prophecy in Israel after the Exile* (New York: Oxford University Press, 1986), has characterized the way in which prophets assume authority beyond the established claims of torah. The shift here in the voice to which Israel is to listen, from torah to prophet, nicely embodies Barton's thesis. In another context with the third canon of Hebrew scripture, Donn F. Morgan, *Between Text and Community: The "Writings" in Canonical Interpretation* (Minneapolis: Fortress, 1990), has shown how authority is processed through quite intentional hermeneutical maneuvers. I suggest that in our text the tradition of Jeremiah makes a similar interpretive move.

ness of 34:4-7. The book of Jeremiah makes a specific judgment about a historical crisis. It understands that crisis in terms of the entire tradition of covenant, and it reads the entire tradition of covenant in terms of that crisis. In this crisis, so the argument goes, submission to Babylon is the way covenant is kept, covenant blessings are assured, and Yahweh alone is worshipped. It is the folly of autonomy (= not listening) to refuse Babylonian reality.

(4) In our own time, these chapters speak eloquently against the ideology of autonomy so powerful in modernity, against our notions of holding initiative for our life, and our mistaken notion of being self-starters.[21] Our refusal to have our life given or derived from another is a core pathology in our time as in the days of Zedekiah.[22] Modernity has scuttled not only the tradition rooted in a scroll, but the large notion that authority which permits life can be and must be rooted in another who both gives and commands. Indeed, the summons to listen is for us a summons to break with the most foundational presuppositions of modernity. One can make a quite concrete case that in many places in the world (though not yet in the United States), there is savage loss of land and loss of power where the ruling group has imagined itself to be autonomous and has failed to listen either to the requirements of God's justice or to the hurts of God's people.

In ancient and in modern contexts, this call to repentance urged so insistently by the prophet touches core assumptions of social power. It is ironic, but perfectly credible, that the Rechabites —

21. Karl Barth, *Protestant Theology in the Nineteenth Century: Its Background and History* (Valley Forge: Judson, 1973), has seen most clearly that the entire "Enlightenment Project" was aimed not primarily at objectivity as an epistemological enterprise, but at human autonomy, i.e., the knowing agent who had reference to none beyond the self.

22. In our own time, Robert N. Bellah et al., *Habits of the Heart: Individualism and Commitment in American Life* (Berkeley: University of California Press, 1985), chronicles the same sort of pathology for those who refuse to receive and derive their lives from another. The healthy contrast to such a sense of autonomy is evident in the work of Emmanuel Levinas, *Totality and Infinity: An Essay on Exteriority* (Pittsburgh: Duquesne University Press, 1969), which characterizes healthy human life in terms of serious engagement with "the others." In the tradition of Jeremiah, that "other" is Yahweh, whom Zedekiah and the people of Jerusalem had disregarded.

those poor in spirit and poor, who have so little to lose and so little to gain — are viable candidates for listening. The contrast of Zedekiah and the Rechabites, a contrast both in choices made and in consequences received, suggests that visible power and apparent social importance are impediments to listening . . . and therefore to living long or well.

THE "BARUCH DOCUMENT"
Jeremiah 36:1–45:5

Chapters 36–45 (or 37–45), in the common judgment of scholars, constitute a peculiar and intentional corpus of materials.[1] This corpus may perhaps be intentionally organized; it is expressed almost exclusively in prose, and seems to be preoccupied with the life of the prophet Jeremiah.

The organization of this extended narrative includes the following elements. It begins with ch. 36, which narrates an account of the way in which Baruch wrote and publicly read a scroll of Jeremiah.[2] The corpus concludes in ch. 45 with a special promise to Baruch. Thus chs. 36 and 45 provide the brackets and boundaries which contain the entire narrative. Because the beginning and ending chapters both feature Baruch, this entire corpus is conventionally linked to Baruch.[3] He is taken variously as either the author or the main character of the narrative, or both.

With these two chapters as the boundaries, we may identify

---

1. The dominant critical judgments of scholarship continue to be those of Bernard Duhm and Sigmund Mowinckel, on which see Childs, *Old Testament as Scripture,* 342-45. A recent consideration of these materials is offered by William L. Holladay, "A Fresh Look at 'Source B' and 'Source C' in Jeremiah," *Vetus Testamentum* 25 (1975): 394-412. It may well be that ch. 36 should not be grouped with the following materials. On that question, see Carroll, *Jeremiah,* 509-510.

2. We have already encountered the role of Baruch in ch. 32.That reference, however, is not germane to the role of Baruch in this extended narrative, for no critical judgment groups ch. 32 with this material.

3. Richard E. Friedman, *Who Wrote the Bible?* (New York: Summit, 1987), 146-49, has rather dramatically suggested Baruch as the author of the book of Jeremiah. Such a claim is a considerable overstatement, but not unrelated to the main tendency of criticism.

three larger sections of material which seem intentionally organized:

(1) Jeremiah 37:1–40:6 is concerned with *the threat of Babylon*
and with Jeremiah's role in urging surrender of Jerusalem to
Babylon. This unit culminates in 40:1-6 with a report that
Jeremiah was recognized by the Babylonians and given preferential
treatment by the invaders. Of special interest in this section is the
role of Ebed-melech (38:7-13), who subsequently receives from
the prophet a special promissory oracle (39:15-18).

(2) Jeremiah 40:7–41:18 constitutes a central section in the
narrative which functions as a transition and a change of focus
and subject in the narrative. This material appears to be straightforward reportage concerning *governance and conspiracy in post-587
B.C.E. Judah*. In this section not only is the prophet Jeremiah
absent, but there is no element of explicit theological reflection
or interpretation. In its present context, this section — which may
indeed be strict reportage — functions to switch the locus, theme,
and problematic of the narrative.

(3) Jeremiah 42:1–44:30 provides a third and final section.
This section concerns the community of Jews who fled to Egypt
and who brought Jeremiah against his will to Egypt. The section
is constituted by a series of *harsh condemnations of the Egyptian
venture* and culminates with a subtle suggestion that this pitiful
flight to Egypt is in fact the inversion and negation of the Exodus.

Thus I suggest that there are two major units of prophetic
material (37:1–40:6; 42:1–44:30), linked together by the descriptive narrative of 40:7–41:18. The two major units have as their
epitomes two preaching articulations in the mouth of the prophet.
These two units are organized in the same way and perform the
same theological function in the narrative. They do, nonetheless,
reflect changed circumstances and therefore changed substantive
arguments. On the one hand, 38:17-18, in a double "if-then"
statement, functions to offer positive and negative possibilities to
the Jerusalem leadership. The prophet offers both a possibility and
a warning to Zedekiah. The positive possibility is surrender to
Babylon as a way to have life. The negative alternative is to refuse
to surrender, that is, to resist, and so to come to a sorry end.

On the other hand, after the transfer of power to Gedaliah and

122

the failure of his leadership, 42:9-17 offers another "if-then" construction with the same basic structure of positive and negative alternatives.[4] In this case, the positive possibility is to stay in the land, and the negative warning concerns flight to Egypt.

Thus the message of the prophetic voice is different in the two summary passages. The positive option in 38:17-18 concerns *surrender to Babylon,* but does not mention remaining in the city. (Presumably refusal to surrender implies remaining in the city to resist.) In 42:9-17 the positive possibility is to *remain in the city* (but the text only alludes to and assumes surrender to Babylon). Thus the issue and argument is different in the two situations because circumstances have changed. The circumstance has been changed through the intermediate narrative (40:7–41:18), in which Gedaliah is established in power and then assassinated. The assassination of Gedaliah is in fact an act of resistance against Babylonian governance.

Despite the two different postures of 38:7-18 and 42:9-17, in the end both pivotal oracles concern submission to Babylon as the only way to survival. In the latter section, remaining in the city implies submission to Babylon, just as flight to Egypt is in fact resistance to Babylon. The middle section of 40:7–41:18 seems to change matters, but does not in fact effect the essential position voiced by the prophet. The entire corpus is committed to Babylonian reality, which must be heeded as the will of God.

The theological and literary intention of this material has been the subject of much scholarly reflection. A number of useful hypotheses are available, each of which contains a useful insight, but none of which adequately accounts for the material as we have it. We may identify the following scholarly contributions as suggestive and useful.

(1) A commonsense view assumes that this material does indeed report developments in the exilic community.[5] There is no doubt

---

4. The "if-then" construction of 42:9-17 is not only more extended but also more complex than the comparable unit in 38:17-18. The purpose, intent, and argument of the two passages are nonetheless closely parallel.

5. Holladay, *Jeremiah 2,* is most inclined among contemporary scholars to this view.

that in broad outline the narrative reflects historical developments. That is, no one seriously doubts the governorship of Gedaliah as a provincial arrangement after the fall of the monarchy.[6] In my judgment, however, the narrative is not such that we may regard it as primarily historical in character. While the broad outline of events is secure, this does not go very far in suggesting why the material is shaped as it is.

(2) Perhaps the most influential interpretive angle is that of Heinz Kremers, who proposes that this extended narrative is the "passion narrative" of Jeremiah, tracing the way in which, as a righteous sufferer and rejected outsider, the prophet comes to an ignominious end.[7] This view places primary emphasis on the person of Jeremiah, who confronts the kings of Jerusalem and is acknowledged by the king of Babylon and then ends, against his will, among the refugees in Egypt. This view can be critiqued because the person of Jeremiah does not seem to dominate the narrative so completely, and the personal suffering of the prophet is scarcely a main theme.

(3) In contrast to Kremers, Martin Kessler and Ernest Nicholson place the account of the narrative not on the person of Jeremiah, but on the speech of Jeremiah which is taken as the word of God.[8] The narrative then traces the way in which that decisive word from God is utterly and consistently rejected throughout the narrative, first by the leadership around Zedekiah (before 587) and then by the Egyptian contingent led by Johanan (after 587). The narrative then is a story about the destiny of the

---

6. On the rule of Gedaliah, see J. Maxwell Miller and John H. Hayes, *A History of Ancient Israel and Judah* (Philadelphia: Westminster and London: SCM, 1986), 421-25. They suggest that Gedaliah was not only governor but in fact succeeded to the throne of Zedekiah.

7. Heinz Kremers, "Leidensgemeinschaft mit Gott im Alten Testament: Eine Untersuchung der "biographischen" Berichte im Jeremiabuch," *Evangelische Theologie* 13 (1953): 122-140.

8. Martin Kessler, "Jeremiah Chapters 26–45 Reconsidered," *Journal of Near Eastern Studies* 27 (1968): 81-88; Nicholson, *Preaching to the Exiles.* Nicholson writes: "To be more specific, the narrative has for its primary purpose a description of rejection of the Word of Yahweh, here enshrined in the scroll of the prophet's oracles, in the actions of the king who is the personification of the nation" (42).

Word. Again, this suggestion greatly illuminates the narrative but does not account for all of the materials. The two emphases on the person of Jeremiah (Kremers) and the word of Jeremiah (Kessler, Nicholson) might usefully be brought together, for the destinies of person and word are not likely to be separated in the intention of the narrative.

(4) Gunther Wanke has provided a shrewd and discerning form-critical analysis of the narrative and has paid special attention to the scenes in which the narrative is cast, and to the way in which various characters are assigned roles in the scenes.[9] While this analysis greatly illuminates the artistry of the narrative, it does not help greatly in discerning the larger intentionality of the whole.

(5) Christopher R. Seitz has paid primary attention to the ideological claims and arguments that operate in the narrative.[10] He has observed that a variety of competing and conflicting ideologies are at work there.

It is likely that none of these analyses adequately illuminates the intentionality of the narrative, but a mixed, eclectic model of intentionality may be more useful. Concerning these several hypothesis, I have only one additional suggestion. As Baruch is presented in ch. 36 as a close associate of Jeremiah and in ch. 45 as especially blessed by Jeremiah, so also he appears in this narrative in one other strategic spot.

In 43:1-3 Jeremiah enters into severe dispute with the leadership of the Egyptian venture. They refuse his word of counsel, which is that they not go to Egypt. They dismiss his word as unauthoritative.[11] Their way of dismissing the word of Jeremiah is enormously suggestive. The adversaries of the word of Jeremiah say:

---

9. Gunther Wanke, *Untersuchungen zur sogenannten Baruchschrift*. Beihefte zur Zeitschrift für die alttestamentliche Wissenschaft 122 (Berlin: de Gruyter, 1971).

10. Seitz, *Theology in Conflict;* and "The Prophet Moses and the Canonical Shape of Jeremiah," *Zeitschrift für die alttestamentliche Wissenschaft* 101 (1989): 3-27.

11. Jeremiah himself is treated in this passage as he himself has done to others in chs. 23 and 27–29.

> The LORD our God did not send you to say, "Do not go to Egypt
> to settle there"; but Baruch son of Neriah is inciting you against
> us, to hand us over to the Chaldeans, in order that they may kill
> us or take us into exile in Babylon. (vv. 2-3 NRSV)

It may be, if the text is historical, that Jeremiah is too venerated
and cannot be attacked directly. As a result, the attack is diverted
and directed against Baruch. Our purpose, however, is not to
determine historicity, but to consider narrative intentionality.
Taken as a "signature" for the narrative, however, this statement
suggests that Baruch was an important operative, and was perhaps
the leader or the symbol of the pro-Babylonian community of
Jewish exiles, that is, the generator of the ideology placed in the
mouth of the prophet.[12]

Thus I suggest that there is a convergence in this material of
three factors: (1) the centrality of *Baruch,* (2) the decisiveness of
the *prophetic word,* and (3) the *pro-Babylonian ideology* that pervades
the material. What is neglected in the several hypotheses of
Kremer, Nicholson, Kessler, and Wanke is the Babylonian bent of
the material. That is, our interpretation requires us to take into
careful account the convergence of *the will of Yahweh* and *the reality
of Babylon.* Or said another way, the resolve of Yahweh is discerned
in, with, and through the socioeconomic-political reality, and any
attempt to understand the word and will of Yahweh in this narrative apart from the "Babylonian-Baruch ideology" misunder-
stands the mode of theology that is offered here. Thus I concur
with Seitz that there is an ideological dimension to this narrative.
Yet as Kremer, Nicholson, Kessler, and Wanke have missed the
political element in the theological affirmation,[13] it appears to me
that Seitz minimizes the theological seriousness and import of the

---

12. For a shrewd and suggestive analysis of the role of Baruch and what
he represents in the Jeremiah tradition, see J. Andrew Dearman, "My Servants
the Scribes: Composition and Context in Jeremiah 36," *Journal of Biblical
Literature* 109 (1990): 403-421.

13. On the "idealist" disregard of the political factor in the theological
affirmation, see the strictures of Gottwald, *The Tribes of Yahweh,* 592-607. On
the power of ideology in the formation of the text, see Mottu, "Jeremiah vs.
Hananiah."

ideological affirmation. It is the convergence and interpretation of the two that become the driving force of the narrative.[14] In the two programmatic passages I have cited, 38:17-18 on surrendering to Babylon and 42:9-17 on remaining in the city, it is the alliance of Yahweh and Babylon that counts to force a truth on the community. And in the two special oracles of blessing cited by Seitz (39:15-18; 45:1-5), it is the supporters of the Babylonian view (Ebed-melech indirectly and Baruch directly) who receive their life as a spoil, while the others receive a death sentence.[15]

Thus the "Baruch document" makes a massive, determined, sustained judgment that the will of God is indeed visible and operative in the flow of international power in the Near East. Refusal to accept this Babylonian reading of the destiny of Jerusalem is taken as a refusal of the prophetic word, and derivatively, as resistance to the will of God. To regard this narrative as a "Baruch document" is not to focus on the person of Baruch.[16] Rather, it is to affirm the theological *Tendenz* which Baruch represents and to accept the way in which theological reality and the conduct of public policy cohere.[17] We can then see why Baruch is so important for this material. It is my judgment that scholars have focused on the right man, but for the wrong reasons.

14. On this methodological convergence, see David Jobling, "Sociological and Literary Approaches to the Bible: How Shall the Twain Meet?" *Journal for the Study of the Old Testament* 38 (1987): 85-93.

15. Seitz, "Canonical Shape," 16-24, suggests that Ebed-melech and Baruch assume roles in the text not unlike Joshua and Caleb in the book of Numbers. On the role of the latter in the shaping of the final form of the text of Numbers, see Olson, *Death of the Old*.

16. I suggest that Friedman does not probe deeply enough concerning Baruch and the authorship of the Jeremiah tradition. While focus on the individual person of Baruch may suit our individualistic tendencies and notions of writing, it likely does not fully recognize the ideological disputes in which the person and party of Baruch are fully engaged as they fashion the literature.

17. Gottwald, *The Tribes of Yahweh*, 608-621, has nicely suggested the ways in which theological and political realities may be functions of each other in a dialectical fashion. In some of Gottwald's own recent work the dialectic does not seem to be fully honored, as the political tends to reduce the theological in importance. For much of scholarship, however, the greater temptation is in the opposite direction; for that reason, I accent the force of political ideology in shaping the text and its claims.

In the end, then, we can suggest that the accusation made against Baruch in 43:3 and the accusation that Jeremiah is a pawn of Baruch contain a powerful element of truth. The pro-Babylonian cast of the material is not simply political ideology or pastoral sensitivity toward exiles, but it is finally a daring judgment of faith about God's will and work in the world.[18] The blessed, in the end, are those who accept this version of reality.

The Baruch narrative itself is an interpretive act which proceeds on the assumption that theological and socioeconomic political realities are deeply enmeshed together and must be held together in a Yahwistic view of reality. As the Baruch narrative itself practices such an interpretive stance, our own interpretive act concerning the same text tradition must not do otherwise. Thus I suggest that the name "Baruch" signifies exactly that inalienable congruence of theological and political realities.

JEREMIAH'S SCROLL (36:1-32)

This chapter occupies a pivotal place in the tradition of Jeremiah, and more broadly in the shaping of Israel's faith for exile. We may identify three related dimensions in its pivotal place. First, the chapter is closely related to ch. 26. In ch. 26, which in turn derives from ch. 7, Jeremiah is on trial for his life. While the prophet is acquitted, he clearly has become *persona non grata* for the royal-temple leadership in Jerusalem. Chapter 36 now completes that process of making Jeremiah an outsider to the establishment, one who is regarded as an unwelcome and unnecessary threat to dominant policies.

Second, the confrontation between the prophet (through Baruch) and the king makes this meeting virtually a classic paradigm for meeting between prophet and king when "truth speaks to power." Whereas the first point above (Jeremiah as a rejected outsider) focuses on the person of Jeremiah, this second point moves our attention away from historical issues to a paradigmatic

---

18. See Brueggemann, "Second Reading," in which I have argued that pastoral and political affirmations come to be taken as a reliable theological claim.

drama that transcends both the person of Jeremiah and questions of historicity.[19] That is, regardless of what happened, this is how such a meeting between king and prophet should have happened. The meeting shows that the field of perception in which the prophet moves cannot be accommodated to the ways of the king. It is fair to say that this narrative has contributed greatly to our understanding of "prophetic ministry" as essentially confrontational.

A third point has recently received primary attention from scholars. What happens in this narrative is that the scroll of Jeremiah takes on independent authority (i.e., independent of the person of Jeremiah) and comes to have a life of its own. This emergence of an authorized scroll is emblematic of the emergence of a canonical "book," and this development is pivotal in the formation of an authorized canon. That is, ch. 36 functions as a model of "Bible-making," so that interest turns from the personality of the prophet to *the book of Jeremiah*. It is the book (scroll), and not the presence of the prophet, which becomes decisive in resisting the king. From now on, establishment leadership must face a book which relentlessly places established power in jeopardy. The scroll is so much more difficult to resist because it cannot, like a person, be intimidated, banished, or destroyed. It keeps reappearing.

36:1-8   The narrative begins with an account of how the scroll came to be written. The narrative is situated in 605 B.C.E., just as the world of the Fertile Crescent was in enormous upheaval[20]

---

19. On the person of Jeremiah as a paradigm, see Sheldon H. Blank, "The Prophet as Paradigm," in *Essays in Old Testament Theology.* Festschrift J. Philip Hyatt, ed. James L. Crenshaw and John T. Willis (New York: KTAV, 1974), 111-130. The person of Jeremiah is no doubt a construct of the canonical process of Jeremiah, heavily influenced by Deuteronomic theology. See Walter Brueggemann, "The Book of Jeremiah: Portrait of the Prophet," in *Interpreting the Prophets,* ed. James L. Mays and Paul J. Achtemeier (Philadelphia: Fortress, 1987), 113-129; and Wilson, *Prophecy and Society in Ancient Israel, 231-251.*

20. On the historical interaction between Jehoiakim and Jeremiah, see Miller and Hayes, 403-6. Marion Ann Taylor,"Jeremiah 45: The Problem of Placement," *Journal for the Study of the Old Testament* 37 (1987): 88-94,

and just as Jehoiakim emerged as a perverse king (v. 1). That is, the "Bible" emerges in the midst of social disorder when there is a profound unsettlement in public life. The "Bible" intends to participate in and be a party to that unsettlement.

The scroll is formed at the impetus of Yahweh (vv. 2-3). The Bible itself strains to make the crucial and difficult claim that a human book is at the instigation of heavenly authority (see also 1:1-3). The scroll is not generated by Jeremiah. It is to contain "the words that I have spoken," not the words of the prophet. The purpose of the scroll, moreover, is to move Judah to hear *(shema')* and to turn *(shub),* and so to avoid evil. That is, the scroll is not designed to give information, nor even to make an argument, but it is to authorize, energize, and evoke a transformed life that will avoid and deter the coming evil. The scroll is intended to alter Judah's public existence. That intention, however, is not guaranteed. We do not know if the scroll will be that powerful, and God does not know either. Even for God the scroll only opens a possibility: "It may be" (36:3).

Jeremiah is obedient to the divine command (v. 4). He dictates the scroll which Baruch writes down. This chapter for a second time introduces Baruch, who is pivotal for the formation of the book of Jeremiah (cf. 32:12-16).[21] The introduction of Baruch indicates that the production of the scroll is a very human, political enterprise, for Baruch himself is a crucial political figure. He is not a mere stenographer, but one who has a deep stake in the argument made by Jeremiah (cf. 43:1-7). As we shall see, the production of the scroll is a deeply political act that advocates a particular slant on policy questions and passionately engages the issues of the day.[22] From the outset, the Bible is not a neutral

---

suggests that the dates linking prophetic material to Jehoiakim are ways of speaking in formulas about the judgment of God.

21. On the person of Baruch, see James Muilenburg, "Baruch the Scribe," in *Proclamation and Presence.* Festschrift G. H. Davies, ed. John I. Durham and J. Roy Porter (Richmond: John Knox and London: SCM, 1970), 215-238; and Friedman, 146-49.

22. It seems likely that Baruch, in the scroll, becomes a cipher and agent for the arguments and ideology of pro-Babylonian policy. On the political and social location of Baruch, see Dearman.

document and its formation is not a disinterested act. Jeremiah's mandate to Baruch (36:5-7) parallels Yahweh's mandate to Jeremiah (vv. 2-3). Jeremiah needs a go-between, because he himself is unwelcome in the public places of promulgation.

The intent of Jeremiah echoes the intent of Yahweh: "It may be . . ." (v. 7). The scroll is no certain thing. It is not known what Judah's response will be, but it is the only chance for Judah in the face of Yahweh's impatience and anger. The obedience of Baruch to Jeremiah (v. 8) is parallel to Jeremiah's response to Yahweh (v. 4). The formation of the scroll is narrated as a twofold drama of command and obedience. Through this twofold process, what is initiated in God's own intent has now been delivered concretely to the place of public address. The "word of God" is intended precisely to be heard in public places, to impinge upon public policy, and to provoke public transformation. Such hearing, impingement, and provocation require a quite human act. In this case, Baruch makes the word of God available, and Baruch himself is a passionate advocate for how the heavenly word of Yahweh touches public policy.

36:9-14   Baruch is obedient to Jeremiah. He reads the scroll in public, as per instruction (v. 10). He does so on a high holy day, which assures a large hearing. He reads the scroll in the temple in a named chamber. As we shall see, that the place of reading is in "the chamber of Gemariah the son of Shaphan" cannot be either incidental or unimportant. It is not possible to know if this reading is a scheduled public event or if it is an intrusive act of personal assertion.[23] We do not know if such a public reading was a routine and acceptable occurrence in the temple or not.

What matters is the response to the reading (vv. 11-14). In such a predemocratic society, appeal is not made to "the masses." What counts is the leadership. The scroll in the "chamber of

---

23. It is not impossible that the presentation of the scroll was like the offer of theses made by Martin Luther, which set in motion the church crisis that became the Reformation. While Luther's act is popularly thought to be a daring act of defiance, in fact he followed a convention in instigating theological discussion and dispute. Baruch's presentation of the scroll may in its context have been such an act of inviting a dispute.

Gemariah" is heard by the son of Gemariah, Micaiah. He obviously belongs to an important and powerful political family, and has easy access to the high councils of government.[24] Micaiah immediately reports what he has heard to the cabinet of the royal government. "All the princes" are assembled, and we notice in the list of high officials his father, Gemariah.

The impact of the report of the scroll is powerful. It must have been like the report of the "Pentagon Papers" of Daniel Ellsburg.[25] It is enough to get the attention of the leadership, and to evoke a response of interest and of anxiety. Thus Jeremiah's strategy for Baruch is effective. The scroll (the content of which we know nothing specific) contains words and claims that require the serious and sustained attention of the government. The narrative intends to model a scroll that cannot be avoided, and a power structure that must respond to the scroll. Baruch is summoned to the cabinet meeting. He answers the summons of the cabinet, apparently willingly and unafraid. The scroll by dramatic moves is making its way into the presence of established power, where it must have its say.

36:15-19   The action shifts from a temple chamber to a government chamber. The stakes grow higher! Baruch now provides a second reading of the scroll which has been initiated in God's own utterance (v. 15). This hearing evokes "dread" *(phd)* among the listeners, who are establishment figures (v. 16). The scroll requires and receives a serious hearing. It makes its way into the high councils of government, not because of Jeremiah or Baruch, but because of its intrinsic claim. The response of the princes is twofold.

First, the king must know (v. 16)! This seemingly innocent statement may be more freighted than it appears. This urging may, of course, only voice the expectation of the alarmed princes that the king will have to deal with the claims of the scroll, for it belongs to the king and not to the princes to respond to the crisis.

---

24. See Dearman, 411-421.
25. On the Pentagon Papers, see Neil Sheehan et al., *The Pentagon Papers* (New York: Quadrangle, 1971).

If the statement is read more cunningly, the princes may now sense that they have (at long last) an available tool which the king cannot avoid.[26] One cannot determine how the princes are positioned in this tense confrontation. They may be only mediating to the king as innocent functionaries. The narrative suggests, however, that at least some of the princes are sympathetic to the argument of the scroll and are relieved to have their own view voiced in the presence of the king, voiced in a way that does not place them in direct opposition to the king.[27] That is, we should not assume that all the princes are "yes men" to the king, but some represent very different interests and views which may concur with those of the scroll. It may be that the scroll weighs in on a government dispute that was already under way.

The second response of the princes to the reading by Baruch is to investigate the origin of the scroll (vv. 17-18). If the princes are to value the scroll and risk something for it, they obviously need to know of its origin, authenticity, and credibility. They do not want to go out on a limb for a document that may be a hoax. The specific question poses a much larger one. How can such a countergovernment opinion be voiced in a relatively closed society? Who could have authored such a dangerous document? Baruch's answer is direct and reassuring. The scroll belongs to

---

26. Whether the decision to take the scroll to the king is an innocent act or a calculating one depends on two things: (1) whether the issues stated in the scroll were already reflected in a tension at work in the government, and (2) whether the scroll is understood by its handlers as enmeshed from the outset in abrasive policy issues. That is, if the scroll is understood in relation to actual policy matters, then the urging of the royal cabinet officers is more likely to be a calculated act. If, however, the scroll is understood only religiously, then the act may be more innocent. I believe political innocence in such a context is not likely.

27. If the family of Shaphan and the family of Baruch are socially located as Dearman suggests (see above, n. 22), then we may imagine they would favor a policy of great prudence which would urge accommodation to Babylon; they may also be very judicious about running personal risks in confronting the king. Thus the strategy reflected in this narrative makes sense when we consider the role of scribes in a royal government. On such functionaries, see Eris W. Heaton, *Solomon's New Men: The Emergence of Israel as a National State* (London: Thomas and Hudson, 1974, and New York: Pica, 1975).

Jeremiah (v. 18). No claim is made by Baruch that the scroll comes from God. Baruch responds concerning the human process of scroll making, for this is a very human confrontation.

The princes seem satisfied with his response. Their concluding advice to Baruch is telling indeed. They advise Baruch to disappear with Jeremiah, to be safe from the rage of the king which is sure to come, for this is a dangerously provocative scroll. This response on the part of the princes is enormously important. It indicates, on the one hand, that the princes recognize the scroll to be inherently dangerous and troublesome, and sure to evoke the passionate hostility of the king. They not only know something of the scroll, but they know a great deal about the king. They have witnessed his temper tantrums before. On the other hand, this advice suggests that the princes are not neutral parties in this conflict. They align themselves with the scroll-makers, and by subtle action they align themselves against the king. That is, they do not want the king to succeed against the scroll-makers. The princes become protectors of this subversive voice that the king cannot tolerate. The seasoned bureaucrats also know to proceed on a "need to know" basis. If the princes do not know where Baruch and Jeremiah hide, it is safe for Baruch and Jeremiah, because they will not be betrayed. Moreover, such an arrangement leaves the princes unimplicated in the hiding. The strategy of the princes is to cut off any traceable connection between themselves and their "informants." Thus the scroll-makers are decisively removed from the scene, and the king is left with only the scroll.

36:20-26   Finally, through a studied and formal development, the scroll arrives at "the court of the king." Neither Jeremiah nor Baruch is there, only the scroll. The meeting between king and scroll is dramatic and tense. The scroll is read to the king while the princes stand in attendance. The princes know and have orchestrated the reading, but now they assume a courtly posture of deference to the king.

The king waits and ostentatiously cuts columns of the scroll after they are read and burns them (v. 23). The king gives no hint of listening to the reading, but makes a great show of contempt for the scroll. The king enacts an early form of "document shredding." He continues his act of disdain until all the scroll is gone. The king has eliminated the scroll! The scroll is gone, and there is only the king. The narrator adds a poignant observation. Neither the king nor his entourage rend their garments. The word "rend" *(qr')* is the same word as "cut" in v. 23. The king would *cut* the scroll in disdain, but he would not *cut* his garments in response or repentance. The king would yield nothing of himself to the claim of the scroll. He shut out the scroll and refused to let it touch his life.

The use of the term *qr'* makes a deliberate and telling reference to 2 Kgs. 22:11, wherein another king, Josiah, bears another authoritative scroll and does indeed "rend" his garments in penitence.[28] Thus our narrative articulates a sharp and unambiguous contrast between Josiah, the good king who responds to the scroll, and Jehoiakim, the resistant king who refuses the scroll — its great demand, and its offer of life. The king wants to be and is "scroll-less" because he imagines he is autonomous and need give no answer. Whereas his princely advisors had responded to the scroll in great fear *(phd)* (Jer. 36:16), now the king and his entourage exhibit no "fear" *(phd)* (v. 24). The contrast between the frightened princes and the unresponsive king is complete. The contrast serves to show that the king is utterly cynical, utterly in opposition to the scroll and to the God who speaks in the scroll.

The princes, including Gemariah, with what must have required considerable courage, defend the scroll against the willfulness of the king and urge the scroll to be taken seriously (v. 25). The king, however, would not "listen." The word "listen" looms large in this narrative and reflects the entire tradition of listening obedience as championed in Deuteronomy. "Listening" bespeaks readiness and willingness to submit to the claim of torah, to yield one's life to the demands of Yahweh.[29] In refusing to listen, the king resists not only this particular scroll but the whole world of demands and promises and Yahweh's will for life in covenant. In rejecting the scroll, the

---

28. Nicholson, 42-46, has clearly seen how this contrast between Josiah and his son works in the text. Cf. also Jer. 22:13-19.

29. For a programmatic understanding of "listen," see Eugen Rosenstock-Huessy, *Speech and Reality* (Norwich, Vt.: Argo, 1969), 16-31, wherein it is seen that living in human community depends on speaking and listening.

king refuses life in covenant with Yahweh. Indeed, the king not only refuses to listen. The king takes aggressive action against the producers of the scroll, dispatching members of his party to "seize" Jeremiah and Baruch (v. 26). The king intends to eliminate those who generate words inimical to his regime.[30]

In the face of the king's cynical and self-serving action, the narrative adds a laconic note: "Yahweh hid them" (v. 26). This note is telling, in light of the princely advice of v. 19. With a reflexive verb, the princes had urged Jeremiah and Baruch to "hide themselves." Now, however, Yahweh is the active subject of a causative verb concerning the process of hiding. By this phrase, the narrative signals that more is at work here than flesh and blood. The confrontation has been escalated, so that the protection of Jeremiah and Baruch is not simply a matter of political expedience, but it requires providential care for the carriers of an alternative politics. The princes are not directly implicated in the hiding of Jeremiah and Baruch, but their counsel in v. 19 is part of Yahweh's involvement. With the complicity of the princes, the reality of the scroll has taken on very large and very ominous proportions. The king imagines he has prevailed. He has not, however, stayed through to the completion of the narrative.

36:27-32   The king imagined that the burning of the scroll finished what was for him only a minor episode. The scroll had been burned and no longer existed. There was only the king. The narrative continues, however, after the king has departed the scene. Two actions are taken in this post-king narrative. First, a powerful and devastating lawsuit speech is spoken against the king (vv. 29-31). It is the voice of the very God who stands behind the scroll who now speaks the decisive word against the king. The

---

30. The elimination of the scroll by the king places Jeremiah (or the tradition of Jeremiah) in the company of those writers, poets, journalists, and novelists who have been silenced by fearful, authoritarian regimes. Such authorities regularly recognize such writers as threats and believe that silencing them can maintain the present order. On contemporary counterparts see Andre Brink, *Writing in a State of Siege* (New York: Summit, 1984); and *The Writer in Human Rights,* ed. the Toronto Arts Group for Human Rights (Garden City: Doubleday, 1983).

king is indicted: "You burned the scroll" (v. 29). That act of burning turned out to be much more significant than the king suspected, or than even the princes understood. Then a harsh sentence is pronounced against the king (vv. 30-32). The articulation of punishment is heavily formulary. It anticipates an ignominious end for the king, whose dead body will be dishonorably exposed (cf. 22:18-19), an end to the dynasty when the king will have no heir (cf. 22:30), and enormous evil against the city. The judgment seems disproportionate to the affront of burning the scroll, except that burning it is an awesome attempt to eliminate the concrete, sovereign word and will of God. The elimination of the word (scroll) is an act of gross disobedience which can only bring death and destruction.

The second act authorized in this oracle is the writing of a second scroll (36:28, 32). The divine authorization of a second scroll (v. 28) is linked directly to the royal burning of the first scroll (v. 27). Two things are evident in this immediate follow-up. First, God is indomitable. God is not deterred in the least by the king's refusal. God is a scroll-maker and will continue to make scrolls.[31] Any particular scroll from the God of Israel can be dismissed as was this first one; but it will be promptly and boldly reiterated. The king is unable to eliminate the scroll because God intends a scroll to be present, sounded, and heeded. Second, the narrative ends with the freighted words: "Many similar words were added to them" (v. 32). Thus the king's resistant activity only evoked a larger, more comprehensive, more demanding scroll. The king's action did not terminate the threat of the scroll as he intended, but only magnified the problem for the king.

It is clear in this dramatic narrative that scroll-making (i.e., Bible production) is a daring, dangerous human enterprise. It is equally

---

31. Jose Faur, "God as a Writer: Omnipresence and the Art of Dissimulation," *Religion and Intellectual Life* 6/3-4 (1989): 31-43, has made a compelling case that Greek religion is metaphysical but that Hebrew religion is literary: "The God of the Hebrews is eminently literate. God communicates in writing" (33). See the more extended study by Faur, *Golden Doves with Silver Dots: Semiotics and Textuality in Rabbinic Tradition* (Bloomington: Indiana University Press, 1986), and the references to Jacques Derrida in his work.

clear that this scroll-making is paradigmatic of the way in which God counters human pretension and resistance. God will not leave the king scroll-less, even if the king wants no scroll. The emergence and reemergence of the scroll thus makes a statement about the theologically constituent elements of the life of this community. Alongside the courage of Jeremiah and Baruch is the resolve and intent of God. God's relentless resolve arises in the form of a scroll summoning to repentance. God will generate as many scrolls as necessary to override the king's zeal for autonomy. The king cannot finally sustain a world where he need not listen. The king's life consists in listening to the reality of the scroll. In this chapter, the power and authority of the scroll have in fact displaced the voice of the prophet. The scroll calls Judah to turn, which is to live.

JEREMIAH ARRESTED AND IMPRISONED (37:1-21)

The last days of Judah are ostensibly ruled over by Zedekiah, the third of Josiah's sons (598-587 B.C.E.). His rule, however, is of little importance, given the larger events of international politics. The great facts of Judah's political situation are the massive powers of Egypt in the south and Babylon in the north. Those two powers are in deep conflict, and the king in Jerusalem sits helplessly in the middle of the conflict. Zedekiah and his city are caught between them and are in fact helpless to effect matters at all. Into this caldron of power politics comes the voice of Jeremiah, carrier of a word from Yahweh. Jeremiah (and the word he carries) are fully cognizant of the international situation. Because the prophet has drawn a conclusion about the shape of that situation, the prophetic word is an urgent, partisan imperative to the king. The king, pitiful political creature that he is, is at risk in the midst of this raging context of great powers, a context made yet more ominous by the prophetic word. The text of Jeremiah is a study of the interface of royal power and prophetic word, and the demanding requirement of daily life in the midst of that interface.[32] This narrative

---

32. Intrusion of the prophetic word into the public life of Jerusalem is a central motif of chs. 37–45. Note also that the word is not only from God

chapter portrays the ways in which the prophetic word intrudes upon royal politics.

37:1-2 Zedekiah is a creature of Babylon (cf. 2 Kgs. 24:17). He rules only at the whim of despised Nebuchadnezzar. The fact that he is an imperial puppet must have evoked resistance from "true patriots." This is the first fact of Zedekiah's rule. For the text, however, that Babylonian fact is only a framing piece of data. The central issue is that the king did not "listen" *(shemaʿ)*. No one listened — not the king, not his royal entourage, not the city nor its citizens. "Listening" becomes the key motif for this part of the text.[33] In the use of that single word, the text makes present not only the urgent advocacy of Jeremiah but the entire torah tradition of obedience and fidelity. "Listening" is to acknowledge that Yahweh and the torah tradition provide the dominant clues to life and to power. Zedekiah's refusal to listen is a decision to ignore the tradition, to reject the prophet, to scuttle a theological identity, and to disregard a transcendent purpose in power politics. A refusal to listen is to imagine that the king is autonomous and therefore destined for self-sufficiency. In his refusal to listen, so the text suggests, the king has sealed his own fate and that of his people. His future depends not upon his ingenuity nor his power, but upon his readiness to accept the theological reality of his life and his rule, that is, the reality of Yahweh's rule.

37:3-5 It is odd indeed that the king who refuses to listen to the prophetic word nonetheless asks the prophet to engage in intercessory prayer. While we may conclude that the indictment of Jer. 37:1-2 comes from a different literary source than the prayer request, we may also take the two as a deliberate textual tension. Taken together the two items suggest that the king wants

---

but is at the same time a partisan, political verdict. Indeed, in the prophetic faith of Israel, one cannot have one without the other; i.e., one cannot have a word from God unless it is also a word pertinent to the social realities of the day.

33. It is most likely that the focus of this exchange on "listen" indicates that we are dealing with Deuteronomic theology. The Deuteronomic theology is insistent on this single accent in appropriating moral demands within the public process.

the aid of the prophet (and of God) (vv. 3-5), but not *the command* of the prophet (or of God) (v. 2). The king's request is a measure of his acute fear and desperation. Verses 3 and 4 nicely juxtapose the reality of the competing armies and the power of prayer. Belatedly, perhaps halfheartedly, the king is driven to appeal for transcendent help when his own devices have failed. His request, however, contradicts his refusal to listen. Such prayer may be desperate; it has, however, no chance of succeeding. Indeed with Jeremiah, the request for prayer is not even acknowledged. The request of the king is simply disregarded by the prophet. The prayers of those who do not "listen" will be scarcely heard, and even their requests for prayer will be disregarded.[34]

37:6-10   These verses constitute the center of our chapter and are representative of the main affirmations of the Jeremiah tradition. This is an oracle which embodies God's intrusion into the crisis of Jerusalem. The king had asked for a word of prayer *addressed to Yahweh* in intercession. Instead, however, he receives from the prophet *a word from Yahweh,* more of the same word to which he would not listen. The king wants God's help, but gets only God's harsh guidance. What he receives is not what he wants. The only help God will give is guidance which the king will refuse to honor.

The oracle is a word to Jeremiah which is then given to the king. The king has no immediate access to God's word, but depends on the word and authority of the prophet. The oracle is astonishing in its threat. Though it is God's own word, it is an analysis of and an anticipation of the behavior of the great empires. The word addresses the king, who is situated exactly between Egypt and Babylon. The present circumstance suggests to the king that Egypt is the significant factor and Babylon is absent. There

---

34. Though it is not explicit, the text suggests yet another example of the correspondence of affront and punishment which Patrick D. Miller, Jr., *Sin and Judgment in the Prophets,* has explicated. Thus Israel's affront is that it did not "listen," though the text does not say so. Jeremiah's disregard of the request for intercession is in turn an act of not "listening," reflecting the nonresponse both of the prophet and of God. Elsewhere Jeremiah is more directly commanded not to pray because God will "not listen" (7:16; 11:14; 14:11-12; 15:1-2).

was a powerful predilection to tilt political-military assessments in Egypt's favor, and Jerusalem is endlessly haunted by Egyptian promises and potential.

The oracle, however, refutes such an analysis. The king has it all wrong, and his entire intelligence establishment has miscalculated. Egypt is no enduring factor in the future, says the oracle. Pharaoh will withdraw, and the Babylonians will come and destroy. The king who relies on Egypt is betting on the wrong horse. The king is advised by those whom Jeremiah regards as false (cf. 27–28). There was an opinion in Jerusalem that the Babylonians would not return to threaten Jerusalem again. Official Jerusalem engaged in a sustained and systemic underestimate of Babylon. Against such a view, Jeremiah is adamant and insistent. The book of Jeremiah is very sure. Babylon will destroy. There is no escape, and there is no alternative. Indeed, if the main force of the Babylonian army does not destroy Jerusalem, a few Babylonian stragglers will, because it is Yahweh's will that Babylon will destroy the city (37:10). The prophet not only identifies the real enemy of the Davidic house. He also announces the outcome of the conflict. Utter destruction! The prophetic word exposes to the king his terrible jeopardy which he apparently had been able thus far to deny. The threat of Babylon is ostensibly geopolitical. It is, however, in fact a theological threat. Yahweh has willed the destruction of God's own people and city. Thus the Jerusalem establishment had not only misread Babylon. It had also misunderstood Yahweh's potential as an enemy.[35]

37:11-15 The remaining verses of the chapter, with one exception, concern the personal situation of the prophet. The prophet's personal life is deeply enmeshed with the burden of his public words. Though the prophet has just asserted the forthcoming Babylonian destruction, he seizes a moment of respite from the Babylonian controversy to tend to personal business with the king. He returns home to exercise his legal right to the land (37:12; cf. ch. 32).

---

35. That misunderstanding is not simply a mistake of judgment. Rather, the miscalculation derives from ideology which distorted perceptions and categories of interpretation, so that the error is not ad hoc but systemic and programmatic.

Jeremiah is a public figure in the city. He is known and his words are known. He is known as the one who has forecast and advocated a Babylonian victory. He is apprehended by a guard as he leaves the city and is accused of deserting to the Babylonians. We are not told, but presumably the city was under tight curfew and none could leave. Predictably, a known imperial sympathizer would be detained. There was sufficient reason from his public message for Jeremiah to be suspect. Jeremiah nonetheless denies the accusation made against him (37:14).[36] He is not a deserter! The guard, predictably, will not "listen" *(shemaʿ)*. Jeremiah's public word from God has already been rejected (v. 2). Now his personal defense is also not heeded. His contemporaries will not *listen,* either to his public oracle or to his personal defense. He is arrested, arraigned, beaten, and imprisoned. His public message is costly. The royal establishment despises his message and therefore abuses the messenger. They find his words unbearable. The prophet is subject to police brutality! His word places him in deep conflict with the royal ideology which refuses to face its true situation of jeopardy. The "princes" are the ones who keep the charade of national security functioning. Public policy in Jerusalem has become the practice of a corporate lie.[37] Jeremiah protests, and therefore he must be harshly silenced.

---

36. The opposition to Jeremiah cannot understand how his words could be anything other than treason. They cannot entertain the thought that his words might indeed be true, i.e., that God wills an imperial triumph over Jerusalem. Ideology, when left uncriticized, renders discernment impossible beyond the close interests of its adherents.

37. Jeremiah's adversaries are indeed on a "March of Folly." Barbara W. Tuchman, *The March of Folly,* characterizes such a strategy of "folly" as a public policy which to any objective observer is self-destructive and which has internal critics who point out the inherent destructiveness of policy. In this case, it is Jeremiah (and no doubt others like Uriah) who point out the folly; the proponents of the policy proceed nonetheless on their self-destructive path. The systemic deception is not unlike that chronicled about Viet Nam by David Halberstam, *The Best and the Brightest* (New York: Random House, 1972); and Neil Sheehan, *A Bright Shining Lie: John Paul Vann and America in Viet Nam* (New York: Random House, 1988). Note that, unlike the episode in ch. 36, here the princes are solidly opposed to Jeremiah. Perhaps this suggests that the crisis is more acute and so the resistance is solidified (if we seek a historical explanation), or perhaps the narrative simply needs a differently positioned opposition to the prophet (if we settle for a literary strategy).

37:16-21 These verses provide an odd conclusion to the chapter. By v. 15 one would have thought that Jeremiah had been effectively disposed of by the government. Certainly the princes thought they had silenced him, and we expect the king to follow the princes in this regard. Zedekiah, however, is haunted. He seems to suspect his own authority. He will not publicly challenge the princes, for they give the appearance of being the true "patriots." They are the ones who "wrap themselves in the flag." Zedekiah also will not, however, settle for their easy affirmation of royal propaganda. Perhaps the king knows better than his princes. In any case, the king questions (i.e., consults) with the prophet "secretly" (v. 17).

The scene of the king in secret with the prophet anticipates the drama in which Nicodemus questions Jesus "by night" (John 3:2). In both cases, the establishment figure comes desperately to the outsider. In both cases, the action of the public official is politically risky and therefore is done surreptitiously. The narrative shows dramatically how the king, as the center of power and authority, grudgingly and desperately reaches beyond official channels of intelligence, suspecting that there is more to be known than his associates tell him. Zedekiah's act toward Jeremiah is an acknowledgement not only of the failure of his official intelligence. It is also a recognition that his own royal power is finally penultimate. He is not master of his own policy. In some way matters are being decided and decreed out beyond his administration. It is as though the governance of affairs has been taken out of his hand. That of course is a main point the prophet has been scoring for a long time. There is another governance which is unfettered by royal policy. Thus the narrative quite indirectly confesses and affirms the rule of Yahweh, a rule which the king mutely acknowledges and which the prophet boldly enacts.

The king's question to the prophet is a desperate, pleading one, for it makes clear that the prophet is the senior partner in this conversation. The king is an empty-handed suppliant, hat (crown) in hand. The king now asks for an assurance from the prophet, though last time he had received another oracle (vv. 7-10), a word which he did not like and which he could not accept. Now he seeks from the same source a second opinion, a better word.

143

Jeremiah must have delighted in the scene. He slows the pace of the interaction. He relishes the moment and makes the king wait. His first guarded response to the king is as though he toys with the king. It is respectful but terse, not at all forthcoming: "There is." Then Jeremiah speaks the word for which the king had come. It is, however, the same relentless word sounded so many times before: "You shall be delivered into the hand of the king of Babylon" (v. 17). Zedekiah surely had hoped for a different word. A different verdict, however, is not to be. The power of the king will be submitted to this other royal, imperial, hostile power. No explanation is given and no compromise offered. It is a settled conclusion.

That brief exchange about policy is followed by Jeremiah's personal petition to the king. The request of the prophet in fact constitutes a statement of his innocence. Cast in the form of two questions, the prophet voices two lines of defense. First, he is innocent (v. 18). He has not undermined the war effort. Second, he is right. He has not wronged the king, nor has he misled the king. The other prophets who refused to take Babylon seriously are surely the discredited ones (v. 19). Jeremiah is a truth-teller, and as such he does not deserve this brutalizing treatment.

On the basis of this self-defense, Jeremiah makes a petition (v. 20). He asks not to be returned to the prison, for if he is returned there he will die. These verses comment no more on the destiny of Jerusalem or Babylon. In the midst of such public issues, personal safety is nonetheless crucial for the prophet. The king makes no verbal response to the new oracle, even as he does not respond after vv. 7-10 or after v. 17. He receives the hard word of the prophet silently. He does, however, act to provide maintenance for Jeremiah, and he places him in a lesser, more humane confinement (v. 21). The narrative is laconic. There are hints, however, that Zedekiah has come to regard Jeremiah as a support and an ally. Presumably the king is able to recognize, albeit reluctantly, that the prophet is indeed a truth-teller. In the finished form of the book, there is a lean suggestion that the king has conceded the prophet's main point. This understated gesture on the part of the king serves as an affirmation of the prophet. It suggests that it is now recognized that the prophet is not a liar or a traitor. He is a truth-teller who seeks no special favor, but only fairness for and acknowledgement of his public role.

In the midst of an urgent public crisis, there is truth to be told. The overriding will of Yahweh cannot be circumvented, certainly not by abusing the messenger. While we are concerned with Jeremiah in this episode, the larger stakes concern the city of Jerusalem. The city is in an awesome jeopardy. The city is not autonomous. God's powerful word matters, and no posturing by king and princes can void that sovereign word. By the end of the chapter the word from the prophet is not heeded. Its bearer, however, receives a modest concession from the king, almost an act of solidarity. That act is very little, but it is no doubt as much as the king dared risk. It is not easy for a king to yield to "another governance." The counterplan of the prophet (and accepted by the king) affirms that, sooner or later, established royal power must yield to the governing word of Yahweh.

JEREMIAH AND ZEDEKIAH (38:1-28)

It is a late, ominous time for Jerusalem and for its king, Zedekiah. Once more, this narrative concerns a confrontation between the king and the prophet. They are the two principal actors in the narrative, and they embody two contrasting perspectives. The king is fragile and desperate. His concern in this narrative is the development of a policy of survival for Jerusalem. His counterpart, the prophet, is by now *persona non grata* among the Jerusalem leaders, for he is not supportive of the dominant policies. While his position has important implications for the survival of the state, that is not his major preoccupation. His concern is the will and purpose of Yahweh as it impinges upon the public life of Judah. The conclusions he draws from his discernment of the will and purpose of Yahweh are not conducive to the survival of Jerusalem, as that survival is envisioned by Zedekiah.

We are very close to the end of the long rule of the Davidic line. No wonder there is tension, hostility, distrust, and panic among the leaders. While the text may reflect the historical realities of the late period of independent Judah, this chapter is primarily interested in the fate of the prophet who is the carrier of a word from God which counters both royal policy and public opinion. The text offers an intense, dramatic confrontation over policy options. As canonical literature, the text does not concern a concrete policy decision about 6th-cent. Jerusalem, but it concerns the odd, destabilizing effect of prophetic alternatives upon a consensus policy. The crisis in the narrative concerns the way in which the holy purpose of God works against the present, perceived well-being of Jerusalem.

The book of Jeremiah in its main parts has a decidedly "pro-Babylonian" slant. It argues repeatedly that Babylon will prevail. According to this view, the better part of wisdom is to acknowledge the dominance of Babylon, submit to it, and live with it (38:2-3, 17-18, 20-23). Moreover, this positive attitude toward Babylon is not simply prudence, though it is that. Submission to Babylon is proposed as a theological judgment: God has legitimated Babylon. Resistance to Babylon is not only poor politics, but also disobedience to Yahweh. This linkage of politics and faith leads to a remarkable and predictably unpopular judgment: *obedience to God* equals *surrender to Babylon*. The book of Jeremiah has made this massive political-theological connection. It is as though life comes through death, well-being comes through submission, security comes through enormous risk. Clearly the discerned will of God collides with the "war effort" of the government.

In addition to the king and the prophet who deal with each other in this account directly and with a mutuality of interest, the third role in this narrative is played by the princes, the body of influential opinion in Jerusalem which seems to control policy. They appear decisively at the beginning of the narrative wherein they vigorously oppose the prophet (vv. 1-6) and at the end of the narrative wherein they greatly intimidate the king (vv. 24-28). The princes advocate a policy of go-it-alone independence and resistance which sounds like a militant kind of patriotism. This position brings them into frontal conflict with the prophet, who believes that resistance to Babylon is suicide. The king seems largely sympathetic to the view of the prophet but lacks either the courage or the political clout to withstand the princes. In this narrative the prophet gives considerable attention to his own well-being and safety. He does not do so, however, in a way that compromises anything of his subversive political opinion. His personal safety is subordinated to the word that he must speak concerning the will of Yahweh and the legitimacy of Babylon. It is this determined convergence of the will of Yahweh and the legitimacy of Babylon, the intersection of theological vision and political reality, that brings him into conflict with the "patriotic" authorities.

38:1-6   In this first episode, Jeremiah preaches his characteristic word, that God is now the active enemy of the Jerusalem enterprise (vv. 2-3). That preaching invites into the narrative the powerful princes, who now appear as a third character in the drama (v. 1). They and not the king appear to be the shapers of policy. They embody the bureaucracy which is impervious outside its own ideology. The population of Jerusalem has only two policy options. It can surrender to Babylon, or it can resist. Surrender, so the prophet asserts, will permit life. Resistance will mean death. The promised death of the people of Jerusalem is by conventional plagues which come with an invading army, sword, famine, pestilence. The statement of the prophet imagines a scenario in which Babylon will lay siege to the city, and the sure consequences of such a siege will be famine and pestilence. That is, the deathliness to come is not like a bolt out of heaven, but is a predictable outcome of an extended siege by the army of the empire. Such a pragmatic reading of the anticipated siege is no doubt realistic. The intent of the verdict, however, is theological. It is because of God's resolve that the choices are "red or dead." Jeremiah's alternative to "dead" is to submit to the empire, that is, to accept the compromise of "red."

The response of the princes is as predictable as Jeremiah is unwavering (v. 4). Jeremiah is a traitor who deserves to die. He is undermining the war effort, and that cannot be tolerated. His is an effective act of sabotage of royal policy because it combines an intelligent political assessment of the chances for Jerusalem with a claim of theological insight. The government does not — indeed dares not — agree with him. It only wants him silenced. On any "realistic" reading of the situation, Jeremiah is an enemy of the government, preparing a counteroption against the "well-being" (*shalom*) of the city as defined by the government. The issue is joined between the government and this formidable dissent. Indeed, this entire chapter is about the problem of public dissent which claims to be the voice of God.

Only now, belatedly, the king appears in the narrative (v. 5). We might expect that the king would be completely allied with the princes against the prophet, but the narrative is more complex than that. Zedekiah does not resist the opposition of the princes who want to retaliate against Jeremiah, though he signals no agreement with them. He acts, not in resolve, but in weakness. He abdicates in the same way that Pilate is later to do (John 19:6). He (perhaps reluctantly) turns the troublesome dissident over to the more zealous authorities. With the king's tacit approval, Jeremiah is placed in a miry cistern, presumably to die through neglect (Jer. 38:6). This first episode features the king as the hapless, helpless man in the middle between "zealous patriots" and the dissenting prophet. The outcome of this episode, however, is that the prophet is eliminated from public discussion. The narrative thus far has accomplished the silencing of the prophet and the stifling of a critical prophetic word.

38:7-13   The carrier of God's counterword appears to have been defeated (cf. Gen. 39:19-23). Now, unexpectedly, a fourth character enters into the plot. Without any explanation, an Ethiopian in the royal entourage attends to Jeremiah (Jer. 38:7-8). We do not know why. The narrative introduces this fourth character abruptly and without comment. Is his appearance a fortuitous accident? Has Jeremiah a special friend among "the king's servants"? (The name of the man means simply "servant of the king.") Is Ebed-melech dispatched by other powerful interests in the court who favor Jeremiah's policy alternative, for we know that Jeremiah did indeed have powerful governmental friends who were hostile to royal policies?[38] Is the appearance of Ebed-melech an "act of God" to save the carrier of the word, and thereby to keep the word "in play"? We are told nothing and left to draw

---

38. On his support among powerful insiders, see Jer. 26:17, 24; 36:19; cf. Dearman, 403-421. On the episode concerning Ebed-melech, see Seitz, "Canonical Shape," 16-27. Both Dearman and Seitz are concerned with the literary, canonical function of these references; it is difficult to determine what operates historically, but we consider the "historical realities" as they are proposed in the final form of the text. Thus the text gives Jeremiah the support of powerful insiders.

our own conclusion. The narrator seems to have no curiosity about the question. The narrative is not embarrassed by the sudden appearance of Ebed-melech. The entry of Ebed-melech into the narrative is crucial, for only he stands between Jeremiah and death. His entry foils the death sentence already decided upon by the princes and now being implemented. His appearance in the narrative puts us on notice that this narrative has working through it a purpose other than straight reportage, a purpose that is not subservient to political pressure or persuasion.

This unexpected servant and the king have a brief but decisive exchange (vv. 9-10). Ebed-melech makes a powerful plea on behalf of the beleaguered prophet which is at the same time criticism of the princes. The king (who did not readily side with the princes in v. 5) is moved by the plea of his servant and authorizes the rescue of the prophet (v. 10). We are not told why the king responds so readily, but he clearly is not one of the bloodthirsty zealots of v. 4. In v. 5 the king does not resist the princes. Now he yields to Ebed-melech. Perhaps Zedekiah yields to whatever is the current pressure. Perhaps he is relieved at this intervention by Ebed-melech. Zedekiah plays no active role either in the condemnation of Jeremiah (v. 5) or the rescue (v. 10) of the prophet. In any case, the authorization of the king and the intention of the servant controvert the plan of the princes. We are told in enormous detail of the rescue of the prophet (vv. 11-13). It is clear that the rescue is of crucial importance to the narrator. The rescue of the prophet is no act of direct divine intrusion, but a determined, detailed human act. The rescue of the messenger is important; not even the will of the government can eliminate this threatening countervoice. Thus far we have seen the effort to silence the prophet, and we learn that effort could not succeed.[39] The action of Ebed-melech brings the prophet back into public discussion. The word works its unwelcome way in the face of determined opposition.

---

39. In the narrative accounts concerning Jeremiah, there are repeated efforts to silence him. Here, as in chs. 26 and 36, these efforts do not succeed because of human intervention on his behalf. Jeremiah is not without important allies, and the word is not without attentive adherents, even in the deep crisis of the city.

38:14-28   The two episodes of vv. 1-6 and vv. 7-13 are accounts, respectively, of imprisonment and release, of sentence and pardon, not unlike crucifixion and resurrection.[40] The carrier of the counterword was for a moment nullified (v. 6), but is inexorably restored (vv. 11-13). The two movements of the narrative are like preliminaries for the main meeting between prophet and king. Finally, now that the princes (vv. 1-6) and Ebed-melech (vv. 7-13) have contributed their parts, the narrative must come to this direct confrontation, for the decisive issue must be faced between king and prophet. It is a meeting fraught with both danger and caution. The stakes are very high. It is not, however, a meeting conducted in hostility. There is a genuine effort by both king and prophet to communicate and even to accommodate. The stakes are now too high for acrimony. Nobody has anything to win in this conversation by abrasiveness. In the end the prophet and the king share in the struggle for a truth that will save the city.

This extended unit is an intense conversation. The text consists almost entirely of an exchange of speeches. In this section the princes hover behind the king but are not present; Ebed-melech is now completely absent. Now it is head-to-head between the two principals:

Speeches of the King	Speeches of the Prophet
v. 14 Inquiry	v. 15 Fearful reluctance
v. 16 Assurance given in secret	vv. 17-18 The regular prophetic options of submission or defeat
v. 19 Royal fearfulness	vv. 20-23 The regular prophetic options
vv. 24-26 Plea for duplicity	v. 27 Compliance to the king (indirect discourse)

The meeting is between the king, who needs to know what his governmental intelligence cannot tell him, and the prophet,

---

40. Parallels to the career of Joseph in Gen. 39–41 are worth noting. There also the authorities who oppose Joseph are unable to resist his destiny. Those designated by God cannot be finally hemmed in by the authorities.

who can provide what the king needs to know. The narrative is crafted to give the prophet the upper hand and to explicate the epistemological embarrassment of the king. The book of Jeremiah is insistent in its claim that the prophet carries the data the king needs, which the king cannot receive from any other source. The government finally must submit to the prophet. The text thus makes a daring epistemological claim. The crucial information is withheld from authorized channels. The government does not "know best."[41]

Jeremiah is not a coward, but he is realistic. He knows his verdict will displease the king (v. 15; cf. Dan. 4:19). If he displease the king, he will again be in a situation not unlike Jer. 38:4. Perhaps Jeremiah imagines his situation as Thomas More imagined his situation. He thought that speaking would bring jeopardy and so he preferred silence, because silence ostensibly maintains safety. It is better not to speak if the word only enrages the government. The prophet is wisely restrained (v. 15).

The prophet is not excessively courageous. He takes care to protect himself and receives the king's assurance (vv. 15-16). The king makes a secret promise to the prophet (v. 16). The king cannot be caught in public protecting a "traitor." The king, however, desperately needs this man as an ally, and perhaps even respects him. We may wonder whether, in that chaotic moment, the king's promise of safety is to be trusted. Perhaps the prophet wondered as well.

The king's assurance, in any case, is enough for the prophet (vv. 17-18). The prophet delivers once again his terrible word for the king. Upon hearing his pronouncement, we may wonder in retrospect why the king bargained so hard to get the prophetic word, for it is the same harsh verdict already well known from Jeremiah (cf. vv. 2-3). Perhaps the king thought he would get a better, reassuring word this time. He does not, however, for the

---

41. The same epistemological inversion takes place in the narratives of Joseph and Daniel, wherein the occupant of the throne must go outside his royal company to an uncredentialed Israelite to learn reality. In the same way, this king must go to the uncredentialed prophet to learn the truth. All these texts witness to the epistemological subversion that is present in the faith and in the text of Israel.

prophet is intransigent and the word is relentless. The king receives once more the same message from the prophet. There simply is no maneuverability in Judah's situation. There are two options: surrender and live, resist and die. The word of God promises a way of survival; it is not, however, the desired word, but only a grudging, compromised way of survival. If the present form of this narrative is from and for exiles, as seems plausible, then this reiterated word is an assurance to the ones deported to Babylon.[42] They have chosen the only way to live, which is the way of terrible submission. There is no chance of life except in reference and accommodation to the empire (cf. 29:5-7). There is no chance of life through self-assertion and triumphalism.

Oddly, Zedekiah does not flinch from or argue against this prophetic verdict (38:19). The king seems almost ready to submit to this word from God, a word he could not have welcomed. The situation of the king, however, is complicated. Zedekiah does not fear the Babylonian army or government, as we might expect. Rather, he fears his own people. In this response, he fears the pro-Babylonian party. Perhaps they are hostile to him because he resisted too long in his refusal to submit to Babylon. Thus Zedekiah does not reject the word of Jeremiah, but recognizes that it is politically impossible for him to be public about it. In his response to the prophet, the king is enormously candid, now treating the prophet as his confidant and ally. The king is immobilized. He is politically incapable of doing what he knows theologically to be correct.

Jeremiah's response to the fear of the king is not terribly surprising, nor does it reflect any great pastoral sensitivity (v. 20-23). Indeed, the prophet sounds the same options yet one more time. The only safety for the king is in surrender (v. 20). The promise is that the king will be safe from his compatriots whom

---

42. This word nicely conforms to the pastoral needs and political interests of the community of exiles in Babylon. Thus it makes most sense to assume that this is a word reflective of the faith of the exilic community, i.e., an exilic redaction of the tradition. A notice of such an interest, however, does not diminish the status of the claim as "canonical." This view of Israel's life and destiny may have arisen out of a vested interest, but it is accepted as normative in the final form of the text.

he fears if he heeds the prophet. The alternative to surrender is most severe. Jeremiah envisions that a refusal to surrender will cause a terrible defeat and punishment. In his vision, all the women of the royal entourage will be treated as women prisoners of war are characteristically treated. The exiled (and abused) women will engage in terrible lamentation. The king will be exiled, the royal family taken, the city burned. The only alternative is surrender. One way or the other, God has determined and decreed the end of the Jerusalem project. Jerusalem is over, either in death or in displacement. There is no third alternative. That is, there is no policy alternative that would be acceptable to the hawkish princes surrounding the king.

Again, upon hearing the devastating verdict of the prophet, the king does not argue or resist (vv. 24-26). The king is only aware that his personal situation is tricky and ominous, so he sets about to do "damage control." This time, unlike that in v. 19, he fears not the ones in Babylon but the princes at home, the ones we have encountered in vv. 1-6. The king pledges the prophet to secrecy. The king fears most his own advisers, not Babylon. It is as though the king is in fact persuaded by the prophet about the hard options. Perhaps his response is in order to buy time. In any case, Zedekiah urges the prophet to dissemble, to avoid the additional danger of internal conflict. Moreover, the prophet complies with the king's request (v. 27). It is as though, in this moment, the prophet is concerned for his own well-being. He is willing to compromise with and accommodate his message. Apparently he had yet another chance to sound his word to the princes; but he declines. The princes are vigilant against him, and he relies on the protection of the king. It is as though these two exhausted, beleaguered figures now must make common cause against impossible odds and enormous hostility.

The last verse of the chapter suggests that the king and the prophet both kept their word to each other (v. 28). They are in collusion against the princes. The prophet is under arrest. The king has received a sure word from the prophet which he does not doubt. The king, however, does not share that word with his advisers or act on it. The princes have both the king and the prophet in hock; they seem to be the ones determining policy.

153

The conversation between king and prophet seems to have no influence on policy. For an instant, the resistant princes have silenced the prophet and intimidated the king. For all the princes know or care, it is as though there had been no word from the LORD. The prophetic word can for a moment be eliminated from the narrative.

This chapter traces the three-way struggle for power. The princes for now prevail against both king and prophet. The prophet is rejected, and the king is intimidated. The chapter alternates between the prophet's hard word and the prophet's personal safety. The overarching drama of the chapter concerns the way in which dominant public policy is on a terrible collision course with God's holy purpose. The collision is under way and near at hand, but we do not know yet of the outcome. For the moment, we are made privy to a peculiar moment of human interaction between king and prophet. Both are at a desperate moment of need. In that moment, they make common cause. Their common work is an act of deception that does not change the larger story line of Jerusalem's ending. It does evidence, however, that even in the throes of such a public crisis, real human persons must act, in the presence of faith, fear, and complexity. Now the die is cast. For the moment, the princes have prevailed against king and prophet. We are still waiting, however, to see about the lean options the prophet has offered the king. The word does offer a way out. It is, however, a lean option, a very narrow gate for survival. In the world of prophetic reality, powerful leaders are offered an option of life, often an option that appears to be too costly politically. The prophetic word is uncompromising and unaccommodating of such political cost. A prophetic reading of reality finally makes no deals. It simply waits for reality to be faced.

THE FALL OF JERUSALEM (39:1-18)

The prophet had long since made clear that Jerusalem had only two choices: surrender and live, or resist and die. Under the leadership of Zedekiah Judah exercised its choice, and made the wrong choice. It resisted Babylon. In 38:1-6 it is clear that this policy had the militant support of "the princes." In so doing, according to the prophet, the monarchy resisted Yahweh and therefore died. This chapter describes the "payoff" of that disastrous choice (39:1-10) and adds two personal episodes derived from the public disaster (vv. 11-14, 15-18).

39:1-10 Most recently in 38:18, Jeremiah had detailed to Zedekiah the deep costs of defiance of Babylon. Now all the threats have come to fruition. While the threats are cast theologically, they also voice political realism. The consequence of resistance to the invader is what an invading, occupying army characteristically does. In this account, there is no mention of the prophet nor of the God to whom Jeremiah bears witness. The devastation of the city is presented simply as the working out of imperial strategy. The narrative is offered simply as reportage and closely parallels the accounts in 2 Kgs. 25:1-12; Jer. 52:4-16.

The taking of the city of Jerusalem was the result of a long siege, perhaps as much as eighteen months (39:1-2). The city could not in the end withstand the resolve of the empire. Finally the commanders of the Babylonian armies occupied the city (v. 3).

Zedekiah fled but was readily captured by the Babylonians (vv. 4-7). Jeremiah had long counselled the king to surrender. In 38:24-26 Zedekiah gives the impression of understanding and accepting the word of the prophet. Now, however, in the midst of crisis, the king is without courage, resolve, or resource. He neither resists nor surrenders, but jumps ship in an ignominious way. He abdicates his royal office and his royal responsibility, leaving his people in the lurch. Read more generously, he intends a "government in hiding." Zedekiah does not, however, get very far in his escape. We may imagine that with such an extended siege the land is saturated, not only with Babylonians but with intimidated informers. The fleeing king is apprehended. As an important prisoner, he is taken to the headquarters of Nebuchadnezzar in the north at Hamath. Nebuchadnezzar is actively present with his armies, no doubt directing the campaign. He is not, however, as far south as Jerusalem, and therefore the prized royal prisoner must be transported north to the field headquarters of Nebuchadnezzar.

Nebuchadnezzar metes out a horrible punishment to this king, who was for so long troublesome to the empire. Zedekiah is forced to watch while his sons are executed, and then he has his eyes put out. The brutal death of his sons is the last thing he sees, the last thing he will ever see, the thing he will see as long as he lives. And then, in his blindness, he is deported. His defiance ends him in Babylon, in any case. It is as though there never was an option for the king except Babylon. Either he would go willingly (as the prophet urged) or violently (as finally happened). Zedekiah is now the second king of Judah in exile in Babylon.[43] One was taken into exile willingly, the other defiantly. The first was treated humanely (cf. 2 Kgs. 25:22-30), the second brutally. Babylon is the place where Judean kings congregate and die. Apparently how they go, willingly or not, influences their treatment in exile.

Having put a decisive end to the royal threat, the Babylonians now seize and raze parts of the city (Jer. 39:8-10). Eight hundred thirty-two persons were deported (52:29). The deportation was not wholesale. The theological claims we are given assert that "significant Judah" was totally in exile. The important elements of society were deported. It is that view of Judah's history which the Bible wants us to accept, being a document produced by the community of exiles. Thus the judgment is not without a self-serving aspect. In fact, life did go on in devastated Jerusalem. Perhaps it was only "some of the poor" who remained, but there were people there. Life, commerce, and religion did resume. This ongoing life, however, figures only slightly in the emergence of exilic and postexilic Judaism. It was the community of Jews in Babylon who had the decisive voice in defining a Jewish future. That continuing Jerusalem operation, however, will in time occupy us in the book of Jeremiah.

Christopher R. Seitz has made a compelling case that the target of the Babylonian invasion was not the city, nor the temple, nor the general populace, but only the Davidic house embodied by Zedekiah.[44] Thus no mention is made of an assault on the temple by the invaders. The Babylonian authorities establish themselves

---

43. See 2 Kgs. 24:12 on Jehoiachin in Babylon.
44. Seitz, *Theology in Conflict*, 264-69.

"in the gate" (39:3), presumably to establish and maintain a semblance of civil order; moreover, that some are left in the land and given vineyards and fields (v. 10) indicates that the Babylonians were concerned to sustain the economic structure of the community.[45] Seitz has observed the important contrast between the consolidating policies expressed in vv. 3, 10, and the violence toward the king which sustains the view that the target is the monarchy. It was not the city nor the general populace, but the royal clique that made imperial rule endlessly problematic and unsettled. When that body of opinion was crushed and its functionaries eliminated, Babylon had reason to believe Judah could be adequately governed.

Perhaps most noticeable in the report of destruction is the restrained understatement. The narrative offers no interpretive comment about the debacle. No didactic point is scored. No moral explanation is offered. No theological connection is proposed, not even a reference to the prophet Jeremiah. It is as though the narrative wants us to attend only to the dread and brutality present in the scene. There will be ample time later to reflect on what has happened and why. There will be opportunity to notice that what happened is exactly what the prophet had envisioned. This is indeed "plucking up and tearing down." All such commentary, however, is held in abeyance. It is enough for now to take in that the holy city has become the humiliated, devastated, abandoned city. Without any direct reference, the narrative witnesses that Jeremiah's "word" has been enacted as deed.

39:11-14   The narrative moves promptly to Jeremiah, our continuing topic of interest. The destiny of the prophet is closely tied to that of the city, but Jeremiah's future is not identical with the fate of the city. Jeremiah remained where Zedekiah had left him, in "the court of the guard" (38:28). That is where he is now found by the Babylonians (39:14). No doubt there is some irony in the fate of Zedekiah and the destiny of Jeremiah, the two

---

45. See Seitz, *Theology in Conflict,* 270, n. 180, and his citation of J. N. Graham, "'Vinedressers and Plowmen': 2 Kings 25:12 and Jeremiah 52:16," *Biblical Archaeologist* 47 (1984): 55-58.

treatments now reported back-to-back. The defeated Zedekiah is brutalized. Jeremiah is found by the Babylonians in a royal prison, an enemy of the king. An enemy of the king, however, figures to be a friend of Nebuchadnezzar.

Before Jeremiah is found in the prison, however, a decree of Nebuchadnezzar is promulgated (vv. 11-12). It is as though Nebuchadnezzar, already before Jeremiah is found in the ruins of the city, knows the name of the prophet and shows that he is recognized as a friend of the empire. It is not unreasonable that the news of a favorable voice in Jerusalem should be known through channels of imperial intelligence. And if not that, the book of Jeremiah wants us to perceive its central character in this way. Jeremiah is singled out by the Babylonians from the general deportation. He is to be well treated. The narrative makes nothing of the irony of Jeremiah's position. He had been accused of being a traitor, of "being soft" on Babylon. Now his preferential treatment by Babylon would seem to vindicate the charge made by fellow citizens of Jerusalem. The narrative passes over the problem in silence. Moreover, the prophet is to have the decisive voice in determining his own future. Jeremiah's person now acts out the positive option Jeremiah had announced for the community. He has urged "submit and live." As one who has *submitted,* he is permitted to *live.* His personal destiny is presented as what might have been available for Zedekiah and for all his cohorts, had they not believed their own war propaganda — their silly, false notion of "well-being" *(shalom).*

Jeremiah is permitted to choose his own future. In a time of chaos and turmoil, his life has become a zone of free choice. His chosen future is marked in two ways. First, he aligns himself with Gedaliah, scion of an influential family, long an important support for the prophet.[46] Gedaliah embodies what was left of "independent Judah." Gedaliah and Jeremiah embody together a middle way for Jews, between the self-destructive shrillness of "the

---

46. Gedaliah is the heir of the family of Shaphan and Ahikam. Cf. Dearman, 410-11. This family is closely allied with Jeremiah and with the views he advocates. Thus Babylon would have been glad to have such a cooperative advocate occupy the new position as governor.

princes" and the easy resignation of the deserters and accommodators. More than that, Jeremiah himself lives out his message. He had proclaimed "submit and live." He had entrusted his future to Babylon, as Nebuchadnezzar here knows. And now he lives, with a decisive say about his future.

The last phrase of v. 14 is telling: "He dwelt among the people." Of course, Jeremiah is not a deserter or one who betrays. He is the one who cared most about his people and who risked the most for them. In the end, there is perhaps an ironic reversal of positions. The king who seemed to care about the survival of his people is now removed from his people and incapable of helping them. Jeremiah, who seemed a defeatist, is the one who now lives in solidarity with the people and who survives in the city. Without any obvious didactic message, the narrative bears witness to the truth, validity, and effectiveness of Jeremiah's message. Jeremiah is indeed the prophet whose word has come to pass (cf. Deut. 18:22). The apparently strong one is nullified, the apparently weak one in this crisis persists and prevails.

39:15-18 These verses appear abruptly and refer back to Jer. 38:7-13. Jeremiah is still in "the court of the guard" (38:28), even though Gedaliah should "take him home" (39:14). In the midst of the destruction, Jeremiah remembers Ebed-melech, who had abruptly and without explanation rescued him. This last episode is such an utter contrast to vv. 1-10. We had been watching the large, public drama of the empire against the state. Now we have an oracle addressed to one, solitary individual who has no standing and about whom we know practically nothing.

The oracle is in two parts. On the one hand, God is relentless in the resolve against Jerusalem (v. 16). God's action will be for evil and not for good. There is no vacillation or reprieve given by the prophet concerning the city. On the other hand, Ebed-melech is singled out for exceptional treatment. He will be delivered *(n-ts-l)*. "I will save you" *(mlt)*. The oracle uses two powerful verbs for God's rescuing action. God promises to do for Ebed-melech exactly what God would not do for Zedekiah or for Judah. Ebed-melech is singled out, an exception is made. The reason for the exception is that Ebed-melech trusted in Yahweh

159

(batah). Long ago, Jeremiah had warned Jerusalem not to "trust" in the claims of the temple (7:4). Jerusalem, however, had misplaced its trust and so was destroyed. Ebed-melech's trust, however, entailed not simply a good attitude, but a quite concrete act. He intervened for Jeremiah; he saved the prophet. He made the presence of the prophet viable. Thus it is his daring service on behalf of the prophet that is his act of trust. He not only trusted God, but trusted God's concrete way in the world.

Jeremiah 39 as a whole makes a complete contrast between Zedekiah, on the one hand, and Jeremiah and Ebed-melech, on the other hand. In the shaping of the chapter, 39:1-10 contains a general report that is unexceptional and known elsewhere. The tradition of Jeremiah has nothing to contribute to that. That report, however, is previously a foil for vv. 11-14, 15-18, which is peculiar to the tradition of Jeremiah and which narrates a certain history which is wrought through fidelity to the prophetic word. Thus vv. 1-10 is history in disobedience to the word and vv. 11-18 is history in obedience to the word. The destruction of Jerusalem is sweeping and comprehensive (vv. 1-10). A critical exception is nonetheless made. Ebed-melech constitutes an important remnant.[47] The destruction wrought by God through Nebuchadnezzar is not morally indifferent or undifferentiated. Even in such a moment of institutional failure, faithful acts of courage matter and are salvific. The chapter ends in a great affirmation of trust, trust which serves and substantiates the person, tradition, and book of Jeremiah.

The saved ones are the ones who adhere to a Jeremianic discernment of reality. Those who are allied with this faith have their life as "war-booty."[48] All the others become "war booty" for the Babylonians. Trust as evidenced by Ebed-melech is a limit and

---

47. Seitz, "Canonical Shape," 16-27, suggests that Ebed-melech and Baruch constitute a remnant not unlike Caleb and Joshua in the book of Joshua; indeed, they may be intentionally patterned after those figures. As such they provide for the community in the harsh transition to exile, as did Joshua and Caleb through the wilderness.

48. The phrasing was used generally in 38:2 and now is applied specifically. The language is war rhetoric, but the image has now been completely transformed as a way of speaking of a surprising rescue from the general destruction of war.

alternative to Babylonian power and devastation. The contrast is sharp even if left without comment: the resisters in the monarchy come to a sorry end. The alternative for a good end comes to Jeremiah, who is uncompromising in his vision of reality, and to Ebed-melech, who allies himself with the prophet and the prophet's word. The chapter as it stands is a belated invitation that others could separate themselves from a deathly royal vision of history and embrace a counterhistory which leads to life.

JEREMIAH'S RELEASE (40:1-6)

In ch. 39 the event toward which the book of Jeremiah persistently pointed has happened (39:1-10). The "end" anticipated by the prophet has happened and is narrated in detail. The prophet is thereby vindicated. God will not be mocked. For mocking God, Jerusalem is destroyed.

Life, however, goes on. The deportation did not empty the land. People still lived there, and because people still lived there, there was need for order and governance. A different governance was required which, unlike the monarchy which was endlessly troublesome to the empire, would be loyal, trustworthy, and committed to Babylon. Babylon now had the "right" and power to have its own kind of government in Judea.

40:1-6   First, however, there is one more telling of the special treatment accorded Jeremiah by the empire, a treatment already told in 39:11-14.[49] His treatment contrasts completely with the fate of Jerusalem. This narrative, as elsewhere, moves back and forth between public events and quite personal matters. Even in the upheaval of 587 B.C.E., the life and destiny of individual persons is not nullified or disregarded.

---

49. The two versions of the capture and release of Jeremiah in 39:11-14; 40:1-6 differ somewhat in detail. Both accounts conclude with Jeremiah's entrustment to Gedaliah, i.e., with those who now come to power and who share his ideological orientation. Thus Jeremiah is in the care of the same family who has long been his advocate. Before that conclusion, however, 40:1-6 shows Jeremiah subjected to the more threatening experience and fate of the exiles.

The narrator reiterates once more in simple, direct fashion the theological significance of the destruction of the city (40:1-3). The narrative even places the theological warrant and explanation in the mouth of a Babylonian military officer, perhaps not unlike the Marcan strategy of placing a final confession of Christ in the mouth of a Roman soldier (Mark 15:39). The Babylonian officer articulates standard prophetic Deuteronomic theology:

> Because you did not obey *(shema')*
> [Therefore] this thing has come upon you. (Jer. 40:3)

The reasons for the devastation are thoroughly covenantal, and in this moment are clear even to the Babylonian. The Babylonian captain of the guard sounds strangely like the prophet.[50]

The narrator, however, is interested in the personal destiny of Jeremiah (vv. 4-6). The contrast of general and personal concern is expressed in v. 4 by "now, behold" *(we'attah)*. The conquerors are attentively deferential to him, as Nebuchadnezzar has commanded (39:12). Jeremiah is released and given the options of going to Babylon or remaining in the land. The important point is that Jeremiah is free and can choose his own future. In this special treatment, there is no doubt high irony. On the one hand, Jeremiah is entirely vindicated. On the other hand, to be well treated by the occupying army can hardly be a popular outcome. It is the treatment given to someone who has become a traitor. Thus Jeremiah, in the very moment of his vindication, is marked as a traitor by the "hawks" among his own people (cf. 26:11; 38:4). Jeremiah 40:5 suggests not only that Jeremiah is given freedom of choice, but also a government allowance.[51]

Jeremiah exercises his choice and identifies himself with the

---

50. The indictment of v. 3 addressed to Jeremiah is odd indeed. Carroll, 699-700, has rightly seen that these verses intermingle a narrative about deportation and an oracle from Jeremiah. In the conflation of the two, however, the oracle of the prophet is placed in a Babylonian mouth and is addressed to the prophet, rather than coming from him.

51. On food guarantees from the king, see 2 Sam. 9:7; 2 Kgs. 25:27-30. In both parallel cases, the guarantee is more than a little threatening and ominous. On material provision given in the moment of release, see Deut. 15:1-11; and David Daube, *The Exodus Pattern in the Bible* (London: Faber & Faber, 1963), 55-61 and *passim*.

provisional government of Gedaliah, which Babylon had authorized and installed. In making this choice, Jeremiah is consistent with his own past urgings. He does not flee, and he does not resist Babylon. He occupies a middle position which is politically prudent and, in his reasoning and in the reasoning of the book of Jeremiah, theologically faithful. Persistently, the interpretation given these events by the tradition of Jeremiah is counter to the popular view that all pro-Babylonian postures are in fact treasonable. The Jeremiah tradition never finishes sorting out the vexed challenge that faithfulness to God seems to some to be treason to royal Jerusalem. Jeremiah's choice about the future must have given powerful, much needed legitimacy to the regime of Gedaliah.

GEDALIAH'S GOVERNORSHIP (40:7–41:18)

This distinct narrative unit is a straightforward account of the brief and tragic history of Gedaliah's governorship. Most scholars take the main outlines of the account as historically reliable, though there clearly is redactional activity. It is most striking that in this narrative about the quick "rise and fall" of Gedaliah, Jeremiah is completely absent. Nothing is said in the narrative that leads to any direct theological interpretation. The narrative traces the sorry events after the occupation by Babylon. One may conclude that the violence and disorder reported here are the residue of a community that long has imagined itself to be autonomous and free to do what it wants.

40:7-12 These verses narrate the solidification of the provisional government of Gedaliah.[52] It is clear that Gedaliah comes from one of the powerful and respected families of Jerusalem politics. His grandfather Shaphan and his father Ahikam have been highly visible before him, and have taken positions that seem sympathetic to the voice of Jeremiah.[53] The posture of his family

---

52. See Miller and Hayes, 421-430.

53. Apparently Gedaliah occupied something of a middle position politically that made it possible for him to govern. He is both trusted by the

seems regularly to be a sane, moderate position that is rooted in covenantal tradition and that is not attracted to the more urgent ideologies of its contemporaries. That is, his family is not tempted with the "extremity" of those who would foolishly resist the power of the empire, that is, the ones who in the end evoked the destructive occupation of Babylon. Gedaliah appears to be sober enough to be trusted by Babylon, stable enough to be trusted by his own people.

The political position of Gedaliah is delicate and mediating. He and his compatriots are forced by circumstance to recognize and come to terms with the power of Babylon. The government of Jerusalem has been defeated and has no bargaining maneuverability. In such a circumstance, it is possible on the one hand to continue to be a firebrand of resistance, but such persons are never permitted power by the conquering command. Zealots in such a situation quickly become irrelevant. On the other hand, it is possible to become a "Quisling," who excessively accommodates foreign power for the sake of personal advantage and who, in the process, betrays the identity of his people and earns their scorn. A mediating possibility is difficult but crucial. It is a position of leadership that cooperates with the occupiers, but which is vigilant for the well-being and independence of his people.

It is plausible to assume that Gedaliah occupied, or sought to occupy, this middle ground. He belonged to a family which had not been empire-baiters. We may imagine, moreover, that he was not excessively an accommodationist, but was respected and trusted by the main body of opinion among his people. Of course, much depends on perception. No doubt he was perceived by some, no matter what he did, as a despicable compromiser. Perhaps in the end his is a "no-win position," sooner or later sure to evoke either the hostile, angry sentiments of independence or the harsh, heavy hand of the empire.

These verses portray the initial consolidation of Gedaliah's authority. There is no doubt that he is a creature of the empire

---

Babylonians and capable internally of governing. His sorry fate, however, suggests that he could not win over or cope with his "right wing," which anticipated independence from the empire.

(40:7). In any case, because of his claim to power his contemporaries, especially the military officers, must deal with him, no matter what their sentiment, ambition, or bias may be. Verse 8 tells of the rallying of a number of significant political forces in Judah to Gedaliah. Of these, the first named, Ishmael and Johanan, will be prominent in the narrative to follow.

Gedaliah receives the leading military figures and enunciates his policy (vv. 9-10). This constituency, as will soon be evident, is crucial to his regime, for this can make him or break him. Gedaliah anticipates and assures that the hegemony of Babylon will not be heavy-handed or unbearable. Of course this is no new conviction on his part. It is a long-held assessment held by those who clustered about Jeremiah. Gedaliah begins his statement with an assurance (v. 9). He promises that submission to Babylon will cause well-being. He issues a nicely balanced statement about "as for me" and "as for you" (v. 10). He nicely differentiates functions and responsibilities, "mine" and "yours." Concerning his own position, Gedaliah asserts not that he will represent Babylon to the Jews, but that he will represent the Jews to Babylon. He will be an advocate for his people. He is not Nebuchadnezzar's man, but he is a man for his people and with his people. The statement evidences strength and resolve to be a faithful and independent agent over against the empire which has authorized him. This enunciation hints at the suspicion with which his office must have been greeted.

The acceptance of this risky role as Judea's advocate, however, also requires something of his restless cohorts: "as for you." They are to work and to be productive in order to make the economy work and generate prosperity. It is as though Gedaliah bargains with the military functionaries who can be either his allies or his adversaries. He nicely distinguishes between political and economic functions. He claims the former for himself and will not compromise; he summons his fellows to economic responsibility. His forceful assertion on the one hand warns his listeners away from any political meddling or interference, and on the other hand it reminds them that they have important work to do. Gedaliah's statement is an assertion of policy that neither asks nor receives assent. Gedaliah's main work is the revival of the economy, and for this he needs a committed, productive work force.[54]

Verses 11-12 report on a generally positive response to the governance of Gedaliah. Apparently many people from Jerusalem had evacuated to avoid the coming Babylonian upheaval and were waiting to see what would happen. For them, the designation of Gedaliah by Nebuchadnezzar evokes a positive response, confidence, and willing allegiance. That so many returned meant that they accepted his authority. Moreover, they went to work (v. 12), as he had hoped (v. 10). Two central issues occupied Gedaliah. On the one hand, he had to secure his own authority and public support. That is, he had to demonstrate that he was serious, could be authoritative, and was not an imperial stooge. On the other hand, his political claim signified nothing if the economy did not recover. Gedaliah's approach to legitimacy is moderate and realistic. His intent is to practice good faith in a context where political independence is not a realistic possibility. Jeremiah had anticipated that the people of God must live on terms other than their own. Gedaliah provides the procedures and structures for this possibility. His moderate government was the best option available, though the arrangement must have been disconcerting, even galling, to those who had treasured memories of better days and who entertained ambitious visions not schooled in present reality.

Gedaliah's modest, moderate regime seems to give concrete political embodiment to Jeremiah's expectations. Jeremiah has eschewed both independence and excessive subordination to Babylon. Gedaliah seems to have struck exactly the right balance. Thus his intentions may be understood as prudential and pragmatic. They also conform to Jeremiah's vision and so reflect an indirect vindication of the prophet. It is telling that, after the Babylonians appoint Gedaliah, he is indeed left on his own without imperial

---

54. The enumeration of wine, summer fruit, and oil indicates attention to "money crops." That is, revival of the economy depends upon production of goods that are useful as export. Attention to such money crops speaks against a self-support peasant economy. This suggests that the economic policies of Gedaliah may have been controversial, thought by some to be too beholden to imperial needs and expectations.

interference. The Jews are given a chance on their own to "make it work."

40:13-16 Gedaliah's government was not only provisional; it was also exceedingly tenuous and, as it turned out, short-lived. It had the backing of the Babylonians (v. 7); it also had the visible support of Jeremiah, who now aligned himself with this government that was a creature of the occupying army (v. 6). The government turned out to be untenable, and the backing of Babylon and Jeremiah must have been distinct liabilities in terms of public support in Jerusalem.

The enduring political questions in Judah now surfaced once again, with enormous passion. The recurring options in Jerusalem were either fierce independence or accommodationist submission.[55] The troubles which now surfaced for Gedaliah may have been in part personal, as his personal advancement through imperial support no doubt blocked the careers and ambitions of others. But the troubles are not primarily personal. They are no doubt deeply felt ideological, partisan disagreements. Gedaliah embodies accommodationist policy, as Jeremiah had earlier championed the same policies. While that policy may have appeared prudent and pragmatic to cool heads, to others it no doubt smelled of betrayal, much as General Philippe Petain was regarded in France. From such a perspective, the theological endorsement of Jeremiah would count for little. Interpretation of this text must pay close attention to the political nuances that are beneath the surface of the narrative. The narrative makes clear that biblical faith, including Jeremiah's advocacy, must be understood and practiced in the midst of real and difficult political realities. There was no supernaturalist or transcendentalist perspective which proved that accommodation was the will of God. The concrete specification of God's will is a judgment call made in a situation of political emergency. It is always in such an emergency that a decision must be made about the will of God. Thus it does not surprise us that such a call does not command universal and immediate assent in the community.

---

55. A third troublesome and always available option was alliance with Egypt. That option, however, is not visible in this particular narrative.

Gedaliah receives an intelligence report from his loyal colleague, Johanan (vv. 13-14). The report is that an assassination plot has been instigated against Gedaliah. It is not news to Gedaliah that he has powerful adversaries. No doubt he already knows their names. The Ammonites must have resisted a "Babylonian satellite" as close as Jerusalem, for this is what Gedaliah represents in international politics. That is, what might be workable for Jerusalem may constitute a threat for its neighbors. That Babylon can plant its governor in Jerusalem constitutes an implied threat to Ammonite independence. Ishmael no doubt was also a known adversary to Gedaliah. Perhaps he is only an opportunist. Because he is identified as "of the royal family" (41:1), however, he surely is not only an opportunist, but the embodiment of an alternative political opinion and likely the leader of a rival party. We are not surprised that a member of the deposed royal family would vigorously dissent from accommodationist policy. Both adversaries, Baalis and Ishmael, are known and no doubt were under steady surveillance.

What is new in the report of Johanan is that the specific plot and plan are now uncovered. Johanan, like many intelligence agents, is prepared to take a preemptive strike against the instigators of the plot.[56] Gedaliah, however, demurs.

We do not know why Gedaliah resists Johanan's eagerness to act. The use of the word "false" (40:16), a characteristic word in Jeremiah, suggests that Gedaliah does not believe the report. Perhaps there were too many such rumors of threat, and the governor could not spend his energy responding to such ostensible threats. Or perhaps at a moment of acute and delicate transition, Gedaliah stands for unity and consensus and so does not want to acknowledge division or vulnerability. We may believe that Gedaliah's rejection of the report and refusal to act on it were not romantic. His was more likely a calculated political judgment, one that had enormous implications for the future. Of such judgments, made at great risk, is the story of Israel's public faith constituted.[57]

---

56. See the close parallel in 2 Sam. 3:22-27. As in the case with Joab, here also political assassination is not a disinterested act.

57. The courage of Gedaliah and the political decision to disregard the

41:1-3   The discussion of Johanan's report (40:13-16) is preliminary to the main action in the crisis. Gedaliah is warned, but boldly
adopts a very different strategy. He conducts himself as though he
were above such a threat. Ishmael is a member of the deposed royal
family and apparently a leader of some significance, and so cannot
be excluded from visible attention. Perhaps Ishmael has dynastic
intentions; such ambition required political independence for his
people and had no patience with the accommodationist governor.
Ishmael is in any case a political force with which Gedaliah must
reckon. At Mizpah, Gedaliah's locus of government, there is a
high-level meeting. Gedaliah is engaged in consolidating his power,
seeking allies, and building a consensus which is necessary to his
government. It is not improbable that hard bargaining between rival
factions was anticipated, but the public meal indicates that there was
a prospect either that Ishmael would join in support of the government or at least acknowledge its legitimacy.

Gedaliah, however, completely misread his situation and underestimated the opposition of Ishmael. Both in rejecting the
intelligence report of Johanan and in conducting a public parley
with Ishmael, Gedaliah misread the danger to himself from Ishmael. The narrative portrays Ishmael in the most ruthless and
despicable terms possible. He violated the hospitality of Gedaliah.
He exploited a friendly public gesture from the governor and, in
complete dishonor, committed an act of outrage. Jeremiah 41:3
is at pains to celebrate Gedaliah both for his long, honorable
pedigree and for his legitimacy from Babylon. He is a noble man
who stands in contrast to Ishmael, who is presented as nothing
more than thug, albeit a royal thug. Gedaliah had made a beginning in new governance, but he had no chance. There was still
active (though unrealistic) public opinion that believed Babylonian
power could be thwarted.[58] The same unrealistic judgment which

---

known threat is not unlike the decision of John F. Kennedy to go to Dallas,
where he was murdered. He made the decision on political grounds, with full
knowledge of the danger.

58. In a quite different context and different form, the unrealistic ambition
of Ishmael continues the perspective of Hananiah (Jer. 27–28). In both cases,
the more hopeful option may be rooted in sound, dynastic faith, but it fails
to reckon with the political reality of the empire.

earlier had so troubled Jeremiah now destroyed a responsible accommodationist effort at governance. Thus Gedaliah's brief effort at governance ends in a bloodbath.

41:4-10 Ishmael, however, is not yet finished with his violence. He is an eager, ruthless man and is increasingly a desperate one. Pilgrims from the great northern cities and shrines came to Jerusalem, dressed in mourning clothes.[59] They did not know of the bloodbath committed the day before; they knew only of the destruction of the city. Their visit reflects the continuing power and attraction of Jerusalem, even for northerners who had been cut off from Jerusalem for more than a century. They came with good intentions and in innocence. They knew nothing of Jews killing Jews; they knew only of Babylonian violence against Jerusalem, and they had come to grieve the wound to the city. Their public gesture is an act of bold solidarity with the suffering city. That gesture, however, is ruthlessly mocked, exploited, and dismissed by Ishmael.

The good intentions of the northern pilgrims contrast sharply with Ishmael's violence. He has no reason to fear these visitors, no cause to despise them or injure them. Perhaps they took him by surprise. Perhaps they disrupted his plans or inconvenienced him. Perhaps they were potential informers against him. In any case, their innocent, good intentions contrast with his vile, negative intention. Ishmael deceives them by word as he invites them to meet Gedaliah, whom he has already killed. He deceives them by deed, for he presents himself sharing the grief which they grieve. His deception is only a device to seduce them into the city. Then he kills them. Ishmael's action is almost inexplicable. We are never told what Ishmael is after, but he seemingly will stop at nothing to secure what he wants. Perhaps the narrative offers this report to exemplify the deep disorder present in a society that will not listen.[60]

---

59. This episode may be taken as evidence that the operation of the cult in Jerusalem did not terminate in 587. See Enno Janssen, *Juda in der Exilszeit.* Forschungen zur Religion und Literatur des Alten und Neuen Testaments 69 (Göttingen: Vandenhoeck & Ruprecht, 1956), 46-56 and *passim.*

60. If, as Seitz proposes, the real trouble for Babylon is not the city or its

Ishmael pauses momentarily to receive a bribe from ten of the visitors (41:8). For the sake of their "wheat, barley, oil, and honey," he spares them. He is indeed an unprincipled man. But that pause is only momentary. The narrative is preoccupied with the man's actions, which are deathly. He made dastardly use of a large cistern, one known to the readers of this text. And he filled it! He filled it with corpses. He filled it with the innocent dead. In their death, Ishmael has killed off whatever chance there may have been for some measure of Jewish autonomy from the power of Babylon. For good reason, Ishmael flees. He goes toward his patrons, the Ammonites. There he will be safe. He takes with him a remnant, no doubt as hostages. Ishmael's moment in the narrative is brief and ugly. He completes the devastation wrought by Nebuchadnezzar. It is as though he wants to save Jerusalem from Babylon and will decimate (or destroy) the city in order to save it. His intervention which destroys Jerusalem is the last gasping measure of the old dynastic ideology which Jeremiah had for so long refuted.

41:11-18 Ishmael fled, and Johanan pursued after him. Ishmael's motives are never probed, and we do not learn either what he wanted or what he accomplished. The pursuers catch up with the pursued at the great pool of Gibeon.[61] But they do not apprehend him. Ishmael escapes to the Ammonites. In the perspective of the narrator, Ishmael is thoroughly discredited both by his violence and by his appeal to the Ammonites.

Johanan, with the death of Gedaliah, has now emerged as a leader to counter Ishmael. Johanan is warmly welcomed by the hostages of Ishmael who had been taken against their will. Johanan is perceived as their savior and rescuer (v. 13). He does not eliminate Ishmael, but he does end his moment of terror. The

---

people but the Davidic dynasty, then Ishmael may be an extreme case of the enduring, self-destructive power of the royal ideology which has already provoked the empire and brought destruction upon the city. If that is correct, clearly Ishmael is impervious and will risk yet another imperial intrusion into Jerusalem for the sake of his ideology and his ambition.

61. The parallel should not be pressed too far, but cf. 2 Sam. 2:13 and another political crisis at the pool of Gibeon.

land, however, is in shambles. The political situation is one of chaos. While abruptly stated, it does not surprise us greatly that Johanan proposes to go to Egypt, as far away from Babylon as is possible (v. 17). The Jews expect that Babylon will fiercely retaliate because their appointee, Gedaliah, has been murdered. The Jews then seek safety in the only place they can think of, Egypt.

The narrative proceeds in great detail. What is most to be noticed is that there is no stable political order. Public life is in total disarray. None of the available options is very attractive. Johanan opts for the extreme alternative to Babylon, namely, Egypt. Notice that this chapter is presented as reportage. There is no reference to the prophet or to the God of the prophet. The action of the chapter is an interplay of principle and prudence. It is time for the prophet to intervene yet one more time, reminding us that the public life of Judah cannot be reduced to mere political calculation.

Jeremiah had long since made clear the only workable option for his people. The three dominant figures of this narrative, Gedaliah, Ishmael, and Johanan, embody these policy options: Gedaliah is a Babylonian accommodator, Ishmael is a fierce actor for resistance and independence, and Johanan now opts for Egypt. While flight to Egypt appears to be the most plausible remaining option, Jeremiah, as we shall see, is unwavering in his pro-Babylonian insistence.

JUDAH REFUSES TO LISTEN (42:1–43:7)

The extended narrative which begins in ch. 37 revolves around three themes: (1) the public adjustment of Judah to the new situation after 587 B.C.E., (2) the intrusion of the word of God into public issues through the speech of Jeremiah, and (3) the personal fortunes of Jeremiah. Jeremiah as an identifiable voice in the narrative was most active in chs. 37 and 38, boldly speaking a pro-Babylonian option to the king and the princes. In chs. 39–41, however, Jeremiah is only marginally visible in the text. In 39:11-14; 40:4-6 Jeremiah is treated carefully and respectfully by the Babylonians and casts his lot with the government of

Gedaliah, thereby giving his measure of legitimacy to the new regime. His only other entry in these chapters is in 39:15-18, a remembrance of Ebed-melech, likely functioning as an earnest of "remnant theology" which now emerges in the narrative. As an active voice concerning public policy, Jeremiah is virtually silent in chs. 39–41.

The reportage of chs. 39–41 serves to vindicate the primary witness of the book of Jeremiah: the "Babylonian card" will be played and change all other options. That has turned out to be true. The decisive impingement of Babylon has happened. In its wake have come in sequence Gedaliah, Ishmael, and now Johanan, but none can reorganize the ruins created by Babylon. By the end of ch. 41 the post-587 venture of Gedaliah has failed, and the *de facto* leadership of the community (first Ishmael and then Johanan) seems to have run out of options. It is exactly when the visible leadership runs out of options that Jeremiah is invited back into the narrative (42:1-2). In the formation of the narrative, the centrality of Jeremiah in ch. 42 (after his silence in 40:7–41:18) seems to connect back to 38:17-18, 20-23, where Jeremiah stated his last argument against King Zedekiah. It is now time for the prophet again to state his Yahwistic option, which again seems too costly and is rejected.

After 587 as before 587, Jeremiah is consulted when the community knows nowhere else to turn. After 587 as before 587, Jeremiah makes a response the community does not want to hear and cannot bear. The response of the prophet is not unchanging and fixed. Before 587 his urging is to *submit to Babylon*. After 587 his urging is to *remain in the land of Judah*. Both responses are unpopular and counteract the easier choice. Moreover, even the latter response, *remain in the land,* is tantamount to submission to Babylon, for the territory is under Babylonian control. Thus, even with a changed response, the large vision of the future in this tradition is unchanged.

The long unit of 42:1–43:7 is framed as a narrative by a *request* for guidance (42:1-3, 5-6) and a *rejection* of that guidance (43:1-7). The community asks for guidance but cannot bear the response it receives. Between the request and the rejection is Jeremiah's long oracle of guidance (42:7-22), which is divided at v. 18 into two distinct speeches. This unit is strikingly different from chs. 39–41, which, even where Jeremiah is mentioned, is cast as a direct report on public events. In our present unit, the text contains very little narrative and no report on public events. It consists primarily of speech which follows a sequence of invitation (42:1-6), response (42:7-22), and rejection (43:1-7). The speech, rather than the narrative, permits Jeremiah direct voice in the life of the fearful, desperate Jews. It does not surprise us that it is in the speech that the text is more directly concerned with theological dimensions of Israel's life. This long response of the prophet is in important ways a summation of Jeremianic theology.

42:1-6   Even before our unit begins, we are told that Johanan and his company "intended to go to Egypt" (41:17). From the perspective of the community of Johanan, Egypt is the premise and conclusion of the entire transaction. The consultation with the prophet seems to be preempted by a decision already made. On the face of it, this seems a simple, concrete decision about geography. It immediately becomes clear, however, that in the purview of Jeremiah such a decision is not simply a political option but is fraught with theological gravity and risk. It is odd that the decision seems to have been made in 41:17, yet in 42:1-3 guidance is sought from the prophet.

The peculiar arrangement of 41:17 before 42:1-3 (i.e., the conclusion before the guidance) is a narrative setup for the harsh polemic of the prophet that is to follow. That is, this community is impervious to prophetic counsel and will work its own stubborn way. Perhaps the request of the community is only a ploy, anticipating Jeremiah's quick blessing. Perhaps the request also reflects the bewilderment and confusion of the leadership in a moment of profound chaos. In any case, the turn of the narrative back to Jeremiah (who has not been consulted since Zedekiah did so in ch. 38) is striking. The turn to Jeremiah is abrupt. It is as though consultation with the prophet seems to all persons as the obvious, uncontested thing to do. That clarity, however, simply reflects the perspective of the book of Jeremiah. Outside the prophetic literature, such an act of consultation might seem less than obvious. When people are fleeing for their lives, prophetic consultation does not always happen — except that it will surely happen in this canonically recommended reality. Because all of Jewish life is lived under God's aegis, consultation with the prophet is not only appropriate but indispensable.

The request of the community is abrupt, wholehearted, and enormously serious. It is made by the entire community, "from the least to the greatest." It asks Jeremiah to pray and seek guidance, fully certain that such guidance will be given and can be followed (cf. Deut. 30:11-14). The request is a statement of profound confidence and trust. The speakers now recognize themselves as "this remnant" (Jer. 42:2). The book of Jeremiah is framed to recognize that after 587 the carriers of Jewish faithfulness are a small, vulnerable community. What that small, vulnerable community does matters enormously, for it carries the future of Jewishness. The statement of self-description is most suggestive: "We are left but a *few of many*" (v. 2). The move from "many" (in times past) to "few" (in the present) is decisive for their situation, and it contrasts programmatically with the celebration of the Exodus which asserts "we were few and became many" (cf. Deut. 10:22).

Thus the phrase "few of many" is a code phrase indicating that this community is a reversal or undoing of the Exodus. That is, the phrasing is not a population report, but a recognition that the whole history of deliverance is now in deep jeopardy and is in a process of reversal.

Jeremiah's response to their request is positive and eager (Jer. 42:4). He will pray, and he has no doubt that an answer will be forthcoming. The exchange assumed that prayer is a mode of guidance, and that the prophet is crucial to that process of guidance. In the time before 587 Jeremiah has been explicitly prohibited from prayer, for God was cut off from and uninterested in the destiny of Jerusalem (7:16; 11:14; 14:11-12; 15:1-2). The devastation of 587 seems to have cancelled that prohibition.[62] In

---

62. The change whereby the silenced Jeremiah can again intercede is not unlike the change in Ezekiel, who is reduced to dumbness and with the fall of Jerusalem is once again permitted to speak. On the latter, see Klein, *Ezekiel,* 37-40.

a situation of genuine need and supplication, Jeremiah is free again to exercise his prophetic function of intercession.[63] Jeremiah thus takes their request at face value and agrees to cooperate.

The response of the commanders and the people to the cooperation of Jeremiah is a vow of unconditional obedience (42:5-6), echoing the response Israel previously made to Moses (Exod. 24:3, 7), to Joshua (Josh. 24:21, 24), and to Samuel (1 Sam. 7:4, 6, 8; 12:19). The language of this exchange suggests that this meeting with Jeremiah is not an incidental conversation. Rather, the text casts this meeting as one of the great dramatic moments in the life of Israel that is community-forming.[64] This "remnant" now pledges to be obedient Israel, to live according to the will and purpose of Yahweh, and to heed the word of the prophet. Yahweh is invited to witness its oath and to hold it to the oath.

The language of the oath is formal, formidable, and even exaggerated: "May the LORD be a true and reliable (RSV 'faithful'; *emet wenne'eman*) witness." This meeting is indeed serious business. The pledge is that Israel will hear *(shema'),* no matter what the command of God is, no matter if it is good or evil, pleasing or not pleasing. This radical pledge made to the prophet is a blank check to follow the will of Yahweh, no matter what. It is as though the narrator seizes the opportunity to sketch out what genuine obedience would look like, since the tradition of Jeremiah looks in vain for compelling models in contemporary Jerusalem (cf. Jer. 5:1). In retrospect, it is clear that the purpose of the narrative is to expose a radical model of *dis*obedience. The textual tradition thus envisions a remnant community prepared to obey, committed to torah, responsive to the prophet. This meeting is their "Sinai,"

---

63. For a review of the role of prophet as intercessor, see Samuel E. Balentine, "The Prophet as Intercessor: A Reassessment," *Journal of Biblical Literature* 103 (1984): 161-173. See his references to Burke O. Long and Georg C. Macholz on 169, n. 24.

64. It is impossible to assess this meeting historically. In terms of the textual tradition of Jeremiah and the canonical intent of the text, it is the voice of the prophet and the derivative text that creates the community. That is, the text serves to assert and enhance the authority of the prophet (and the prophetic text) as the way in which faithful Israel is formed.

and they will now go to their wilderness (exile), fully faithful.[65]
That is, the exchange within the text ostensibly reports a full and
ready obedience. But the text as text uses the example of ostensive
obedience in order to demonstrate rank disobedience.

42:7-17   Jeremiah reconvenes the assembly of Israel after ten
days. We are told nothing about Jeremiah's reception of God's
guidance, for the Bible simply takes such a reception for granted
(42:7). There is now convened a formal "assembly," which is not
a private or casual consultation. It is a meeting of all Israel from
the least to the greatest, now being reconstituted after the debacle
of recent events (v. 8).

This speech of Jeremiah is constructed around a series of "if-
then" pronouncements, positive and negative, which affirm that
public policy choices have profound public consequences, for they
are in the end acts of faith and unfaith.[66] The skeletal structure
of the speech consists in three "if-then" statements. First, there is
a positive "if-then" statement in vv. 10-12, matched by a negative
"if-then" statement in vv. 13-15a. That negative statement,
however, is then commented upon in greater detail by a second
negative "if-then" statement in vv. 15b-17. The threefold rhetorical
pattern of protasis and apodosis (vv. 10-12, 13-15a, 15b-17) is
employed to make a clear policy recommendation and to issue a
stern warning. The rhetoric of this speech, in the long tradition
of Moses, Joshua, and Samuel, is a pattern of blessings and curses

---

65. Seitz, "Canonical Shape," helpfully demonstrates how the tradition of
Jeremiah appeals to the wilderness tradition as a type for the exile Israel now
faces. The juxtaposition of Joshua-Caleb and Ebed-melech–Baruch shows how
the same issues are again present at a crisis point when the community faces
the issue of continuity and discontinuity. The abrasive quality of this conversation in 42:1-6 is evident in the reference to "your God" (v. 5) and "our
God" (v. 6).

66. The "if-then" structure of the rhetoric reflects an assumption and
affirmation of a "deeds-structure" notion of the relation of actions and outcomes. On that notion, see Klaus Koch, "Is There a Doctrine of Retribution
in the Old Testament?" in Crenshaw, *Theodicy in the Old Testament*, 57-87.
On the power and problem of such a practice of structure legitimation, see
Walter Brueggemann, "A Shape for Old Testament Theology, I: Structure
Legitimation," *Catholic Biblical Quarterly* 47 (1985): 28-46.

which is determined completely by covenant obedience *(shema')* or disobedience *(lo' shema')*.

Jeremiah first states his positive recommendation, which is God's intention for the remnant. The "if" is terse: "Remain in the land" (v. 10). This is the sum of God's command, expressed with the intensity of an infinitive absolute. This is the key statement of the entire unit, and everything else follows from this decision. The "then" that follows is more extended and exceedingly rich. It consists in four rhetorical patterns, each of which carries extraordinary theological force:

(1) The oracle reverts to the four verbs which seem to govern the book of Jeremiah, "build, break down, plant, pluck up" (cf. 1:10; 18:7-10; 24:6; 31:28). If the remnant remains in the land, Yahweh will implement the two good verbs, "build and plant," and not work devastation. One might have thought the work of "breaking down and plucking up" had already been completed in the Babylonian occupation. But no, more such destructiveness is in purview, unless the remnant stays in the land. The choices of the people can change the resolve of God. Moreover, a decision to remain in the land of the devastation will evoke new life from God. This quite explicit theological reasoning is anticipated in the syllogism of 18:7-10, which asserts that Israel's decisions impinge upon God's intentions. Now that general theological pattern is given quite concrete substance.

(2) God can and will change course, that is, "repent."[67] The "evil which I did to you" refers to the destruction of 587. So quickly God pulls back from that harsh act. Faithful obedience does change God's mind. The anger of that occasion of destruction (587) does not fate Israel forever to judgment (cf. 31:27-38). God now pines to do good for Israel, but God's goodness will require obedient residence in the city. Already here are the seeds of restoration. The destroyed city is immediately the object of God's positive and attentive concern. It is, however, a concern

---

67. On God's capacity for repentance, see Fretheim, *The Suffering of God.* Overtures to Biblical Theology 14 (Philadelphia: Fortress, 1984); and Francis I. Andersen and David Noel Freedman, *Amos.* Anchor Bible 24A (Garden City: Doubleday, 1989), 638-679.

that depends upon Israel's decision to stay present to the crisis. If Israel changes, God will change.

(3) The prophet then delivers a salvation oracle with a twice stated "do not fear."[68] This speech echoes the initial promise made to Jeremiah (1:8, 19; cf. also 30:10-11), which is now transferred from the prophet to the whole community. God will be a decisive force to intervene on Israel's behalf. The rhetoric is more intense than those initial assurances in ch. 1, for in addition to the verb "deliver" *(n-ts-l)* which was previously used, it is seconded by the verb "save" *(y-sh-ʿ)*. God will be an active, intervening agent. In 1:13-15, however, Jeremiah's danger did not come from "the north," but from his compatriots.[69] Thus our oracle forms a counterpart to 1:13-15. Babylon was sent by God, and now God intervenes to protect the community from Babylon. The salvation oracle quite concretely and practically assures exilic Judah that God will prevent Babylon from being the threat it fears.

(4) Finally, in a most remarkable statement, God promises "compassion" for the displaced community (cf. Isa. 54:7-8). Then, dramatically, it is asserted that because Yahweh gives mercy, therefore "he" (i.e., Babylon) will have mercy and "let you remain in your own land." The statement is crucial because it witnesses to the precise convergence of *Yahweh's covenantal resolve* and *Babylon's foreign policy.* It is the mercy of Yahweh which will make Babylon a merciful overlord, who will make living in the land a viable option.[70] The prophet inserts a theological, covenantal dimension into the fearful realities of international politics.

This entire statement is an argument that the remnant must not leave, but must stay in the land and in the city, present to its troubles and open to its future. The exiles, it is argued, have no other future and no other business. Moreover, Yahweh's own commitment to the rehabilitation of land and city is massive and

---

68. On the form in this text, see Conrad, *Fear Not Warrior,* 49-55.

69. In that text there is, to be sure, an enemy and a threat to come from the north. The salvation oracle, however, is to protect the prophet from his own people, who react against his word of threat and judgment.

70. On the interplay of mercy and Babylon, see Brueggemann, "At the Mercy of Babylon."

overriding. The oracle gives every thinkable theological warrant for not running away from the trouble. God wants God's people present both to the trouble and to the possibility.

The prophetic oracle proceeds like a syllogistic argument. Finally the negative "if-then" is voiced, stating the costs and risks of leaving the land (Jer. 42:13-15a). The "if" equates not staying with not listening *(shemaʿ)*. That is, departing, especially to Egypt, constitutes disobedience to Yahweh. The seduction of Egypt is the assumption that such "flight" is an escape from punishment, threat, and curse. Egypt appears to this desperate, frightened community to be a peaceable place, where there is no threat of war and no famine. Egypt regularly offers itself as an escapist alternative, both from the troubles of the land and from the dangers of Babylon.

The "then" that follows from this negative "if" is rhetorically complex. The "then" is stated in v. 15 but is further developed into an additional, albeit derivative, "if-then" formulation. The derivative "if" of v. 15 is simply a reiteration of v. 13. The "then" of vv. 16-17 in fact completes the "if" of v. 13. That is, the protasis is a proposal to escape the curse and the apodosis is an assertion that Egypt is saturated with deathliness. When the remnant flees to Egypt, it will find death waiting, in three stylized forms: sword, famine, pestilence. In Israel's long theological tradition, Egypt is a place from which to escape, not a place to which to flee. To go to Egypt now will be to rush to receive deathly curses. An inclination to go to Egypt as an escape from deathliness is a grievous misreading of social reality. While the "then" clause is stated in stylized and formal theological language, the argument is that Egypt is not a hospitable place; to go there is to go from the frying pan into the fire. To go to Egypt is to act out a death wish, for it is a sure way to guarantee the complete eradication of the Jewish community.

The threefold pattern of "if-then" argument is simple, forceful, and direct:

positive:	*if:*	remain in the land
	then:	mercy, life, and well-being.
negative:	*if:*	we will not remain

	then:	hear,
negative:	*if:*	you enter Egypt
	then:	death!

Jeremiah has previously stated simple, unambiguous options to
Zedekiah (38:17-18, 20-23). Now, in a quite different context, a
parallel pronouncement is given. The proclamation is thoroughly
theonomous: God wills a concrete community policy. The proclamation is cast in conventional covenantal formulations of blessing and curse. This formalistic theology is also a thoughtful "judgment call" about concrete sociopolitical reality. The land,
dangerous and devastated as it is, is Israel's destiny. Anything else
will lead to death. Israel must learn to live in this land, even
though Babylon looms large and threateningly. The fidelity of
Yahweh counters the Babylonian danger, as Yahweh will not
counter the deathliness of Egypt.

42:18-22 As is characteristic of stern covenantal (Deuteronomic) theology, the negative warning of the prophet receives
much more extensive coverage than the positive invitation. In
42:7-17, vv. 10-12 voice a positive invitation, whereas all of vv.
13-17 is negative warning. In the second speech (vv. 18-22) there
is no positive invitation at all, but only severe warning.[71] A parallel
is drawn in this second speech between Jerusalem already destroyed and the remnant now under threat of like destruction.
(The preaching of ch. 7 had earlier made the same argument,
drawing a parallel between already-destroyed Shiloh and about-
to-be-destroyed Jerusalem. Only now, Jerusalem is not in the role
of the about-to-be-destroyed, but embodies what has already been
destroyed. Thus the parallelism is even more poignant here than
in ch. 7.) The appeal to Jerusalem destroyed and the warning
against further destruction constitute the claim that God will not
be mocked and disobeyed. The flight to Egypt, which seemed like

---

71. The disproportion of the length of the curse in relation to the blessing
is not unlike the disproportion in length in the recitals of Lev. 26; Deut. 28,
where the curse passage is so much longer than the blessing statement. Our
passage has important parallels to the curse recital of Deut. 28.

an escape, is in fact a sure death sentence. The sequence of the curse is not unlike the formal recital of Deut. 28:37. The remnant community, when it disobeys, will become an object of scorn and derision, utterly humiliated. The outcome of the anger of God finally is this: "You shall see this place no more" (Jer. 42:18). No doubt the remnant community, any remnant community, imagines its displacement is temporary; there will come a time, sooner or later, when there will be a return to the homeland.[72] The prophetic oracle rejects such a hope. This remnant, if it leaves the land, will never come back. The present moment is the only chance for life in the land; if that chance is forfeited, there will be no other chance.

In v. 19 the verdict of the prophet escalates covenantal rhetoric as much as is imaginable. It is as though the prophet said, "A new commandment I give to you." This is a new command, cast in the characteristic language of commandment: "Thou shalt not go into Egypt."[73] This is as strong and unambiguous as the prophet can be. It is a remarkably concrete statement and leaves nothing to the imagination. The conclusion is consistent with the earlier advocacy of the book of Jeremiah, though the issue is somewhat reconfigured. The earlier command had been "Do not resist Babylon." The command against going to Egypt in fact serves the same social policy and is another version of the same perspective. Not going to Egypt inevitably means submission to Babylon and to its occupying force.

The theological claim of this prophetic assertion is enormously important. It affirms (1) that new commandments are given; (2) they are given through prophetic authority, the voice of newness, even when the command is not rooted in old tradition; and (3) the new command concerns concrete issues of public policy

---

72. The imagination and therefore expectation of an imminent return to the homeland is, I suspect, inevitable among exiles. This is certainly the case with contemporary communities of exile, including deposed monarchies and communities of refugees.

73. The negative, to be sure, is *'al*, bespeaking an immediate provision, and not *lo'*, which would suggest a permanent prohibition. That is, the prohibition is something less than an abiding command. On the two negative particles, however, see Gerstenberger, *Wesen and Herkunft*, 50-54 and *passim*.

in the midst of public crisis. The prophet reminds the listeners that they have promised allegiance to his teaching. Now they are reneging. The danger is double. It is wrong to go to Egypt. It is wrong to vow to listen to the prophet and then to disobey. On both counts, this remnant community has placed itself in profound jeopardy.

The final verses of this speech voice a clear prophetic lawsuit (vv. 21-22). The indictment is that the community did not *shema'*. The indictment is sweeping and comprehensive. Israel's refusal to listen is massive and systemic. It pertains to everything the prophetic tradition has ever uttered. The sentence is the standard list of covenant curses. The remnant is under death sentence for its policy decision. It has made the wrong historical decision and now lives under an inescapable death sentence. Death by sword, famine, and pestilence is the predictable outcome of enemy occupation. These curses are caused, however, by not listening.

43:1-7   The negative rhetoric of Jeremiah in 42:13-22 has prepared us for the outcome of this confrontation. We are led by Jeremiah's indictment to anticipate a gross act of disobedience, for the rhetoric clearly expects such a negative response. And that is what we find in the concluding section of the narrative (43:1-7). The prophetic oracle had been so earnestly sought and devoutly yearned for by the fugitive community (42:1-6). The response made to the prophetic oracle by the community, however, is immediate, total, belligerent rejection (43:1-7). One wonders: Did the remnant think it would receive a different oracle? Did it imagine Jeremiah would not reverse course and become oddly and capriciously anti-Babylonian? If we stay inside the text, which is clear and uncompromising, we have the simple, predictable process whereby the prophet condemns this errant remnant community.

We may, however, step outside the text and ask about the intended sociopolitical function of the text. It becomes plausible that the voice of Jeremiah in this text is in fact the voice of the Babylonian community of exiles, in deep dispute with its counterpart, the Egyptian community of exile.[74] The dispute in the

---

74. The sweeping claim of the narrative is that the land was completely

midst of the Exile is not between simply prophet and people (as the text ostensibly has it), but between two communities who vie for legitimacy as the true carrier of the Jewish tradition. That is, the text is a witness and party to a conflict about legitimacy. Clearly the figure of Jeremiah has become a mouthpiece for the community of Babylonian exiles, which seeks to assert its own exclusive legitimacy and the corresponding illegitimacy of every rival community. The canonizing process has clearly settled the matter of legitimacy in favor of the Babylonian community.[75] The interplay of *vested interest* and *theological affirmation* is both evident and unavoidable. The text is not disinterested, but it operates on the conviction that the intent of God and the interest of this community of Babylonian exiles do indeed converge.

The response of Jeremiah (and the community for which he speaks) to the Egyptian community of exiles, therefore, is predictable. The text loses no time in labelling the adversaries of Jeremiah. They are "insolent men," that is, they presume on their own to know better about what to do (v. 2). They set themselves against the authority of God (or Jeremiah) which is given to us as canonical.

Jeremiah has with due solemnity announced the will of God in the form of a command: "Do not go to Egypt" (42:19). There is no room in the command for hermeneutical playfulness. It will not do to argue about the meaning of such a command. The only way to counter such a command is to reject it. It must be dismissed wholesale. That is what the Egyptian community does. It labels the command "a lie" *(sh-q-r)*. It rejects the notion that Yahweh would give such a command. The use of the term "false" *(sh-q-r)* in this way is remarkable. Characteristically, it is Jeremiah who labels other opinions as "false" (cf. 23:14; 27:10; 28:15; 29:21).

---

emptied. "All the people . . . all the remnant of Judah" went to Egypt. The ideological character of the narrative asserts that there was no third alternative and forces this simple, sharp either/or. Either one succumbed or one fled with this party to Egypt.

75. Clearly the canonizing process is a political process: in this case it represents achievement and triumph for the community of Babylonian Jews. To say that the process is political does not in principle deny that the final shape is theologically faithful. Theological faithfulness and political interest are not by definition mutually exclusive.

Now the word is turned back on Jeremiah, and he is the one who is dismissed as a fraud. We note, of course, that there is no objective ground by which to adjudicate this dispute.[76]

In severe fashion, Jeremiah's earlier controversy with "false prophets" is now turned against him. Of Jeremiah himself and therefore the exilic community for which he speaks, this recalcitrant group led by Johanan can have God say to Jeremiah, as Jeremiah earlier said himself:

> I did not send the prophets,
> yet they ran;
>
> I did not speak to them,
> yet they prophesied. (23:21)

From the perspective of the Egyptian remnant, the verdict against going to Egypt is not God's word, but is the self-serving ideology of a countercommunity for which the prophet has no transcendent authority. Of course! How could it be otherwise? Each side in this deep conflict argues that the other side is acting autonomously and claiming its own perspective as God's will. We have no way to adjudicate these claims (as they did not), except to note the canonical outcome of the dispute. In the canonical outcome of this text, the Babylonian opinion is accepted as God's truth.

In a desperate attempt to establish "the lie," 43:3 makes an unexpected accusation. It is as though Jeremiah himself is too powerfully situated to attack successfully, and therefore the attack is turned on Baruch. This is a stunning maneuver on the part of Jeremiah's adversaries, though perhaps if we knew more we would understand better. All we know is that Baruch is Jeremiah's faithful colleague who shared in the risks of his vocation. We have had no evidence heretofore that Baruch, beyond his loyalty to Jeremiah, represents a political or ideologically partisan position. Indeed, we would not even know that Baruch is a known political figure. This reference suggests to us that Baruch, and therefore the entire productive process of the book of Jeremiah, is not an

---

76. See Crenshaw, *Prophetic Conflict,* 48-61.

innocent enterprise but is an ideological assertion that champions some positions and counters others.[77]

We may make no claim that Jeremiah's (and Baruch's) theological position is less than reputable and faithful. That theological position, however, if it has any significance at all, inevitably takes sides on public questions. That is, the book of Jeremiah is not neutral in the great contested issues of the day. In the circumstance of this text, it was impossible to speak of God's will among the exiles without in the same moment taking sides on the conflict among exilic communities and therefore recognizing that no claim is politically disinterested. Thus while the accusation in v. 3 may be overstated and/or gratuitous, it is surely not unfounded. Baruch and the pro-Babylonian party not only stood against the Egyptian remnant, but were also decisive in the formation of the book of Jeremiah and in its canonizing powers. This is not an argument that they were simply political operatives; it is rather to recognize the inescapable fact that interpretive questions (i.e., questions of God's will and questions of canonization) are always set in the midst of and intimately connected to difficult public issues. That is how the Bible came to be and where it came from. Johanan and the others of the Egyptian remnant understood well the process. Since they are losers and outsiders to the canonical verdict, they do what they can to discredit both the process and the outcome. As a last effort, they employ one of Jeremiah's best words in order to critique ideology. They label the entire position of the Jeremiah-Baruch community as "false" *(sh-q-r)*. In that utterance, the Egyptian remnant dismisses the entire canonical process of Jeremiah and disengages itself from the powerful legitimating advocacy of the Babylonian community of exiles.

The argument of Johanan in vv. 2-3 is situated in the canonical text, however, to refute the charges made against Jeremiah. The speech of the Egyptian remnant is sandwiched in v. 2 by the label "insolent" and in v. 4 by "they did not listen/obey." The Egyptian remnant refused to submit to what was becoming a canonical judgment.

---

77. That ideological reality is evidently pro-Babylonian; moreover, it seems linked to the great scribal families, of which Baruch is a representative member.

Acting against the word of the prophet, the community led by Johanan went to Egypt (vv. 5-7). They themselves went, with considerable resolve. They also took all those who had been exiled and had returned. They took all those who remained under the regime of Gedaliah. They took the entire population! Astonishingly, they also took Jeremiah! And they took Baruch! The report ends in indignation and sadness (v. 7). We do not know why they took Jeremiah. It is sometimes said that they did so to protect the prophet, but his life was not in any danger in Jerusalem. Perhaps Jeremiah and Baruch are taken as hostages against the dangers from the pro-Babylonian party. Surely Jeremiah and Baruch must have been taken against their will. The Egyptian company forced Jeremiah and Baruch to act and to live exactly against their own deep conviction. There must be powerful irony in this last act. Jeremiah, all through the book, has been "over against" some dominant ideology (cf. 1:18). He has been powerless in the face of dominant ideology. He has been endlessly rejected and in jeopardy. And now, at the end, even as he is vindicated by the outcome of events in Jerusalem, he is once more abused, rejected, dishonored, and powerless. He is, so the text says, utterly defeated, certainly not delivered and protected as had been promised him at the outset (1:8, 19).

The text adds its terrible verdict: "They did not listen!" (43:7). They imagined they were autonomous. Even when they had sworn to listen to the prophet, they did not. In marginality as in power, in jeopardy as in strength, Jeremiah's constituency always and characteristically resisted his word. The text has no doubt that in its failure to heed Jeremiah the remnant failed to heed Yahweh. And "not listening" can only lead to death.

"They arrived at Tahpanhes" (v. 7)! Of course they did. That is where they had been headed. That is where they were resolved to go. That is where they wanted to go, even against the counsel of the prophet. That is where they went to be "out of reach" of the Babylonians. The culmination of this confrontation is indeed ironic. Johanan and his companions imagined they had escaped the threat. Jeremiah had made clear that they had chosen poorly. In pursuit of life, they had chosen death (42:22). According to the prophet, they were closed off forever to the homeland. They had, on such a reading, no future. They ended up where the story of Israel had begun, back in Egypt, back in a bondage they misread as freedom.

No doubt the text intends to report geographical specificity. It names the place of their arrival. Israel, however, can never read such geography without attending to the historical drama that surrounds the geography and works through it. In such a dramatic reading, the end has come. Johanan has opted out of Yahweh's saving drama. The scenario or rescue that began with Moses in this pitiful moment ends in exhaustion, failure, defeat, and despair. Jeremiah at the end, like Moses at the beginning, had labored mightily to preserve another option for his people.[78] For all his fidelity, however, Jeremiah is defeated by the power of a false reading of reality which he could not finally counter. The end result is not only a defeat for Jeremiah. It is an awesome defeat for the God whose work has begun in an escape from Egypt. Defeat for the prophet and for God all pivots on "not listening." And the end of not listening is death!

JEREMIAH IN EGYPT (43:8-13)

The community led by Johanan ended in Egypt (Tahpanhes) against the strong counsel of the prophet. Jeremiah himself arrived with them, against his will and against his perception of the will of Yahweh. In 43:8-13; 44:1ff. Jeremiah repeatedly rebukes the community of Jews in Tahpanhes for what he perceives as its utter defiance of the purposes of Yahweh. According to Jeremiah, continued presence in Jerusalem under the hegemony of Babylon is Yahweh's intention for the Jews, which this community has blatantly defied. Our present text is organized as a symbolic act (43:8-9) and an oracle occasioned by the symbolic act (vv. 10-13).

43:8-9 This report of a symbolic act is not unlike Jeremiah's earlier actions concerning a broken pot (19:1-13), an iron yoke

---

78. See Richard E. Friedman, "From Egypt to Egypt: Dtr[1] and Dtr[2]," in *Traditions in Transformation.* Festschrift Frank M. Cross, ed. Baruch Halpern and Jon D. Levenson (Winona Lake: Eisenbrauns, 1981), 189-192.

(27:2), and especially a hidden loincloth (13:1-7). This act is like the latter act, in that it consists in hiding something that has no immediate power or significance but which is left as a sign and gesture, the power and significance of which will emerge only later. It is not helpful, as some interpreters do, to regard such acts as "magic," as though they could only be committed or only matter to a primitive, precritical mind. Such a reading of a symbolic act reflects a kind of positivism which is unaware of the strange power exercised by such acts. It is more helpful, in taking the text seriously, to see the act as a poetic, sacramental gesture.[79] Such a gesture makes an assault on presently construed reality, and stakes out a power-laden expectation for the future that works in the imagination of the observing community. It is the kind of gesture that is characteristically committed by communities of marginality and oppression. Such communities possess no conventional form of power and must rely on sacramental gestures as modes of power which the dominant power cannot resist. Such gestures often take on enormous social power and significance, enough to reshape the community.

In this sacramental gesture, the prophet places large stones underneath the mortar pavement of Pharaoh's palace. In doing so, the prophet dramatically "undermines" the palace, the throne, and the authority of Pharaoh. What is "underneath" Pharaoh — more basic, more reliable than Pharaoh's throne — works to destabilize and threaten the perceived absoluteness of Pharaoh and his governance.

43:10-13 The gesture itself could admit of other significance than "undermining." It is the interpretive oracle that gives the act its subversive thrust. The oracle depends upon the stones for its concrete poignancy; the stones depend upon the oracle to gain this special significance. The commentary on the symbolic act is

---

79. The reported action must be accepted as given in this narrative account. That is, it is not useful or possible to determine the "historicity" of the event. The textual report may be simply a literary presentation, but that does not detract from the cruciality of the event in bringing this part of the Jeremiah tradition to closure.

in the mouth of Yahweh: "Behold, I." The "I" of Yahweh becomes the basis and premise for all that follows. In this extended oracle, Yahweh enacts only two verbs: "I will send, I will take." The object of those verbs is Nebuchadnezzar, who is identified in two ominous ways. Nebuchadnezzar is "king of Babylon" and "my servant." Nebuchadnezzar is the carrier of imperial might and authority, and is the embodiment of Yahweh's resolve; *imperial might* and the *resolve of Yahweh* converge. The utterance of the twofold identity on the one hand threatens the political claims of Egypt. On the other hand, the utterance jeopardizes the religious legitimacy of the empire which appeals to Egyptian gods. Thus the twofold title for Nebuchadnezzar is an act both of political critique and of theological subversion.

It is a daring act to utter the name of Nebuchadnezzar in the throne room of Pharaoh. The mere utterance of this awesome name already deabsolutizes Pharaoh, for there is now another, more powerful name in the presence of which Pharaoh must exist. Nebuchadnezzar's primal act, according to the oracle, is to engage the stones of the symbolic act. The hidden stones, now brought into public play, are the base (and warrant) for Nebuchadnezzar's throne which is now to be established in Egypt. The throne of Nebuchadnezzar does not belong in Egypt and has no right to be there. The prophet, however, has provided a place to put the throne, a place not borrowed from Pharaoh, but newly formed by prophetic authority and prophetic speech. Thus the prophetic act (43:9) makes the political act of Nebuchadnezzar possible (v. 10).

The hidden stones are the base for the throne of Nebuchadnezzar, and they have been put there by the prophet. That is, the prophet has symbolically created the "place" for this odd throne. The stones are hidden as they wait for a revolution in power. They are as hidden as is Nebuchadnezzar's promised and inchoate power. But what is hidden will be revealed, to the great cost of the pharaoh. What is hidden cannot be stopped. Nebuchadnezzar will come here to power.[80] His power will be public, visible,

---

80. On the historical ground for this alleged episode, see John Bright, *A History of Israel*, 3rd ed. (Philadelphia: Westminster and London: SCM, 1981), 351-52.

magnificent, expansive, embodied in a spreading "royal canopy." The canopy will be a sign of awesome royal power which must be protected. Nebuchadnezzar will establish a magnificent presence, in the very throne room of Pharaoh!

Then follows a series of harsh verbs, specifying how this new rule will be conducted. Nebuchadnezzar will "ravage" (*nkh;* RSV "smite") the land of Egypt. The verb is the same as that used with the old plagues of Moses (Exod. 3:20; 7:25; 9:15; 12:13; Ps. 136:10). The land of Pharaoh will be visited with a severe threat, as it was in the beginning of Israel's life, when the Egyptian government was confronted by a power it could not resist. Nebuchadnezzar will come and place the empire of Egypt under curse, the curses most threatening in Israel's rhetoric (cf. Jer. 15:2), the curses that come with an invading army: pestilence, captivity, sword. Egypt has always imagined itself protected, isolated, and immune to danger (cf. Ezek. 29:3). It is so no longer. The power of death will have its intrusive way in the empire, as it did with Moses (cf. Exod. 11:4-6).

Nebuchadnezzar will carry out a complete devastation of the religious symbols of Egypt, the symbols of legitimacy, the signs of ideology, the emblems that maintain the claims of the imperial order. Fire will burn the temples where the symbolic power of the empire is housed. The gods of the empire will be confiscated, shown to be not only vulnerable but finally powerless. Nebuchadnezzar will possess the Egyptian gods; that is, he will possess their power and authority to govern. Moreover, he will "delouse" the land, in the way a shepherd shakes out his coat.[81] A shepherd, living very close to the sheep, may get fleas and vermin, and the coat must be shaken out. So Nebuchadnezzar will shake out the vermin of Egypt, which may mean both the gods of the empire and its enormous wealth. The imagery thus denigrates what Egypt values, dismissing it as "lice," and it places the denigrated wealth and gods of Egypt under threat. Nebuchadnezzar will destroy ("break, burn") all the imperial symbols of power and authority. This recital of verbs of violence and destruction is not unlike the command of Deut. 12:1-3, in which Moses commands Israel to

---

81. On this rendering, see Holladay, *Jeremiah 2*, 302-3.

destroy all religious symbols of Canaan that seduce Israel and
resist Yahweh. In a parallel way, Nebuchadnezzar will break all
the symbolization which supports Egyptian power, in order that
his own power may prevail.

Thus the act (Jer. 43:8-9) and the oracle (vv. 10-13) open
Egypt to the threat of Nebuchadnezzar. It is worth noting that
nowhere in this unit are the Jewish fugitives mentioned. They are
not on the horizon of this oracle. The larger threat against Egypt,
however, does indeed touch the Jewish community in Egypt. On
the one hand, the oracle asserts that Egypt is no safe place to
which to flee. It is a place of deep danger, and the Jews with
Johanan have gone from the frying pan into the fire (cf. Amos
5:19). On the other hand, the oracle asserts that there is no place
in which to hide from Babylon. Thus the Babylonian accent of
the Jeremiah tradition persists until the end. It reaches into the
most unlikely place; Egypt, in geopolitical terms, is the furthest
extreme from Babylonian power. As the Psalmist cannot finally
escape from God (Ps. 139:7-12; cf. Amos 9:2-4), so the Jews
cannot finally escape Nebuchadnezzar, who is "my servant."

In the end, this oracle is one more reiteration of a consistent
claim of the Jeremiah tradition. Because Yahweh governs, Jews
must live in a Babylonian world. This assertion of *Babylon over
Egypt* is an anticipation of the first of the Oracles against the
Nations in Jer. 46:1-28. In that long poem, Egyptian power is
broken by Yahweh because of Egypt's inordinate arrogance. In
the prose commentary of 46:2, 13, 25-26 that Yahwistic threat is
embodied in Nebuchadnezzar and the Babylonians. The mistake
of the Egyptian community of Jews is that they thought they
could have Yahweh without Babylon. This text, like much of
Jeremiah, insists that Yahweh is regularly and inescapably accompanied by Babylon. The fugitives have completely miscalculated.
They stand under the threat made against the Egyptians, for it is
with Egypt that they have placed their misinformed trust.

JEREMIAH'S LAST KNOWN WORDS (44:1-30)

The narrative account of Jeremiah's life ends in 43:7 with the
arrival of the Johanan community in Tahpanhes. The so-called

"Baruch document" concludes with three oracles (43:8-13; 44:1-30; 45:1-5). In these oracles there is no more narrative account, only a voice. The three oracles are summary theological statements, as though the shapers of the canonical book want to have one last chance to make their powerful, partisan statements of advocacy.

The most extended, elaborate, and interesting of these concluding statements is 44:1-30. It is divided into three statements by Jeremiah (vv. 1-14, 20-23, 24-30), with one "answer" given to the prophet by his Egyptian adversaries (vv. 15-19). This material is aimed, in the first instance, at the Egyptian community whom it purports to address.[82] It has a wider interest, however, because it makes a more general theological point. Because the material makes a general theological point, it may indeed be that the ostensive answer to the prophet (vv. 15-19) is in fact not an answer but a deliberate foil designed to serve the larger argument. In general, the point of this extended discussion is that Israel must be committed *only to Yahweh*.[83] Any compromise of this singular loyalty is unacceptable and is sure to bring trouble and death.

44:1-14 This section makes an argument that assumes a world of cause-and-effect payoffs governed by Yahweh. It is filled with conventional covenantal language which affirms that "evils" committed against Yahweh will produce "evils" wrought by Yahweh.[84]

---

82. To state the matter this way means that the historical dimension of the reported oracle is bracketed out. Our concern is with the canonical placement of the oracle and the canonical function of the oracle as a form of theological advocacy and instruction. Its canonical placement and function focus attention on its enduring assertion and not its meaning for the first alleged listeners.

83. The "only Yahweh" theological position is powerfully articulated in the tradition of Deuteronomy and in the part of the book of Jeremiah governed by that theology. It likely is rooted in the role and memory of Moses in the community, and has not only theological but also socioeconomic politcal implications. Robert M. Polzin, *Moses and the Deuteronomist* (New York: Seabury, 1980), has explored some of the interpretive issues involved in the "only Yahweh" theology.

84. The term "evil" *(ra')* is variously rendered in the NRSV as "disaster" and "wickedness." Such varied translations are unfortunate, because they

The statement appeals to recent judgments enacted by Yahweh against Jerusalem and Judah as a didactic example and warning for the Egyptian community of Jews.

The basic argument of the oracle is succinctly stated in vv. 2-3, in a conventional lawsuit pattern. The sentence implemented by Yahweh is "evil" (NRSV "disaster") worked against Jerusalem and the cities of Judah, that is, the destruction wrought through the Babylonian invasion (v. 2). (Note well, the Babylonians are not mentioned.) The indictment against Judah which caused the destruction is the "evil" (RSV "wickedness") committed by Judah, which is essentially the violation of the First Commandment (v. 3). That is, loyalty to Yahweh has not been singular and unambiguous. Such divided loyalty has caused the failure of Jerusalem.

This tight syllogism, reflective of a morally rigorous notion of historical reality under Yahweh's governance (vv. 2-3), is momentarily modified in vv. 4-5 by the standard mitigating factor of prophetic theology.[85] Though vv. 2-3 present a closed and compelling case, in fact Yahweh has been gracious over a long period by sending prophets who warn Israel and seek to provoke repentance.[86] (This is the intent of Jeremiah, according to Jer. 7:4-7; 26:3; 36:3.) That is, the prophets are not a threat against Israel, not a negative force, but are God's gracious gift through which repentance and rescue might occur (44:4). The prophets, however, in fact make no effective difference in the future of Israel, because Israel characteristically will not listen (v. 5). Indeed, "not listening" is a foundational attitude of Israel. The outcome of v. 6 is the same as in v. 2, a massive judgment wrought by God, who will brook no rival and who will act against those who engage a rival.

---

destroy the rhetorical effect of matching the offense with the punishment. On the close and intentional connection between offense and punishment, see Patrick D. Miller, Jr., *Sin and Judgment in the Prophets*. In this passage, the correlation is evident in vv. 2-3.

85. Cf. 2 Kgs. 17:13-14; Zech. 1:3-6.

86. The Deuteronomic assumption reflected here is that there was an intentional, identifiable series of prophets all with the same charge. This assumption is rooted in Deut. 18:9-22 and comes to its culmination in the Deuteronomic casting of Jeremiah. Cf. Wilson, 156-252.

Thus vv. 2-6 are built around very conventional themes, and are arranged in chiastic fashion:

a God does "evil" (v. 2)
   b Israel disobeys (v. 3)
      c God sends prophets to rescue (v. 4)
   b′ Israel refuses and does "evil" (v. 5)
a′ God works destruction (v. 6).

The prophets constitute God's "second effort" to save, but to no avail. This argument in vv. 2-6 is a reflection on the past. It is not an assault on Jerusalem, but reflects on a judgment that has already been implemented and that is well known among the Jews in Egypt here addressed.

Now the text ends its review of Jerusalem's destiny and focuses on the present implied audience in Egypt: "And now" (*we'attah*, v. 7). The Egyptian community is invited to order its present life differently because of this review of the past. While the shift of v. 7 leads us to expect an imperative, in fact the tone of vv. 7-9 is accusatory. The Hebrew poses an accusatory question in vv. 7 and 9, while the two elements rendered as questions by the RSV in v. 8 properly reflect the tone of the whole. Thus four questions are asked: Why? Why? Will you? Have you? All of the questions imply that the addressed community is indeed doing "evil," much like the earlier community in Jerusalem. Moreover, this "evil" will lead to being "cut off," that is, excommunicated and declared illegitimate. We likely hear in this threat the strident voice either of the community of exiled Jews in Babylon, which regards all other Jews as less than adequate, or the community of Jews who remained in Jerusalem, which regarded Egyptian Jews as outside the pale. The cause of illegitimacy is attentiveness in the Egyptian community of Jews to other gods which were indeed attractive and which led to a compromise of "pure Yahwism," sponsored by the accusing party. In effect, this community of Jews in Egypt had learned nothing and has refused to change, thus rejecting the torah (v. 10).[87] Thus what purports to be a probe and invitation

---

87. The concrete data that the Egyptian community of Jews broke the

by the prophet is, in the end, a severe condemnation, with the verdict rendered in v. 10.

The verdict in v. 10 is now given a full and exceedingly harsh response in vv. 11-14. God says, "I will set my face" (v. 11). God is utterly resolved to bring "evil" on this community. The reference is to "all Judah," but that seems in this context to refer only to all those who did not yield to Babylon but opted for Egypt. For that community, according to this text, there are no longer any options, no choices, no alternatives, no escape. The term twice rendered "perish" (*tmm;* RSV "be consumed") means "completed." That is, the community will be "totalled," with nothing left, nothing salvageable. The totality of destruction will be accomplished by sword, famine, and pestilence. The reiteration three times of "sword" and "famine" may indicate redactional activity. More likely it suggests the passion of the verdict. The outcome will be a community which is an utter humiliation. In v. 13 the text asserts a historical analogy, not unlike vv. 2-9: as with Jerusalem in the past (vv. 2-6), so with Egypt in the present (vv. 7-9). What Yahweh has done in the recent past that everyone can already see, now Yahweh will again do here. None will escape . . . except a few fugitives. If the community is a rescued remnant as it thought itself to be, now there will be only a remnant of a remnant, survivors who are not of any value (cf. a like figure in Amos 3:12).

44:15-19   The prophetic oracle receives a defiant answer from the community. This may be a genuine answer, and if it is, it is a very bold response to the prophet. But because the answer is so recalcitrant, it may rather be a response placed in the mouth of the Egyptian community by the prophetic tradition.[88] That is,

---

torah is presumably offered in evidence of the Elephantine community; cf. Miller and Hayes, 434-36. The theological verdict of the text may follow such evidence. It is nonetheless at the same time a highly polemical, partisan verdict made by a rival community.

88. On the practice of placing a quote in the mouth of an opponent, see Hans Walter Wolff, "Das Zitat im Prophetenspruch," *Gesammelte Studien zum Alten Testament.* Theologische Bücherei 22 (Munich: Kaiser, 1964), 36-129. Such a device often creates an adversarial position against which the prophet can then speak.

such resistance in action by the opponents of the Jeremiah tradition is credible. Such determined resistance in actual speech, however, is more difficult to imagine, because one would expect at least a surface effort at compromise. This resistant response either reflects a very hard-nosed community, prepared to challenge the prophet, or it is a device by the framers of the text to make the community of Egyptian Jews appear as ignoble as possible. In this answer (either a serious one or a contrived one to thicken the dispute) there is no signal of accommodation to the prophetic word. From the perspective of the Jeremiah community, this response is resistant, arrogant, and death-choosing. The community is portrayed as completely and militantly resistant to the prophetic program of "Yahweh alone."

This community of response blatantly and defiantly answers, "We will not listen" (Jer. 44:16). That statement constitutes a rejection of Jeremianic theology. The book of Jeremiah (especially its prose elements) has endlessly accused the community of "not listening," and now here is an explicit, frontal refusal, without embarrassment or shame or any mitigating factor. The alternative to "listening" (i.e., keeping the torah) is to keep faith with alternative gods, in this case with "the queen of heaven."

With this defiant assertion, the answering community now makes a programmatic theological defense of its religious commitment. The reason for holding to this alternative faith is simple: It works (v. 17)! The queen of heaven delivers the goods. The worship of this god has led to "peace and prosperity." Negatively, the neglect of the worship of this god has led to the loss of well-being (v. 18). The point seems irrefutable. It is the argument that every religion seeks to make, that a god is judged by the gifts that are given. On its own terms, the argument is unanswerable.

44:20-23 Jeremiah will nonetheless answer. His answer does not engage the argument just offered, for one cannot challenge an argument made on those premises. Instead, perhaps wisely, perhaps of necessity, Jeremiah ignores the assertion of his opponents and simply restates his own Yahwistic, covenantal, prophetic argument. The oracle accepts the analysis just made by his

197

opponents, but turns the argument on its head and draws an antithetical conclusion.

The offering made to other gods does indeed matter decisively for the community, as the opponents have asserted. These offerings are not, however, causes of well-being. They are rather causes of covenantal curse. The very religion that the community of Egyptian Jews thinks has caused it to prosper is in reality the religion that has brought trouble. The worship of this other god is in fact the trigger for the evil that will be worked against them by Yahweh. Thus there is indeed blessing and curse; the disagreement is over which god can bless and which god will surely curse.

44:24-30   The text adds one more paragraph, yet another oracle to clinch the argument. The prophet now sarcastically acknowledges that the resolve of this recalcitrant Egyptian community is fixed; the prophet will no longer dispute with them (44:25). The statement of the prophet includes a twofold infinitive absolute that greatly strengthens the verse: "you shall *surely keep* your vow and you shall *surely do* your sacrifices." The tone of this concession by Jeremiah is not unlike the prophet's concession to Hananiah, when Jeremiah finally recognizes that an argument is futile (28:6). Thus the prophet abandons the community to its own deathly choice, and will protest no longer.

Given that unshakable conclusion drawn by the Egyptian community of Jews and now grudgingly accepted by the prophet, we are not surprised that this severe God will speak yet again (44:26-28). Now Yahweh makes a statement that disassociates God's own self from this community. God no longer evidences a concern for this community, but now God is preoccupied only with Yahweh's own sovereignty and authority.[89] Yahweh will completely withdraw from this community and will be for it an absent, unavailable God. Or perhaps we may even say a "dead God." The community will no longer say, "As Yahweh lives," for they will have no reference points for such a bottom-line statement. This community is alone and without God in the world.

---

89. See the same self-concern on God's part in Exod. 14:4, 17; Ezek. 36:22-32.

God is, in this oracle, not yet finished with this community. God will do what God has been doing since the beginning of the book of Jeremiah. God is "watching," that is, staying at an attentive distance, overseeing the working out of God's resolve (cf. 1:11-12). For the community of exiles presumably in Babylon, God is "watching" for good (cf. 24:6-7; 29:11; 31:28). But for this community in Egypt, the same "watching" will yield only evil. The statement of 44:27 employs for negative use two statements made positively in other, earlier contexts. Thus "for evil and not for good" (v. 27) inverts "for welfare and not for evil" (29:11). Moreover, the negative "watching" here counters the watching of 31:28, in which the watching is for planting and building. Thus God is not absent nor dead for this community, but worse: God is alive and attentive to work a terrible destiny for this community. That terrible destiny will be termination.

Jeremiah 44:28 constitutes a climactic statement in two ways. The phrase "few in number" is a direct reference to Israel's miraculous origin in Egypt, when it was clearly Yahweh alone who took "the few" and made a people (cf. Deut. 10:22; 26:5).[90] Yahweh was the only reason Israel happened at all. Now that whole saving process is being inverted.[91] The community is reverting to "few in number," which inevitably happens when the strong support of Yahweh is absent, for Yahweh is the only source of life and well-being for this community. This community has cut itself off from that one reliable source, and now Yahweh will let this community have its choice . . . complete nullification.

The last phrase of Jer. 44:28, "mine or theirs," is an acknowledgement that the difficult theological issue has been joined in vv. 15-19, that more than one argument has been made, and that no conclusive point has been scored. "Their" argument is in vv. 17-18; "my" argument is in vv. 21-23. The community must wait

---

90. Deut. 28:62 has a curse quite parallel in its intent.

91. The "return to Egypt" thus is not simply a geographical development, but constitutes the nullification of the Exodus. In this terminal moment, Israel is as it was before God's primal event of rescue. This foolish community has, by its conduct, cancelled Israel's entire history of rescue.

to see how the pragmatic outcome of the case will finally adjudicate
the argument.

Finally this dismissive statement by Yahweh accepts the criteria
by which the theological question will be decided. Yahweh offers
a "sign" for the future, a piece of future concrete data which will
decide the large theological issue (vv. 29-30). The "sign" is a deed
wrought by Yahweh. Pharaoh Hophra (Apries) will be done to
death. To be sure, Pharaoh does have enemies, but Jeremiah argues
(as he earlier argued concerning Babylon as an enemy) that it is
Yahweh who will dispatch these enemies.[92] Thus the test of "mine"
or "theirs" (i.e., the vindication of Yahweh or the queen of heaven)
will be manifest in the destiny of the pharaoh who hosts this
refugee community of Jews. The reference to Zedekiah as a model
for Hophra is a reiteration of the "then-now" "there-here" argument of vv. 2-9. That is, the argument about the fate of Jerusalem
(vv. 2-6) is used as an argument about Egypt (vv. 7-9).

The die is cast; but the community must wait, as the biblical
community must always wait, to see how the die lands.[93] The
recurring problem of biblical faith, upon which the prophets
always insist, is that the community of faith must act in the middle
of things. This community of faith does not have the luxury of
waiting until the end to see how things turn out. Thus a decision
for Yahweh or for the queen of heaven cannot wait until the
destiny of Hophra is clear. A decision of faith must be made now.
And of course, the prophets know that a refusal to decide, a
decision to wait for more data, is itself a decision, usually a wrong
one as well as a cowardly one.

We may pause over the serious theological adjudication which

---

92. The same argument is made in Jer. 50–51; there it is Babylon who is
attacked by enemies dispatched by Yahweh. In every case, the destruction can
be understood in political, military terms, but the tradition of Jeremiah insists
upon a Yahwistic construal of such political, military events.

93. The actual turn of events concerning Hophra did not in fact turn out
as this text anticipates; cf. Bright, 347-352. If, however, the text be taken
canonically and not historically, then the crucial point is that the future of
Jews cannot rely upon Egypt which this pro-Babylonian text perceives as
disobedience to Yahweh. In the end, the judgment here pronounced against
Egypt is matched by the final judgment against Babylon in chs. 50–51.

is invited by this chapter. For the question between "mine" or "theirs" is in fact the large question of prophetic faith and is in contemporary theology the crucial issue between "foundationalism" and confessional theology.[94] That is, it is a question of what "reasons" and warrants can be given for faith in the God of the Bible. I suggest three useful lines of reflection.

(1) In the first instance, it is clear that intellectually Jeremiah's case is no more convincing or compelling than is that of his opponents. The argument is a stalemate, moving from different assumptions, waiting for data. Each side operates from premises that the other side cannot afford to grant. James Moulder has made a powerful case that arguments about God acting in history are impossible arguments that cannot be made convincingly, and that are not needed by anyone.[95] Every such argument is in fact not an argument from data, but is an argument imposed on the data, which insists that the data must be read in a certain way. Robert P. Carroll takes considerable delight in the recognition that the same "experience" can be used by two conflicting ideologies, because each ideology presses the experienced data into its service.[96] At the level of logical analysis, there really is no serious issue that can be joined, and the two sides talk past each other. The outcome is that each party remains convinced, not by experience or by data, but by its own premise, assumptions, and interests.

(2) Such a reading of the matter, however, does not take us very far in interpreting the text. Our interpretation of Jeremiah cannot leave the matter there if the text is to be taken on its own terms. For into this rather sophisticated intellectual argument there intrudes the matter of canon. At a second level, it

---

94. For a judicious review of that contemporary debate, see William C. Placher, *Unapologetic Theology: A Christian Voice in a Pluralistic Conversation* (Louisville: Westminster/John Knox, 1989). The vexed question of "foundationalism" is not unlike the debate here conducted between Jeremiah and his opponents.

95. James Moulder, "Skepticism and Agnosticism about Theology and Historiography," in *Being and Truth*. Festschrift John Macquarrie, ed. Alistair Kee and Eugene T. Long (London: SCM, 1986), 437-452.

96. Carroll, 737-38.

is the text of Jeremiah that has emerged as a "classic," [97] that is, as an important and prevailing text to which we continue to turn for authorization and reflection. The matter of "canon" does not require a theory of inspiration or revelation, nor is it an escape hatch to defend an absolutist ideology. Rather, the canonical shaping of the argument insists that the canon both (a) recognized the serious nature of the argument and (b) proposed an answer which intended to refute the counteranswer. Our interpretation must at least reflect on why the canon came to this conclusion and what it means that the canon so decides. That is, to conclude simply that one answer is as good as another is to ignore the fact that the argument is lodged in this way in this text. If we are to hear this text at all, it requires — at least for a moment — standing inside that community of interpretation to give its rendering a serious and preferential hearing. Whatever the outcome may be, the canonical nature of the text makes the matter more complex than simply calling the argument a draw.

(3) If we seek to go underneath the intellectual "balance" of the question about "which God" and beyond the formal fact of canon, we are led to theologically substantive issues. That is, the matter of "Yahweh versus the queen of heaven," or more broadly, "Yahweh versus other gods," is not simply a multiple-choice question among gods with different names, one of which is as credible as another.

The question of "which god" is a question which has a long-term history and a theological density, a history and a density which the book of Jeremiah seeks to exposit.[98] That is, each God

---

97. On the notion of classic, see David Tracy, *The Analogical Imagination: Christian Theology and the Culture of Pluralism* (New York: Crossroad, 1981), 99-229.

98. I use the term "density" here with deliberate reference to the notion of "thick description" so crucial to Clifford Geertz. Geertz has written of the social process and reality in many places. I find especially helpful "Blurred Genius: The Refiguration of Social Thought," *American Scholar* 49 (1980): 165-179. In this article Geertz variously proposes that life is "a game," "a stage," "a text." For his more programmatic statement, see Clifford Geertz, *The Interpretation of Cultures* (New York: Basic Books, 1973), 3-30.

is embedded in a certain history, and when one chooses a god, one chooses with it a history.[99]

The claims of Yahweh (as voiced in vv. 21-23) are rooted claims, and not just the ideological self-serving, *ad hoc* arguments of one party to an exilic dispute about power. The rootage of the claim goes back behind Jeremiah and the prophetic traditions to the earliest recitals of Israel, to Moses, and to some fundamental decisions about covenant at Sinai. These are not merely the biases of contemporary religious authorities (though that factor is not absent), but they are claims about the moral, communal dimension of social power and social order, and the force of religious legitimation that supports certain moral, communal claims.

To put the matter another way, the argument between the two claims concerns an intense interface between theological symbolization (creedal recital) and socioeconomic, political practice that brings together the holiness of God and the value of the neighbor. Such a claim in which the tradition of Jeremiah stands may or may not be true, but it is not a matter of indifference. The counterclaim of the queen of heaven (which has yielded no canonical, classical literature and no interpretive community) makes no witness about the holiness of God which refuses harnessing holy power for immediate social ends, and makes no claim about the value of the neighbor who is an end and not a means. In the end, a cavalier notion that one argument is as good as another is not wrong, but it is terribly innocent. It is innocent because it imagines that theological choices are not choices about social power. It is innocent because it imagines that an even-handed refusal to choose is in fact also a choice, not only about theological symbolization but also about social power. Such a perspective finally does not understand the linkage, explicit at least since Karl Marx, that every theological claim carries with it a socioeconomic claim.[100] And

---

99. Manifestly the "queen of heaven" lacks a history, i.e., produced no continuing community of interpretation. In Tracy's terms, the queen of heaven generated no "classic." In adjudicating the rival claims of the two parties at this late date, it is evident that Yahweh and Yahwism has a kind of historical density not matched by the queen of heaven. It is the difference in density that tells in the canon-making claim of Yahwism.

100. Marx's programmatic statements as quoted in McLellan, *The Thought*

these claims are not a matter of indifference to the ongoing work of interpretation.

This chapter is remarkably honest in recognizing the difficulty of an advocated theological claim and in refusing to voice an easy answer. The last verses of the chapter do invite reflection. How is it that Zedekiah fell? Is the end simply raw power, so that Nebuchadnezzar finally has his turn? Or is there a moral texture even to such imperial power? The text intends to leave the Egyptian community of Jews haunted by that question. It may also leave us haunted in the same way for the same reason by the same question.

BARUCH'S DESPAIR (45:1-5)

This brief chapter brings to a close the section of the book of Jeremiah commonly called the "Baruch document." Chapter 46 is the beginning of the Oracles against the Nations, which obviously constitute a very distinct body of material. Chapter 45 is not only dated to 605 B.C.E. ("the fourth year of Jehoiakim," v. 1), but explicitly refers to Baruch's writing of the Jeremiah scroll, an event described in ch. 36 (45:1). Moreover, the dating formula is exactly the same as in 36:1. Thus chs. 36 and 45 are explicitly related to each other, both of which feature Baruch. It is probable that these two chapters are placed as they are to provide brackets at the beginning and at the end of the narrative material commonly referred to as "the Baruch document." Thus ch. 45 gives closure to an account begun in ch. 36.[101]

This chapter is of peculiar interest because it expresses the concern of an individual, and shows the prophet responding to that individual. For our interpretation, the most important issue is to inquire about the identity of Baruch, to wonder why he

---

of Karl Marx, 22, are the criticism of heaven as thus transformed into the criticism of earth, the criticism of religion into the criticism of law, and the criticism of theology into the criticism of politics. See the comment on the passage by McLellan, 21-27.

101. On the placement and function of this narrative unit, see Taylor.

merits special attention for the prophet and why he is given such structural importance in the redactional shaping of the book of Jeremiah. The easiest and perhaps most convincing thought about Baruch is that he was a person close to Jeremiah and loyal to the prophet at great risk. That is sufficient reason for this good word to him. Baruch greatly aided the prophetic vocation of Jeremiah, and now the prophet responds appropriately.

If, however, we pay careful attention to 43:2-3, we may suggest another way of understanding the Baruch of ch. 45. In 43:2-3 Baruch is blamed by the adversaries of Jeremiah for inciting Jeremiah to betray Jerusalem to the Babylonians. This has the effect of softening the direct criticism of Jeremiah. I suggest that the name "Baruch" may also have come in this material to be a cipher for all that body of opinion and all those persons who championed a pro-Babylonian view of the crisis in Jerusalem. Thus Baruch may be a tag-word for all those "right-minded" people who with Jeremiah equated the purpose of Yahweh with the oppression of Babylon. This is not to deny that Baruch is a person, but to suggest that he is a representative person. Mention of Baruch is a convenient way of referring to all those who stood with Jeremiah in his radical "Babylonian reading" of his time and place in God's history. This concluding oracle then is a commendation and vindication of those who have shared the faith and discernment of Jeremiah.

After the identification of the time and place of the oracle (45:1-2), the oracle itself combines two quite different rhetorical maneuvers. On the one hand, there is the intimate transaction of lament and response concerning Baruch. The lament of Baruch is ostensibly quoted and reiterated by Jeremiah, perhaps prayed to God by Jeremiah on behalf of Baruch. It is a cry of exhausted, unrequited faith which has run great risks, but without any good response from God. That Baruch finds "no rest" means that he has gotten the consequence appropriate to the wicked, but he himself is a righteous, obedient man. Thus the complaint of Baruch voices a question of theodicy, not unlike the question of Job, already anticipated in Jer. 12:1-4.

The response of God to Baruch through Jeremiah consists of two distinct phases. First, Baruch is rebuked for expecting and demanding too much.[102] The RSV expresses the warning in 45:5 as an interrogative. But it is not a question; it is, rather, a reprimand. Baruch seeks "great things" for himself, and he should not, because they are not to be given, and he has no ground on which to make such an insistence. That is, Baruch's risky faith is an end in itself and should not be utilized as a means toward a self-serving end.[103]

Second, soon after the rebuke by the prophet comes a promise (v. 5). Baruch will receive his life as "spoil." The phrase "prize of war" is a military phrase referring to captive booty that victorious soldiers can take home from their enemies. Baruch will not be given material war booty. There is indeed a victory, and there will be "booty." What Baruch will receive is more lean than normal war booty, but also more precious: his life! God promises Baruch that the outcome of risky faith is survival into the future. As is often the case in Jeremiah, the response of God does not adequately meet the terms of the complaint. Baruch is not the promised rest for which he prayed, but survival.

That promise of personal survival, however, is more poignant if we consider the countertheme of the divine oracle. In addition to the personal, intimate word to Baruch, the occasion of the personal address is used for one more public oracle in vv. 4-5. Again, this prophetic response from God is in two parts. The oracle utilizes four of the strong verbs of 1:10.[104] The two negative verbs "break down and pluck up" will prevail over "plant and build." One last time, Jeremiah recites the sentence of death which God has decreed. In this odd usage of the four verbs, the action of "plant and build" is regarded as all in the past, for the present

---

102. The uncompromising response to the complaint of Baruch, which is a reprimand, is not unlike the response made by Yahweh to the complaints of Jeremiah, which are also characteristically reprimands rather than reassurance; cf. 12:5-6; 15:19-21.

103. We do not know what "great things" are for Baruch; perhaps it is some ambition for leadership in the community of Babylonian Jews. The argument of Dearman, 411-421, suggests that such an ambition could be credible and cogent, given Baruch's apparent family ties. The same term *gedolot* is used in the same way in Ps. 131:1.

104. See the analysis of these verbs in their several contexts by Taylor, 90-91.

and immediate future belongs to the verbs of destruction. Moreover, the hard sentence now pronounced is not aimed simply at Jerusalem and Judah, but the scope is "all the land," perhaps "all the earth." That is, the known world of power arrangements in its totality is under assault from God; nothing will be spared.

This massive negative message is reinforced by the second public element in the oracle: "I am bringing evil upon 'all flesh.'" The "evil" (disaster) God will bring is commensurate with the evil found in the human community. The term "all flesh" is used elsewhere in exilic texts to refer to the whole of creation (cf. Gen. 6:12; 9:15; Isa. 40:5).

The public element of this oracle has a forward thrust as the Hebrew text of the book of Jeremiah is now arranged. The reference to "all the earth" and "all flesh" suggests a transnational scope to the oracle which anticipates the Oracles against the Nations in Jer. 46–51. Thus the themes of "prophet to the nations" and "pluck up and tear down" from 1:10 are here taken up to give closure to the book of Jeremiah.

In light of that massive judgment which dominates much of the tradition of Jeremiah, we are in a better position to appreciate the promise made to Baruch. There will be wholesale destruction, but there is an exception. The exception (remnant) is for those who have supported and accepted Jeremiah. The formula "your life as a prize of war" is used in 38:2 to refer generally to all those who submit to Babylon, who are a party to a Babylonian reading of Yahwistic reality. More specific use is made of the formula only in our text and one other time, to refer to Ebed-melech (39:18). Ebed-melech is also a functionary in Jerusalem who intervened to save the life of Jeremiah (cf. 38:7-13). Thus the two recipients of the formula, Ebed-melech and Baruch, have in common only that they have been allied with Jeremiah. It is clear that both of them did so at enormous personal risk.

Thus this brief oracle asserts *massive judgment* and an *exceptional rescue*. Christopher R. Seitz has suggested that the two recipients of the rescue formula, Ebed-melech and Baruch, function in the book of Jeremiah as did Caleb and Joshua in the book of Joshua.[105]

---

105. Seitz, "Canonical Shape," 16-27; cf. Olson.

That is, they are the two who had faith in the promises of God, who ran risks for their faith, and who therefore became the only survivors into the next generation of Israel, when all the others had been abandoned by God to death. This formula signals a self-conscious remnant theology and identifies the two addressees (Baruch and Ebed-melech) as the means by which God will open a faithful way into the future. The oracle concerns not only remnant theology but also a practical way forward in the community of faith, identifying those who are the carriers of real faith for the future. That these two have their lives ensures a survival of a faithful community in the midst of massive destruction.

There can be little doubt that Baruch at least (and perhaps Ebed-melech) is situated in the Babylonian community of Jews who are the wave of God's future (cf. Jer. 24).[106] This good word to Baruch thus offers a direct counterpoint to the oracles of 43:8-13; 44:1-30, which dismiss the Egyptian Jews to death. The destruction there is wholesale, as indicated by the unrestrained rhetoric of those oracles. Conversely, the good hope of Baruch, perhaps the quintessential Babylonian Jew, is voiced in very lean verbiage because it is a very lean hope. It is nonetheless hope, the most hope given in the midst of a world now destined for upheaval and chaos. The Oracles against the Nations which follow choreograph that coming upheaval and chaos. This little oracle asserts, in the face of the upheaval, that there is still a live hope and a concrete chance for faithful Jews.[107] That hope, as always for Israel, is based only in the promissory word of God.

---

106. See Jer. 51:59-64, where the brother of Baruch is mandated to go to Babylon, so that it is not unreasonable that Baruch also went there.

107. Perhaps this oracle performs the same function as the concluding narrative report of 52:31-34 (2 Kgs. 25:27-30). On that passage, see Gerhard von Rad, "The Deuteronomic Theology of History in *I* and *II Kings*," *The Problem of the Hexateuch and Other Essays* (1966; repr. London: SCM and Philadelphia: Fortress, 1984), 219-220.

THE ORACLES
AGAINST THE NATIONS
Jeremiah 46:1–51:64

It is conventional in the prophetic literature of the OT to have collections of oracles which are Yahweh's word to (and against) the nations, as in Amos 1–2, Isa. 13–23, and Ezek. 25–32.[1] The history and development of this genre of prophetic speech is not well known to us.[2] It may be that the oracles emerged in the midst of liturgic celebrations of the sovereignty of Yahweh, and served to voice the claim that God's sovereign rule extended not simply over Israel but over all peoples. Thus in Ps. 96:10 the imperative is issued: "Say among the nations, 'The LORD is king!'" (NRSV).[3] The oracles may then be the concrete way in which it is announced to the nations that "The LORD is king."

That genre, which no doubt has liturgical antecedents, is utilized in the book of Jeremiah to implement the assertion of Jer. 1:10 that Jeremiah is summoned to be "a prophet to the nations." Indeed, the book of Jeremiah makes very little coherent sense unless the claims of the text are set initially in the context of the

---

1. A splendid introduction to the genre and various texts is Norman K. Gottwald, *All the Kingdoms of the Earth* (New York: Harper and Row, 1964). In this volume Gottwald is still focused on historical-critical questions and does not greatly reflect the penetrating social criticism of his later work.

2. The origin of the genre is perhaps liturgical. See one bold proposal in that regard by Aage Bentzen, "The Ritual Background of Amos 1:2–2:3," *Oudtestamentische Studiën* 8 (1950): 85-99.

3. See the discussion of the psalm and this formula in Walter Brueggemann, *Israel's Praise: Doxology against Idolatry and Ideology* (Philadelphia: Fortress, 1988), 29-53. There is no doubt that the formula used in the Jerusalem temple carried with it triumphalist tendencies for the Davidic house; cf. John Mauchline, "Implicit Signs of a Persistent Belief in the Davidic Empire," *Vetus Testamentum* 20 (1970): 287-303.

history and politics of the Near East. The life of Israel and Judah in the 7th and 6th cents. is dominated by Babylonian policy and power. It is the work of the book of Jeremiah to relate that imperial policy and power credibly to the claims of Yahwism.[4] The book of Jeremiah makes use of the genre Oracles against the Nations to assert the rule of Yahweh over the nations as well as over the people Israel.

In the present ordering of the Hebrew text of the book of Jeremiah, the Oracles against the Nations (chs. 46–51) are situated following the end of the Baruch narrative in ch. 45.[5] Indeed, ch. 45 functions in its present locus as a transition between the Baruch narrative and the Oracles against the Nations. As the last word of the Baruch narrative, ch. 45 asserts that Baruch, great defender of Jeremiah's message (and perhaps generator of pro-Babylonian ideology), will have his life as a prize of war (45:5). In contrast to that comforting word to Baruch, however, the same oracle asserts that God is about to bring disaster *(ra'ah)* against "all flesh" (v. 5). The phrase "all flesh" is paralleled in v. 4 with the phrase "the whole land."[6] That is, God is about to disrupt all present power arrangements. The statement provides an appropriate lead-in to the Oracles against the Nations.

These oracles in chs. 46–51 voice a single recurrent theme: God is sovereign. The nations must honor Yahweh's sovereignty. Honoring Yahweh's sovereignty often entails positive regard for Yahweh's people.[7] Nations which do not honor God (and God's

---

4. I take this in a quite general sense concerning the broad flow of geopolitical power. I am most reluctant to become as specific or precise as is Holladay, *Jeremiah 2*.

5. The LXX, which places these texts in the midst of ch. 25, does not concern us here. It is evident that the collection of Oracles against the Nations was something of a free-floating collection. Differing placements in the final form of the text no doubt serve different canonical intentions.

6. The phrase can be rendered "all the land."

7. The oracles often concern abuse of Israel, but not always. Thus the other nation may be an agent of Yahweh against Israel, or the judgment of a nation may concern cruelties not perpetrated against Israel. This is noticeably the case in some of the oracles of Amos 1–2. Israel may be a subject of such oracles but is not necessarily present. The horizon of the genre can be more comprehensive.

people) stand under judgment and will be destabilized. This argument is articulated in a variety of stylized forms. Because Yahweh is sovereign, no nation, no matter how powerful, is finally and ultimately an absolute value.

This theological argument is exceedingly difficult in our context of modernity, where the rule of Yahweh in public matters is intellectually problematic. I suggest, however, that Paul Kennedy's study, *The Rise and Fall of the Great Powers,* may be understood as a contemporary, secularized form of the same affirmation.[8] Kennedy proposes that every nation-state, because of its population, territory, and natural resources, is entitled to a certain share of the world's wealth. When a nation-state overreaches that share in an act of self-aggrandizement, that nation places itself in jeopardy and stands at risk in the process of world politics. To be sure, Kennedy bases his argument completely on economic, political, and military considerations; as might be expected, he introduces no explicit theological categories into his argument. In the end, nonetheless, Kennedy's argument is that no nation-state dares to conduct itself as though it were an ultimate end in itself. A viable and survivable nation-state must understand its own life and security in the context of a larger dynamic to which it must submit and of which it is a part.

Mutatis mutandis, I suggest that the argument of Kennedy is the same as the argument in the prophetic Oracles against the Nations. That "larger dynamic" which relativizes and endlessly jeopardizes every absolutist political claim is articulated in the prophets as the will of Yahweh. The prophet Jeremiah and the other prophets were not obscurantist supernaturalists. Perceiving the world theologically, they were able to discern that when a nation violates the larger dynamic of the political process which has a coherent moral purpose, trouble comes. Thus it is indeed possible to understand the role of Babylon in terms of Yahweh's governance, or alternatively (with Kennedy), in terms of a larger relativizing dynamic. My point is not to claim Kennedy for the theological process, but to suggest that the prophetic categories of criticism of the nations are not remote from our own sense of

---

8. Kennedy, *Rise and Fall.*

the historical process. Yahweh is the character in the drama of world history who overrides national pretensions and chastens every self-serving idolatry. It is this character to whom the nations must finally make reference, and with whom they must come to terms.

Having affirmed the theme of Yahweh's sovereignty, the Oracles against the Nations in Jeremiah require a more nuanced consideration. As we have seen in the Baruch narrative, the pivotal reality of Babylon decisively shapes the view of international reality held in the book of Jeremiah. Thus it will not do simply to treat chs. 46–51 as an undifferentiated mass of materials on a common theme. We may make three differentiations in the materials that are appropriate in the context of the book of Jeremiah.

(1) The oracles concern Egypt, the Philistines, Moab, Ammon, Edom, Damascus, Kedar, Elam, and Babylon. Although all these oracles belong to the same genre, a distinction is to be made in the context of the book of Jeremiah between the oracle against Babylon (chs. 50–51) and all the other oracles (chs. 46–49). Two formal grounds for such a distinction can be noted. First, the oracle concerning Babylon is much longer than any of the others. Second, that oracle stands in the final position, clearly designed to conclude the collection.

The primary distinction, however, is not finally formal but substantive. In the context of Jeremiah, it is Babylon who is "the destroyer" of all the other peoples. That is, Babylon is likely the agent of Yahweh in working trouble for the nations in chs. 46–49. Such a view is congruent with the historical performance of Babylon under Nebuchadnezzar, who did indeed trouble the other nations. Moreover, such a role for Babylon fits the conviction of the Jeremiah tradition that Nebuchadnezzar is the servant of Yahweh working the will of Yahweh (cf. 25:9; 27:6; 43:10). Thus Nebuchadnezzar is the tool of Yahweh in governing and chastening the other peoples. The text implicitly voices the triumph of Babylon over the nations, and a great affirmation for Babylon. That is, I suggest, the first point concerning the oracles of chs. 46–49. Yahweh triumphs over the nations through the work of Babylon.

In the second part of this corpus, however, the tradition does a complete about-face. The second point is that in chs. 50–51 Babylon in turn is decisively crushed and its power is nullified. Penultimately, the purposes of Yahweh converge with the interests of Babylon. Ultimately, God's purposes converge with no earthly arrangement, and certainly not with Babylon. Thus the book of Jeremiah is penultimately pro-Babylonian, until the very end. At the end, however, in an act of profound hope and assurance for exiled Jews (exiled by Babylon), Babylon is nullified — which permits a homecoming for exiled Jews.[9]

The prose commentary in the Babylonian oracle (cf. 50:8-10, 18-20, 44-46) anticipates the rise of the next world power (Persia) who will overwhelm Babylon. This oracular tradition, however, does not simply provide political commentary on the coming and going of nations. It is a theological assertion that finally no world power, not even mighty Babylon toward whom Jeremiah (and Baruch) are so well disposed, can claim special privilege with Yahweh. The text asserts that Babylon has finally run afoul of Yahweh in its pretension. Alternatively, Kennedy might say that Babylon has overreached in its pretension and is sure to fall. The very Babylon so useful to Yahweh (and to Jeremiah) finally is destroyed by Yahweh (Persia). Such a sovereign destruction is the ground of hope for Jews in the 6th century. The oracles are arranged in a two-stage way, first celebrative of Babylon (chs. 46–49), then utterly dismissive (on theological grounds) of Babylon (chs. 50–51).

(2) The oracles against the other nations (chs. 46–49) seem to be all of a piece. We may only notice that Egypt stands in the first position (ch. 46). Assuming such an arrangement is not happenstance, we may suggest two reasons for this priority. First, Egypt is named first as the major power which is able to counter and cope with Babylon. Given the pro-Babylonian propensity of the book of Jeremiah, Egypt as the main counter to Babylon would be perceived as the greatest threat, and so needs to be dealt

---

9. In a later generation, Isa. 40–55 celebrates the fall of Babylon as a permit wrought by God so that the exiled Jews can go home. In Jer. 50–51 the tradition of Jeremiah moves toward this affirmation, but does not yet make such a complete affirmation.

with first and most decisively. Of all the powers who resist the Yahweh-Babylon axis, Egypt is foremost.

Second, the Baruch narrative ended in chs. 43–44 with harsh words against Egypt and against the Jews who fled to Egypt. In 43:10-13; 44:30 the text is specific and concrete in its dismissal of Egypt. To be sure, there stands between the concrete judgment of chs. 43–44 against Egypt and the oracle of ch. 46 the Baruch oracle in ch. 45. Nonetheless, the placement of the oracle against Egypt in ch. 46 helps make a direct connection between the Baruch narrative which ends with Egypt and the Oracles against the Nations which begin with Egypt. Yahweh has pledged to work a judgment against "all the earth" (45:4) and against "all flesh" (45:5). Such a massive judgment begins against Egypt.

Thus the primacy of Egypt in the Oracles against the Nations lets the rule of Yahweh be initiated most aggressively against Yahweh's (and Babylon's) greatest enemy. The capacity of Egypt to evoke such hostile commentary is no doubt rooted in 7th-6th cent. politics, where Egypt is a primary threat to a pro-Babylonian reading of political reality. That historical-political reality concerning Egypt is perhaps reinforced for the prophetic text by seeing the ignoble flight of the Jews to Egypt (chs. 42–44) as the full circle which began in Exod. 1–15.[10] All the pharaohs from the time of Moses until the 6th cent. fall under a common negative symbolization in ancient Israel. All of them are dismissed as the quintessential enemy of Israel and of Yahweh. For all these reasons, historical-political and symbolic, Egypt receives special focus in this corpus. Egypt is a primary cipher for all that resists the purposes of Yahweh.

(3) The Oracles against the Nations end with an odd narrative in Jer. 51:59-64. Such a narrative is not at all usual in such a collection, and it clearly departs from the genre. Our purpose is not to comment on the historicity of the narrative about Seraiah. Rather, we consider the function of the narrative in the arrangement of the text in the book of Jeremiah. This remarkable narrative permits the text concerning Babylon to stand as an enduring testimony against Babylon. It is as though chs. 46–49 are only

---

10. See Friedman, "From Egypt to Egypt," 189-192.

prelude to chs. 50–51. In the end, it is the defeat of Babylon and none other that matters to the exiled Jews and to the book of Jeremiah. If Yahweh is to evidence sovereignty anywhere, it will most compellingly be sovereignty over Babylon.

The role of Seraiah, brother of Baruch, is especially important for the shape of the book of Jeremiah. (Again, our concern is a structural, not a historical one.) The text is arranged so that the two brothers, Baruch and Seraiah, are preoccupied with two scrolls which well embody the two-stage philosophy of history in the book of Jeremiah (cf. ch. 36 on Baruch's scroll and then, to a lesser extent, Baruch with the property document of ch. 32). On the one hand, as we have seen, Baruch is the great pro-Babylon voice who believes Jerusalem must submit in order to trust Yahweh. As a pro-Babylonian, Baruch can see that it is indeed God's will that Jerusalem be "plucked up and torn down" by Babylon. On the other hand, the future of the Jews, the future of "building and planting," depends upon being free and having the power of Babylon broken. This latter requirement is the burden of the scroll and witness of the second brother, Seraiah. Thus the two brothers in turn are custodians of two scrolls that celebrate Babylon and then nullify Babylon.

In the two-stage view of Babylon, the two brothers evidence how it is that God, through the historical process, first "plucks up and tears down" (through Babylon) and then "builds and plants" (beyond Babylon). Both turns of history vis-à-vis the empire are evidence of Yahweh's rule over Israel and over the nations. In the end, the Oracles against the Nations are a theological statement, not to be explained away by historical correlations. In the end, the historical process, the rise and fall of the great powers, is an unmistakable witness to the relentless rule of Yahweh.

ORACLE AGAINST EGYPT (46:1-28)

In the Oracles against the Nations Yahweh's governance over the international world around Jerusalem is asserted. In the assertion of this claim, Egypt is addressed first. In the pro-Babylonian tendency of the Jeremiah tradition, Egypt is the main diplomatic alternative to Babylon, and is considered a deathly alternative.[11] Thus on political grounds Egypt most needs to be brought under the aegis of Yahweh. Moreover, Egypt has come to be a primal metaphor for worldly power that is organized against the purposes of God. For both political and metaphorical-theological reasons, Egypt is named first in this list of nations, for when Egypt is brought under the rule and purpose of Yahweh, in effect Yahweh's governance will be fully established. This extended discussion concerning Egypt is organized into three rhetorical units (46:3-12, 13-24, and 25-26). After this relentless and sustained address concerning Egypt, the unit culminates with a good and reassuring word to Israel (vv. 27-28). Before the good word for Israel can be spoken, however, the hard word against Egypt must be effected.

Before taking up the actual oracle, the text in its present arrangement is introduced by two editorial comments, first a general foreword to the collection (v. 1) and then a historical note concerning Egypt (v. 2).

46:1 This verse functions as introduction to the entire unit of chs. 46–51, connecting the rule (word) of Yahweh and the future of the nations. Jeremiah, the speaker of these oracles, is the one who connects *the rule of Yahweh* and *the future of the nations*. That connection is not self-evident; it is established by the daring and critical oracles that follow. The final phrase of 46:1, "concerning the nations," provides an important clue to the final form of the Jeremiah text, for this phrase deliberately refers back to the mandate of 1:10. From the outset, according to the "call narrative," the prophecy (and book) of Jeremiah have been concerned with God's governance of the nations through the words of Jeremiah. Thus 1:10 and 46:1 form an inclusio, framing the book of Jeremiah and providing a literary context for the concern for Israel and Jerusalem within the inclusion. These framing verses suggest, in tension with the materials in between, that the book of Jeremiah in the end is concerned with the rule of Yahweh and the coming

---

11. On the theological issues in the Exile as pertains to the Jeremiah tradition, see Seitz, *Theology in Conflict.*

of Yahweh's kingdom over the kingdoms of the world (cf. Rev. 11:15). A serious hearing of this textual tradition requires us to think again about that large governance which in the end transcends even the well-being of Israel.[12]

46:2 The text moves specifically to implement the mandate of 1:10 and the concrete substance of 46:1. The initial words, "concerning Egypt" (NRSV), are daring and abrupt. Indeed, the utterance of this phrase makes an outrageous theological claim, for it is not easy or obvious that Yahweh and Egypt belong together in the same world of power or in the same utterance. By the utterance of this phrase, the text preempts our field of perception. The claim, that a speaker for Yahweh should address the great Egyptian empire, should leave us dazzled. The warrant given for the utterance is no more compelling warrant than we have seen heretofore in the book of Jeremiah: it is a speech from Yahweh. It is the "word of Yahweh," a word beyond known reason and conventional logic that dares draw the empire into Israel's theological discourse.

This verse seeks to give historical placement for the oracle that follows, though the specific historical placement is subordinated to the canonical-theological claim asserted. The claim concerns the rule of Yahweh over the empire in every time and in all times. The historical specificity asserted is the battle of Carchemish in 605 B.C.E., when Babylon emerged as a world power, thus jeopardizing Egyptian hegemony.[13] This prose editorial comment appeals to the outcome of that battle as a reference point for Yahweh's governance amid world powers. That is, the outcome of the battle is claimed as a show of Yahweh's will and power. Notice that the connection between *theological claim* and *historical experience* depends on the large, bold assertion of the prophet.[14] The Egypt

---

12. It is envisioned that all the nations will be either willingly or reluctantly brought under the rule of Yahweh. This is evident in the Enthronement Psalms, in the Yahwist theology, as well as in the prophets. On the rule of Yahweh as a political construct, see Wright, "The Nations in Hebrew Prophecy."

13. On the battle, see Miller and Hayes, *A History of Ancient Israel and Judah,* 403.

14. It is evident that the claim of the oracle is not self-evident. It is rather

now addressed is a "Carchemish-conditioned" empire, when everything about the old hegemony had become unglued, and its vaunted power was now exposed as fraudulent. Everything is placed in danger for Egypt, and everything is now open for the peoples long intimidated by Egypt. The danger and the openness are here acknowledged to be Yahweh's fresh action in the world. The prophetic world governed by Yahweh becomes more daring and imaginative, and in such a casting, more ominous for the empire.

46:3-12 The poem invites us into the middle of a dangerous and uneven battle. The poem is not completely clear, because the antecedents of the pronouns are ill-defined. The poem is not a report of a battle, but it is an act of imagination whereby the poet construes a harsh conflict and a rout of the great empire. The purpose of the poetry is to redescribe international reality. International powers seem so stable, so entrenched, so enduring. The poetry intends to subvert all such presumed political givens and to propose an alternative scenario for the shape of worldly power.

In vv. 3-4 we do not know who is addressed with the series of imperatives. It is a summons to battle, a summons and dispatch of well-armed, well-prepared, responsive troops. They are to move immediately into action; they are to do so because the speaker has already noticed that the enemy is in frantic retreat (vv. 5-6). Early in the Jeremiah tradition the poetry speaks of a great invading army and the humiliating rout of Judah and Jerusalem (5:15-17; 6:1-8, 22-26). Now the poetic strategy is to take up the same sort of language and apply it to the seemingly invincible Egyptians. The rhetoric of invasion and attack is the same as in the earlier poems, but now the rhetoric has been redirected from Judah toward Egypt. The attacked are said to be in complete panic; their situation is so desperate that they cannot even escape. They are indeed in a hopeless situation.

---

an imaginative construal that reads reality in this way rather than in some other way. On the power of imagination to "take as," see David J. Bryant, *Faith and the Play of Imagination* (Macon: Mercer University Press, 1989), 115-128 and *passim*.

The poet has shrewdly withheld identification of any of the actors in this scenario. We do not know who is attacking (46:3-4) or who is retreating (vv. 5-6). Now in vv. 7-9 we are to have the earlier dramatic portrayal specified. In v. 7 we are asked about the cast of characters. The question provides a hint of the answer: "Who is this rising like the Nile, the great surging river?" (author's translation). The "Nile question" (v. 7) prepares us for the "Egypt answer" (v. 8). Now finally we are told: Egypt! That is who is surging desperately in retreat. Egypt — arrogant, powerful, threatening — had thought to "cover the earth" with its aggressive drive for domination (v. 8). Verse 9, however, counters that imperial intention with disaster and abrupt imperatives. Horses, chariots, warriors with shield and bow, all are now summoned and addressed. They are addressed like the invader in v. 4, only now it is the one attacked who is addressed. The question is asked (v. 7), the answer is given (v. 8), and now in a mocking way the Egyptians (men of Ethiopia, Put, and Lud) are addressed and advised to go out in retreat (v. 9). Thus vv. 7-9 portray an international conflict between the old established power of Egypt, now on the run, and the new power of the north that arises ominously against them. We are able to see that the new power in the north is addressed in vv. 3-6, and the old fading power in vv. 7-9. The shape of the rhetoric helps present a drastic contrast between awesome power and frantic retreat, between Babylon on the attack and Egypt in desperate withdrawal.

Thus far the poem could be only ordinary war poetry, dramatizing the waxing and waning of battle, the rise and fall of nations, the sudden disarray of a long vaunted power.[15] It is not until we reach v. 10, however, that the prophetic claims of the oracle are made explicit. We could have forgotten, in the poem and in the powerful imagery of battle, that this poem is prophetic, Jeremianic,

---

15. The sudden disarray of a long vaunted power seems on the face of it to be implausible. Yet in our very own experience, the abrupt demise of the power of the Soviet Union makes clear such a realistic possibility. The text itself does not depend on concrete examples, but proceeds in confidence of the power of its own speech to redescribe reality. We can nonetheless observe a convergence between the intention of the poetry and our own recent, observable public experience.

Yahwistic. Now abruptly in v. 10, everything is named and becomes focused. The day of battle is a day with a special reference and sponsor and purpose. The day belongs to the LORD, "Yahweh of hosts." The naming of God is in an exaggerated military formula (twice named LORD, God of the troops) to accent God's powerful, decisive presence in the conflict. This assertion redescribes what is happening. What we witness at first glimpse is simply a conflict between Egypt and "the north." The naming of the name of Yahweh now provides a clue for what is in fact happening. This is no ordinary context, no routine battle. This is not simply a battle between world powers, war as an instrument of state politics. This is a theological happening, attesting to the decisive power and purpose of Yahweh.

And the purpose? It is that God may avenge God's own foe! That is, the real enemy of Egypt is not the Babylonians; it is the God of Israel. We are not told wherein Egypt has offended Yahweh. We only know that the full establishment of Yahweh's governance requires the terrible demise of Egypt.[16]

Perhaps the poetry against Egypt takes Judean listeners clear back to the Exodus, and we are hearing one more reiteration of the old, foundational hostility between Pharaoh and Yahweh, a hostility primally voiced in the Exodus liturgy (Exod. 1–15). More likely we are in the midst of a theological verdict pertaining to the 7th-6th cents., when the flow of the future is to Babylon (cf. Ezek. 28).[17] Egypt is judged by the Jeremiah tradition to be a deathly impediment to the coming ordering of world power. Either way, as an allusion to the Exodus or as a more contemporary critique of Egyptian power, we have a theological verdict and not simply a political analysis. That verdict is that God will take up the whole of the Egyptian army as a bloody "sacrifice" (Jer. 46:10).

The rhetoric shocks us. This is not the sort of poetry that suits our propensity to reconciliation. This is indeed brutalizing rhetoric. I suggest three ways to understand what happens in such a

---

16. On the ways in which Yahweh established rule, see Mendenhall, *The Tenth Generation,* 69-104.

17. Cf. Donald E. Gowan, *When Man Becomes God.* Pittsburgh Theological Monograph 6 (Pittsburgh: Pickwick, 1975), 69-92.

text. First, the poetry is no doubt making use of rhetorical conventions.[18] This is the stock formulation of war poetry that inevitably includes a theological (self-serving, ideological) dimension. The convention mocks the enemy for the sake of our well-being. Second, such brutalizing poetry does not claim to be evenhanded and nonpartisan, but no doubt reflects a quite partisan judgment made in the midst of heavy conflict where one cannot abdicate or practice neutrality. In this poetry, there is no ambiguity about where the future lies and where the right is being enacted. Third, however, this use of literary convention and the partisan judgment of the poem are in the service of a larger theological claim. Yahweh stands at the center of this harsh dispute. Yahweh stalks the map of the Near East as only Yahweh is authorized to do. The nations will sooner or later have to come to terms with Yahweh's powerful will. International politics does not consist simply in power and cunning and strategy and ruthlessness. There is a purpose that overrides all such human posturing. Whoever stands over against that transcendent purpose, as Egypt here does, is sure to fail.

After the massive theological assertion of v. 10, vv. 11-12 provide a dramatic contrast. Now there is almost a tone of pity and momentary sympathy. The poet again uses the old formula concerning healing in Gilead. As there had been no healing in Gilead for beloved Israel (cf. 8:22), so Gilead offers no remedy for Egypt! As Israel had been beyond healing, so Egypt is utterly beyond healing. Egypt now receives what God's own people had received earlier. There remains for the empire only shame and cry, a cry that fills the earth (cf. Exod. 11:6). In the end there is "stumbling and falling" (Jer. 46:12), the same words sounded in v. 6. The poet crafts the way in which Yahweh prevails; and when Yahweh prevails, Egypt is gone!

46:13-24   The same themes of conflict and defeat are sounded again, though now the imagery is more poignant. The prose

---

18. On the genre of war oracles in relation to Jeremiah, see Duane L. Christensen, *Transformations of the War Oracle in Old Testament Prophecy.* Harvard Dissertations in Religion 3 (Missoula: Scholars Press, 1975), 183-280.

introduction of v. 13 provides a simple political summary: it is Babylon (Nebuchadnezzar) against Egypt. That is so simple, and anyone could have seen such a visible development. Poets, however, can never stand so far outside events and take them so simply as would other observers. The poet wants us to go inside the text, inside the experience of pain and defeat and humiliation. Our work is not just to draw a geopolitical conclusion (easy enough), but to linger over the hurt that belongs to imperial arrogance, and to notice the futility of such restless domination.

In the initial statement (vv. 14-17) the invading enemy is not even mentioned. The poet focuses completely on Egypt. The key cities of the empire are named — Memphis, Tahpanhes — centers of power, now to be centers of pain and shame.[19] The poet speaks in ironic imperative. These great imperial cities are to "stand ready and be prepared," but prepared only for wholesale defeat. The massiveness and depth of defeat are evidenced in the retreat of the god Apis (v. 14). As the god leaves the field in shame, so the armies of the empire become hopeless. And why has the god fled? Because Yahweh has defeated him. Yahweh has done so directly, according to this rhetoric — no enemy army, no mediating agent. This is the rhetoric of a daring poet who is willing to read historical reality theologically. As in the old exodus, the holy God overrides the gods of the Egyptian empire. And when the gods of the empire are defeated, the empire is indeed lost.

One more time the word pair "stumble-fall" is repeated (v. 16; cf. vv. 6, 12); Egypt's last strategy is a retreat back to the safety of the invulnerable homeland. The ambitious imperial claims of Egypt, which extended far up into the Fertile Crescent, far beyond its conventional sphere of influence, have been defeated. The poet cannot resist one more cutting jab at the failed empire. Verse 17 is almost like a political cartoon in which the pharaoh is mocked

---

19. The mention of Tahpanhes is here made without special emphasis. Nonetheless, the attentive reader cannot fail to remember that it was to Tahpanhes that the Jews led by Johanan fled and to which they carried Jeremiah (43:7-8; 44:1). Thus in connecting the Oracle against the Nations corpus (chs. 46–51) to the Baruch document (chs. 36–45), that Egyptian city is now mentioned as a place under threat. Almost incidentally, the threat sounded in chs. 43–44 is here given added emphasis.

as the boisterous leader who fails in the moment of crisis. Of course such a ruler will fail, because he seeks to act against the purpose of Yahweh. Israel's poets have known since Moses that pharaohs will always lose when Yahweh prevails.

The next section of the poem begins with an oath or decree in the mouth of God (vv. 18-24). This is Yahweh's only substantive appearance in this section of the poem. Yahweh does only one thing, but it is done in the name of Yahweh's massive military authority. The one who swears is the "LORD of the troops." Yahweh authorizes one "who will come" (v. 18). That is all. Yahweh does nothing more; the coming one is not named anywhere else in this poem. All else that happens is human action, all conflict enacted by human agents. But what a coming one! He is like Mt. Tabor towering all alone over the hills, like Carmel, jutting out prominently and all alone into the sea, massive in presence, sure to be noticed, unavoidable, dominating the entire landscape. The struggle for power and domination in the Fertile Crescent is an uneven one. The poet, however, does not explicate. The poet avoids concrete political reference, because he wants Yahweh (specified only once) to be the key factor in this geopolitical revolution. The "coming one" evokes a pathos-filled imperative for Egypt: "prepare for exile" (v. 19)![20] The judgment on Memphis echoes the earlier judgment on Jerusalem. God has decreed a terrible dismantling of royal power; the same "coming one" who ended Jerusalem will also end Memphis.

The juxtaposition of vv. 18-19 is telling. In v. 18 the "coming one" is sketched out with powerful, exaggerated rhetoric. The counterpart of Egypt (v. 19) bespeaks failure and defeat, a pitiful counterpart to Yahweh, unable to perform any effective role in the drama of power.

Verses 20-24 are framed with the ominous phrase "from the north" (vv. 20, 24; cf. 1:13-15). The one who comes is not named. We know his identity. It is not his identity that counts, however; it is his detailed characterization that interests the poet. This ominous one from the north is like a "gadfly" who comes to sting,

---

20. The phrasing and imagery of "baggage for exile" is the same as in Ezek. 12:7-16; only here it is the great empire who is to pack for deportation.

before whom Egypt, the "beautiful heifer," is helpless.[21] The image
then changes abruptly. The "gadfly" (46:20) becomes "enemies
marching in force" with axes, attacking the land and destroying
primitive forests (vv. 22-23). The figures of an insect (v. 20) and
an invading army (vv. 22-23) are brought together by the poet
in the image of the locust (v. 23). The locust is both a pesky insect
and an invading, irresistible army, too numerous to count, irresistible, destructive, intimidating, making one utterly helpless.

Against that awesome power from the north, Egypt is a "beautiful heifer," attractive, dumb, helpless, vulnerable, and exposed
(v. 20). The image of Egypt shifts slightly; the "beautiful heifer"
is now the "fatted calf" (v. 21). The first image was of the empire,
the second is of the soldiers. They are the ones entrusted with
resistance to "the coming one," but they are in fact only a valuable,
attractive sacrifice, to be done handily to death. At the edge of
the images of heifer and fatted calf, military language again intrudes language of retreat, calamity, and destruction (v. 21).

The image of Egypt now changes. The heifer has become a
serpent, quietly, stealthily sneaking away, sneaking to safety, but
a creature whose very name is one of shame and humiliation
(v. 22). The serpent may seek to hide in the underbrush, but the
coming one will destroy it. Even in the form of a devious, hiding
snake, Egypt cannot escape.

This poet voices a remarkable richness of images: beautiful *heifer,*
exposed to the pain-inflicting *gadfly,* the *fatted calf* vulnerable and
designed only for sacrifice (cf. v. 10), the *serpent* vulnerable to the
woodsmen, utterly exposed; finally comes the *locust* devouring all
that is still standing (cf. v. 14; 5:17 on devouring). The richness of
the imagery serves to dramatize and detail the uneven contest, the
hopelessness of Egypt and its sure defeat before the irresistible
invader. The images of Egypt are all of passivity and vulnerability.
There is nothing Egypt can do or will do. The images of the "one
who comes" bespeak aggressive and effective activity. The conflict is
so uneven, and the outcome is so unavoidable. Jeremiah 46:24 does
not advance the rhetoric, but only reiterates the now familiar themes
and drives to the inevitable conclusion: "Egypt will be handed over!"

---

21. Holladay, *Jeremiah 2,* 331-32, reads "horsefly" instead of "gadfly."

46:25-26   These prose verses now draw the explicit historical verdict that has been sketched in the foregoing poetry. It is as though the prose intends to name and identify (and inevitably flatten) the metaphors of the preceding. This explanatory comment is dominated by two powerful first person verbs, the first a participle and the second a perfect verb. These two verbs place Yahweh at the center of the action, attributing to Yahweh both enormous resolve and enormous power. The first verb asserts Yahweh's mustering of power against Egypt: "I am bringing punishment" *(pqd)*. The verb is followed by six uses of the preposition "against" *('yal)*: against Pharaoh, against Egypt, against its gods, against its kings, against Pharaoh, against all who trust Pharaoh. The grammar could not more relentlessly voice Yahweh's "againstness."[22]

This sweeping negative assertion is then explicated in v. 26 with the second strong verb, "I will deliver" *(ntn)*. Now we learn that the "againstness" of God is to be by the hand (power) of Nebuchadnezzar, who is now explicitly named as "the coming one" (v. 18; cf. v. 13). In this section the strong verb is followed by a threefold use of "the hand of"; "into the hand of those who seek their life, into the hand of Nebuchadnezzar, into the hand of his officers." This threefold usage matches the sixfold preposition of v. 25. The two series of uses thus juxtapose the unequal adversaries. In v. 25 the sixfold inventory names all those who are now at risk. The threefold usage in v. 26 counters by naming those who will prevail. Thus vv. 25 and 26 respectively explicate the "beautiful heifer," who is six times vulnerable, and the "gadfly," who is three times powerful. The outcome of this confrontation could hardly be more dramatically articulated.

At the end of v. 25 we are offered one more surprise: "afterward!" (cf. 25:12; 27:7, 20). The text dares to comment upon ancient Near Eastern politics, to anticipate the destiny of Egypt after the hegemony of Nebuchadnezzar which has been the subject of the poetry. One can, of course, imagine that this concluding

---

22. See the same negative preposition in a series in Isa. 2:12-16; Jer. 1:15; and in 48:18 with a weaker preposition. In each case God is said to be "against" everything that is established.

assertion only reflects historical experience after Nebuchadnezzar, for the Babylonian threat against Egypt could not be sustained very long. On such historical grounds, the line seems to retreat from the sweeping rhetoric of the preceding. The line, however, need not be taken simply as a reflection of subsequent historical events. It can be taken canonically as awareness that even Nebuchadnezzar and even Babylon are penultimate. The Babylonian army and empire are not the real determinants of the historical process, and even such a massive political construct as Babylon finally cannot endure.

If the Babylonian achievement is penultimate, then what is ultimate? Who is then ultimate? It is Yahweh who governs the two strong verbs of 46:25-26. It is Yahweh who speaks this oracle, who concludes "says the LORD." It is Yahweh and not Babylon who will fix the long-term destiny of Egypt. That long-term destiny willed by Yahweh is that Egypt will live as in "the days of old." The Babylonian invasion is an episode for Egypt, not an irreversible development. After this episode which lacks staying power, God intends even Egypt to live in its own land, as it used to be. Egypt had indeed been too ambitious (cf. v. 8). When that imperial ambition is defeated, however, Egypt can return to its proper role in its proper sphere.[23] God does not want to destabilize this great power endlessly.

The great powers, however, must learn (again and again, it appears) that they are not autonomous agents free to act according to their unbridled power. The historical process, governed by Yahweh, will in savage and cunning ways curb such arrogance, leaving the aggressor unhealed (v. 11) and displaced (v. 19). The large future of the historical process cannot be nullified, even by imperial pretension. The purpose of Yahweh, who stands sovereign within the historical process, cannot be mocked. There is indeed an "afterward," even for Egypt. The route from self-serving ag-

---

23. A return to a proper sphere of power, influence, and ambition is what Kennedy, *The Rise and Fall of the Great Powers,* urges and believes possible. That is, an overextended great power need not disintegrate. It can be changed for a realistic chance at life. The anticipation of this text and the analysis of Kennedy are agreed in an alternative to destruction.

gressiveness to well-being in one's own proper sphere, however, is a route of terror, brutality, and suffering. Egypt stands, in the final form of the text, as a cipher for all the great powers, who learn again and again, so reluctantly and so painfully.

The poem, cast in the voice of Yahweh, exhibits a sober, balanced view of the public process of history. It refutes and rejects a view which says that the historical process is endlessly submissive to raw power. It asserts, as the only viable alternative to raw power, an ordered governance from Yahweh which limits, curbs, and chastens. One option for the public process (embodied here by Pharaoh) allows no Yahweh to speak or act. The other option, carried in the mouth of the prophet, portrays Yahweh indefatigably at the center of the international process. To be a prophet "to the nations" (cf. 1:10) means to portray the process of public power as a process under a larger purpose and not as an end in itself.

The final phrase of 46:26 is telling: "says the LORD." Yahweh is the ultimate and decisive speaker of the historical process. Yahweh does not want to force the great powers out of history, but Yahweh does relentlessly insist that the great powers must accept their proper and therefore limited role. That Egypt will again be inhabited means that it belongs inalienably in the public process. Egypt's life and power are, however, penultimate, as is Nebuchadnezzar's great conquest. What prevails in the end is only "says the LORD."

46:27-28 Throughout this long poem Israel, Judah, and Jerusalem have not been mentioned (except for the historical notation of v. 2). Indeed, Israel, Judah, and Jerusalem are nowhere on the horizon of this poem. The issue of the poem concerns the imperial power of Egypt coming to terms with the governance of Yahweh, without reference to any privileged role for the biblical community. Verses 25-26 have provided something of an interpretive conclusion for the poem.

Then, however, vv. 27-28 appear at the end of the poem as an extrapolation from the preceding action. These verses constitute an odd, unexpected development in the poem. Two things are clear. First, the assertion of the rule of Yahweh over Egypt has crucial derivative implications for Israel. It is not that Yahweh has taken action against Egypt for the sake of Israel; God's actions are only because of Egypt's arrogant overextendedness, which mocks Yahweh. Nonetheless, when Egypt comes under the governance of Yahweh, as it now will do through the agency of Babylon, Israel finds itself in a new position. Thus the odd continuation of the Egyptian poem in vv. 27-28 dramatically asserts that benefit to Israel is derivative from Yahweh's sovereign dealing with the nations. This odd derivative effect is nowhere more clearly articulated than in Ezek. 36.[24] God's actions are undertaken not because God loves Israel, but because Yahweh will be honored (Ezek. 36:22, 32). Yahweh's desire to be honored by the nations benefits Israel. So in our passage, God's actions are not because God loves Israel, but these acts nonetheless benefit Israel.

Second, the benefit to Israel in the preceding poetry is stated in a traditional formulation we have already considered in Jer. 30:10-11. As the "war oracle" against Egypt in 46:3-4, 9 uses old formulations which were used against Judah in chs. 4-6, so now the good news for Israel also uses an old formula already used in ch. 30. What interests us is not the text itself (already discussed in its locus in 30:10-11), but the placement, use, and intent of the text in this location.

These verses constitute a salvation oracle, with the double assertion, "Fear not" (46:27-28).[25] Each assuring imperative is followed (as is characteristic of the form) with a reason why Israel should not fear. The reasons are (1) "I will save you," and (2) "I am with you." This is the God who will end exile, bringing Jacob safely home and giving security. This is the God who will deal severely with the exile-causing nations. Thus the oracle concerns the end of Judah's exile. In terms of its specific statement, this is an odd announcement here, because it seems concerned with Babylon who caused exile, rather than with Egypt, the subject of vv. 1-26. That, however, only evidences that these two verses are an old poem reused and redirected.

Now the salvation oracle, the homecoming, and the gift of

---

24. See Brueggemann, *Hopeful Imagination,* 68-87; and Gowan, *Eschatology in the Old Testament.*

25. See Conrad, *Fear Not Warrior,* 108-115.

well-being and security are connected to the judgment against Egypt. The oracle of Yahweh against Egypt has made the world a safe place for Israel.

As v. 28 sorts out Yahweh's intention for the nations and Israel's benefit, the poem uses two rhetorical structures which are very different. On the one hand, there is a contrast between the host nations of exile and the people of Jacob. For the former, there is "a full end." For Jacob there is no "full end," that is, Jacob can and will endure beyond exile.[26] On the other hand, the last two lines of the unit concern only Jacob, the other nations now being absent. The destiny of Jacob at the hands of Yahweh is twofold and delicate. There will be appropriate chastening, as when a father chastens a son. The historical process has abundantly delivered the chastening. Jacob will not be off scot-free (cf. Isa. 40:2). The counterpoint to this verse is unstated. We expect a statement that says, "but I will not destroy." This is not stated but is perhaps implicit in the adjective, "in just measure" *(mishpat);* that is, the chastening is appropriate punishment, but not capricious or ultimate nullification. This carefully wrought verse delicately asserts that Judah's position vis-à-vis Yahweh is very different from the position of the nations that host the Exile. That difference is perhaps rooted in the old covenant tradition, though nothing is said of covenant.

Or perhaps Judah's special future is rooted in the difference Yahweh makes between perpetrator nations and victim nations, as though God cares differently for the victim nations. No such

---

26. On the contrast of "make an end" and "not make an end," see also Amos 9:8; Jer. 4:27; 5:10, 18. The prophetic tradition struggles relentlessly with the question of God's making an end of God's people. Cf. Frank Crüsemann, "Kritik an Amos im Deuteronomistischen Geschichtswerk," in *Probleme biblischer Theologie.* Festschrift Gerhard von Rad, ed. Hans Walter Wolff (Munich: Kaiser, 1971), 57-63; Rudolf Smend, "'Das Ende ist gekommen': Ein Amoswort in der Priesterschrift," in *Die Botschaft und die Boten.* Festschrift Hans Walter Wolff, ed. Jörg Jeremias and Lothar Perlitt (Neukirchen-Vluyn: Neukirchener, 1981), 67-72; and Klaus Koch, "Das Profetenschweigen des deuteronomistischen Geschichtswerks," in Jeremias-Perlitt, 115-128. To be sure, these reflections concern *qets,* not the word for "end" in our text. The questions nonetheless are much the same with the use of the two terms.

distinction, however, is explicit in the poem. What is clear is that after the massive rhetorical assault on Egypt (Jer. 46:3-26), there is here a modest counterpoint. God values the little one, God notices the abased one, and God gives to this oppressed one a future. Egypt is given a future: "Egypt shall be inhabited as in the days of old" (v. 26). Jacob is given a future; "Jacob shall have quiet and ease" (v. 27). Both the great power and the beloved community are given futures, and the two futures are not incompatible.[27]

It is as though the poem witnesses to and sanctions a moment in geopolitics which is chaotic and disruptive, when power is turned loose against all established normalcies. The poem, in the end, envisions a settled normalcy when all the powers are back in their proper places and proper perspectives. When that happens, Jacob can resume its life. For both the empire and the beloved community, everything depends on Yahweh's sovereign rule. Without that sovereign rule, all these states are left in disarray and under threat. When Yahweh's sovereign rule reemerges, as it does through this poem, well-being comes. Both the long military mock-sing (vv. 3-26) and the brief salvation oracle (vv. 27-28) are rhetorical acts in the service of God's reestablished order. That order in the end will serve both Egypt and Israel well. It is worth noting that Babylon, the agent of reestablished order, receives no word of a future here. That comes later in the tradition of Jeremiah (chs. 50–51). The "prophet to the nations" has reenvisioned the ancient Near East as a map of well-being where there is just chastening but not an end. Rather, Yahweh's reestablished rule is a new beginning. There must be endings, but here they serve only to begin again.

ORACLE AGAINST THE PHILISTINES (47:1-7)

The Philistines are an old, traditional enemy of Israel, especially prominent in the time of Saul and David. Later, by the time of

---

27. In a quite different tradition (Isa. 19:24-25), the great powers and the beloved community finally come to share in the favor and blessing of the God who presides over the affairs of both.

Jeremiah, they do not figure as a political force, but are pawns of the great powers. The region of the Philistines, however, continued to be a strategically crucial position in the path between Egypt and the threatening power "of the north." In practice, the Philistine region had become a satellite of Egypt, exercising no independent political position. As satellite, it was of course exposed to and vulnerable before the same threat as was Egypt. Consequently it is useful to regard this brief poem of ch. 47 as a satellite to the larger poem of ch. 46.

This is a poem that does not develop very much; that is, it contains no plot. Its single idea is to assert in the most vivid way possible that the Philistines are under threat "out of the north" (47:2). The poem uses highly stylized formulas to convey that single motif.

47:1 This verse again identifies the poem as God's word to Jeremiah; in other words, we are again hearing "the prophet to the nations." The timing of the oracle "before Pharaoh smote Gaza" is a curious one. That phrasing suggests a threat from Philistia's south, but the poem itself concerns the threat "from the north." We lack sufficient data to determine what is intended by the phrasing of v. 1.

47:2-7 The poem begins with the metaphor of "waters, overflowing torrent" (v. 2). The image of "waters" bespeaks the surging threat of chaos that is relentless, irresistible, and endlessly destructive. Already in Isa. 8:7-8 Assyria had been pictured as a great chaotic threat against Judah, and now the same image is used to allude to a subsequent power from the north which will again bring chaos, destruction, and death. The waters of chaos will fill the land and inundate the cities. Nothing will be exempt from the threat to come. The danger will evoke terror and fear, dread and grief — an enormous cry of need, helplessness, and hopelessness.

The image is changed in Jer. 47:3, or perhaps better, the metaphor of surging waters is now connected to a concrete reference. The "chaotic waters" are in fact the onslaught of a savage army. Again using the standard formulas of military poetry, v. 3 evokes a sense of ominous power and massive danger — of huge stallions, rushing chariots, and rumbling wheels. The poet seeks to bring the listeners into the specific action of the one-sided battle. That picture of brutal and determined force from the north is sharply contrasted with the Philistine fathers, the ones formerly of military prowess, now unable even to protect their own children, now utterly weak, and failed, and helpless. The rhetoric draws a powerful and complete contrast between power and weakness, between success and shame, between action and passivity.

The metaphor of rushing waters and the image of charging soldiers finally converge at the first poetic climax. It is "the day" (v. 4; cf. 46:10)![28] It is Yahweh's day, the day of armed assertiveness, of vengeance, of raw unrestrained power. It is Yahweh and none other who dares this awesome deed of destruction. The name of Yahweh is now evoked for the first time in the poem. It is Yahweh who comes against the Philistines. (The reference to Tyre and Sidon here is enigmatic; apparently these coastal cities are here grouped with the Philistine cities, also subject to the terrible threat of the day.)

The juxtaposition of 47:2-3 and v. 4 reiterates what we have seen in 46:3-10. The ostensive enemy is "from the north," that is, Babylon. The theological accent of these poems, however, makes clear that the real destroyer is not Babylon, but Yahweh. It is Yahweh who is at work to establish or reestablish Yahweh's own hegemony. The poem is a theological act that insists upon a drastic rereading of political reality.

The Philistine response to the massive threat of Yahweh is pictured in a derisive way (v. 5). Reference is made to two Philistine cities, Gaza and Ashkelon, which have been centers of power, but are now centers of grief. The third line of the verse appears to be mocking. The men of the Philistines had been powerful and formidable, before whom the ancient Israelites stood in awe. Now, because of this massive reversal wrought through an invasion, there is only a remnant, only the feeble descendants and leftovers of the

---

28. The notion of "the day" is rooted in military references that indicate the coming of massive devastation dispatched by God. See von Rad, *Old Testament Theology,* 2 (1965):119-125.

great ones. Perhaps this is a comment on how few they are. More likely the phrase suggests that the great ones have come upon pitiful days. Indeed, David's grieving song, which he did not want overheard by the Philistines, said of Saul and Jonathan, "How are the mighty fallen!" (2 Sam. 1:25, 27). Keeping that poem in mind, there is perhaps high irony here.[29] The Philistines were the mighty ones, and now the mighty ones among the Philistines have fallen. They are reduced not only to ordinary folk, but to pitiful soldiers who cringe before the invasion, who have not the energy ever to be effective fathers! Their characteristic acts are "baldness" and "gashing," either desperate attempts to bring and motivate their impotent gods or, more likely, acts of terrible grieving over the loss of their known world.[30] Either as desperate religion or as pitiful grief, the former "giants" are now helpless. The rhetoric helps render them helpless, making their impotence and hopelessness palpable. Indeed, no "helper" remains (cf. Jer. 47:4). The poet carefully offers a sketch of an old power that has failed; warriors now grieve, soldiers falter, fathers fail even their own little children. The poem itself is a powerful rhetorical act of diminishment. The great ones are indeed fallen, and their own pious acts of impotence measure their futility and despair.

The poem concludes with a harsh vocative (vv. 6-7): "Ah, sword of the LORD!" The one addressed is unnamed, indeed not named anywhere in the poem. In v. 2 we know of one "out of the north," but that is all. From the context and from ch. 46, we surmise that the one addressed is Babylon, or even Nebuchadnezzar who is to be "Yahweh's sword." The poet, however, is either restrained or judicious, leaving everything open and unspecified. The one addressed is some human agent, some historical threat, authorized by Yahweh to move "against Ashkelon and against the seashore" (47:7).

The vocative address performs a trick. The ostensive question

---

29. The same inscrutable reversal of the Philistines is narrated for an earlier period in the "Ark narrative" of 1 Sam. 4:1–7:1. The Philistines have their season of success and power, but they are pitiful and helpless when Yahweh's power is mobilized against them.

30. In 1 Sam. 6:1-9 the Philistines are portrayed as helpless and frantic to avoid the threat of God. On frantic ritual activities in the face of God's power, see 1 Kgs. 18:28-29.

of v. 6 is "When will you stop your destructiveness? When will you have done enough? When will you finally desist, either in exhaustion or in satiation?" The question is put as though the questioner (the poet, Yahweh) is exhausted with the feverish activity of "the sword of Yahweh" and wants the devastation to stop. The question implies an exasperated "Enough!" Or perhaps the question is wishful thinking in the mouth of the Philistines? Or if the questioner is in fact Yahweh, then the question sounds as though Yahweh's destructive sword is autonomous, out of control, and no longer subordinate to Yahweh. Then the question suggests that the sword is indeed "out of hand."

Whatever the intent of the question, it receives a harsh answer. How can the sword be quiet? How can the sword rest or how can it be sheathed? It cannot be rested; it dare not be, because it has been mandated (commanded) by Yahweh and must do its terrible work for Yahweh against the Philistines. The sword is not out of control. It is appointed and authorized by Yahweh, and it must do its obedient work. That is, the destruction now happening in the Philistine cities is not just northern aggression. It is an act commanded by Yahweh.

The poem revolves around one idea, namely, destruction from the hand of Yahweh. No reason for the destruction is given. There is nothing here of Philistine arrogance or brutality or disobedience.[31] The poem simply anticipates terrible military devastation; four times the poem connects the devastation to the purpose of Yahweh: "day" of Yahweh (v. 4), "Yahweh destroys" (v. 4), "sword of Yahweh" (v. 6), and "Yahweh gives charge" (v. 7). Everything that is happening is credited to Yahweh. The historical process is not on its own.

The poet ostensibly wants the Philistines to notice and understand what is happening. The poet intends that the Philistines should be theologically alert. Behind that ostensive purpose, however, the poem is an acknowledgement of Yahweh's unqualified governance, wrought here as terrible violence.

---

31. This is in contrast to the Oracles against the Nations in Amos 1–2, where there are reasons for the destruction, reasons related to barbarism and massive cruelty. Such reasons may be inferred here, but they are not stated.

Interpreting this text requires both candor and criticism. The candor is to confess that the poem affronts us. It is so severe and so raw, and indeed shameless, unbothered about the theological authorization of brutality. We might wish it otherwise, but this is what we have. The criticism we must do is to ask what is intended in this speech. What response does the poem intend to evoke? Perhaps the poet wishes only to assert the unqualified and unprincipled rule of Yahweh, unprincipled because in this text we are given no warrant or sanction for what Yahweh is doing.

More likely, in the assertion of Yahweh's unqualified role, the poet intends to establish a ground of hope outside all established normalcies. Yahweh is not domesticated by any of our conventionalities, but acts in sheer freedom, owing no one anything. Listeners to this poem are invited to face this undomesticated God who may violate our sensitivities, this God who may be the only hope for the Philistines as for Israel. Of course the point is not to do "theology." The poet wants to understand and embrace life in the world. It is evident that a force of chaos is set loose, flowing like volcanic lava. The foe from the north may be only sheer chaos. The poet dares to assert, without denying the severity of the threat, that even this flow of chaos has a name, an unmocked name. The brutality evident in this poem is nothing less than brutal. It is in the end, however, a "connected brutality," connected to the name of Yahweh and therefore to large purposes. It is an odd way *in extremis* to assert moral coherence in public reality. Whatever moral coherence there is depends on the undomesticated one, who works God's own way, savagely and relentlessly. Moreover, all the calculated response of the Philistines (baldness, gashing) does not curb this raw holiness, which permits no explanation but only evocative, shrill speech of testimony.

ORACLE AGAINST MOAB (48:1-47)

Upon finishing with the Philistines in ch. 47, the text moves abruptly east across the hill country and the Jordan River to address Moab. When the address begins, it goes on and on, yielding a long and complicated poem, longer even than that addressed to mighty Egypt.

235

This long poem is exceedingly difficult, and scholars are uncertain on a number of preliminary points: (1) It is exceedingly difficult to locate *political-historical events* that correspond to the poetry, though William L. Holladay makes a characteristically valiant effort.[32] (2) It is impossible to identify geographically many of the *place names,* and the poem invites considerable speculation among scholars. (3) The poem is disordered so that a *literary analysis* is complicated, even assuming that sense can be made of it. There is no doubt that this poetry utilized traditional materials that must have belonged to an established pattern of rhetoric concerning the nations and especially concerning Moab. (4) It is difficult to determine why *this poem concerning Moab is so extensive,* compared to any of the others in the corpus. Clearly the poem became a "catchall" for traditional materials, variously judged "authentic" and "secondary." Very likely Moab as a close competitor and immediate rival evokes a hostility and resentment greater than found elsewhere.

Because we can reach no reliable conclusions concerning political-historical, geographical, or literary matters related to the poem, we are largely limited to the claim of the text itself (not a bad limit), which requires no great speculation about matters outside the text. We may better ask, what rhetorical effect does the text intend to evoke in its listeners, listeners who ostensively are Moabites but who are likely to have been Judeans?

48:1-9 This poetic unit makes an abrupt beginning, linking two unlikely items (48:1a). First, the subject is Moab! The utterance of the name no doubt evokes in Judah a host of negative sensitivities. Second, Israel's "LORD of the troops" is about to speak. In quick fashion, the *destiny of Moab* is drawn into the sphere of *Yahweh's sovereign speech.* That national destiny will be powerfully impinged upon by this sovereign speech.

The first word this ominous God speaks is "Woe," that is, trouble, death, judgment (v. 1b). The long chapter to follow is a complicated exposition of this simple utterance. The "woe destiny" of Moab is presented, in the beginning, by two rhetorical devices

---

32. Holladay, *Jeremiah 2,* 353-364.

(vv. 1b-5). On the one hand, the cities, the great centers of economic power and military pride, are named: Nebo, Kiriathaim, Heshbon, Madmen, Horonaim, Zoar, Luhith. The poem sounds like an intelligence report for a coming invader. The poem knows the terrain of Moab well. On the other hand, the poetry couples with the naming of centers of power and pride phrases concerning suffering, destruction, and death: "Laid waste, put to shame, taken, put to shame, broken down, cut off, brought to silence, pursued by a sword, desolation, great destruction, destroyed, cry, weeping, cry of destruction." The connection between the *centers of power and pride* and the *phrasings of loss* pound at the listener. What had seemed permanent and secure is rhetorically undermined and placed in jeopardy. Indeed, these two incongruous rhetorical elements fight each other; in their fight, the poem accomplishes a massive inversion, for the centers are, through the poem, emptied of pride and power.

Having anticipated the devastation, the poem now addresses those who live in the midst of the devastation (vv. 6-9). Verses 6 and 9 provide an inclusio; v. 6 is an imperative urging flight out of the city to escape the devastation;[33] v. 9 oddly differentiates between "Moab" (presumably its people) and the destroyed cities. The people are urged to separate themselves from the cities (and perhaps from the royal-urban ideology which drives those cities toward destructiveness). In both verses the listeners are urged to escape, for the coming attack will focus on those centers of power and pride.

Within that inclusio, vv. 7-8 voice a prophetic lawsuit. The indictment in the first line focuses on "false trust" *(bth)*, which is in fact idolatry. The sentence now announced is that Chemosh, the Moabite god, will go into exile *(glh)*, along with priests and princes. Thus the assault is upon the power structure, its leaders, and its religious ideology which has fostered and legitimated a

---

33. See Robert Bach, *Die Aufforderung zur Flucht und zum Kampf im alttestamentliche Prophetenspruch.* Wissenschaftliche Monographien zum Alten und Neuen Testament 9 (Neukirchen-Vluyn: Neukirchener, 1962); and Patrick D. Miller, Jr., "The Divine Council and the Prophetic Call to War," *Vetus Testamentum* 18 (1968): 100-107.

false perception of reality. In v. 8 the poet utters the ominous "the destroyer" *(sh-d-d)*. The term *sh-d-d* is the same as the term "laid waste," which began the deathly recital of v. 1b. "The destroyer" is not named, but the threat is real and concrete. Though the focus of the poem has been on cities and strongholds, now the horizon of the "destroyer" includes cities, valleys, and plains, that is, everything everywhere. The assault is twofold, as is characteristic in Judah, for it includes both the prospect of exile and the danger of devastation. Thus the destiny of Moab is the same as the fate of Judah previously announced in the book of Jeremiah. Both Judah and Moab receive the same from the hand of Yahweh, and both receive the same from the action of Nebuchadnezzar. Both receive for the same reason: "Because you trusted . . . !"

48:10-13 These verses provide a reflective pause, an interlude, in the poetry. They consist in a brief poetic statement (v. 11) enveloped in what appear to be two prose elements (vv. 10, 12, 13). The poetic element presents the situation of Moab under the metaphor of wine-making (v. 11). Moab has had a long, pleasant career as a winemaker and producer. The winemaker has been at ease, prosperous, and indolent, content not to remove the sediment in the wine (lees). On "ease," see Amos 6:1 for the same term of complacency applied to Zion. On complacency concerning the process of wine-making, see Zeph. 1:12. In Zephaniah the indifference and complacency is because it is believed that "The LORD will not do good, nor will he do ill." That is, the indifference and indolence are because the God of Israel is not taken seriously as a norm, a demand, or a threat. The life of the complacent and indolent winemaker has been unbothered and untroubled, perfectly at ease. Now the poem shifts the image. Now Moab is not the winemaker, but the wine that has been left undisturbed, not moved around, not poured out, that is, not taken into exile *(glh)!* (Again that ominous word!) The result of the lack of disturbance is that the taste and smell of the winemaker has gone unchallenged and unchanged. Moab has gone to sleep in its well-being.

That idyllic picture of untroubled Moab is juxtaposed to the two incongruous prose verses. Everyone is to do the destructive work of Yahweh with vigor (Jer. 48:10)! The time is coming for the ominous days of dismantling (vv. 12-13). The text returns in v. 12 to the imagery of the middle portion of v. 11. There will be poured out Moab, poured out like wine, and the containers will be empty, broken, smashed. The theological conclusion is that the Moabite god Chemosh will have failed (cf. v. 7). This odd sequence of statements holds together poetic metaphor (wine-making), political analysis (exile for Moab), and theological verdict (failure of Chemosh). The destiny of Moab (like the destiny of Israel) partakes of and requires all three elements for its full articulation. The last word in v. 13 is "confidence" *(bth)*, the same root as the powerful indictment of v. 7. Thus Moab trusted in its own strength (v. 7) and in the power of its god who sustained that strength (v. 13), even as Israel placed its trust in the wrong object. Both politically and theologically, the season of Moab's ease is over, brutally terminated.

48:14-20   In this poetic section the language and images echo vv. 6-9. Again it is the "LORD of hosts" who speaks (v. 15). This time the title is escalated. Yahweh is "the King," thus providing a direct challenge to the rule of Chemosh, who is in process of being dethroned and displaced. Twice in connection with the mention of Israel's God there is also mention of "the destroyer of Moab" *(sh-d-d,* vv. 15, 18). By the verdict of Yahweh, the God of Israel, a terrible destructive force has been unloosed in the political arena against Moab.

Again the rhetoric engages in sharp reversals to voice the dismantling of Moabite power and pride. The mocking address is to the "heroes," the "mighty men," "the choicest of his young men," "the mighty scepter," "the glorious staff." The poet with great extravagance names and acknowledges all the well-being, prestige, and grandeur of Moab. Such a naming, however, is part of a larger strategy of humiliation. The great ones are named only to be attacked.

The poem urges Moab to change its speech, in order to bring its speech into contact with the new reality caused by Yahweh. They did say, "We are heroes" (v. 14). They are now urged to say, "How the mighty scepter is broken" (v. 17). The first speech is

obsolete and now illusionary; the poet urges Moab's speech to
embrace the new reality of devastation. The poet seeks to break
the power of ideology which keeps speaking about a reality that
no longer exists. There follows once again a rich vocabulary of
devastation: "calamity, affliction, bemoan, destroyed, flee, put to
shame, broken, wail, and cry." This collage of words contrasts
totally with the preceding cluster of "heroes, mighty men, choicest,
and so forth." What had been is no more. What will be is deathliness, wrought by "the King" (v. 15). Between what has been
and what will now be stands the decree of Yahweh and the
unnamed "destroyer." The unit ends with "laid waste" (*sh-d-d*,
v. 20), thus referring back to the opening of v. 1b. The whole
poem thus far is situated between "laid waste" (v. 1b) and "laid
waste" (v. 20); between these two dread-filled verbs lies Moab's
future.

48:21-28   These verses in prose (except the conclusion, v. 28,
in poetry) introduce no new themes, but state the issue of Yahweh
against Moab with rich and varied metaphor. It is helpful to see
that these lines express the two motifs of a prophetic lawsuit,
indictment and sentence.

The indictment against Moab is twofold. First, Moab made
himself great against Yahweh; that is, Moab asserted autonomy
from Yahweh (v. 26). The indictment, on the face of it, is more
than a little curious, because Moab would not have imagined itself
in any way in relation to Yahweh. The text, however, never reflects
upon or explains why Moab should be responsive or submissive
to Yahweh. The text simply assumes this to be the case, and further
assumes that Moab should know about this definitional relation.
That Yahwistic claim, which is foundational to all these "Oracles
against the Nations," is a daring act of rhetoric which insists upon
connections where others do not notice or acknowledge them.
Moab's failure is a failure to come to terms with the rule of Yahweh,
a rule which is the driving power of this poetry.

Second, the specific way in which Moab "magnified itself" is
that it made a laughingstock of Israel. The language is not unlike
that of the Psalms of Lament, which complain of people treating
Israel with contempt (Ps. 59:8; Lam. 1:7; Jer. 20:7). Moab has

treated Israel with contempt. This is the way in which Moab has violated Yahweh. Thus sin against the "brother" here is indeed sin against God. Moab does not love the brother whom it has seen, and surely does not love God whom it has not seen (cf. 1 John 4:20).

From such a foundational indictment comes a severe sentence. The punishment for defying Yahweh and mocking Israel is stated in three sets of metaphors. First, "judgment" *(mishpat)* of a political-military kind is described which is massive and comprehensive (Jer. 48:21-25). The attack envisioned includes the "tableland" and "all the cities." That utter devastation has broken the power ("horn," "arm") of Moab (v. 25), so that Moab is reduced to a helpless subject state.

The second set of metaphors is more venturesome. Moab will be made drunk and will wallow in his vomit (v. 26). The image suggests humiliation, weakness, helplessness, and instability, the depth of pitiful degradation. The third element in the characterization of Moab's new situation is to be "held in derision" *(sh-h-q,* v. 26), that is, treated with contempt (a punishment which corresponds verbally to the indictment of v. 27). That is, Moab will now be treated the way Moab has cynically treated Israel.[34] It is no wonder that this section concludes in v. 28 with poetry echoing v. 9. The only counsel the poem offers is to leave, escape, and go hide in remote places in the hinterland, for the destruction is severe and wholesale. There is no hope except to flee.

48:29-33   The poetry now resumes after the prose unit, utilizing lines from Isa. 16:6ff. This unit is a lawsuit which turns on the "therefore" in Jer. 48:31. Verses 29-30 are the indictment, which is completely lacking in specificity but which piles up the vocabulary concerning defiance, arrogance, and autonomy. This language is an extrapolation from the pivotal indictment of v. 26. Moab is guilty of "pride, pride, loftiness, pride, arrogance, a haughty heart." All but the last of these six words either is derived

---

34. Again, notice the precise correspondence between offense and punishment, as noticed programmatically by Patrick D. Miller, Jr., *Sin and Judgment in the Prophets.*

from the same root or sounds alike. The rhetorical effect is cumulative. Moab has thought it was outside the arena of Yahweh's sovereignty and could do what it wanted, for the indictment of haughtiness and insolence has substance only in a world where Yahweh is the decisive point of reference. The conclusion of the indictment in v. 30 is terse and abrupt: "not so in his hand, not so they do" (author's translation). What Moab does has no substance, because there is a quality of unreality about its life, an unreality rooted in a lack of reality about its relation to Yahweh. Moab treats Yahweh as unreal; the outcome, however, is not that Yahweh is made unreal by Moab, but that the life of Moab becomes a self-destructive unreality. Yahweh stands "real" in the poem, to the harsh cost of Moab.

The sentence against Moab bespeaks the coming devastation and suffering (vv. 31-33). Verse 32 hints at the well-being and effectiveness of the Moabite economy, which in the past was extensive and productive. Against all that prosperity, however, "the destroyer" has come. Again the poet uses the term as we have seen repeatedly, *sh-d-d*. We do not know if "the destroyer" is Yahweh or some human agent designated by Yahweh. The poet gives us no hint and lets the rhetoric make its own intimidating case.

As a result of "the destroyer" who will devastate Moab, there is occasion for mourning, weeping, crying. The poet conducts a national funeral. This motif of sadness over the ruin was already anticipated in the first word of the poetry, "Woe" (v. 1b). The word bespeaks the sadness and grief of death, and now the poet explicates that large initiatory word. Thus the coming practice of grief, sadness, and mourning (vv. 31-32) is nicely juxtaposed with the gladness and shouts of joy which have been heard but which now are silenced (v. 33).[35] The harvest time is a time of exuberant celebration, a time of rich profit, an assurance of blessing, and no doubt of exaggerated drinking. All of that extravagant celebration, however, will now cease. The wine-making will stop, and with it

---

35. On the contrasting sounds of grief and joy, see the suggestive metaphor of Jer. 7:34; 16:9; 25:10; 33:11. On similar imagery for drastic reversal, see Luke 6:20-21; John 16:22.

all glad occasions of profit, blessing, and imbibing. The poet anticipates an abrupt end to all joy and celebration so characteristic of the community. The regular patterns of social life which generate celebration, well-being, and identity are all halted; in their place come grief and mourning. By the cluster of the words for *mourning* and for *joy*, the poet has enacted a dramatic reversal of the fortunes of the community.

The poem has made use of the figure of wine-making in different ways. In vv. 11-12 the images are mixed, whereby Moab is a producer of wine but then is also the wine poured out (in exile). In v. 26 Moab is the victim of wine. Now in these verses the reference is the joy evoked in wine-making time. By the use of this metaphor, along with other images, the poet has effected a complete and dramatic reversal. In both the positive reference to joy (now terminated) and in the negative reference to grief (now anticipated), the vocabulary is reiterative and cumulative. Indeed, in this unit we may identify three clusters of terms which express intensity, passion, and certitude about the future:

Moab's offense:	Moab's loss:	Moab's destiny:
pride	summer fruits	wail
proud	vintage	cry out
loftiness	gladness	mourn
pride	joy	weep
arrogance	wine	
haughtiness	shouts of joy	
insolence	shouts of joy	

These clusters of words revolve around a very simple argument urged by the poet. *Arrogance* causes enormous *loss,* which evokes profound *grief.* At the center of the process of arrogance-loss-grief stands Yahweh in uncompromising sovereignty.

48:34-39 These verses are dominated by the first person asseverations of Yahweh: "I will bring an end to Moab" or, alternatively, "I will cause a sabbath to Moab" (v. 35). Yahweh's resolve is to cause Moab to disappear. That verdict of God dominates this section and, indeed, the entire chapter. From that verdict, the other elements of this unit follow: (1) There is grief over Moab, because of its wretchedness and death (v. 34). (2) Moab is indicted as a worshipper of false gods (v. 35). (3) There must be deep grief (moaning) of a ritual kind (i.e., set to music) because of the massive, visible reversals of fortunes (v. 36).

From the verdict comes an outpouring of overwhelming grief (vv. 37-38). Four acts of public grief are named: shaving heads, cutting off beards, gashing hands, and dressing in sackcloth (cf. 47:5-6). The extremity of the lament indicates the depth of the loss. The reason for the loss is that God's own self has broken the vessel "no one wants" (NRSV). The poem uses a metaphor used earlier for Israel, for Jerusalem, and even for a deposed king.[36] Jeremiah 48:39 seems to be almost a quote of the lament itself. In grief, this is what the mourner might say: "How it is broken!"[37] The poet comes close to the edge of language, beyond which nothing dare be uttered. The rhetoric provides no coherent statement, but almost an ejaculation of disconnected words: "broken, wail, shame, derision." Moab is completely dismantled; nothing coherent can even be voiced about it.

48:40-47   The concluding poetic unit on Moab again sounds the notes of devastation and ruin. In vv. 40-43 we have a description of the threat. The one who is to come (we are not told whom) comes as a massive, hovering dangerous eagle, who will swoop up Moab. The metaphor of eagle quickly yields to more concrete, graphic description. The attack will be against the centers of power (cities and fortresses), and the hearts of the Moabite soldiers will melt in fear. The poet uses a startling metaphor to contrast the would-be valor and courage of the soldiers with the anguish and hurt of labor pains. This metaphor is not unlike that of the failed fathers of 47:3. The outcome of such a terrible threat that reduces to helpless trembling is "terror, pit, and snare"

---

36. See 22:28; 30:12-17. On the latter, see Brueggemann, "The 'Uncared for' Now Cared for."

37. On the same imagery, though with different terminology, see 19:11. Here the broken pot is Moab; there it is Israel and Jerusalem. In this oracle Moab receives the same devastating treatment earlier enacted against Israel.

(48:43), that is, places of utter defeat and hopelessness. The poem does not linger long to tell us why this will happen. The reason, already stated in v. 26, is that Moab has magnified itself against Yahweh, that is, acted in defiance against the rule of Yahweh. Such an act of self-magnification can only bring ruin and devastation.

The theme of "terror, pit, and snare" is an especially powerful alliteration in Hebrew: *phd, pht, ph*. While the triad is offered in v. 43 only as a conventional formula,[38] in v. 44 the poem arranges in a more meaningful sequence. Now one moves from one danger to the next. The cumulative effect of the three terms is a sense of inescapability and therefore hopelessness. There will be no way to circumvent the harsh destiny of judgment now set in motion. The general theme of inescapability of judgment echoes Amos 5:18-20, but the specific wording of these verses is more paralleled by Isa. 24:17-18, in which the same phrasing is utilized in an apocalyptic context.

The long rhetorical assault on Moab culminates in Jer. 48:45-47. These lines refer again to Heshbon, center of power (v. 45). Heshbon, however, is now surrounded by desperate fugitives trying to escape the devastation. The great city is burning; the monarchy is up in flames. The threat reaches to the center of power, of autonomy, of arrogance. It touches the crown and core of what had been limitless pride. The "sons of tumult" have, by the end of the poem, reached their sorry destruction.

The "political job" done on Moab in v. 45 is matched in v. 46 with a theological reference. The verse begins with "woe," reiterating the ominous beginning point of v. 1b.[39] Moab is now "undone"; in other words, Moab will perish as a vulnerable, helpless community, sons and daughters (i.e., everyone into exile). It is stunning that this is now "the people of Chemosh," Moab as known by its god. In v. 7 it is Chemosh who goes into exile. In v. 13 Moab is ashamed of Chemosh. The defeat of Moab is in actuality the defeat of this god who is no god at all. The fall of Moab is in fact the defeat of Chemosh at the hands of Yahweh, thus replicating once again the

---

38. On one member of this triad, see Hillers, *Treaty-Curses*, 69-70.

39. Here the term is *'oy*, whereas in v. 1 it is *hoy*, but the connection seems clear enough.

theological conflict of Yahweh over the Egyptian gods (Exod.
5–15), of Yahweh over Dagon (1 Sam. 4–6).[40]

The poem ends, oddly enough, with an act of hope (Jer. 48:47).
The phrase, "I will restore their fortunes," is a common Jeremianic
term for restoration after exile (cf. 29:14; 30:3, 18; 31:23; 32:44;
33:11, 26).[41] Now the phrase is applied even to Israel's enemy.
In Hebrew the phrase is *shabti shebot*, a phrase not unlike the
double use of "captivity" *(shebi)* in v. 46. Thus the same sound is
used to voice exact opposites, exile (v. 46) and return (v. 47). The
concluding verse, however, cannot be understood simply as a play
on words. The point of the reverse is a theological one. There
are, even for Moab, "latter days." There is more promised for
Moab than ultimate destruction. The assertion of v. 47 can of
course be understood simply as an editorial maneuver to tone
down the awful threat of the foregoing. Read theologically,
however, the verse suggests that Yahweh's primary business with
Moab is not destruction. The destruction so passionately voiced
is a "strategic necessity" in order to establish Yahweh's sovereignty,
out of which will come Yahweh's powerful newness.[42] The final
verse of the poem hints at a reestablished international order in
which Moab has a positive role to play and in which Moab will
have better days of well-being as a gift from Yahweh.

This complex and difficult poem voices in an acute way the
question raised by all of the Oracles against the Nations. The
question is acute here because the oracle goes repeatedly over the
central points. We are left to ponder the intent of such an oracle
that seems to work a rhetorical "overkill." Two suggestions about
the intent of the poem come readily to mind. First, the poem
voices deep Israelite venom felt toward its near and troublesome
neighbor. The poem is an act of vengeful ventilation and catharsis.

---

40. On the Ark narrative as a struggle between Yahweh and Dagon, see
Miller and Roberts, *The Hand of the Lord,* 40-51.

41. See Bracke, "Coherence and Theology," 148-155.

42. On "vengeance" for the sake of sovereignty, see Wright, "The Nations
in Hebrew Prophecy"; and Mendenhall. The burden of Wright and Mendenhall is that Yahweh's destructive action is not capricious but is an instrument
of policy, legitimated by a rightful claim to sovereignty. The conclusion of
this poem supports such a scholarly verdict.

No doubt this element is present whenever the poem is recited. Such a view, however, does not reckon with the clear claim that this is God's speech, though it is not difficult to imagine such passionate ideology placed in God's mouth.

Second, it can be suggested that this oracle (and others like it) are not addressed to the ostensive addressee, but are designed for Judah's hearing and overhearing. No doubt there was "overhearing" and some intended overhearing, but the poem is too specific and didactic for that to be an adequate explanation of the poem.

If we are to be "realistic" and take the poem on its own terms, this is an oracle from God's mouth. Then the question is, Why does God speak this way? The answer is that God, this particular God, speaks this way because the establishment of Yahweh's hegemony over the nations is crucial to their well-being. One does not need to deny the operation of Israel's political ideology in this claim, but such ideology does not exhaust the theological claim expressed. The God who speaks in this poem is not simply a petty partisan and patron of Jerusalem. There is more to the speech of God than the political claim of Jerusalem. This is the God of the whole Israelite tradition, the LORD of heaven and earth, the initiator of the Exodus who withstood the Egyptian empire for the sake of the slaves. This is the God who destabilizes and deabsolutizes every pretentious and petty political claim for the sake of a larger ordering that makes human life possible.[43]

To be sure, this large claim of Yahweh's sovereignty ill fits with the harshness of the threat against Moab. The threat mouthed by Yahweh anticipates the awesome policy of "destroying villages in order to save them." Governments in the real world of power, however, act in such a way. This poem is exactly the voice of the government of Yahweh that intends to reestablish its authority and prerogative. Moab's failure, according to the poem, is that this kingdom resisted Yahweh's authority by trusting in "strongholds and treasures" (v. 7), by mag-

---

43. Notice that in the oracle against Moab in Amos 2:1 the indictment concerns Moab's brutal treatment of Edom. The indictment thus suggests an international governance in which Israel, at least in this oracle, is not even a player. Yahweh's moral agenda is not coterminal with Israel but has a direct connection to the nations and their policies.

nifying itself at Yahweh's expense (vv. 26, 42), by treating Israel in derision (v. 27), and by pride and arrogance (vv. 29-30). Such policy will not work! Nations in the end cannot act in such a way with impunity. There is a terrible accounting.

That theological claim which interprets the international order according to the intention of Yahweh finally leads us to an observation about these oracles in their present place in the book of Jeremiah. The corpus of chs. 46–51 makes a decisive canonical statement in the tradition of Jeremiah. The book of Jeremiah wants to assert that there is indeed the free, unfettered, dangerous power of Yahweh released into the public process. That free, unfettered, dangerous power will not be domesticated or disregarded. Israel may try to domesticate the power of Yahweh, and Moab may seek to disregard Yahweh. Judah and Moab both try to treat Yahweh as irrelevant. And both bring upon themselves massive danger. In the end (i.e., the end of the canonical corpus), however, this free and dangerous One does speak and act decisively. In that speech the whole of the world, even the particular claims of the kingdoms, is sharply reshaped and even preempted. Moab, like all the nations, must come to terms with Yahweh's sovereign resolve. A mocking disregard of this holy intention will bring deep trouble, visible even in the public process. From the beginning, Jeremiah had struggled with the public reality of "exile" (1:3) and was a "prophet to the nations" (1:10). Now the theme of *exile* plays heavily among the nations. There may be a restoration of destiny (48:47), but first there is an exile (48:7, 11, 46). Because there is a powerful, passionate Yahweh, there will be an inescapable exile.

ORACLES AGAINST OTHER NATIONS (49:1-39)

This chapter includes oracles concerning five peoples. None of these peoples receives the extended attention of Moab in ch. 48. All of them, however, are discussed with reference to the same themes as were present concerning Moab.

49:1-6 The oracle against *the Ammonites* falls into two distinct units, plus a conclusion in v. 6. Verses 1-2 are dominated by the fourfold occurrence of the root *yarash*, variously rendered as "heir"

(v. 1), "dispossess" (v. 1), and "dispossessor" (v. 2 twice). In v. 1 the first three lines are introduced by an interrogative triad characteristic of Jeremiah, *ha-, 'im, maddua'*.[44] The first two questions, "has . . . has . . . ," require a negative response: no, it is not true that Israel has no sons or no heirs. The third line then functions as an indictment against Ammon, based on the implied answers to the first two questions. If Israel had been without sons and heirs, then Ammon and its god Milcom might rightly take over the land. But because Israel does indeed have heirs and sons, Milcom (and Ammon) have wrongly, improperly, and illegitimately taken over the land of Israel (Gad). The indictment thus is that Ammon has wrongly seized Israelite territory and disregarded Israel's legitimate claim as heir of the land. Ammon has taken what is not rightly his. Thus land-taking military aggression is voiced in a metaphor concerning sons, heirs, and family rights.

The sentence against indicted Ammon is introduced, "Therefore, behold . . ." (v. 2). God declares war on Ammon, causes a savage cry of attack, and dispatches armies which will devastate and destroy Ammon. In the end, Israel will dispossess those who dispossess; the term *yarash* can be rendered "possess" or "dispossess," so that Israel will now possess that from which it has been dispossessed.

Thus the indictment concerns illicit seizure of the land, no doubt as royal policy. The sentence concerns the reseizure of the land by Israel, which implies a great loss to Ammon. The oracle lives amid the recurring tension over land among peoples, tensions which may be very old, but which continue to be passionately felt by succeeding generations. Families and tribes never forget when an unfair land seizure has been perpetrated, whether by war or by dishonest adjudication. Ammon will not in the end be able to hold the land inappropriately taken. Moreover, because of its aggressive greed, Ammon will not only lose that land but will have its homeland abused as well, burned and reduced to an abandoned heap. These two verses offer a reflection on a primary dynamic of world history. That dynamic consists in (1) illicit land seizures and (2) sudden, inexplicable reversals whereby land is

---

44. On the form, see Walter Brueggemann, "Jeremiah's Use of Rhetorical Questions," *Journal of Biblical Literature* 92 (1973): 358-374.

given back to those to whom it rightly belongs. The poet discerns the story of Judah within this recurring dynamic.

In vv. 3-5, the second element of this oracle, the mode of rhetoric is very different. Verse 3 is a summons to public ceremonies of grief: "wail, cry, gird, lament, run." Ammon is summoned to respond to its grief-evoking situation. The reason for the grief is that both its god (Milcom) and its human leaders (priests and princes) will go into exile, that is, will experience severe defeat and humiliation. Verse 4 is a taunting dismissal of Ammon, which has been excessively complacent, which trusts in its own resources, and which feels utterly secure (cf. 48:11). The security reflected in 49:4 is in fact a terrible illusion. The key term is again "trust" *(bth)*. Ammon has placed its confidence in its own powers, powers which are inadequate when real trouble comes.

Verse 5 counters that illusion with a heavy dose of theological reality. The central reality is introduced by "Behold, I." This is the historical power and purpose with which Ammon has not sufficiently reckoned. It is this "I" of Yahweh who cracks the complacency of Ammon and breaks open the illusion. Yahweh will cause exile and displacement, that is, a dispossessing of this settled people. There are no alternatives to Yahweh, who will prevail. Thus vv. 3-5 bespeak the terrible loss and hurt that derives from the lawsuit of vv. 1-2. Because of its infringement upon Israelite land, Ammon is in deep jeopardy.

The conclusion in v. 6 reflects a complete change of tone. It looks beyond the present moment of vexation. The verse anticipates the reversal of Ammonite destiny. The One who will do a good deed of rescue for Ammon is the same One who will cause the exile. Thus Yahweh will do for Ammon as Yahweh will do for Judah, causing both exile and homecoming (cf. 31:10, 27-28 for these actions toward Israel). The oracle concerns both Ammon's immediate fate (devastation) and Ammon's long-term destiny (well-being). Both are in the hands of Yahweh.

49:7-22 This more extended oracle concerning *Edom* seems to be built out of a variety of traditional pieces.[45] Jeremiah 49:7-16

---

45. Verses 9, 14-16 are closely related to Obadiah. It is not necessary or possible to determine the direction of influence.

constitutes an extended poem interrupted by the prose argument of vv. 12-13.

Verses 7-10 make up something of a rhetorical unit. Edom is traditionally a place of wisdom and understanding.[46] The rhetorical question of v. 7 appeals to that tradition. The wise decision now for Edom, if indeed Edom still possesses wisdom, is to flee from the coming trouble (v. 8). Thus the question of v. 7 does not clearly imply a certain answer. If there is still wisdom, Edom will flee. Not to flee would be "foolish." Whether Edom flees from the devastation will evidence whether wisdom is still present in Edom. The threat announced is the "calamity of Esau" (v. 8). No specifics are given. We only know that the unspecified threat is very large and very grave.

In vv. 9-10 the poet engages two images to accent the threat Yahweh poses to Edom. Grape-gatherers do not pick the vines completely clean, but leave a residue (cf. Deut. 24:19-22). Thieves in the night do not take everything available, but only what they need. Both grape-gatherers and thieves leave something behind.[47] Yahweh, however, is unlike conventional grape-gatherers and thieves. Unlike grape-gatherers, Yahweh will leave no residue in Edom. Unlike a thief, Yahweh will take everything from Edom. Thus the images of grape-gatherer and thief are involved in order to make a contrast, to state how radical and massive will be Yahweh's actions — so radical and massive that nothing will survive and life is not possible.

In light of that massive warning and threat, Jer. 49:11 voices an odd footnote. In such a war-devastated society, there will inevitably be orphans and widows, without resources or protection. They are the predictable products of war. These, however, unlike the subjects of vv. 7-10, will be safe with Yahweh (cf. Hos. 14:3b). They are invited to trust *(bth)* Yahweh, and Yahweh will give them life. The inclination of Yahweh in Jer. 49:11 is quite in contrast to the ferocious Yahweh of vv. 9-10. The contrast is a

---

46. See Hans Walter Wolff, *Amos the Prophet* (Philadelphia: Fortress, 1973), 37, n. 91.

47. The argument itself is cast in a sapiential mode. That is, the argument proceeds by questions, anticipating that the answer will come from the expeience of the listener. If there is sufficient reflection, the listener can find the answer which condemns without being told directly.

strange one, indicating that only the abandoned and defenseless will find succor in Yahweh; all others will be devastated. Thus even this exceptional note functions in the total context of the poem to underscore the destruction everywhere else anticipated.

The prose interlude of vv. 12-13 seems again to underscore the imminent danger to Edom. The "cup" is a cup of suffering and devastation (cf. 25:15-29). Innocent peoples have had to drink from that cup; that is, innocent peoples have been caught in the flow of international upheaval caused by Yahweh. How much more will Edom drink such a cup, Edom who deserves the upheaval! There will be no escape for Edom. The punishment is as sure as God's own oath; it is aimed first against Bozrah, a proud capital city now to be utterly dismantled, subject of a massive curse, object of Yahweh's devastating action (cf. Deut. 28:37).

In light of the "no exception" statement of Jer. 49:9-10 and the curse formula of v. 13, vv. 14-16 now simply restate the threat. The poet "reports" on a "rumor" that has gone among the nations (v. 14). God is mobilizing all the nations together against Edom. This daring verse thus suggests a convergence of divine resolve and savage international strategy. The rumor among the nations is rooted in God's own resolve (v. 16). Because of pride and arrogance, there will be no escape, no hiding place, no refuge. God and God's agents will search out every hiding, fleeing Edomite.

In the reprise against Edom, three powerful metaphors are employed (vv. 17-22). First, Edom will be *like Sodom and Gomorrah,* utterly devastated, without any qualification or rescue (vv. 17-18). Second, God will be *like a lion* who will attack the flock of sheep that is Edom and will devastate and terrorize (vv. 19-20). No shepherd (king) in Edom can withstand the terrible threat. The sheep are completely exposed when the lion comes. Third, the one who will attack (i.e., a human agent) will be *like a great eagle,* who with huge wings will intimidate and terrorize, causing warriors to quake like women in labor (v. 22).

Sodom and Gomorrah, lion, and eagle are all images summoned in order to voice the impending threat against Edom. Behind the threat in these various images is the intention of Yahweh. In vv. 19-20 the poem comes to theological focus in the awesome person of Yahweh. The claims made for Yahweh in this assertion are threefold. First, there are first person verbs: "I will cause to run, I will appoint." Second, there are three interrogatives of defiance: "Who is like me, who will summon me, what shepherd can stand before me?" The questions are in fact assertions of authority and defiance. The claim implicit is "none like me, none can summon me, no shepherd can withstand me." Third, it is asserted that Yahweh has a "plan" against Edom, that is, a resolve from the very throne of heaven. All three of these devices — the verbs, the questions, the "plan" — establish the lion-God who dispatches the eagle-scavenger as the key actor in Edom's life. Against such a force Edom has no option, no chance, no future. This is an extraordinarily powerful statement of destruction. Its passion is matched by a complete lack of concrete reference or reason. We only hear of the "calamity of Edom," but know nothing about its motivation. That "calamity" looms large in the purpose of Yahweh.

49:23-27   Damascus here represents all of Syria (cf. Isa. 7:8). Syria is now named among those under assault from Yahweh. Three cities are named which refer to all of the kingdom: Damascus, Hamath, and Arpad. All of these have heard "rumors" of threat, all are anxious, all are uneasy (v. 23). Damascus receives more particular attention than the other two cities named (vv. 24-26). The great city and fortress of Damascus is feeble, unstable, and upset as a woman in labor (cf. v. 22). The mocking lament of v. 24 leads to the great reversal of vv. 25-26, contrasting "before" and "after." The joyful city is forsaken.[48] The best young men are now dead. Soldiers are destroyed. Strength is gone; the glory is departed. The mood is not even one of threat, but only of grief, for a great city has been destroyed. Verse 27 concludes the poem with a standard formulary against Damascus and its king (cf. Amos 1:4). This brief poem lacks every historical reference, every cause for such an action on God's part. The poem functions to destabilize every historical-political claim. The poem asserts that even great concentrations of human power (as in

---

48. The same language of reversal concerning Jerusalem is expressed in Isa. 62:4-5, though there the reversal is a positive one.

monarchies) are enormously pliable and tentative in the face of Yahweh's "tidings" and Yahweh's "plan." None can withstand the resolve of God.

49:28-33 The horizon of the poet now makes a sweep toward the Arabian tribes of the East. "Kedar" is generally taken to refer to Bedouin peoples of the East, indeed, as far East as is thinkable in the geography of the ancient world.[49] "Hazor" is less certain. Apparently it cannot here refer to the great Palestinian city of the book of Joshua. Holladay proposes that the term refers not to a specific city but to the sedentary Arabs who are not nomadic, and Robert P. Carroll, following Jer. 49:31, leaves it as "unwalled villages."[50] The reference is in any case indefinite.

This oracle is again an announcement of invasion and devastation. It includes the two standard elements: (1) an imperative which mobilizes the enemies of the addressed people (vv. 28-29), and (2) an urging that the inhabitants under attack should escape to safety (v. 30).

The most interesting element in this poem is the explicit reference to Nebuchadnezzar, who is said to have a "plan" and a "purpose." This reference is worth noting, because in none of the other oracles in this collection has Nebuchadnezzar been explicitly named. (He has been named, to be sure, in some of the editorial introductions). Even here, however, the mention of Nebuchadnezzar may not be secure, for the LXX lacks the name. If the historical reference to Nebuchadnezzar is retained, then we have a more concrete setting for the oracle. If not, then we have, as in other places, a large theological assertion about Yahweh's resolve. And indeed, after v. 30, the poem concludes with a claim for Yahweh, not for any human agent.

Thus Nebuchadnezzar is in any case not pivotal for the primary assertion of the oracle, which is theological. It is Yahweh who speaks the imperative, "Rise up" (v. 31), as in v. 28. It is Yahweh

---

49. See Jer. 2:10, where "Kedar" is juxtaposed to Cyprus as the furthest thinkable reference to the eastern edge of reality, as Cyprus represented the western edge.

50. Holladay, *Jeremiah 2*, 382-83; Carroll, *Jeremiah*, 809-811.

who attacks this people who dwell secure (*bth*, v. 31). It is Yahweh who claims the verbs "I will scatter, I will bring" (v. 32). Because of Yahweh's resolve, the loss of camels and herds is reported, and the utter devastation of the city is accomplished. At best, Nebuchadnezzar is a "bit player" in Yahweh's large intention. There is no doubt that Nebuchadnezzar hovers over and around these oracles against the nations. The poet, however, is never confused on the name of the primary actor. Nebuchadnezzar may indeed have a plan and purpose. It is, however, Yahweh who presides in plucking up and tearing down, as Yahweh has done even in Judah.

49:34-39   In the last of these brief oracles, the poet reaches the far northeastern horizon of the available world. No reason and no historical occasion is given for this harsh pronouncement of judgment against *Elam*. Unlike the preceding oracles in this collection, this oracle is rhetorically simple. Most of the rhetorical features found in the other poems are absent here. The poem is dominated by a single rhetorical pattern, namely first person verbs with Yahweh as the subject. After the initial "behold" (v. 35), the sequence of verbs is impressive:

I will break,
I will bring,
I will scatter,
I will terrify,
I will bring (evil),
I will send . . .
    until I have consumed,
I will set . . .

The recital is unambiguous, without reservation, unqualifiedly negative and destructive, and without any historical agent. Yahweh resolves to nullify the power and the governance of Elam, and to replace it with Yahweh's own direct rule.[51] The language is

---

51. The political threat involved in "direct rule" is enormous. It happens when a hegemonic power loses patience with its underlings. Such a loss of patience suggests that "direct rule" will be much more severe and serve to squelch any autonomy or move toward independence. A recent case in point has been the refusal of the Soviet Union to allow independent rule in the

thoroughly military. The fate of Elam is sealed in Yahweh's asser-
tive intention.

The oracle, however, adds one other active verb for Yahweh,
which follows after the threat (v. 39). For Elam, as for Egypt
(46:26), Moab (48:47), and Ammon (49:6), there are more days,
other days, better days intended by Yahweh. After the massive
devastation, Yahweh will restore the fortune of Elam. God's ultimate resolve is the well-being even of Elam. That well-being can
only happen, however, when Yahweh's throne is firm in the land
and all other claimants to the throne have been eliminated.[52]

ORACLE AGAINST BABYLON (50:1–51:58)

This extended and complex oracle concerning Babylon belongs to
the same genre as other "oracles against the nations" in chs. 46–51.
Indeed, it is regularly grouped in interpretive discussions with all the
others in this corpus. The argument of this oracle is not unlike the
others: Yahweh summons new enemies against Babylon and decrees
the downfall of the arrogant empire, much as Yahweh has summoned
enemies against the previously named nations in chs. 46–49.

Though this oracle is like the others in the corpus in terms of
genre and rhetoric, it is a mistake to group it with the other
Oracles against the Nations in the book of Jeremiah. Indeed, chs.
50–51 represent a countertheme in the book of Jeremiah, counter
to chs. 46–49. In the end, in the final form of the text, Babylon
dominates the book of Jeremiah, as the empire of Babylon dominated the politics of the period of Jeremiah.[53] Babylon is the
superpower par excellence, and it utterly preoccupied Jeremiah
and his contemporaries, as well as subsequent generations of
Judean exiles who established the final form of the text of Jeremiah.
Babylon is everywhere in the text of Jeremiah, explicitly in much

---

Balkan states but to insist upon direct rule. Ezekiel 34:11-16 is a case in
which Yahweh as the hegemonic power undertakes direct rule at the expense
of the Jerusalem "shepherds." In that case, however, the direct rule of Yahweh
will be benign.

52. On this rule, see Patrick D. Miller, Jr., "The Sovereignty of God."

53. See Miller and Hayes, 416-436.

of the prose, by allusion and implication in much of the poetry. Moreover, the argument of the book of Jeremiah is that Babylon is implementing the judgment of God against Jerusalem.[54] For that reason, Jerusalem's obedience to God entails submission to the power and policy of Babylon.

In the Oracles against the Nations, the situation is not different for the other nations from the situation of Judah and Jerusalem. As Babylon dominates the horizon and destiny of Judah and Jerusalem, so in chs. 46–49 Babylon will dominate the future of the other nations. The central threat of the book of Jeremiah is that *the resolve of God* and *the policies of Babylon* converge completely and are to be equated. Thus a Yahweh-governed world is a Babylon-dominated world. The religiopolitical outcome of such an argument is that for Jerusalem there can only be a Babylon-shaped future, even as the nations must face a Babylon-dominated future. Babylon is indeed Yahweh's mode of sovereignty. Neither Jerusalem nor the other nations can entertain any alternative to Babylon. Thus the political preeminence of Babylon, in itself overwhelming, is given theological legitimacy by the tradition of Jeremiah, seemingly to perpetuity.

Chapters 50–51, however, provide an unexpected and decisive turn in the final form of the text of the book of Jeremiah. The poetry which has so consistently summoned the "foe from the north" (i.e., Babylon) now turns against the "foe from the north," and thereby transforms the role and position of Babylon. That great empire now is not the means of attack, but the object of Yahweh's attack.[55] Yahweh, who has made such good and

---

54. Seitz, *Theology in Conflict,* has shown that the interpretive disputes concerning the meaning of the Exile pivot on divergent understandings of the role of Babylon and the place of the exiles within that Babylonian hegemony.

55. Brevard S. Childs, "The Enemy from the North and the Chaos Tradition," in *A Prophet to the Nations,* ed. Leo G. Perdue and Brian W. Kovacs (Winona Lake: Eisenbrauns, 1984), 151-161, has observed that the nature of "the enemy" is expressed in rhetoric in chs. 50–51 different from the rhetoric of chs. 46–49. In chs. 50–51 the rhetoric becomes apocalyptic and the enemy "has taken on a trans-historical, apocalyptic coloring" (159). Such a difference may be required because of the stature and massive threat of Babylon. In any case, Childs's analysis supports the important distinction between the two bodies of text.

sustained use of Babylon, now acts against that same Babylon. All the pro-Babylonian sympathy of the Jeremiah tradition is in this utterance nullified and negated. A sharp divergence is voiced which breaks apart the sovereign purpose of Yahweh from the imperial policies of Babylon. The two do not converge, but are at strong odds with each other. By the end of the book of Jeremiah, trust in and obedience to Yahweh do not equal submissiveness to Babylon, for Babylon now stands under judgment and will soon disappear from the map of world power. Babylon is therefore not the shaper of the future, not the perpetual power with which to reckon, but only one more pretender to power who cannot endure the ultimate power of Yahweh.

Thus by the end of the book of Jeremiah we are left not with *Yahweh and Babylon,* but with *only Yahweh.*[56] At the most, Babylon has been for Yahweh only a convenience; at the worst, Babylonian power has been a brutalizing interlude which cannot be sustained or extended. This oracle in chs. 50–51 thus makes two claims. First, only the sovereign power of Yahweh matters. That sovereign power is allied with nothing else and is dependent on no other power (cf. Isa. 25–28).[57] That sovereign power will on its own terms and in its own way prevail, and must be accepted. Second, adherence to Yahweh's sovereign power is not only unavoidable. It is good news for Judah and Jerusalem, for it makes a post-Babylonian, postexilic future thinkable, available, and do-able. In this shaping of the final form of the text, Jer. 50–51 not only play against chs. 46–49. They also exercise a theological role in the

---

56. Thus in a very odd way even the Oracles against the Nations serve the "Yahweh alone" theology voiced in the tradition of Deuteronomy which is so decisive in shaping the final form of the book of Jeremiah. While the Oracles against the Nations contain none of the rhetorical marks of Deuteronomic shaping, the theological import of the oracles is congenial to that theology.

57. In his comments on Isa. 40:13-14, R. Norman Whybray, *The Heavenly Counsellor in Isaiah XL 13-14* (Cambridge: Cambridge University Press, 1971), has shown how in the Exile Israel reasserted "Yahweh alone" theology. In Isa. 40 the poet intends to refute any claim of credibility for the gods of Babylon, thus making a point parallel to that of Jer. 50–51.

book of Jeremiah disproportionate to their extent, for they counter much of what has gone before in the book. They make the claim that the dynamic of public history is indeed a theological dynamic, and not a matter of power politics. There is a purposefulness to the public process that is not coterminous with raw power. Thus the appearance of Babylonian power is not to be taken at face value.

The passing of such a superpower is good news for the little, subjugated peoples who had resigned themselves to long-term domination. The passing of a superpower, such as happens in this text, raises large questions not only about political possibilities, but about moral coherence in the world. These two chapters assert that a profound moral coherence continues in, with, and beyond Babylon. That profound moral coherence is visible not only in the emergence of the power of Babylon, but in the disappearance of Babylon as well.

50:1 These chapters receive a formal and ponderous introduction. The structure of this introduction is not unlike 1:1-3; in both cases we deal with *the word of Yahweh* and with *the role of Jeremiah,* who is explicitly named in both introductions. The two sources of text are intimately linked to each other, but the two are not to be equated. The explicit naming of Jeremiah here suggests a reflective, canonical intention. The framers of this text know they are "making Scripture." They seek to balance the *"Exile"* (1:3) with an address concerning the proximate *cause of exile* (i.e., Babylon) and the *end of exile* when that proximate cause is overpowered by the ultimate cause of exile, that is, when Yahweh overpowers the ostensive superpower, Babylon.

50:2-10 With a mixture of poetry and prose, these verses announce the main themes for the two long chapters to follow. Instruction is given to the implied messengers: "declare, proclaim, set up, proclaim, do not conceal, say" (v. 2; cf. Isa. 40:9; 52:7 for a like implied messenger). The poem proposes a major announcement which is the outcome of a battle that is now completed, an announcement which is stunning in its import, unexpected but to be eagerly received by "the nations," that is, by the subjugated

259

peoples.[58] The battle has been fought elsewhere (we are not told where or how), but the news will now change the circumstance and destiny of those addressed in the announcement.[59] The whole of the ancient Near East was contained in the Babylonian hegemony, and the Babylonian gods seemed beyond challenge. Now, in an instant, only as long as it takes to issue the news bulletin, that brutal hegemony is ended, and with it the seemingly all-powerful Babylonian gods are terminated. This is a moment the bondaged peoples savored!

The announcement is terse and to the point. First, Babylon is captured! The verb is passive. No agent is named. What counts is that the invincible one has been overthrown. Second, the fall of the empire has a theological dimension. The failure of Babylon is the failure of its gods, Bel and Merodach.[60] The verbs are each repeated, "put to shame, dismayed." Politically and theologically, the announcement completely revamps the landscape of public life. There will be ample time later for details. This is only the lead bulletin, but it says all that needs to be said.

Verse 3 provides a modest explanatory note. Babylon has fallen because a nation has come "out of the north." The phrase is filled with irony. In terms of *Realpolitik,* the reference is to Cyrus and the Persians. What counts for the text, however, is not the concrete political reference, but the fact that Babylon which has for so long been the ominous foe "from the north" should now be displaced by a new "foe from the north" which in turn threatens Babylon. History has turned decisively, and the turn is bad news for Babylon.

---

58. As Babylon is larger than life, so the report of the defeat of Babylon is voiced in speech that is larger than life, or as Childs ("The Enemy from the North," 161) has observed, Israel has "'mythologized' an historical tradition." The report requires Israel to push to the limits of language to speak adequately about this most welcome, quite unexpected turn of the historical process.

59. On the battle there being effective here, and the battle then being effective now, see Brueggemann, *Israel's Praise,* 29-38; and Garrett Green, *Imagining God: Theology and the Religious Imagination* (San Francisco: Harper & Row, 1989). The capacity to transfer the effect of the battle from there to here, from then to now, is operative in the imagery of apocalyptic which Childs finds in this text.

60. See Carroll, 819.

The new "foe from the north" makes the old "foe from the north" helpless, wretched, and devastated.

Now the oracle reflects on the implication of the news bulletin concerning Babylon for Israel and Judah (vv. 4-5). The defeat of Babylon entails the end of displacement and exile for the Jews, and the capacity to come back home! The book of Jeremiah has had as its central theme the Exile (cf. 1:3). In a moment, in the twinkling of an eye, exile is over. The deported ones are now returning in weakness, grief, and penitence to Jerusalem, to the site of the temple, to God. The return home signifies a return to covenant with God, a relation disrupted by exile. The covenant is now said to be "everlasting." It is precisely at the end of the Exile that the renewed, restored relation with God is celebrated as everlasting and beyond disruption.[61] That is, at the very moment of discontinuity deep continuity is asserted.[62] The rhetoric of return clearly intends that the Exile is not one of many disruptions, but is the only one of its kind. Such a rupture will not happen again (cf. Isa. 54:7-10; Gen. 9:8-17). Judah and Israel are now assured a solid, enduring destiny with Yahweh.

The poem reflects on the circumstance of exile (Jer. 50:6-7) and on the reversal and return (vv. 8-10). Verses 6-7 reflect on the reasons for exile. "My people" are understood as a flock of sheep; the sheep, however, have been at the mercy of their shepherds (= kings; cf. 22:22; 23:1-4; Ezek. 34:1-10). The Exile has been caused by the terrible failure of Israel's kings. Indeed, even the conquering enemy, Babylon, knows the cause of exile. The Babylonians here are presented as theologically astute enough to understand both Israel's *sin* and the certitude that Yahweh is Israel's *hope*. The Babylonians understood better than Israel's kings both the cost of sin and the root of hope.

The oracle, however, does not linger over the Exile and its causes. It wants rather to assert the end of exile and the capacity for homecoming (Jer. 50:8-10). It is time to leave Babylon! Those

---

61. See Gen. 9:8-17; Lev. 26:40-45; Jer. 31:35-37; 33:19-26; Ezek. 34:25-31; 37:24-28.

62. On continuity in the midst of the discontinuity of exile, see Brueggemann, "A Shattered Transcendence?"

addressed are urged to act as "he-goats." "He-goats" are the strong leaders of the flock who take bold initiatives and act with courage, in order to lead the flock in a determined way. The departure from exile will require strong courage and resolve, and will therefore necessitate determined leadership. Thus v. 6 is an authorization of leaders who must dare to act against the residue of Babylonian power which continues to be intimidating. The imperative of the poem urges an end to fearfulness. The ground for such daring action is that Yahweh is creating an enemy against Babylon who will now plunder Babylon. For that reason, emerging leadership among the exiles need not be intimidated. Thus the daring Israelite action now authorized and required takes place in a context of enormous international upheaval.[63] The Jewish leadership can reckon with unnamed allies authorized by Yahweh who make their escape possible.

50:11-16   This poetic unit in turn addresses two different subjects. First, Babylon, the defeated and humiliated power, is addressed (vv. 11-13). It is Babylon who has been a reckless plunderer (v. 11), acting as greedy as a hungry cow which can gorge itself to death, as aggressive and brazen as a lusting stallion. Both the heifer in pasture and the lusting stallion act for their appetite and know no restraint or boundary to their desire. Babylon has imagined it could do whatever it wanted by way of abuse and self-serving exploitation; now, however, comes the reckoning of shame and disgrace and dismantling (v. 12). Babylon's autonomy has failed to reckon with Yahweh, with Yahweh's anger which now retaliates against Babylon. Babylon has for too long violated Yahweh and Yahweh's "heritage." The richness and power of the images assert that Yahweh's overriding purpose and sovereignty will curb and limit Babylon's self-indulgent freedom. The empire must now answer for its self-indulgence. Such self-serving license can run loose in history only for so long, and then Yahweh acts against the violator.

---

63. Childs, "The Enemy from the North," has seen that the upheaval is not only international but transhistorical. The poem strains to find imagery and language adequate for the deep turn that is here anticipated.

In vv. 14-16 there is a second address, this time to the new unnamed enemy of Babylon. This address is largely a series of imperatives, urging and authorizing brutal military action against Babylon. Yahweh is portrayed as a king who declares unconditional war against the empire. No doubt such poetry reflects the accumulated hostility of the Jews toward their oppressor. The poetry, however, is more than a venting of resentment; it is a theological assertion that Yahweh will not finally tolerate such a strident abuse of public power. Thus the series of authorizing imperatives is marked by utterances about Yahweh. Babylon has sinned *against Yahweh* (v. 14). The coming action is *the vengeance of Yahweh* (v. 15). The poem refuses the notion that, to paraphrase automaker Henry Ford, history is "just one damn empire after another." History is the working out of Yahweh's righteous will. Because Babylon has stridently violated that righteous will, a turn in the public process is now authorized and will not be resisted.

50:17-20   These prose verses provide an explicit review of Israel's history under the metaphor of sheep and shepherd. Israel is a vulnerable flock, exposed to ravenous lions. (One can detect various philosophies of power at work in this material. Whereas v. 6 has asserted that Israel's own shepherds have caused the trouble, here the problem is marauding lions from the outside. These lines do not acknowledge, as earlier prophets including Jeremiah had asserted, that these imperial lions were indeed dispatched by none other than Yahweh. Here the lions are presented as greedy self-starters.) The history of Israel has consisted in the long-term threat of Assyria and more recently the dangerous, destructive presence of Babylon.[64] Israel's life has been lived under the threat of and shaped by the reality of these two empires for a very long time. The relation of Israel to these empires (much like the relation of Lithuania to the Soviet Union or the relation

---

64. The history of Israel and Judah as portrayed by Miller and Hayes, and by J. Alberto Soggin, *A History of Ancient Israel* (Philadelphia: Westminster and London: SCM, 1985), makes clear that Israel and Judah are states characteristically dominated by larger powers who decisively impinge upon and shape Israel's life and policy.

of Nicaragua to the United States) is as sheep to lion. In that unequal relation, the sheep is exposed and helpless, and the lion would seem to be authorized to govern to perpetuity.

But now, all of that sheep-to-lion relation is to change (v. 18)! In turn Babylon, like Assyria, will be "visited" by God. When the great powers are "visited" by God, good things happen for Israel. Israel returns to its land, which has been occupied and exploited. The flock receives back its pasture from the real shepherd. The very flock which had strayed (v. 6) is now free, safe, innocent, and unmarked by sin. Israel going into exile and Israel coming out of exile are two different peoples. The difference is that Yahweh will pardon. The pardon from Yahweh permits Israel's life and history to begin again, afresh, with new potential. In these few verses the oracle reflects on recent imperial history. In doing so, however, it insists that the real determinants for Israel's life are not the policies of the empires, but the purposes of Yahweh. It is Yahweh, the good shepherd, who gives Israel its life and restores its good pastures. Unlike much of the book of Jeremiah, here Babylon is not a tool of Yahweh, but only a rapacious lion. Yahweh presides over all such threats and then pardons.

50:21-34   This section, made up of quite different and distinct literary units, is largely preoccupied with Yahweh's direct dealing with Babylon. The oracle reflects the standard genre of taunt songs and victory songs. Only in vv. 28, 33-34 is there comment on Israel, which is a by-product of the main theme. The oracle concerns Yahweh's relation to and governance of the empire, almost without reference to Israel.

In vv. 21-27 three themes interplay. First, the unnamed attacker is authorized to proceed against Babylon in a most determined way. That agent of Yahweh is to "slay, and utterly destroy" (v. 21), to seize grain and "destroy . . . utterly" (v. 26), to kill all its bulls and destroy all its wealth (v. 27). Babylon is to be showed no mercy. "Bull" here may be taken to mean all the potency of the empire — sexual, military, and economic.

Second, the countertheme of the attack is to taunt and gloat over the massacre of Babylon. This is especially evident in vv. 23-24. The rhetoric is the voice of lament and grief, but the expression of grief is ironic. It is as though Yahweh, the perpetrator of destruction, can say with mock innocence, "I can hardly believe what has happened to Babylon!" In v. 24 Yahweh addresses the empire directly, so that there is no misunderstanding. The core argument is reiterated: "Babylon is taken."

The authorization of the attack and the taunting of Babylon are held together by a third rhetorical feature asserting that this action is indeed the action of Yahweh. Thus the attacker does "all that I have commanded you" (v. 21). It is Yahweh who has "opened his armory" (i.e., his stock of weapons; v. 25), who has had work to do. Indeed, the fall of Babylon is for a theological reason: "You strove against Yahweh" (v. 24). The term "strive" elsewhere refers to political, personal, or military conflict of a physical kind. Here it is an odd usage, for no such conflict is identifiable between Yahweh and Babylon. This oracle suggests, however, that Yahweh and Babylon have been in dispute over who should control Israel and the land of Israel. In that hard dispute, Babylon has lost and must now be punished. Clearly the theological interpretation of Babylon at the end of the Exile is very different from the role earlier assigned to Babylon in the days of Zedekiah. The intent of the whole is to assert the sovereign rule of Yahweh, now implemented through an unnamed attacker whose role is to destroy the usurping empire of Babylon.

Verse 28 adds an isolated note that is derivative from the poem. The double use of the word "vengeance" suggests that Yahweh's vengeance consists in the reestablishment of Yahweh's rule and Yahweh's honor, both against Babylon and for Jerusalem (the temple). Thus "vengeance" is the abrasive factor in sovereign rule and order. Political authority depends on the capacity to enforce! It is in Zion that this vengeance/rule of Yahweh is now to be proclaimed. Yahweh is back in charge. Note that in the exilic proclamation of Isa. 40:9 it is Zion who receives the news of Yahweh's reasserted governance.

Again, in a prose reflection, the familiar triangle is mobilized. There is in this interaction *Babylon,* who is to be destroyed; there is the *unnamed attacker,* who is summoned and authorized by Yahweh; and there is *Yahweh,* who initiates the action of the one against the other. At a human level, the anticipated action is simply one superpower against another superpower. Read theologically, however, as the oracle insists, the key actor in the world of the superpowers is none other than Yahweh. Read theologically, two factors are decisive. On the one hand, Babylon has "proudly defied" *(zd)* Yahweh. Indeed, Babylon's very existence as an aggressive, arrogant imperial power is an act of defiance (cf. Dan. 4). On the other hand, there is in the historical process requiting *(sh-l-m)*. That is, even great powers may expect to receive back in kind for their actions and policies. The great powers finally are not free and autonomous. Thus the triangle serves in a dramatic way to articulate that even the superpowers live in a world of theological, moral accountability. The world around Jerusalem is theologically ordered; none can escape or circumvent that resilient ordering.

In the following poetic section (Jer. 50:31-32) the oracle takes up the theme of the "proud one" *(zd,* as in v. 29). Babylon is the arrogant one par excellence. Such presumptious, rebellious posturing inevitably makes Babylon the sworn enemy of Yahweh, who will not tolerate such posturing.[65] Yahweh is definitionally against such arrogant power. In such an enmity, Babylon cannot prevail. Those who resist Yahweh, so the poem insists, will always lose and always pay. Verse 32 then offers a consequent lament which is largely in stylized, formulaic language. The second line is not unlike an earlier lament over Israel (Amos 5:2), a statement of total hopelessness and helplessness. The only difference is that instead of the subject being "virgin Israel," now it is proud Babylon (cf. Isa. 47:1-3 on the disrobing of "virgin" Babylon). The intent of this poem is to accomplish and enact the rhetorical dismantling of the empire, so that the speech itself makes available and visible the terrible ending of the empire.

Again, the demise of Babylon yields the liberation of Israel. This brief unit begins with a powerful abruptness, with an inverted word order in the Hebrew (Jer. 50:33): "Oppressed is the people of Israel." Verse 33 characterizes the oppression. Verse 34 counters

---

65. See Gowan, *When Man Becomes God,* 22, for the term *zd* and more generally on the arrogance of states which mock Yahweh. It is instructive that most of Gowan's exposition concerns precisely Babylon.

the oppression with a strong first word: "liberator" (*ga'al;* RSV "Redeemer"), the one who ends oppression. Thus the resolve of God is to override the practice of the empire.

This little unit (vv. 33-34) is crafted around four rhetorical features. First, the central one of "oppress/liberate" is decisive. Second, the terms "held fast" and "strong" are the same Hebrew word (*hzq*). Thus as the oppressor is strong to confine, so the Redeemer is strong to release. Third, the phrase "surely plead their cause" is made of three uses of Hebrew *rib (rib yarib et-ribam)*. The Redeemer goes to court in order to secure the right of the one illicitly held captive. Fourth, the contrast of "rest/unrest" is expressed in a Hebrew wordplay: "rest" = *rg'*, "unrest" = *rgz*. The term rendered "earth" may mean "land" (i.e., the land of Israel), so that when the land is set free of Babylon it also can become a peaceable land. The lines nicely develop the total contrast between two systems of power which have enormous implications for the future of Israel.

50:35-40   In a stunning and remarkably disciplined piece of poetry, we are offered an "ode to a sword." This poem is striking first because it has no verbs in its main clauses; the phrase concerning the sword is reiterated in all its stark power. Second, the sword is not identified politically or linked to any historical process. It stands barren as a contextless threat. That is all there is, just a sword. It is a sword, perhaps from Yahweh's armory (cf. v. 25), which will do its singularly devastating work. It is attached to no human agent. This sword as a bald threat is aimed at every significant element of imperial society — princes, wise men, diviners, warriors, horses, chariots, mercenaries, treasures. Every part of public life is to be denied power and stability. And in each case, there is to be a radical and total reversal, so that diviners (wise men) become fools,[66] warriors are shattered, troops become women, treasures are plundered, waters are dried up. Everything is reduced to weakness, lifelessness, and dysfunction. One can

---

66. The ultimate foolishness is to imagine that one is autonomous and self-sufficient. Von Rad, *Wisdom in Israel*, 65, terms such foolishness "practical atheism"; cf. Isa. 10:12-14.

imagine a slow, eerie camera shot silently scanning the lingering ruin, Babylon, "stumbled and fallen" and "none to raise him up" (v. 32). All of this will happen because of images and idols (v. 38), all because of self-deceiving ideology that seduced the empire into a false discernment of its place in life.

The upshot of this sword-visited state follows with a "therefore" (vv. 39-40). The land is now emptied of all agents and symbols of power, life, and effectiveness. Instead there are only the most despicable scavengers who can live where there are no life supports: wild animals, hyenas, ostriches, and nobody else, now or ever.[67] Like Sodom and Gomorrah, Babylon is now emptied of human life and human possibility — no people, no persons, nobody, no future! The language strains to convey the utter nullity of the old order, an order which so recently seemed so settled and so secure (cf. Isa. 47:7-10).

50:41-46 This section consists of two quotations of materials we have already considered elsewhere. First, Jer. 50:41-43 reiterates 6:22-24. The quote is verbatim with only minor changes. Obviously the names are changed, so that "daughter of Zion" becomes "daughter of Babylon." What is most important in the reuse of the material is that the poet accomplishes an exact inversion of the role of Babylon. In 6:22-24 it is to be assumed that the enemy people from the north is indeed Babylon who terrifies and who will show no mercy. In the present passage it is Babylon who is terrified and to whom no mercy will be shown. In 6:24 it is Babylon who devastates Jerusalem and "we" who have pain as in labor. Now it is the "king of Babylon" (no less) who hears and who is reduced to pain and anguish. The poem deftly makes the strong one into the weak one and portrays for us the total reversal of power in public history. The first one dramatically becomes the last one! We are permitted to watch while the great king of Babylon, a syllable at a time, is reduced to frailty, intimidation, weakness, and dysfunction.

---

67. Here I am following the NRSV. For a very different rendering, see John Bright, _Jeremiah_. Anchor Bible 21 (Garden City: Doubleday, 1965), 355; and Holladay, _Jeremiah 2_, 420-21.

The prose section of vv. 44-46 is likewise a quote, this time paralleled in 49:19-21. Again the inversion is total, for in ch. 49 the invader is presumed to be Babylon, whereas here it is Babylon who is the helpless, vulnerable flock. What counts now is the "plan" and "purposes" of Yahweh made against Babylon. No shepherd, no king — not even a Babylonian king — can withstand the purpose of Yahweh. Yahweh will appoint whomever God chooses. In 2 Isaiah the one chosen and appointed is Cyrus (Isa. 44:28; 45:1). Here the candidate is not named. In any case, Babylon has no voice in the coming leadership. The phrase "appoint whomever I choose" is taken up in Dan. 4 as a threat against Nebuchadnezzar (Dan. 4:17, 25, 32). The claim is powerfully made that Yahweh and not Babylon will order power in the world. The nations will hear and will know that the old ordering of public reality, which was dominated by Nebuchadnezzar, has come to an abrupt, decisive ending. The poet must work intensely so that this chapter can counter the main claims of the book of Jeremiah. When this chapter is finished, it is clear that *the purpose of Yahweh* and *the role of Babylon* are no longer compatible. It is that startling incompatibility which is the theme of the poem and which becomes the basis for new hope on the horizon of Jeremiah. Jerusalem is invited to look beyond the Babylonian episode to the future intended by Yahweh.

51:1-23   This long unit consists of several distinct pieces that could be variously divided. The main themes, however, are abundantly clear.

The sovereign voice of God begins with a statement of resolve (Jer. 51:1-5). The initial "behold" alerts us to a new, decisive announcement which entails a new action. The word is followed by two first person verbs: "I will arouse, I will send." The remainder of vv. 1-4 concerns the result of these two promised actions. The one aroused, that is, stirred to action (so RSV) and authorized, is a destroyer who will utterly destroy Babylon. In v. 1 it is a single destroyer who is aroused; in vv. 2-3 the destroyer comes with other agents, no doubt elements of an invading army. The ones sent will come to "winnow," that is, to judge and devastate the land. No one will be spared, not even the chosen youths (v. 3). Babylon will become an area for massive suffering and death because of the resolve of God. This rhetorical unit ends with a motivational clause in two parts (v. 5). Positively, this action is taken because Israel and Judah are still the object of God's concern. The term rendered "forsaken" is an adjective form of "widow." That is, this people is not without the strong protective husband who will intervene on its behalf.[68] Negatively, the action against Babylon is because of the guilt of Babylon (contrast 50:7). Thus the poem contains a triangle:[69] Yahweh is for Israel; Yahweh is against Babylon. We are given no specifics, but we may imagine that Babylon's guilt that is "against the Holy One of Israel" was enacted as abuse against Israel (later on; see 51:49). Thus Yahweh's forceful ultimatum is because of the violation of Israel, Yahweh's "wife." Babylon becomes the outsider in this triangle, at great cost.

The same voice of sovereign resolve now makes direct address (vv. 6-10). The addressee is not clear. Verse 6 suggests, in characteristic fashion, that the inhabitants of Babylon are urged to flee the coming attack. However, in v. 9 the address suggests the exiles (Israelites and others) who have been forcibly gathered in Babylon are now urged to leave, because the coming trouble is not aimed at them. In either case, the urging to flee serves to underscore the coming judgment. This unit is framed in juridical language. In v. 6 the coming judgment is identified as Yahweh's "vengeance" (i.e., restitution of rule) and as "requital" (i.e., as an equitable response to the acts of Babylon). In v. 9 it is "judgment" against

---

68. On "widow" as a designation for the socially vulnerable, see Paula S. Hiebert, " 'Whence Shall Help Come to Me?': The Biblical Widow," in *Gender and Difference in Ancient Israel,* ed. Peggy L. Day (Minneapolis: Fortress, 1989), 125-141.

69. On "triangling," see Murray Bowen, *Family Therapy in Clinical Practice* (New York: Aranson, 1978); and Edwin H. Friedman, *Generation to Generation: Family Process in Church and Synagogue* (New York: Guilford, 1985). Claus Westermann, *Praise and Lament in the Psalms* (Atlanta: John Knox and Edinburgh: T. & T. Clark, 1981), 169 and *passim,* has shown that the Psalms of Lament in Israel are triangles of God, speaker, and enemy. In the laments the speaker asks God to triangle with the speaker against the enemy. The outcome of such triangling is evident in our oracle.

Babylon that is being enacted, and in v. 10 the vengeance, requital, and judgment against Babylon are said to be "Zion's vindication" *(tsedeqah)*. Thus the action against Babylon is at the same time action for Israel, again the same triangle operative as in vv. 1-5.

At the center of this unit (vv. 7-9a), Babylon is characterized in a way that sharply contrasts its previous state and its present crisis. Previously, Babylon was "Yahweh's golden cup," that is, the means whereby God punished other peoples (v. 7).

It was through Babylon that all the other nations were required to drink the punishment that made them reel in drunkenness, helplessness, and humiliation. The entire unit turns dramatically at the beginning of v. 8: "Suddenly!" In an abrupt way, almost beyond explanation, Babylon has now been broken and devastated and worthy of grief. When healing was offered, Babylon in its recalcitrance refused. This unit offers something of a ring composition and pivots on the transition in v. 8. In an instant, the prosperous empire has become pitiful and ineffective. The changed circumstance of Babylon has come about because Yahweh is now reestablishing order and paying attention to the well-being of Israel. The reference to the righteousness *(tsedeqah)* of Israel in v. 10 is parallel to the mention of Israel and Judah in v. 5. While Yahweh deals directly with Babylon, the spin-off of that relation for Israel is never far from the horizon of the poem.

Now Yahweh addresses both parties to the coming conflict (vv. 11-14). On the one hand, the attacker is summoned (vv. 11a, 12a). On the other hand, Babylon is addressed in order to be forewarned that it faces "your end" (v. 13). Yahweh manages the battle so that the fate of both the attacker and the attacked are centered in Yahweh's rhetoric. In v. 11 we are given a prose interpretive commentary to identify the parties to the coming conflict. It is Yahweh who stirs up the Medes against Babylon (cf. v. 1 on the same verb). In the end, it was the Persians and not the Medes who nullified Babylon, but the confusion or uncertainty about these historical references is not crucial to the rhetorical intent of the text. In both the prose of v. 11 and the poetry of v. 12, attention is focused on Yahweh's "purpose." That is matched in v. 14 by reference to Yahweh's "oath" to destroy Babylon. Thus the named people (Medes) are proposed as the concrete way whereby Yahweh's intention is implemented!

We have seen attention given to Israel in vv. 5, 10, and less directly in v. 11. In the next poetic unit (vv. 15-19) the climactic statement of this unit again concerns Israel. This entire unit is a quote from 10:12-16, which celebrates Yahweh's power, contrasts that power with the powerlessness of the idols who lack "breath," and asserts the special status of Israel (51:19). The same triangle is again asserted, with the claim that God is indeed actively partisan to this people, while punishment comes to the other peoples. The power, wisdom, and understanding of Yahweh, which have cosmic proportion, are in fact correlated to the well-being of Israel. The connection between v. 15 and v. 19 suggests that the great, cosmic power of Yahweh through which the world exists is now mobilized for and developed toward the well-being of Israel. Sandwiched between the claim for Yahweh (vv. 15-16) and the assurance of Israel (v. 19) is the acknowledgement that the image-worshippers have neither power from God nor capacity to recognize the special place of Israel (vv. 17-18). Notice that in this poetic unit there is no reference to Babylon nor any concrete reference to punishment. It is striking how much the context of chs. 50–51 causes us to read the text (from ch. 10) with reference to Babylon, while the poem itself is silent in its reference.

51:20-24 The poem of 51:20-23 is one of astonishing intensity and discipline, paralleling 50:35-38. The opening line is difficult only because the pronoun "you" lacks a clear antecedent. The poem is addressed to one who will destroy the empire. In context that would seem to be the new attacker/destroyer named in 51:11, but that is never specified. Whoever is addressed is a "war club" (NRSV) in the hand of Yahweh to work havoc on Yahweh's enemies.[70] The term rendered "hammer" is from the same root as "break" *(n-p-ts)* in vv. 20-23. Whoever is addressed is instrumental to the active resolve of Yahweh. The verb "I will shatter" (RSV "break") dominates the poem, being reiterated in each line. The direct object of the verb in vv. 20-23 indicates (as in 50:35-

---

70. See Isa. 10:15, where the image of "axe" is used for the same purpose.

38) that every and all aspects of the life of the enemy will be terminated. This includes military power (51:21), every facet of the civilian population (v. 22), and the operators of the rural economy, as well as the urban managers of power (v. 23). This is one of the most extreme cases of God's massive assault against God's sworn enemy. The term "shatter, break" recurs in Ps. 137:9, where it is conventionally rendered "dash," while it might better be rendered "smash," as the NRSV does in Jer. 51:20-23. In both the Psalm and in this poem, the violent verb is used with reference to Babylon.

Verse 24 adds a prose commentary, perhaps to justify the brutality of the preceding lines. In this verse Yahweh will repay *(sh-l-m),* that is, settle accounts. The evil to be repaid has been perpetrated against Zion, that is, Babylon has violated Judah and Jerusalem. The response of Yahweh is to violate Babylon. Here the theological connection is made explicit that is implicit throughout this long oracle. The theological connection made is daring indeed. It asserts that the fall of Babylon is related as cause and effect to the damage done to Jerusalem.[71] This daring claim is like a claim that the Soviet Union will be leveled because of the violation of Prague, or the United States because of its violation of Managua. Babylon cannot outflank the resolve of Yahweh concerning the ordering of the nations. Any effort to escape Yahweh's rule leads to massive brutality against the perpetrator.

51:25-33 The opening line of this section announces the main point, and it does so even without a verb: "Behold, I (am) against you." Out of that clearly articulated premise, everything else follows. Babylon is a destroying mountain who destroys. (The term "destroy" *[mashhit]* is the same as the one mobilized naming the agent against Babylon in v. 1.) Yahweh announces only one action against this destroyer, with one strong verb: "I will stretch out my hand" (v. 25). Yahweh will mobilize and enact Yahweh's full power. As Yahweh has saved with an outstretched hand (Deut. 4:34; 26:8; cf. Jer. 21:5), so Yahweh will now destroy in the same way. Because God acts so

---

71. On the direct connection of cause and effect, see Koch, "Doctrine of Retribution," 57-87. On the verb *sh-l-m,* see Koch, 60.

frontally and so decisively, the power of Babylon is completely broken. Nothing from its proud ruins can be salvaged. Nothing will be of any worth at all — no stone for the corner, no stone for a foundation, nothing useful. The imagery is extreme, for it takes enormous devastation to so crush stones that they cannot be reused. It is difficult to imagine a more comprehensive or total act of savagery beyond any salvage. The crushing of the stones may appeal back to the verb "shatter" *(n-p-ts)* in 51:20-23.

Through a series of seven imperatives, Yahweh now authorizes those who will move against Babylon. Among the imperatives, the verb "prepare" *(q-d-sh,* i.e., to "sanctify") is used twice, suggesting that this is indeed God's holy war — holy in its purpose, holy in its stratagem. While the military vocabulary and the naming of historical enemies is evident, v. 29 makes clear that it is Yahweh's *purposes* that are the main issue. It is clear in Isa. 55:6-9; Jer. 29:11 that at the end of the Exile Yahweh has "purposes" for Judah, that is, purposes of homecoming. The purposes of Yahweh against Babylon here form a countertheme, for Babylon's demise makes Jerusalem's homecoming possible.

We now have described for us in vivid detail the outworking of Yahweh's purposes for Babylon (51:29b-32). The poem makes an inventory of the aspects of the life of Babylon which now have failed. Verse 29b is a large thematic summary statement. To be "a desolation, without inhabitant," includes the complete failure of the army, which has been as weak and cowardly as women.[72] Moreover, the walled cities are in flames. Verses 31-32 dramatically suggest a relay arrangement of royal messengers. They have news to bear, and it is as urgent as it is ominous. The news of defeat cascades in and must be reported, in all its power and detail. The messenger carries this report to the king: "The city is taken." The phrase is the same as the theme line of 50:2. This devastating piece of news which terminates Babylon as a world power is the

---

72. The reference to women refers to weakness and cowardliness. There is no doubt that such a reference bespeaks a macho, sexist horizon. Such a usage does not need to be defended, but can be understood amid the savage rhetoric of war. The usage ironically reflects arrogant masculinity and wants to make the contrast as sharply as possible.

theological counterpart of the announcement, "Your God reigns" (Isa. 52:7). "His city is taken" and "Your God reigns" are two renderings of the same news. For the exiles it is good news; for the king of Babylon it is unbearably bad news. Because the city is taken, the poet can detail the scene of fire and pain and confusion, perhaps not unlike the most desperate scenes from *Gone With the Wind*.

This unit concludes with an ominous and awesome statement: "Yet a little while." The phrase moves to the edge of apocalyptic rhetoric, anticipating a "time of harvest," that is, a full and total judgment against the city.[73] There will be trampling on the city like the trampling of a threshing floor, only the trampling will be of the pride, power, and prestige of the imperial city.

51:34-58 This long poem consists of many smaller units that make use of various literary conventions.

In Jer. 51:34-40 the poem is a lawsuit structured in two parts. The first part, the indictment, is placed in the mouth of an inhabitant of Zion and constitutes a lament concerning Babylon's maltreatment of Jerusalem (vv. 34-35). In this indictment cast as lament, Nebuchadnezzar is explicitly named as the perpetrator. He is the subject of harsh verbs, "devour, crush, swallow." The accusation made against Nebuchadnezzar is that he has emptied Jerusalem (i.e., deported its people) and swallowed the city whole. Nebuchadnezzar has behaved like a sea-monster, like the very embodiment of chaos and evil. Verse 35 brings the cosmic metaphors down to concrete cases. Nebuchadnezzar has wrought enormous violence in Jerusalem. The last line of the verse is a formula assigning bloodguilt to the Babylonian king.[74] That is,

---

73. Such a phrasing belongs congenially with the apocalyptic tilt given to the text by Childs, "The Enemy from the North."

74. On the power and acknowledgement of bloodguilt, see H. Graf Reventlow, "Sein Blut komme über sein Haupt," *Vetus Testamentum* 10 (1960): 311-327; and Klaus Koch, "Der Spruch 'Sein Blut bleibe auf seinem Haupt' und die israelitische Auffassung vom vegossenen Blut," *Vetus Testamentum* 12 (1962): 396-416. On a major narrative effort to avoid "bloodguilt," see Walter Brueggemann, *Power, Providence, and Personality: Biblical Insight into Life and Ministry* (Louisville: Westminster/John Knox, 1990), 49-85.

Nebuchadnezzar must answer for the blood he has shed. What he regards as state policy is redefined by this poet as murder. The whole of the indictment-lament is an enormous condemnation of Babylon for its wholesale abuse of Jerusalem.

The second part of this unit is a juridical sentence in the mouth of Yahweh, introduced by "therefore" (vv. 36-40). The statement of Yahweh, in response to Zion's lament, begins with juridical language concerning a lawsuit. Yahweh will go to court on behalf of Jerusalem. The language moves immediately toward "vengeance" and the implementation of terrible judgment against Babylon. Yahweh promises to dry up the sources of water and of life, until the great city shrivels and dies and becomes only a habitat for jackals, without human life and without political power. Thus in one terse verse, the poet brings a dramatic and decisive end to the empire.

Then Yahweh details the additional punishment (vv. 38-40). This little section begins with lions and ends with lambs and he-goats. The poet imagines the Babylonians to be desperate for food and for drink, starved, ravenous, and parched with the passion of a hungry lion, ready to gulp down everything and everyone within reach. Yahweh, however, will give the lion bad, destructive food that it will immediately seize and consume. From that bad food the lion will become drunk and die in a perpetual sleep. Then Yahweh will slaughter and offer the Babylonians like helpless sacrificial animals, done to death at the hand of Yahweh. The drama of these verses is like the injection of a tranquilizer into a ferocious animal that is quickly reduced to helplessness. When the wild animal turns to drunkenness and sleep, Yahweh can do the act of termination as easily as a lamb is slaughtered.

Upon the execution of Yahweh's judgment against Babylon, the poet gloats over and taunts the defeated, destroyed city (vv. 41-44). The lead phrase echoes the governing theme of 50:2. Jeremiah 51:41 narrates a total reversal: Babylon as an object of praise has become Babylon as a horror. The "sea" is the primordial threat of chaos which has now inundated Babylon (v. 42). Though the language is cosmic and mythical, the actual mode of such inundation is likely a historical enemy, even though no reference to such an enemy is made. The delicacy of interpretation is to see that such cosmic claims are not at all removed from concrete experience into an irrelevant supernaturalism. The sweeping power of chaos (embodied in an invading enemy) destroys all the infrastructure and life-support systems of the empire, and reduces a once productive region to a lifeless wilderness (cf. 2:6).[75]

Jeremiah 51:44 returns to the sweeping themes of vv. 41-42. With the fall of the city, the patron god of the empire is also brought under severe judgment. It has been this empire-god who has swallowed Jerusalem (v. 34). Now Yahweh takes out of the mouth of the Babylonian god the city that has been swallowed but not digested. It is as though Jerusalem is unchewed meat in the mouth of this god and Yahweh retrieves it from such a destructive chewing. That is, the monster-god-empire is forced to relinquish the city of Jerusalem and is not free to devour it. Yahweh has snatched the life of Zion out of the mouth of the empire in the same way that a shepherd snatches a lamb out of the mouth of a lion (cf. 1 Sam. 17:37). On the one hand, the imagery suggests that Jerusalem was saved very late, at the last minute. On the other hand, the image exhibits Yahweh as strong and determined, and in the end stronger than the monster-god of Babylon. Yahweh has prevailed! The last lines of Jer. 51:44 return to the sober verdict of v. 41. Babylon no longer commands the respect or obedience of the nations, receives neither their booty (tax) nor allegiance nor amazement. Babylon has been emptied of its capacity to dominate its world. It has fallen (cf. 50:32).[76]

This section of the poem is arranged in something like a chiastic fashion.

  a   the verdict (51:41),
     b   mythic allusions (v. 42),
        c   the city as wilderness (v. 43),
     b' mythic allusions (v. 44a),
  a' the verdict (v. 44b).

---

75. The imagery of chaos requires an awareness, as Childs sees, that this is more than one nation invading another. This poetry concerns the reappearance of primordial powers of chaos which Babylon had thought tamed.

76. Bel is now emptied (51:44), as Jerusalem had been emptied (v. 34).

Now the abused exiles are addressed as "my people" (vv. 45-46). The exiles are now admonished to depart the empire. Yahweh is about to execute fierce anger against the empire.[77] That "fierce anger" is not now aimed at the Israelite exiles, but they must leave Babylon to avoid the general destruction that is to come. The admonition to flee the general destruction is not unlike the rescue of Lot in the face of the destruction of Sodom (Gen. 19:15-23). The exiles are beset by endless "rumors" (*nishma'ah,* used three times; RSV "report") concerning the empire, its violence, its instability, and its patterns of intrigue. The exiles are tempted to get caught up in such turmoil; paying need to such gossip, however, can only compromise and weaken the resolve of the exilic community. Thus these imperatives urge the exiles to become involved in no imperial games, to remember their own identity, and to act only in response to the initiative of Yahweh. The mandate from Yahweh is to "go out," a word already used for the Exodus (cf. Isa. 49:9; 52:11-12).

The concluding poetry in the oracle is a reassertion that Babylon will be defeated, destroyed, and terminated (Jer. 51:47-58). Twice the poet uses the awesome anticipatory formula, "Behold, the days are coming" (vv. 47, 52). Three times the poet invokes a coming "destroyer" (vv. 48, 53, 56, twice in the plural). The defeat of the gods of Babylon, who are empty, powerless images, bespeaks the fall of a haughty imperial power everywhere feared and deeply resented. The defeat of the gods who legitimate such power will be welcomed everywhere, in the heavens as on earth (v. 48).[78] The elimination of the theological, ideological intimidation of Babylon will permit the whole world to breathe a sigh of glad relief.[79] The

---

77. The phrase in v. 45 is the same as in 4:26. Childs, "The Enemy from the North," 157-161, notes the connection between chs. 50–51 and 4:23-26.

78. The rejoicing in heaven and on earth is not unlike the rejoicing in Ps. 96 when the news comes that "Yahweh is king." While Ps. 96 is liturgic and cosmic whereas this oracle is more political and historical, the point of celebration is the same. Babylon is crushed and Israel is free precisely because the rule of Yahweh has been decisively reestablished.

79. The sigh of glad relief on a cosmic scale is like the sigh of glad relief when any totalitarian oppressor finally falls. The cosmic dimension of this fall expressed in apocalyptic language permits all of creation to rejoice, even the nonhuman creation, as is evident in Ps. 96:10-13.

specific reason for the defeat of Babylon is that the empire has produced the "slain of Israel" (v. 49). The fall of the empire is connected to the peculiar treasure which Israel is to Yahweh. While the second line of v. 41 does acknowledge that the imperial destruction has not been confined to Israel and has the larger destruction in purview, it is the "slain of Israel" which is the specific ground for the end of the empire.

In vv. 50–51 the surviving Jews are addressed, the ones who were not already destroyed by the empire. They are admonished to go out and not to linger in the empire. A basis for their departure is that they must remember. If they forget, they will try to come to terms with the empire. When these Jews remember, they remember Yahweh, even though they are distanced from the holy place. They are to remember the holy city, and they are to remember the shame and humiliation of the abused temple (cf. Pss. 74, 79). That is, they are to remember that they are Jews, to remember the peculiar hurt and desperation of recent time and then to act as Jews.[80]

The departure urged upon the Jews may indeed be geographical. It may also be a departure, the hard part of which is emotional. The victimized exiles may have come excessively to terms with Babylon, both by being excessively fascinated and by being excessively dependent and therefore grateful. An embrace of Jewish memory is the ground for disengagement from geographical, economic, political, and emotional connections to the empire.

Jeremiah 51:52-53 reiterate themes already heard. The poem knows about the "coming time." God will work justice against the empire. Babylon will suffer and the destroyers will come. There is nothing Babylon, even in its best strength, can do to resist the coming destruction, because God has authored the destroyers.

The large hope of vv. 52-53 is "at hand" in vv. 54-57. The poet

---

80. On the cruciality of memory for the survival and buoyancy of Jews, see Yosef Hayim Yerushalmi, *Zakhor: Jewish History and Jewish Memory* (Seattle: University of Washington Press, 1982); and Ozick, *Metaphor and Memory,* 265-283. On Ps. 137 as a powerful act of memory among exiles, see Stephen Mitchell, "Lamentations," in *Congregation: Contemporary Writers Read the Jewish Bible,* ed. David Rosenberg (New York: Harcourt Brace Jovanovich, 1987), 387-390.

is the one who hears before others hear. What this poet hears, well ahead of anyone else, is a voice, a cry of Babylon (cf. Exod. 11:6). It is a cry of fear and terror and wretchedness. It is the shriek of people under assault, fleeing from the fire and from trampling horses. It is a cry among the secure and serene who suddenly find themselves in deep jeopardy, utterly helpless, bewildered, and with no resources.

The cry is an appropriate response. The cause of the voice is that Yahweh is destroying Babylon. The word NRSV renders "laying waste" (*shoded*, "destroy") is one we have seen earlier in this long oracle. Now it is Yahweh alone who destroys, the sure and determined enemy of Babylon. It is Yahweh who is denying voice to the empire. Wave upon wave of enemy assault lap at Babylon and drown out the cry. The cry of need and hurt is drowned out by the waves of chaos unleashed by Yahweh. The whole of the political-military establishment is terminated.

The ruin evoked here is not wrought through any identifiable geopolitical means. It is wrought solely and singularly by Yahweh, the God of recompense, the God of requital *(sh-l-m)*, the God who repays, who gives people what they have coming. It is Yahweh who defeats and places in a deathly stupor the entire power structure — princes, wise men, governors, commanders, warriors, all the great and significant ones now rendered innocuous, helpless, and pitiful.

The oracle ends with a magisterial formula: "says the King" (Jer. 51:57). This is the real king.[81] The others, including Nebuchadnezzar, have been transitory pretenders. This One is the one with the name of power, "LORD of hosts," "ruler of the troops," before whom empires cannot stand and before whom oppression and violence will not be tolerated. History in the empire is bent irresistibly toward the undiminished rule of Yahweh.

----

81. Reference to "the King" concerns Yahweh. Thus the text asserts the authority of the real king and the dismissal of the pseudo-king, Nebuchadnezzar. The juxtaposition of the two is not unlike Isa. 6:1, wherein Yahweh the real king displaces Uzziah, who was not the real king. On Yahweh as king, see Marc Zvi Brettler, *God is King: Understanding an Israelite Metaphor.* JSOT Supp. 76 (Sheffield: Sheffield Academic Press, 1989).

This long oracle ends in an understated reprise (v. 58). This same LORD of the troops speaks one more time, offering a simple, descriptive verdict. The walls are levelled, and the gates are burned. The efforts of such as Babylon (peoples and nations) are utterly futile in the face of Yahweh. It is worth noting that this last reference to "peoples and nations" is plural. It is as though the poem at the last moment looks beyond Babylon, which has been the insistent agenda of the oracle, to a larger, more comprehensive horizon. The concrete word has become a more philosophical, comprehensive reflection. Perhaps this concluding formula provides a conclusion to the larger corpus of chs. 46–51.[82] Perhaps the verse expresses a canonical awareness, so that the text makes the Babylonian statements reusable in other contexts. In any case, the concluding term rendered "nothing" (NRSV) is Hebrew *riq,* "emptied." The efforts of the nations as autonomous agents are empty efforts. The world cannot be enacted without God. Power cannot be claimed without Yahweh. That affirmation is good news for displaced Jews. For Babylon, it is a late lesson learned repeatedly at enormous cost.

A WEIGHTY LETTER (51:59-64)

This prose passage has in purview the oracle against Babylon just completed (50:1–51:58). The prose paragraph seeks to guarantee the future significance and effectiveness of that just completed oracle for the community of exiled Jews. At the same time, however, this paragraph is a redactional piece that is concerned with the canonical shaping of the book of Jeremiah. The text is quite aware of the need to give closure to the corpus of Jeremiah and knows that this is Jeremiah's last utterance (51:64b). The prophet will be permitted to say nothing more.

The unit begins with the identification of Seraiah, who is pressed into the service of the prophet and who is commissioned to preside over Jeremiah's crucial document. Seraiah is a son of Neriah and therefore, presumably, a brother to Baruch. It is therefore inevitable that the transaction of this narrative con-

---

82. See the same affirmation in Hab. 2:13.

cerning the scroll should be related to the oracle of ch. 45 and to the involvement of Baruch in two of Jeremiah's crucial documents (32:12-16; 36:4-32).[83] This connection of Seraiah and Baruch supports my suggestion that Baruch is representative of the Babylonian community of Jews. In any case, Seraiah is charged with Jeremiah's (now written) words, to make them available and effective in Babylon as they have been uttered and written (perhaps by Baruch) in Jerusalem. The text self-consciously knows that the text must be promulgated to have a future.

The paragraph then deals with the preparation, administration, and deposit of the scroll. (1) *The preparation* of the scroll attributes to Jeremiah the actual writing of the scroll (51:60), unlike ch. 36 where Jeremiah orally dictates the scroll. What matters most is that Jeremiah has now opted for a written medium, surely reflective of the fact that we are well on our way toward a canonical literature.[84] The editors of this material (if not Seraiah) know that they are involved in producing something like "Scripture." The substance of the scroll concerns "evil" (disasters) against Babylon, which surely indicates that the scroll refers to chs. 50–51, the prophet's climactic word against the empire.

(2) *The administration* of the scroll is quite specific and equally odd (51:61-62). First, Seraiah is to read (proclaim) the scroll, that is, to make it a matter of public record (as in chs. 32, 36). Clearly Seraiah is to do something as dangerous as the action of his brother Baruch in ch. 36. Whereas Baruch acts in defiance of the king in Jerusalem in ch. 36, Seraiah acts in defiance of the empire. Second, Seraiah is to "say" to Yahweh, that is, to pray. The prayer is to remind God of what God has said in God's resolve to destroy the Babylonian Empire. The act on the part of Seraiah

---

83. This family, which includes both Baruch and Seraiah, was presumably a family of scribes. See Dearman, "My Servants the Scribes." It seems plausible that this family was both instrumental in championing the role and significance of Jews exiled to Babylon (cf. 42:2-3) and active and instrumental in the canonical production of the book of Jeremiah.

84. On the significance of the move from oral to written communication, see Werner H. Kelber, *The Oral and the Written Gospel* (Philadelphia: Fortress, 1983); and Walter J. Ong, *Orality and Literacy* (New York: Methuen, 1982).

suggests a most interesting motif concerning God and a telling theological understanding of the scroll.

The point about the character of God is that the prophet is concerned to remind God what God has resolved to do. It is as though God might neglect or even forget, unless God is reminded.[85] But then, when did God issue this threat against the empire? Presumably in chs. 50–51. We are given a picture of the scroll being waved in God's face in order to remind God of what God has decreed in the preceding oracle.

The scroll is brought into play because the scroll itself is where God issued the threat. That is, the scroll is indeed God's word.[86] Thus the scroll comes to exercise a pivotal role not only for Jeremiah and for the community of the canon, but in God's own life. The tone of this reminder to God seems not unlike Moses's prayer in Num. 14:17-19, in which God is reminded of God's own verbalized commitment in Exod. 34:6-7. The theological function of the scroll is to provide a guide and norm for Yahweh's exercise of sovereignty. It is as though the scroll functions to say to God, "This is what it means to be God, and this is how to be God."

(3) *The deposit* of the scroll follows its administration (Jer. 51:63-64a). The deposit of the scroll is presented as though it were a formal, public, and sacramental act. The scroll is to be thrown into the Euphrates, the river which is the lifeline of Babylon. It is, however, to be thrown into the river with appropriately ominous words. The deposit of the scroll into the river evokes an announcement that Babylon will sink (like a scroll with a stone tied to it), sink to death, never to rise . . . because of evil.

The speech accompanying the deposit of the scroll evokes two connections. On the one hand, the sinking is not unlike the sinking of Pharaoh, the imperial embodiment of evil now assigned into the powers of the chaotic waters.[87] On the other hand, the scroll

---

85. On God's memory, the chance of forgetting, and reminders to God, see Ralph W. Klein, *Israel in Exile: A Theological Interpretation*. Overtures to Biblical Theology 6 (Philadelphia: Fortress, 1979), 135-36; cf. Isa. 63:7-9.

86. On God's own work in and through scrolls, see Faur, "God as a Writer."

87. The image is not unlike that of Exod. 15:4-10, though the verb is not the same.

in the Euphrates which bespeaks the termination of Babylon is parallel to the waistcloth in the Euphrates bespeaking the termination of Judah (13:1-11). Thus the river is a place where the prophet deposits more than one ominous, deathly message. The scroll, the speech, and the deposit together tell decisively against the empire.

The act of the deposit need not be dismissed as "magic." It can as well be understood as a freighted political act which serves both to undermine the absolutist claims of Babylon and to invite Jewish hope away from its mesmerizing fear of the empire. Insofar as the act is a short-term political act, observers are put on notice that this is a moment when changed allegiance is possible. Insofar as the act is a long-term political act, it creates an abiding clue about the way history will work. Against all present available data, this is an awesome reminder that God, who seems so irrelevant, has taken a profound decision that eventually and inevitably will prevail.

We have, however, no access to the event itself. What we have is a paragraph describing an alleged event. We, with the long succession of interpreters, struggle with the narrative report which is strategically placed in the book of Jeremiah to enhance the oracle of chs. 50–51 and to indicate that, of all the things Jeremiah said or could have said, this is his last testimony to his people. It is a testimony that invites Israel to perceive itself in a peculiar way in a historical process where the sovereign, hidden power of God is decisively at work. It is a testimony that moves beyond most of the book of Jeremiah, which has seen Babylon as God's great partner in judgment. Now, against all of that, Yahweh terminates Babylon. This testimony reminds the community that the shape and clue to life is not given by the will or whim of an empire. Babylon is penultimately significant. In the end, however, Babylon faces a demise with no Easter, a sinking with no rising. After the empire has sunk like a rock into the river, Israel still has the scroll, the promise of the scroll, and the God who speaks in and through the scroll.

No wonder the words of Jeremiah ended (51:64)! Nothing more need be said. This act is like a great belated, exalted cry: "It is finished" (John 19:30)! The empire is finished, and the God of Jeremiah has finished the painful rescue of Israel. This is not "magic." It is a political act of a special, lyrical kind. We must not reduce the power of communal symbol into our straitjackets of rational positivism. Such an act as the deposit of the scroll in the river is a gesture which lingers with power in the community of remembering and hoping. The act invites courage, and it resists resignation. It gathers the community in energy and focuses on its identity, not as the people of Nebuchadnezzar but as the people of Yahweh.

In the end this narrative is, however, not only awesome politics. It is faithful testimony to the God of exile and homecoming, of death and new life. The sinking of Babylon will indeed happen. As the empire sinks from view into chaos, new futures are opened for Israel. They are opened by the God who is both a God "nearby" and a God "far off" (Jer. 23:23). For much of the book of Jeremiah God was far away, in the company of the empire. Now this same God has come near to this subjugated, intimidated people. The river keeps bubbling as the scroll sinks. It bubbles the death of the empire. It also bubbles the rule of Yahweh and the future of Israel. No more need be said; for that reason the prophet stops. His words are ended!

AN ENDING AND A CHANCE
Jeremiah 52:1-34

This chapter, which serves as a conclusion to the book of Jeremiah, is derived from other historical sources and does not mention the prophet Jeremiah at all. With the exception of Jer. 52:28-30, the material is parallel to 2 Kgs. 24:18–25:30, and most scholars believe is derived from it. In the construction of the book of Jeremiah, however, material pertinent to the final events of Jerusalem has already been included in Jer. 39:1-10. Moreover, the material on Gedaliah in 2 Kgs. 25:22-26 is not used in Jer. 52, but appears earlier in 40:7–41:18. Thus questions of literary priority are exceedingly difficult. We can only recognize that the material has had a complex editorial process. With that recognition, we can consider the material as it is presented to us. For even if the process has been complex, it does not follow that the present shaping is unintentional.

52:1-3a This material, which is paralleled in 2 Kgs. 24:18-20, reflects the standard royal formulas from the book of Kings. The harsh verdict rendered upon Zedekiah is noteworthy in two regards. First, Zedekiah receives major credit for the royal policies which led to the destruction and is likened in his destructive effort to Jehoiakim. Both Jehoiakim and Zedekiah are mentioned in Jer. 1:1-3 in relation to the Exile. In general, Jehoiachin may be reckoned as the more troublesome of the two (cf. 2 Kgs. 23:36–24:7), but here the two kings are linked together. Zedekiah receives primary blame in a way that seems to override even the verdict on Manasseh (2 Kgs. 21:1-16). Second, the concluding line of Jer. 52:3a renders an unqualified theological verdict with the verb "cast out." The Exile is Yahweh's work, evoked by anger,

not just with the king but with the city and with the nation. At
last Yahweh does what the book of Jeremiah has long anticipated.
In doing so, a major bonding between God and this people is
harshly nullified. It is remarkable that this is the last and only time
in this extensive chapter that the intervention of Yahweh is mentioned. The remainder of the account proceeds on the basis of
human, historical action.

52:3b-11   While vv. 1-3a rendered a theological verdict concerning the anger of Yahweh, vv. 3b-11 render a political verdict
concerning the provocation of the Babylonians. The juxtaposition
of the two, vv. 1-3a and vv. 3b-11, political and theological
verdicts, is dazzling in its twofold statement of cause and in the
ill-defined connection between the two.[1] Clearly there is a link
between the theological and political verdicts. Clearly the text
intends a connection between the two. We are, however, given
no clue or indication about that connection. Likely we are to
conclude that the provocation of the empire is derived from the
anger of Yahweh, but we have no hint of that. Verses 3b-11 are
completely disciplined as a political description which carefully
avoids any theological allusion. There are two renderings of the
crisis, and either interpretation is valid and permissible. In the
context of the book of Jeremiah, the two cannot be separated and
likely they are understood to be synonymous. Thus Yahweh's
"expulsion" of Judah is not a "supernatural" act, but happens in
a perfectly understandable way which everyone can observe. Given
either interpretation, or given both interpretations together, the
political project of an independent Jerusalem initiated by Yahweh
in fidelity to David is now effectively and decisively finished. We
are at a terrible and irreversible ending in Israel's life.

The account of the Babylonian ending of Jerusalem is closely
paralleled in 2 Kgs. 25:1-7 (see also Jer. 39:1-7). It is the story
of a powerful, determined empire using its force and authority

---

1. The relation between the two is left unspecified, which permits an
enormous range of interpretive options. For these two renderings of the
treatment of Jeremiah, the narrative account employs a parataxis, so that the
grammatical connection between the two is left deliberately unspecified.

against a recalcitrant patronage state. In the wake of the invasion and occupation comes famine (52:6), one of the usual threats (curses); of the other two traditional curses, the "sword" is implicit in the events of destruction, but pestilence is not mentioned explicitly. In any case, Judah and Jerusalem receive all the threats that characteristically come with such an invasion. In the ensuing crisis Zedekiah did not distinguish himself by his courage or nobility. He ran for his life, but not fast enough (vv. 7-11). He was apprehended and treated to an ignoble, cruel ending. Verse 11 reports (as the parallel accounts do not) that he was in prison until his death. The narrative does not explain to us, as would be plausible, that this terrible ending to the life of the king derives from the theological force of v. 3a.

52:12-16   While vv. 3b-11 have been preoccupied with the fate of the king, these verses describe the fate of the city at the hands of a ruthless occupying army. Whereas vv. 3b-11 had been located by the chronology of Zedekiah ("his ninth year"), now the reckoning is by the chronology of Nebuchadnezzar ("his nineteenth year"). Likely the change in chronological reckoning reflects a shift in the horizon of power, for Nebuchadnezzar has now become the point of political reference. It is his power and his longevity on the throne which now determine the shape of events.

Three items are reported from the occupation. First, there was a great destruction of the temple, the walls, and many houses (vv. 13-14). The narrative offers a poignant statement with a fourfold use of "house," suggesting massive destruction by fire, destruction of all that gave stability and security. Second, there was an extensive deportation from the city (v. 15). This verse does not support the conventional wisdom that deportation involved only leading citizens, as this company of deportees seems much more to be a cross section of the population. Third, there were left in the land some whose responsibility it was to continue the work of the agricultural economy (v. 16). This is congruent with the directive of Gedaliah, who worked at revitalization of the economy (40:10-12), though that report does not make the remnant in the land sound as marginal and pitiful as is suggested here. In any case, enough persons are left in the land to make clear that the deportation was part of an imperial strategy for a continued economy in the land, not designed to "empty" the land.

Thus the policy of Babylon reflects political realism, for the empire had a stake in the continuation and revitalization of the economy. Such political stratagems are likely to be less extreme than theological verdicts, one of which might be that the land was "emptied." In such a verdict, theological rhetoric overruns the political realism of the empire. In any case, the fabric of communal life was not destroyed, but every element of the population which might give encouragement to resistance or autonomy was obviously dispatched.

52:17-27 Now the narrative becomes more specific about the action of the occupying force against the city. Two elements are noted. First, there was seizure and confiscation of the temple vessels (52:17-23). This act of violation involved two dimensions. On the one hand, the temple vessels constitute a great storehouse of wealth. We may imagine that the occupying army greedily took what was of value. Invasion is profitable! On the other hand, however, that the wealth is in the temple artifacts adds a theological dimension to the act.[2] The seizure of the temple vessels signifies a removal of all the small signs of theological legitimacy of the temple. The loss of the temple vessels means the loss of prestige for the God who presides over the temple. Writ large, the confiscation asserts that the Babylonian gods have prevailed over the God of Israel. This seizure of the temple artifacts is a highly symbolic as well as highly profitable act that must have been salt on the open wounds of Jerusalem. Peter R. Ackroyd has traced through the literature the fact that the loss and restoration of the temple vessels is a literary device for asserting continuity of the community through the Exile.[3] Here, however, because there is only loss and no restoration, their seizure bespeaks discontinuity. The wealth of the city and the prestige of Yahweh are both forfeited in a single act. This is indeed the Good Friday of the temple!

---

2. This may indeed be an example of "commodity fetishism," for transcendent value is attached to these objects.
3. Ackroyd, "The Temple Vessels."

The second element of the abusive occupation is the seizure and execution of leading citizens (vv. 24-27). The ones seized are enumerated quite specifically. This must have been an act that was highly visible in the city and one that was passionately remembered. The company of those arrested includes the two ranking priests, three lesser priests ("keepers of the threshold"), a military officer, seven members of the king's cabinet, a military secretary, and sixty other citizens. We are not told why the violence is against these seventy-four men. Perhaps this is an accidental roundup of those who happened to be available; perhaps these particular persons were sought out as known resisters to imperial policy. We are not told. We only know that it is a company of influential people. They are given the same ruthless execution as the king, at Riblah. The empire is thorough and ruthless in destroying not only the wealth and structures of legitimacy in Jerusalem, but in destroying any political will for independence among the Jews. The symbols of legitimacy and the possible candidates for leadership are together brought under total and harsh imperial rule.

52:28-30   This concluding statement now adds a summary of the three waves of deportation undertaken by the empire. The reckoning (as in v. 12) is now according to the time line of Nebuchadnezzar, perpetrator of the deportations:

"in the seventh year"	= 598 B.C.E.	3023 persons
"in the eighteenth year"	= 587 B.C.E.	832 persons
"in the twenty-third year"	= 582 B.C.E.	745 persons
Total		4600 persons

This material does not appear in the parallel accounts. Three things strike one about the material.

First, the double use of the term "exile" (*glh*) rings in our ears. This has been the target of the book of Jeremiah since 1:3. The goal of the entire Jeremiah tradition is to tell the tale toward exile, and now the tale is completed.

Second, the numbers are relatively small. (Of course, they are not insignificant numbers for those taken away, or for those whose families were taken away. The situation of exile was no doubt a threatening one and must have been experienced as something like the end of a world.[4]) Small numbers notwithstanding, the structure of the OT is organized around this event which is given a significance all out of proportion to its data. Most specially, the deportation of 587 is the smallest. It is nonetheless that event which has taken on paradigmatic theological significance which has become definitional for Jewishness.[5] Thus in this chapter we are witnessing the primal event for Jewish identity, an event matching in significance the crucifixion of Jesus for the identity of Christians.

Third, the care and comprehensiveness of the dates and numbers of exiles gives a sense of completeness and finality to the summary statement. Nothing is said of all those who remained in the land. They are not counted in the recorded numbers, and they do not count in the horizon of this narrative. The deported ones are the ones who are counted in this reckoning, and they are the ones who count in this version of Jewish reality. The text is reflective of and perhaps generative of the decisiveness of exile for the shaping of long-term Jewish imagination. Nothing is said here of God's absence or God's fidelity. The Exile is a political event worked by Nebuchadnezzar. Nonetheless for Jewish sensitivity, it is the verb "cast out" *(sh-l-k)* in 52:3a that looms over all these statistics: only Yahweh can be the subject of that awesome, decisive verb.

52:31-34   This final paragraph is chronologically removed from the preceding narrative. The last datum in v. 30 concerns 582. Now in v. 31 we are suddenly at 561. The king exiled in 598, Jehoiachin, is alive and still recognized as king after thirty-seven years, but still in exile, still not free, still not able to return home, still not on his throne. He is king, but something less than fully king. His Babylonian overlord is Evil-merodach (Awel-Marduk). Thus we have moved to a new generation after Nebuchadnezzar,

---

4. Daniel L. Smith, *The Religion of the Landless: The Social Context of the Babylonia Exile* (Bloomington, Ind.: Meyer-Stone, 1989), has argued persuasively that the Exile was indeed an experience of acute hardship.

5. On the paradigmatic significance of the Exile for all Jews, see Neusner, *Understanding Seeking Faith,* 137-141.

whose son now will reign only two years (562-560). It is this
new king who "lifted up the head" of Jehoiachin (v. 31).[6] The
Babylonian overlord "spoke kindly," that is, acted as a friend
toward him. Jehoiachin is treated with recognition and with dignity, as a royal person cared for and sustained by his benefactor
. . . "until the day of his death" (v. 34). He died, then, without
ever going home (cf. Jer. 22:24-30, where Jehoiachin is called
Coniah).

The text is uncommonly laconic about this boy-king now
grown older in exile. It is as though the narrative managed to
balance finely and delicately the awareness that he is a captive
with the acknowledgement that he is a recognized, royal captive.
The narrative does not claim so much as to sound hopeful, but
the narrative also does not claim too little to end in despair.[7]
Beyond the fact of theological sensitivity and cunning, this narrative articulation is perhaps precisely faithful to the realities, with
the outcome unknown.

The last paragraph in the narrative states a modest outcome to
what has preceded in this chapter. The main line of the plot of
ch. 52 is one of destruction, despair, and deportation. In the midst
of that sorry plot line, this little paragraph permits an opening
which may let God keep God's powerful promise.[8]

The most important and most difficult question of ch. 52 is
its intentionality in its present locus. Why did the shapers of the
book of Jeremiah include this historical data which is securely
recorded elsewhere? Very likely the chapter intends to make a
theological statement, so that we will misread if we focus too
much on the historical data.

---

6. On the phrase "lift up the head," see the rich wordplay in Gen. 40:16-23.

7. On the promissory dimension of this text, see von Rad, *Old Testament
Theology,* 1:343, n. 22; and the comments of Frank Moore Cross, *Canaanite
Myth and Hebrew Epic* (Cambridge, Mass.: Harvard University Press, 1973),
275-78.

8. This paragraph thus seems to play upon the great promise of 2 Sam. 7:1-16.
Although the statement of Jer. 22:24-30 anticipates the end of the dynasty, it is
evident from 33:14-16, 19-22, 23-26 that the promise made to David is still active
and visible in Judaism. The closing paragraph of the book of Jeremiah makes an
allusion to that promise but does not make any precise claim.

The book of Jeremiah does not end easily or quickly, which suggests that many hands were at work deciding how to end the book. One ending might have come in 43:8-13; 44:1-30, an ending dismissing the Jews in Egypt and implicitly celebrating the Jews in Babylon. A second ending might have come in ch. 45, which anticipates a "disaster" for "all flesh." Such an anticipation opens the way for the Oracles against the Nations (chs. 46–51). We have seen that these oracles are organized in a two-stage arrangement, (1) the victory of Babylon over all the nations, including Egypt (chs. 46–49), and (2) the harsh demise of Babylon (chs. 50–51). The arrangement of these texts favors Babylonian Jews at the expense of the Egyptian Jews and to the neglect of those who remained in Jerusalem. The narrative also asserts, however, that Babylon as a world power is a provisional and passing matter, because Yahweh gives rule to whomever Yahweh will (cf. 49:19; 50:44). Thus God can give dominion to Babylon (chs. 46–49) ("my servant," 43:10) and God can take it from Babylon (chs. 50–51). In 52:1-30 power is given to Babylon. In 52:31-34 Babylon still has power; but there is another visible king, Jehoiachin, who continues to be present and known. Might Yahweh choose to give power back to him? We do not know. Such a turn is politically unlikely; it is nonetheless theologically possible.

Thus the book of Jeremiah thinks and speaks intensely and in various voices about a Babylon-dominated world. That empire might be acknowledged as uncommonly powerful, but not ultimately powerful. Thus the tradition asserts that on occasion the rule of Yahweh and the policy of Babylon converge and are identical. (That is the meaning of the juxtaposition of 52:1-3a and vv. 3b-11.) But the two do not converge everywhere, not always, not finally. Finally it is Yahweh and only Yahweh who governs. Jer. 1:3 introduces us to the tale of exile. Now the story culminates in exile, but the story is not yet ended as we reach the end of the text.

The last paragraph is a theological acknowledgement of Yahweh's sovereignty (vv. 31-34). With that acknowledgement comes a vindication of Jeremiah as well. Jeremiah has known first and most clearly that the city of Jerusalem would fall. Well, it has fallen (vv. 1-30)! It has fallen in every way possible. The prophet cannot finally say "with one to raise it up" (cf. 50:32; Amos 5:2). Perhaps, but perhaps not. Jeremiah is exactly right. Jeremiah knows fully about the sovereignty of Yahweh, but he does not imagine he knows how that sovereignty will out. In Jer. 52:31-34 neither Evil-Merodach nor Jehoiachin knows how Yahweh's rule will out. History is cunning and inscrutable. It is nonetheless the arena where power is given and taken back, assigned and reassigned. In the end, both the great empire and the exiled king must deal with the God of the powerful verb in v. 3a. The verb "cast out," however, is not the only powerful verb in the vocabulary of this God. There are others, which we know from 1:10. The God of the powerful verbs is visible and active nowhere else in this chapter except in v. 3a. Nonetheless, this is the God who dispatches empires and reassigns human power (cf. 49:19; 50:44). At the end we do not know about the destiny of Jehoiachin. Our inability to know, however, is not a problem of failed reportage, so that we wish the narrator had told us more. Rather, our inability to know is a function of Yahweh's sovereignty that requires listening and waiting. More than that we cannot do. This people, because of the odd way of its life with Yahweh, must listen and wait.

SELECTED BIBLIOGRAPHY

Books

Bracke, John M. "The Coherence and Theology of Jeremiah 30–31" (Ph.D. dissertation, Union Theological Seminary, Richmond, 1983).

Bright, John. *Jeremiah*. Anchor Bible 21 (Garden City, N.Y.: Doubleday, 1965).

Carroll, Robert P. *Jeremiah*. Old Testament Library (Philadelphia: Westminster and London: SCM, 1986).

Holladay, William L. *Jeremiah 2*. Hermeneia (Minneapolis: Fortress, 1989).

Nicholson, Ernest W. *Preaching to the Exiles: A Study of the Prose Tradition in the Book of Jeremiah* (Oxford: Blackwell, 1970).

Overholt, Thomas W. *The Threat of Falsehood: A Study in the Theology of the Book of Jeremiah*. Studies in Biblical Theology, 2nd series 16 (Naperville: Allenson and London: SCM, 1970).

Seitz, Christopher R. *Theology in Conflict: Reactions to the Exile in the Book of Jeremiah*. Beihefte zur Zeitschrift für die alttestamentliche Wissenschaft 176 (Berlin: de Gruyter, 1989).

Articles

Anderson, Bernhard W. "'The Lord Has Created Something New': A Stylistic Study of Jer 31:15-22," *Catholic Biblical Quarterly* 40 (1978): 463-478. [Repr. in *A Prophet to the Nations: Essays in Jeremiah Studies,* ed. Leo G. Perdue and Brian W. Kovacs (Winona Lake: Eisenbrauns, 1984), 367-380.]

Brueggemann, Walter. "The Book of Jeremiah: Portrait of the

Prophet," *Interpretation* 37 (1983): 130-145. [Repr. in *Interpreting the Prophets,* ed. James L. Mays and Paul J. Achtemeier (Philadelphia: Fortress, 1987), 113-129.]

————. "Israel's Sense of Place in Jeremiah," in *Rhetorical Criticism.* Festschrift James Muilenburg, ed. Jared J. Jackson and Martin Kessler. Pittsburgh Theological Monograph 1 (Pittsburgh: Pickwick, 1974), 148-165.

————. "A Second Reading of Jeremiah after the Dismantling," *Ex Auditu* 1 (1985): 156-168.

————. "A Shattered Transcendence? Exile and Restoration," in *Biblical Theology: Problems and Prospects.* Festschrift J. Christian Beker, ed. Steven Kraftchick et al. (forthcoming).

————. "The 'Uncared for' Now Cared for (Jer 30:12-17): A Methodological Consideration," *Journal of Biblical Literature* 104 (1985): 419-428.

Childs, Brevard S. "The Enemy from the North and the Chaos Tradition," *Journal of Biblical Literature* 78 (1959): 187-198. [Repr. in *A Prophet to the Nations,* ed. Perdue and Kovacs, 151-161.]

Dearman, J. Andrew. "My Servants the Scribes: Composition and Context in Jeremiah 36," *Journal of Biblical Literature* 109 (1990): 403-421.

Holladay, William L. "God Writes a Rude Letter (Jeremiah 29:1-23)," *Biblical Archaeologist* 46 (1983): 145-46.

Kessler, Martin. "Jeremiah Chapters 26–45 Reconsidered," *Journal of Near Eastern Studies* 27 (1968): 81-88.

Ludwig, Theodore M. "The Shape of Hope: Jeremiah's Book of Consolation," *Concordia Theological Monthly* 39 (1968): 526-541.

Miller, Patrick D., Jr. "Sin and Judgment in Jeremiah 34:17-19," *Journal of Biblical Literature* 103 (1984): 611-13.

Mottu, Henri. "Jeremiah vs. Hananiah: Ideology and Truth in Old Testament Prophecy," in *The Bible and Liberation,* ed. Norman K. Gottwald (Maryknoll: Orbis, 1983), 235-251.

Seitz, Christopher R. "The Prophet Moses and the Canonical Shape of Jeremiah," *Zeitschrift für die alttestamentliche Wissenschaft* 101 (1989): 3-27.

Taylor, Marion Ann. "Jeremiah 45: The Problem of Placement," *Journal for the Study of the Old Testament* 37 (1987): 79-98.

Other Works

Brueggemann, Walter. "At the Mercy of Babylon: A Subversive Rereading of the Empire," *Journal of Biblical Literature* 110 (1991): 1ff.
———. *Hopeful Imagination: Prophetic Voices in Exile* (Philadelphia: Fortress, 1986).
———. *Israel's Praise: Doxology against Idolatry and Ideology* (Philadelphia: Fortress, 1988).
———. "The Kerygma of the Deuteronomistic Historian: Gospel for Exiles," *Interpretation* 22 (1968): 387-402.
Childs, Brevard S. *Introduction to the Old Testament as Scripture* (Philadelphia: Fortress and London: SCM, 1979).
Crenshaw, James L. *Prophetic Conflict: Its Effect upon Israelite Religion*. Beihefte zur Zeitschrift für die alttestamentliche Wissenschaft 124 (Berlin: de Gruyter, 1971).
Diepold, Peter. *Israels Land*. Beiträge zur Wissenschaft vom Alten und Neuen Testament 95 (Stuttgart: Kohlhammer, 1972).
Friedman, Richard E. *Who Wrote the Bible?* (New York: Summit, 1987).
Gottwald, Norman K. *The Tribes of Yahweh: A Sociology of the Religion of Liberated Israel, 1250-1050 B.C.E.* (Maryknoll: Orbis, 1979).
Gowan, Donald E. *Eschatology in the Old Testament* (Philadelphia: Fortress, 1986).
Mendenhall, George E. *The Tenth Generation: The Origins of the Biblical Tradition* (Baltimore: Johns Hopkins University Press, 1973).
Miller, J. Maxwell, and Hayes, John H. *A History of Ancient Israel and Judah* (Philadelphia: Westminster and London: SCM, 1986).
Miller, Patrick D., Jr. *Sin and Judgment in the Prophets*. SBL Monograph 27 (Chico: Scholars Press, 1982).
———. "The Sovereignty of God," in *The Hermeneutical Quest.*

Festschrift James L. Mays, ed. Donald G. Miller. Princeton Theological Monograph 4 (Allison Park, Pa.: Pickwick, 1986).

Miskotte, Kornelis H. *When the Gods Are Silent* (New York: Harper & Row, 1967).

Neusner, Jacob. *Understanding Seeking Faith*. Vol. 1: *Debates on Method, Reports of Results*. Brown Judaic Studies 116 (Atlanta: Scholars Press, 1986).

Ollenberger, Ben C. *Zion, the City of the Great King*. Journal for the Study of the Old Testament Supplement 41 (Sheffield: JSOT Press, 1987).

Olson, Dennis T. *The Death of the Old and the Birth of the New*. Brown Judaic Studies 71 (Chico: Scholars Press, 1985).

von Rad, Gerhard. *Old Testament Theology*. 2 vols. (New York: Harper & Row and Edinburgh: Oliver & Boyd, 1962-1965).

————. *Wisdom in Israel* (Nashville: Abingdon and London: SCM, 1972).

Smend, Rudolf. *Die Bundesformel*. Theologische Studien 68 (Zurich: EVS, 1963).

Smith, Daniel L. *The Religion of the Landless: The Social Context of the Babylonian Exile* (Bloomington, Ind.: Meyer-Stone, 1989).

Wanke, Gunther. *Untersuchungen zur sogenannten Baruchschrift*. Beihefte zur Zeitschrift für die alttestamentliche Wissenschaft 122 (Berlin: de Gruyter, 1971).

Wilson, Robert R. *Prophecy and Society in Ancient Israel* (Philadelphia: Fortress, 1980).

Wright, G. Ernest. "The Nations in Hebrew Prophecy," *Encounter* 26 (1965): 225-237.